Edited by
David Silverman
Qualitative Research

Issues of Theory, Method and Practice

Third Edition

Los Angeles | London | New Delhi
Singapore | Washington DC

Chapter 1 and editorial arrangement © David
   Silverman 2011
Chapter 2 © Giampietro Gobo 2011
Chapter 3 © Marie Buscatto 2011
Chapter 4 © Thomas S. Eberle and Christoph
   Maeder 2011
Chapter 5 © Paul Atkinson and Amanda Coffey
   2011
Chapter 6 © Lindsay Prior 2011
Chapter 7 © Annette Markham 2011
Chapter 8 © Jody Miller and Barry Glassner 2011
Chapter 9 © James A. Holstein and Jaber F.
   Gubrium 2011
Chapter 10 © Sue Wilkinson 2011

Chapter 11 © Jonathan Potter 2011
Chapter 12 © John Heritage 2011
Chapter 13 © Michael Emmison 2011
Chapter 14 © Christian Heath 2011
Chapter 15 © Tim Rapley 2011
Chapter 16 © Kathy Charmaz and Antony Bryant
   2011
Chapter 17 © Catherine Riessman 2011
Chapter 18 © Mary Dixon-Woods 2011
Chapter 19 © Clive Seale 2011
Chapter 20 © Anssi Peräkylä 2011
Chapter 21 © Amir Marvasti 2011
Chapter 22 © Michael Bloor 2011
Chapter 23 © Anne Ryen 2011

First edition published 1997. Reprinted 2003
Second edition published 2004. Reprinted 2006 (twice), 2008, 2009
This third edition published 2011. Reprinted 2011 (three times)

SAGE Publications Ltd
1 Oliver's Yard
55 City Road
London EC1Y 1SP

SAGE Publications Inc.
2455 Teller Road
Thousand Oaks, California 91320

SAGE Publications India Pvt Ltd
B 1/I 1 Mohan Cooperative Industrial Area
Mathura Road
New Delhi 110 044

SAGE Publications Asia-Pacific Pte Ltd
33 Pekin Street #02-01
Far East Square
Singapore 048763

Library of Congress Control Number: 2010923831

British Library Cataloguing in Publication data

A catalogue record for this book is available from the British Library

ISBN 978-1-84920-416-3
ISBN 978-1-84920-417-0 (pbk)

Typeset by C & M Digitals (P) Ltd, Chennai, India
Printed and bound in Great Britain by the MPG Books Group
Printed on paper from sustainable resources

For Andrew and Lily who gave me a very happy year

Contents

Notes on Contributors

Paul Atkinson is Distinguished Research Professor of Sociology at Cardiff University. He and Sara Delamont edit the journal *Qualitative Research*. His publications on research methods include: Hammersley and Atkinson, *Ethnography: Principles in Practice* (Routledge, 2007); *The Ethnographic Imagination* (Routledge, 1990); *Understanding Ethnographic Texts* (Sage, 1992); Atkinson, Coffey and Delamont, *Key Themes in Qualitative Research* (AltaMira, 2003); Atkinson, Delamont and Housley, *Contours of Culture* (AltaMira, 2007). He is currently researching masterclasses for performers and artists. He is an Academician of the Academy of Social Sciences.

Michael Bloor is a medical sociologist and holds a part-time professorial fellowship at Cardiff University. His most recent book (with Fiona Wood) is *Keywords in Qualitative Research: A Vocabulary of Research Concepts* (Sage, 2006).

Antony Bryant is currently Professor of Informatics at Leeds Metropolitan University. He has written extensively on research methods, being Senior Editor of *The SAGE Handbook of Grounded Theory* (Sage, 2007) – co-edited with Kathy Charmaz with whom he has worked extensively within the area of grounded theory and research methods in general. His current research includes an investigation of the ways in which the Open Source model might be developed as a feature of the re-constructed financial sector in the wake of the economic melt-down.

Marie Buscatto is Professor of Sociology at l'Université Paris 1 Panthéon Sorbonne (France). She has led several intensive ethnographic surveys in modern organisations and in the French jazz world. Her most recent book is *Femmes du jazz. Musicalités, féminités, marginalisations* (CNRS Editions, 2007). For further information: www. cmh.pro.ens.fr/hopmembres.php?action=ficheperso&id=223&id_rub=8.

Kathy Charmaz is Professor of Sociology and Director of the Faculty Writing Program at Sonoma State University. She is the author of *Constructing Grounded Theory: A Practical Guide Through Qualitative Analysis* (Sage, 2006) and a co-author for two multi-authored texts, *Developing Grounded Theory: The Second Generation* (Left Coast Press, 2009) and *Five Ways of Doing Qualitative Research: Phenomenology, Grounded Theory, Discourse Analysis, Narrative Analysis and Intuitive Inquiry* (Guilford, forthcoming).

Amanda Coffey is a professor in the School of Social Sciences, Cardiff University. She has published widely on qualitative research methods and in the sociology of education. She is currently an editor of the journal *Sociology*. Her publications include *Making Sense of Qualitative Data* (with Atkinson; Sage, 1996), *The Ethnographic Self, Education and Social Change* (Sage,1999) and *Reconceptualising Social Policy* (Open University Press, 2004).

Mary Dixon-Woods is Professor of Medical Sociology at the University of Leicester. She has research interests in methodologies for synthesis of diverse forms of evidence; quality and safety in healthcare; and regulation and bioethics.

Thomas S. Eberle is Professor and Co-director of the Institute of Sociology at the University of St Gallen in Switzerland. His research areas are the sociology of culture and of organization, phenomenology and ethnomethodology, methodology and qualitative methods. His most recent publication in English is on Alfred Schutz.

Michael Emmison is Reader in Sociology, School of Social Sciences, University of Queensland. His interests are in language and interaction, the use of visual methodologies in social research and the archiving and reuse of qualitative data. His current research is on children's helplines. His publications include *Accounting for Tastes* (Cambridge University Press, 1999, with Tony Bennett and John Frow), *Researching the Visual* (Sage, 2000, with Philip Smith) and the edited collection *Calling for Help: Language and Social Interaction in Telephone Helplines* (Benjamins 2005).

Barry Glassner is Professor of Sociology at the University of Southern California. He is the author of seven books on contemporary social issues. His most recent books are *The Culture of Fear* (Basic, 2010) and *The Gospel of Food* (HarperCollins, 2007). He has published papers in *The American Sociological Review*, *American Journal of Psychiatry* and other leading journals in the social sciences.

Giampietro Gobo is Professor of Methodology of Social Research and Evaluation Methods, and Director of the centre ICONA (Innovation and Organisational Change in the Public Administration), at the University of Milan. His books include *Doing Ethnography* (Sage, 2008), *Qualitative Research Practice* (Sage, 2004, co-edited with C. Seale, J.F. Gubrium and D. Silverman) and *Collecting Survey Data: An Interviewee-Centred Approach* (Sage, 2010, with Sergio Mauceri). He is currently undertaking projects in the area of workplace studies.

Jaber F. Gubrium is Professor and Chair of Sociology at the University of Missouri. He has had a longstanding programme of research on the social construction of care and treatment in human service organizations, and has pioneered the reconceptualization of qualitative methods and the development of narrative analysis. His publications include *Living and Dying at Murray Manor* (St. Martin's Press, 1975), *Oldtimers and Alzheimer's* (JAI Press, 1986) and (with James Holstein) *The Self We Live By: Narrative Identity in a Postmodern World* (Oxford University Press, 2000) and *Analyzing Narrative Reality* (Sage, 2009).

Christian Heath is Professor at King's College London and leads the Work, Interaction and Technology Research Group. He specializes in video-based studies of social interaction drawing on ethnomethodology and conversation analysis. He is currently undertaking studies of auctions, healthcare, the control centres on London Underground and museums and galleries. He has published seven books including *Video in Qualitative Research* (with Jon Hindmarsh and Paul Luff; Sage, 2010) and *Technology in Action* (with Paul Luff; Cambridge University Press, 2000).

John Heritage is Professor of Sociology at UCLA. His most recent work includes *Talk in Action: Interactions, Identities and Institutions* (Blackwell, 2008, with Steven Clayman) and *Communication in Medical Care* (Cambridge University Press, 2006, co-edited with Douglas Maynard).

James A. Holstein is Professor of Sociology in the Department of Social and Cultural Sciences at Marquette University. His research and writing projects have addressed social problems, deviance and social control, family, and the self – all approached from an ethnomethodologically informed, constructionist perspective. Along with Jay Gubrium, he has published *What Is Family?* (May Field, 1990), *Constructing the Life Course* (AltaMira, 2000), *The Self We Live By* (Oxford University Press, 2000) and *Institutional Selves* (Oxford University Press, 2000). Their methodological publications include *The New Language of Qualitative Method* (Oxford University Press, 1997), *The Active Interview* (Sage, 1999). *The Handbook of Interview Research* (Sage, 2002) and *Analyzing Narrative Reality* (Sage, 2009).

Christoph Maeder is a sociologist and Research Director at the University of Teacher Education TG in Switzerland. His most recent publication in English (with Eva Nadai) is on multi-sited ethnography as a theory-driven research strategy for sociology.

Annette N. Markham is a senior research fellow in the Center for Information Policy Research at the University of Wisconsin–Milwaukee, researching the connection between method and ethics. Her primary research focuses on sensemaking in technological mediated spaces and ethical practices in qualitative internet research. Her book *Life Online: Researching Real Experience in Virtual Space* (AltaMira, 1998) has been regarded as a foundational sociological study of lived experience of the Internet.

Amir Marvasti is Associate Professor of Sociology at Pennsylvania State University, Altoona. His research interests include race and ethnicity, deviance and social theory. He is the author of *Being Homeless: Textual and Narrative Constructions* (Lexington Books, 2003), *Qualitative Research in Sociology* (Sage, 2004), *Middle Eastern Lives in America* (with Karyn McKinney; Lexington Books, 2003), and *Doing Qualitative Research* (US edition, with David Silverman; Sage, 2008).

Jody Miller is Professor in the School of Criminal Justice at Rutgers University. She is the author of *Getting Played: African American Girls, Urban Inequality, and Gendered Violence* (New York University Press, 2008) and *One of the Guys: Girls, Gangs, and Gender* (Oxford University Press, 2001), as well as numerous articles and book chapters.

Anssi Peräkylä is Professor of Sociology at the University of Helsinki. His research interests include interaction in medical and psychotherapeutic settings, emotion and conversation analysis. He is editor of *Conversation Analysis and Psychotherapy* (Cambridge University Press, 2008).

Jonathan Potter is Professor of Discourse Analysis and Head of the Department of Social Sciences, Loughborough University. He has a longstanding interest in discursive and qualitative methods and reworking the nature of psychology.

Lindsay Prior is Professor of Sociology and an associate of the Northern Ireland Centre of Excellence for Public Health at Queen's University Belfast where he teaches social research methods. He is author of *Using Documents in Social Research* (Sage, 2003) and is currently editing a four-volume collection on the same theme to be published by Sage during 2011. His current research interests relate to the investigation of health policy networks in the UK and Ireland.

Tim Rapley is a staff scientist at the Institute of Health and Society, Newcastle University. He has written a book, *Analysing Conversations, Discourse and Documents* (Sage, 2007), and keeps contemplating writing another one on qualitative data analysis.

Catherine Kohler Riessman is a medical sociologist and *Emerita* at Boston University. She is Research Professor in the Sociology Department at Boston College. Her most recent book is *Narrative Methods for the Human Sciences* (Sage, 2008).

Anne Ryen is Associate Professor of Sociology at the University of Agder, Norway. She has been doing research in East Africa for twenty years and is leader of the research programme Governance, Gender and Scientific Quality (GGSQ) with Mzumbe University, Tanzania. Her many publications on cross-cultural research include 'Ethnography: Constitutive Practice and Research Ethics' in *The Handbook of Social Research Ethics* (by Mertens and Ginsberg, 2009).

Clive Seale is Professor of Medical Sociology at Queen Mary, University of London, working in the medical school. His research focuses on communication in health care, mass media coverage of health topics, and end-of-life decision-making. He is the author of *The Quality of Qualitative Research* (Sage, 1999).

David Silverman is Emeritus Professor of Sociology at Goldsmiths' College and Visiting Professor, Management Department, King's College (both University of London). He is also Visiting Professor in the Business School at the University of Technology, Sydney. His research interests focus on medical encounters. He is the author of several textbooks on qualitative research.

Sue Wilkinson is Professor of Feminist and Health Research in the Department of Social Sciences at Loughborough University. She has published widely in the areas of gender, sexuality, health and qualitative methods. Her current research uses conversation analysis to examine helpline interactions, and she is particularly interested in the practices and actions of conversational 'repair'.

PART I

INTRODUCTION TO THE THIRD EDITION

Introducing *Qualitative Research*

David Silverman

This book seeks to provide a guide to the latest developments in qualitative research. A reader on the Amazon website, reviewing the previous edition of this book, neatly summed up what I aim to do here:

> Silverman has compiled a nice collection of papers on qualitative research. Firstly, it covers a broad range of research methods (observation, textual analysis, interviews). Second, they are covered in good depth, starting from the approach (how to think about it) to its practice (how to do it). But best of all, I like the values Silverman espouses in this book. It really gets you motivated to do good qualitative research and gets you thinking about the right things. This book will add to your conceptual and technical 'toolkit' for conducting qualitative research. (Minh Tran, November 2009)

I am most grateful for Minh Tran's comments. I think this third edition is even better. It offers a newly updated introduction to cutting edge issues, written by leading scholars in our field. Chapters from the second edition have been revised by their distinguished authors. In addition, reflecting the changing face of qualitative research in the past decade, the book has been transformed. Ten new chapters have been written for this book so almost half its contents are entirely new. Recognizing the need for practical advice on doing qualitative research, there is an additional section on qualitative data analysis containing seven, highly readable chapters. There are three new chapters on ethnography and, recognizing the impact of qualitative research on society, the section on the wider community now includes a chapter on research ethics. Finally, to enhance the reader-friendliness of this book, all chapters contain abstracts, summaries, recommended readings, self-assessment questions and links to relevant websites.

Like the first edition, this text aims to build on the success of the editor's *Interpreting Qualitative Data* [IQD] (Silverman 2006). Like that book, it was generated by a number of assumptions set out below:

1   The centrality of the relationship between analytic perspectives and methodological issues and the consequent requirement to go beyond a purely 'cookbook' version of research methods.
2   The need to broaden our conception of qualitative research beyond issues of subjective 'meaning' and towards issues of language, representation and social organisation.
3   The desire to search for ways of building links between social science traditions rather than dwelling in 'armed camps' fighting internal battles.
4   The belief that a social science, which takes seriously the attempt to sort fact from fancy, remains a valid enterprise.
5   The assumption that we no longer need to regard qualitative research as provisional or never based on initial hypotheses. This is because qualitative studies have already assembled a usable, cumulative body of knowledge.
6   The commitment to a dialogue between social science and the community based on a recognition of their different starting points rather than upon a facile acceptance of topics defined by what are taken to be 'social problems'.

Each of these assumptions is, implicitly or explicitly, highly contested within contemporary qualitative research. This is largely, I believe, because such research has become a terrain on which diverse schools of social theory have fought their mock battles. Ultimately, the assumptions set out here try to move the terrain of our field towards an analysis of the everyday resources which we use in making our observations. This point, which is implicit in many of these contributions, is set out in detail in *A Very Short, Fairly Interesting, Reasonably Cheap Book about Qualitative Research* [VSB] (Silverman 2007).

Of course, avoiding such battles, in the context of a commitment to a cumulative social science, is far more likely to make our trade appear relevant to the wider community. As we look outwards rather than inwards, with confidence rather than despair, the way is open for a fruitful dialogue between social scientists, organizations, professionals and community groups.

Moreover, it is worth noting that we present ourselves not only to the wider community but also to the students we teach. Both *Doing Qualitative Research* (Silverman 2010) and IQD derive from 30 years of teaching methodology courses and supervising research projects at both undergraduate and graduate levels. That experience has reinforced the wisdom of the old maxim that true learning is based upon doing. In practice, this means that I approach taught courses as workshops in which students are given skills to analyse data and so to learn the craft of our trade. Like many contemporary teachers, I believe that assessments of students' progress are properly done through data exercises rather than the conventional essay in which students are invited to offer wooden accounts of what other people have written.

It follows that I have little time for the conventional trajectory of the PhD in which students spend their first year 'reviewing the literature', gather data in year 2 and then panic in year 3 about how they can analyse their data. Instead, my students begin their data analysis in year 1 – sometimes in week 1. In that way, they may well have 'cracked' the basic problem in their research in that first year and so can spend their remaining years pursuing the worthy but relatively non-problematic tasks of ploughing through their data following an already established method.

Like IQD, my hope is that this book will be used by students who are not yet familiar with the approaches involved, their theoretical underpinnings and their research practice. In IQD, student exercises are designed to allow readers to test their understanding of each chapter. In this book, worked-through examples of research studies make the arguments accessible. Moreover, the chapters are not written in standard edited collection style as chapters addressed to the contributors' peers but inaccessible to a student audience. This means that the presentation is didactic but not 'cookbook' in style.

The particular contribution of this reader lies in its assembly of a very well-known, international team of researchers who share my commitment to rigorous, analytically derived but non-polarized qualitative research. Nine US researchers join twelve from the UK, two from Switzerland and one each from Italy, France, Norway, Finland and Australia. While the majority of the contributors are sociologists, psychology, feminist studies, health studies and educational studies are also represented. In any event, I believe that all contributors have succeeded in making their presentations accessible to a multidisciplinary audience.

Rather than denying their own analytic position in favour of some woolly centre ground, these authors have clearly set out the assumptions from which they proceed while remaining open to the diverse interests of their readers. Each has written a chapter which reflects on the analysis of each of the kinds of data discussed in IQD: observations, texts, talk, visual data, focus groups and interviews. Following IQD, each author uses particular examples of data analysis to advance analytic arguments.

The three chapters on observational methods seek to rescue observational work from the pitfalls of mere 'description' and lazy coding and towards exciting methodological and analytic directions for observational research. In Chapter 2, Giampietro Gobo shows how observation is the basic tool of ethnographers. Using examples from political science, Gobo demonstrates why, if we want to understand behaviour and interaction, it is not enough to ask questions. We must also observe the routines and practices of social actors. And we can do this reliably and consistently. Moreover, as Gobo notes, ethnography, like any other methodology, is not simply an instrument of data collection. It is born at a particular moment in the history of society and embodies certain of its cultural features. Gobo's concept of the 'Observation Society' focuses upon why ethnography has come into fashion.

Marie Buscatto builds on Gobo's comments about the limits of purely interview-based research. Her aim is to describe and explain the specific contributions of the ethnographic method to analysis of gender differences in work settings or situations.

Using cogent examples from her research on female jazz singers and musicians and trade unionists, she reveals the specific contributions that the ethnographic method makes to the study of gendered social relations at work. Drawing upon the ideas of Erving Goffman, she makes 'the arrangement between the sexes' the entry point for her analysis. Her methodologically illuminating chapter reveals how ethnography can allow researchers to spot disparaging gender stereotypes, describe 'male' occupational networks, and identify gendered norms and conventions.

While Buscatto shows the power of ethnographic method for our understanding of the construction of gender relations, Thomas Eberle and Christoph Maeder give us insights into how ethnographers go about studying organizations. As they argue, abstract organization theory is not a necessary starting point for research and there is a continuum between theory- and data-guided ethnographic studies. Their chapter contains some illuminating case studies which demonstrate the methodological strengths of observing routine practices within organizations. They conclude with a helpful account of practical considerations in doing organizational ethnography such as field access and participation, data collection and data analysis, informant and field relations, reporting back, ethical questions, and finally writing up.

Part III on texts shows how ethnographic reading of texts can fruitfully work with a diverse set of analytic traditions. Paul Atkinson and Amanda Coffey draw upon ethnomethodology's study of 'the documentary method of interpretation' and literary accounts of narrative and genre. They apply these contemporary concepts to the documents through which organizations represent themselves and the records and documentary data they accumulate. Taking the example of 'audit', they show how we can fruitfully analyse financial statements produced by accountants and accounts of their work by university departments. They also remind us of the 'audit trail' as documents refer to other documents. Following Atkinson and Coffey, we are given the tools to explicate systematically how texts are organized through the concepts of 'authorship', 'readership', 'intertextuality' and 'rhetoric'.

In Lindsay Prior's chapter on texts, we move from literary theory to theories of discourse. However, unlike the stultifying theoretical level of some introductions to this topic, Prior has written a delightful, accessible chapter which shows, in practice, what it is like to 'do things with documents'. Avoiding references to a knowing 'subject', Prior shows us how we can instead focus on the ways in which a text instructs us to see the world. Using examples as diverse as a statistical summary of prevalence rates of mental illness and talk between scientists in a cancer genetics clinic, he reveals a thought-provoking toolbox that we can use when working with textual material.

In the twenty-first century, however, conventional documents are not the only textual material that circulate in the world. The Internet is now perhaps the prime site where words and pictures circulate. Annette Markham's new chapter develops this insight and, in so doing, offers readers an invaluable guide to interpreting such data. In a revealing phrase, she points out that the Internet is *chrono malleable*.

Not only does it collapse distance, but also it can disrupt the way in which time is relevant to interaction since it can accommodate both asynchronous and synchronous communication between individuals and groups. Markham shows the importance of distinguishing research studies which simply use the Internet as a way to gather data (e.g. online interviews) from studies of Internet practices as phenomena in their own right (e.g. the mechanics of online dating or chatrooms). Following this latter option, we learn, as in the other chapters on texts, how participants actively construct meaning.

This idea of the 'active' reader is carried over into Part IV on interviews and focus groups. All three chapters in this section remind us that both respondents and social scientists actively construct meaning in each other's talk. Jody Miller and Barry Glassner address the issue of finding 'reality' in interview accounts. I argue in IQD that the desire of many researchers to treat interview data as more or less straightforward 'pictures' of an external reality can fail to understand how that 'reality' is being represented in words. Miller and Glassner set out a position which seeks to move beyond this argument about the 'inside' and the 'outside' of interview accounts. They fruitfully draw upon their research on gender inequality in youth gangs and on violence against African American young women in urban neighbourhoods. Based upon this research, they argue that interview accounts may fruitfully be treated as situated elements in adolescents' social worlds, drawing upon and revising and reframing the cultural stories available in those worlds. For Miller and Glassner, the focus of interview research should be fixed upon what stories are told and how and where they are produced.

In their chapter, James Holstein and Jaber Gubrium show us how a focus on story and narrative structure demands that we recognize that both interview data and interview analysis are active occasions in which meanings are produced. This means that we ought to view research 'subjects' not as stable entities but as actively constructed through their answers. Indeed, in Holstein and Gubrium's telling phrase, both interviewee and interviewer are 'practitioners of everyday life' who 'animate' the interview. Thus the issue that should confront qualitative researchers is not whether interview accounts are 'distorted' but the interpretive practices present within each interview. Using examples from their research on nursing home residents and on carers of elderly family members, they invite us to locate the interpretive practices which generate the 'hows' and the 'whats' of experience as aspects of reality that are constructed in collaboration with the interviewer to produce a 'narrative drama'.

Sue Wilkinson's chapter on focus groups carries forward Holstein and Gubrium's concern with how we construct the social world with our respondents. Using illuminating extracts from her own data on breast cancer patients, Wilkinson reveals the complicated interpretive activities between members of focus groups as they try to make sense of each other (and the researcher). This close attention to the details of short data extracts is contrasted with how most focus group (and interview) research is usually conducted. Wilkinson's concern with theoretically driven, detailed data analysis stands apart from the dominant tendency to treat focus group talk as a straightforward means of accessing some independent 'reality'. Above all, Wilkinson shows us that content analysis and a concentration on the mechanics of how to run a focus group are no substitute for theoretically informed and detailed data analysis of talk-in-action. Like all the contributors to this volume, Wilkinson underlines the fact that we must never overlook the active interpretive skills of our research subjects.

Part V is concerned with audio data. Jonathan Potter discusses 'discursive psychology', more commonly known as discourse analysis (DA), as a way of analysing naturally occurring talk. Potter shows the manner in which DA allows us to address how versions of reality are produced to seem objective and separate from the speaker. Using examples drawn from television interviews with Princess Diana and Salman Rushdie and a newspaper report of a psychiatrist's comment, he demonstrates how we can analyse the ways in which speakers disavow a 'stake' in their actions.

Potter argues that DA focuses on rhetorical organization, while conversation analysis (CA) is concerned with sequential organization. John Heritage's chapter presents an accessible introduction to how conversation analytic methods can be used in the analysis of everyday interaction. He clearly presents the assumptions and basic principles of CA. From a methodological point of view, Heritage then helpfully sets out the nuts and bolts of doing CA. Using extracts of talk, he shows us how he goes about deciding whether a conversational practice is distinctive, how to locate it in a sequence and then how to determine its role or function. He concludes with a powerful reply to critics who maintain that CA cannot deal with the social context of talk.

The elegance of Heritage's account of everyday talk is matched by the two chapters in the next Part on visual data. Like Sue Wilkinson (in her chapter on focus groups), Michael Emmison argues that visual researchers have worked with inadequate theories. For instance, most tend to identify visual data with such artefacts as photographs and, to a lesser extent, cartoons and advertisements. Although such work can be interesting, it is, in a sense, two dimensional. If we recognize that the visual is also spatial, a whole new set of three-dimensional objects emerge. By looking at how people use objects in the world around them (from streetmaps to the layout of a room or urban street to the design of a hospital), we can study the material embodiment of culture.

Emmison cites Christian Heath's discussion of face-to-face interaction in museums as one way of looking at three-dimensional data in fine detail. Like Emmison, Heath differentiates the wide-ranging interest in the 'visual' in sociology and cognate disciplines, from research that uses video-recordings to analyse conduct and interaction in 'naturally occurring' day-to-day settings. Beginning with a clear account of CA's focus on sequential organization, Heath shows how CA can be used to study visual conduct and how the physical properties of human environments are made relevant within the course of social interaction. Like Heritage, Heath uses a series of telling examples from auctions to London Underground control rooms. He shows how Goffman's idea of a 'participation framework' can be used to analyse the unfolding interactional order present in a video of an auction. Heath also provides highly practical information for students about field relations when using video and how best to record and transcribe such data. Heath concludes by showing the relevance of these insights to studies of the workplace, including human–computer interaction.

As I have already pointed out, the next Part on qualitative data analysis is entirely new to this third edition. Tim Rapley clearly and informally reveals what he calls the 'pragmatics' of qualitative data analysis. As Rapley shows, the hard work begins when we try to explore and explain 'what is "underlying" or "broader" [in our data] or to "distil" essence, meaning, norms, orders, patterns, rules, structures etcetera (the level of concepts and themes)'. Rapley goes on to offer invaluable advice about how to do good qualitative data analysis, emphasizing the importance of detailed readings, reviewing and refining your categories and using your provisional analysis to inform how you collect, transcribe and analyse data when you return to the field. As Rapley argues, good qualitative research is about 'living in the detail'. However, like any good research, we must not rush to offer generalizations but actively seek out contrary cases.

Like Rapley, Kathy Charmaz and Tony Bryant seek to remove the veil from what they call 'the almost magical emergence of theories and concepts from data'. They elucidate the elements of grounded theory (GT) and show what, in their view, has been right and wrong about criticisms of the GT approach. They then go on to demonstrate how GT already contains underused strategies that increase both its methodological power and the credibility of its data analysis. Using helpful illustrations from their own data analysis, they demonstrate what a 'constructivist' GT methodology can look like in practice, showing how we can work with credible data and achieve analytic and theoretical credibility.

In her chapter on narrative inquiry (NI), Catherine Riessman continues this hands-on, student-friendly, approach to the pragmatics of data analysis. Her aim is to distinguish such work from GT and from other methods of analysing interview data. For Riesman, NI, like oral history, is concerned with case-centred research. Hence the leap to broader theories or generalizations is slowed down or even avoided in favour of the interrogation of particular instances, sequences of action, the way participants negotiate language and narrative genres in conversations, and other unique aspects of a 'case'. For Riessman, NI involves resisting what she calls the 'seductive power' of stories. Instead, it asks: Why was the story told *that* way? What do the specific words a participant uses carry on their backs from prior uses? What other readings are possible, beyond what the narrator may have intended? Using two long interviews (reproduced in full at the end of her chapter), Riessman shows how we can answer these questions by examining the way a segment of data is organized and the local context, including the questioner/listener, setting, and position of an utterance in the broader stream of the conversation.

As every student is taught, elegant data analysis presupposes a well-defined research topic, based on a review of earlier studies. Mary Dixon-Woods asks how we can make our literature reviews more robust. Systematic review methodology treats the production of a review as a scientific process. It typically uses pre-specified protocols for the conduct of a review, which formalize and codify the review question; eligibility criteria for studies to be included; searching strategies to be used; quality appraisals to be undertaken; and methods to be used in synthesizing the included studies. Dixon-Woods clearly describes the extent to which the conventional systematic review template is appropriate to qualitative research. As she argues, a key question concerns the extent to which conventional systematic review methodology, with its origins in the 'what works' template, and its focus on estimating the effectiveness of a particular intervention on average, can be consistent with the aspirations of those aiming to produce more interpretive forms of overview of bodies of research evidence.

From the point of view of the research student, there remains the problem that we can spend so much time on literature reviews that we have too little time to gather and analyse our data. As I suggest in DQR, one quick solution to this problem is to work with secondary data. Clive Seale shows that the chief reservation expressed about secondary analysis of qualitative data is that secondary analysts will not have the kind of detailed contextual knowledge about the circumstances of data collection possessed by the primary researcher. Seale argues that this rests in part on an unexamined stereotype of the way secondary analysis of quantitative data sets proceeds, and does not recognize that archived data may be analysed with methods and for purposes that do not require in-depth knowledge of context. He supports his argument with two case studies which show the degree to which general methodological debates are relevant to this form of research practice. Once one gets involved with a data set it is often possible to show the value of secondary analysis without falling into the pitfalls imagined by the critics. As he sagely suggests: 'Just do it'!

Like Seale and Dixon-Woods, Anssi Peräkylä is concerned with the credibility of qualitative research. He is particularly interested in how qualitative research can offer reliable and valid descriptions of its data. Following Heritage's chapter, Peräkylä illustrates his argument with CA research. Validity questions are discussed in terms of the comparative method and conventional 'deviant case analysis' as well as specifically CA methods, such as validation through 'next turn'. He also demonstrates one way of generalizing from case studies and discusses the uses and limits of quantitative techniques in qualitative research. Overall, Peräkylä is right to claim that his chapter is the first systematic attempt to discuss such matters in relation to CA. At the same time, his discussion has a much broader relevance to all serious qualitative research. As I argue in my VSB (Chapter 3), paying attention to sequences of data, rather than apparently striking instances, is a hallmark of all good qualitative research rather than something confined to CA.

Ultimately, good qualitative data analysis is expressed in how well we write. Amir Marvasti argues that novice researchers need to learn the basic skills or craft of writing. In qualitative research, there is no such thing as a format for 'the standard scientific paper'. Marvasti shows that different genres are available to us and describes the stylistic choices available and their advantages and limitations. He also comments upon the strategic choices authors have to consider as they try to publish their work and make it accessible to various audiences. He suggests that a 'perfect paper' is one that strikes a balance between craft skills, genre and intended audience.

One audience for our research may be policy-makers, practitioners, clients or research subjects. The final Part of this book positions qualitative research within the wider community. Michael Bloor's chapter deals with a topic that concerns most qualitative researchers: the ability of our research to contribute to addressing social problems. Bloor argues that our focus on everyday activities makes it particularly relevant in helping practitioners to think about their working practices. He demonstrates his argument by detailed discussions of case studies which he conducted of male prostitutes in Glasgow and of eight therapeutic communities. Both sets of studies illustrate Bloor's point about the ways in which rigorous qualitative research can have relevance for service provision, even if, at least in the UK, it is unlikely to have much impact upon policy debates at the governmental level. Finally, Bloor reviews (and rejects) the argument that social scientists should not be practitioners' helpers.

The final chapter by Anne Ryen addresses how ethical issues arise within qualitative research. As she shows, ethics involves many more interesting matters than the tedious business of form-filling in order to satisfy ethical review committees. Our search for 'rich' data can mean that we organize long stays in the 'field'. Ryen uses her data from research on Asian businesses in East Africa to illustrate and discuss the complexity of research ethics in ethnography. Working in the field involves emergent ethical dilemmas which are different from survey research and cannot be sorted out at the outset. This means that the underlying biomedical model of most guidelines may unduly simplify the social world as understood by qualitative researchers. Instead, we must unpick difficult issues involved in the ethics and politics of matters like rapport, intrusion and harm. As she concludes: 'Qualitative research calls for moral responsibility in a field scattered with dilemmas, not quick answers.'

Not all of the contributors to this volume are in agreement about every issue. Nonetheless, I believe that my authors share enough in common to make this a coherent volume. Many of my contributors, I suspect, would agree with most of the six points at the start of this chapter. With more certainty, I would claim that we share a fairly common sense of what constitutes 'good' qualitative research. For instance, even though we come from different intellectual traditions, I would be surprised if we were to have any fundamental disagreement about, say, the assessment of an article submitted to us for refereeing. This common sense of what we are 'looking for' derives, I believe, from our common attention to the mundane properties of everyday description (VSB, Chapter 2).

I would like to express my gratitude to my contributors for tolerating my schoolmasterly messages about deadlines and for the brilliant work they did in offering suggestions on each others' draft chapters. I thank my Sage editor, Patrick Brindle, for his helpful suggestions about this volume. As always, my thanks are also due to Gilly for putting up with me, to Sara Cordell for keeping my back in working order, and to my friends at the Nursery End for giving me summers to which I can look forward.

References

Silverman, D. (2006) *Interpreting Qualitative Data: Methods for Analysing Talk, Text and Interaction*, Third Edition. London: Sage.

Silverman, D. (2007) *A Very Short, Fairly Interesting, Reasonably Cheap Book about Qualitative Research*. London: Sage.

Silverman, D. (2010) *Doing Qualitative Research*, Third Edition. London: Sage.

Using This Book: A Student Guide

I recognize that academic books are not usually read in the same way as novels. For instance, although you may want to resist the temptation to skip to the final chapter of a whodunnit, no such prohibitions are sensible when using a textbook. So, for example, if you are currently having troubles with your data analysis, you may want to begin by reading Tim Rapley's chapter. Each chapter is more or less self-contained and so there should be no problems in zigzagging through the book in this way.

As I commented in DQR, zigzagging also makes sense because qualitative research rarely follows a smooth trajectory from hypothesis to findings. Consequently, most readers will want to move backwards and forwards through the book as the occasion arises. Alternatively, you may find it useful to skim-read the book in advance and then work through certain chapters in greater detail to correspond with different stages of your research.

As already noted, all the chapters found here have helpful student-oriented features. However, in my view, certain chapters stand out as particularly relevant to a student audience. So, if you are a novice, you might want to begin by reading Gobo's chapter on ethnography, Holstein and Gubrium on interviews, Markham on Internet research, Rapley on data analysis, Marvasti on writing and Ryen on research ethics.

PART II

OBSERVATION

Ethnography 2

Giampietro Gobo

Abstract

Ethnography is a methodology based on direct observation. Of course, when doing ethnography, it is also essential to listen to the conversations of the actors 'on stage', read the documents produced by the organization under study, and ask people questions. Yet what most distinguishes ethnography from other methodologies is a more active role assigned to the cognitive modes of observing, watching, seeing, looking at, gazing at and scrutinizing.

Ethnography, like any other methodology, is not simply an instrument of data collection. It is born at a particular moment in the history of society and embodies certain of its cultural features. This chapter, embracing a theory of method, focuses upon why (right now, notwithstanding more than one century of history) ethnography has come into fashion.

Keywords:

observation, ethnography, methodology, theory of method, applied methods.

Ethnography is a methodology with more than a hundred years of history. It arose in the Western world as a particular form of knowledge about distant cultures (typically non-Western ones) which were impenetrable to analysis since we had only fleeting contact or brief conversations. Despite its good intentions (to gain deeper understanding), ethnography is still a colonial method that must be de-colonialized.

Competing Definitions of Ethnography

Defining a term is always difficult because there are as many definitions as there are different points of view. Atkinson and Hammersley (1994) observe that the definition of the term *ethnography* has been subject to controversy. For some scholars it refers to a philosophical paradigm to which one makes a total commitment, for others it designates an instrument that one uses as and when appropriate.

But the controversy extends further. Since the 1980s the meaning of ethnography has been expanded to such an extent that it encompasses forms of research extremely diverse from a methodological point of view. Everything is now ethnography: from life stories to analysis of letters and questionnaires, from autobiography to narrative analysis, from action research to performance, to field research lasting from a few days to several years. Leading scholars such as James Lull and David Morley have pointed out that what passes as ethnography in cultural studies fails to fulfil the fundamental requirements for data collection and reporting typical of most anthropological and sociological ethnographic research. *Ethnography* has become an abused buzzword and has been diluted into a multitude of sometimes contrasting and contradictory meanings, sometimes becoming synonymous with qualitative studies.

Amid this multiple meaning, there are at least three terms that merge with 'ethnography': 'participant observation', 'fieldwork' and 'case study'. However, they should not be mixed up:

- 'Case study' denotes research on a system bounded in space and time and embedded in a particular physical and sociocultural context. Research is conducted using diverse methodologies, methods and data sources, like participant observation, interviews, audiovisual materials, documents, and so on.
- 'Fieldwork' stresses the continuous presence of the researcher in the field, as opposed to 'grab-it-and-run' methodologies like the survey, in-depth interview, or analysis of documents and recordings. In this case, too, diverse methodologies and methods may be used.
- 'Participant observation' is a distinctive research strategy. Probably, participant observation and fieldwork treat observation as a mere technique, while the term *ethnography* stresses the theoretical basis of such work stemming from a particular history and tradition.

An Updated Definition

The stretching of the term *ethnography* has emptied it of its original meaning. Ethnography was born as a technique based upon direct observation. By contrast, interviews and surveys are mainly based upon listening and asking questions. Of course, it is also essential in ethnography to listen to the conversations of the actors 'on stage', read the documents produced by the organization under study (diaries, letters, class essays, administrative documents, newspapers, photographs and audio-visual aids), ask people questions, and so on. However, they are ancillary sources of information because what most distinguishes ethnography from other methodologies is a more active role assigned to observation.

Ethnographic methodology comprises two research strategies: *non-participant* observation and *participant* observation. In the former case the researcher observes the subjects 'from a distance' without interacting with them. Those who use this strategy are uninterested in investigating the symbolic sphere, and they make sure not to interfere with the subjects' actions so as not to influence their behaviour. Of course there are several intermediate situations between the two extremes of participant and non-participant observation.

Participant observation has the following characteristics:

1   the researcher establishes a direct relationship with the social actors;
2   staying in their natural environment;
3   with the purpose of observing and describing their social actions;
4   by interacting with them and participating in their everyday ceremonials and rituals; and
5   learning their code (or at least parts of it) in order to understand the meaning of their actions.

An Historical Sketch

The birth of ethnographic methodology is commonly dated to the period between the late nineteenth and early twentieth centuries.

Anthropology

Ethnography developed internally to ethnology, a discipline which in the first half of the nineteenth century split from traditional anthropology, which was then dominated by physical and biological assumptions. Ethnology was more concerned with studying peoples (through comparison of their material artefacts) and their cultures, and with classifying their salient features. Before the advent of ethnographic methodology, ethnologists did not collect information by means of direct observation; instead, they examined statistics, the archives of government offices and missions, documentation centres, accounts of journeys, archaeological finds, native manufactures or objects furnished by collectors of exotic art, or they conversed with travellers, missionaries and explorers. These anthropologists considered the members of native peoples to be 'primitives': they were savages to be educated, and they could not be used as direct informants because they could not be trusted to furnish objective information.

Ethnographic methodology did not suddenly erupt in anthropology; rather it arose gradually through the work of various authors, among them the English anthropologist of Polish origin, Bronislaw K. Malinowski (1884–1942), and the English anthropologist Alfred R. Radcliffe-Brown (1881–1955). British social anthropology of an ethnographic stamp assimilated the positivist intellectual climate of its time and put itself forward, according to Radcliffe-Brown (1948), as a 'natural science of society' which was better able to furnish an objective description of a culture than the other methods used by anthropologists at the time. Radcliffe-Brown's polemic was directed against the then dominant speculative or 'desk' anthropology, which preferred to rely on secondary sources rather than undertake direct observation of social facts (customs, rituals, ceremonies) in order to uncover the 'laws' that govern a society.

Malinowski is commonly regarded as being the first to systematize ethnographic methodology. In his famous *Introduction* to *Argonauts of the Western Pacific* – the book which sets out his research conducted in the Trobriand Islands of the Melanesian archipelago off eastern New Guinea – Malinowski described the methodological principles underpinning the main goal of ethnography, which is to grasp the native's point of view, his relation to life, to realize his vision of his world. To this end, Malinowski lived for two years (between 1914 and 1918) among the Kula of the Trobriand Islands. He learned their language (Kiriwinian), used natives as informants, and directly observed the social life of a village, participating in its everyday activities. Malinowski inaugurated a view 'from within' that American anthropologists of the 1950s would call the 'emic' perspective – as opposed to the 'etic' or comparative perspective, which instead sought to establish categories useful for the analyst but not necessarily important for the members of the culture studied.

From the 1920s onwards, ethnographic methodology was incorporated into sociology – where it was adopted by researchers who mostly belonged to the Chicago School – and then into psychology and (recently) political science. Although it was imported from anthropology, however, fully 70 years previously the French mining engineer and later sociologist Pierre Le Play (1806–1892) had used primitive forms of participant observation, when he had stayed with the working-class families that he was studying. The English philanthropist Seebohm B. Rowntree (1871–1954) also used primordial forms of participant observation (after 1886) for his enquiries into poverty and living conditions in the London slums.

Sociological Approaches to Ethnography

Ethnography has a long tradition in sociology, so much so that there is not a unique mode but several approaches, sometimes in opposition.

The Period of 'Nosing Around' and the *Ex-post Facto* Construction of a Myth: the 'First' Chicago School

In the conventional view, ethnographic methodology was first introduced in sociology at the end of the 1910s by teachers and researchers in the Department of Sociology at the University of Chicago. Its director, Robert Ezra Park (1864–1944), urged his students in the following way:

> You have been told to go grubbing in the library, thereby accumulating a mass of notes and a liberal coating of grime. You have been told to choose problems wherever you can find musty stacks of routine records based on trivial schedules prepared by tired bureaucrats and filled out by reluctant applicants for aid or fussy do-gooders or indifferent clerks. This is called 'getting your hands dirty in real research'. Those who counsel you are wise and honorable; the reasons they offer are of great value. But one more thing is needful: first-hand observation. Go and sit in the lounges of the luxury hotels and on the doorsteps of the flophouses; sit on the Gold Coast settees and on the slum shakedowns; sit in the Orchestra Hall and in the Star and Garter Burlesque. In short, gentlemen, go get the seat of your pants dirty in real research. (Personal note by one of Park's students reported in Bulmer 1984: 97)

However, except for some particularly scrupulous and systematic researchers like Frederic M. Thrasher and Clifford Shaw, the research methods used by most of the Chicago School's members were rather primitive. As Madge recalls, 'a concern with method was left very much to the initiative of each investigator' (1962: 117) because 'the abiding fact [...] is that it is unified by its field of interest rather than by its methods' (1962: 125), which were always of secondary concern. Participant observation was given no particular importance, being just one of the many methods that the Chicago School used. Indeed, strictly speaking, the Chicago's School's methods cannot be termed 'ethnography', and its members themselves only expressly used the terms *ethnography* and *participant observation* after the 1940s. What authors since the 1960s have retrospectively called 'ethnography' (thus creating a myth – see Platt 1983; Hammersley 1989) was nothing but a general form of qualitative research. If anything, the Chicago researchers produced case studies (Platt 1983, 1992; Hammersley 1989), monographs produced using a melange of methodologies and methods. But the marked methodological pluralism of the Chicago School was not the result of a deliberate choice. Observation was one of the methods that the criminologist Sheldon Messinger (1925–2002) called 'nosing around' (see Lofland 1980: 4) and which were unconcerned with the methodological problems – access to the field, the ethics of research, the relativity of informants' points of view – which only became important much later.

The Institutionalization of Ethnography:
The 'Second' Chicago School

During the 1930s the Chicago Faculty of Sociology was joined by new members of staff, among them Louis Wirth (1897–1952), Herbert Blumer, Lloyd W. Warner (1898–1970) and Everett Cherrington Hughes. These scholars were distinguished, among other things, by a greater methodological awareness which had a strong impact on their pupils and followers (most notably William Foot Whyte, Howard Becker, Blanche Geer, Anselm Strauss, Melville Dalton, Erving Goffman, Fred Davis and Rosalie Wax), who after World War II produced a series of studies which revolutionized the current theories of deviance, education and work. And it was in this period, too, that ethnographic research became institutionalized by being taught, described in articles, subjected to methodological reflection, and eventually (in the 1960s) codified in textbooks. Ethnographic methodology as we know it today came into being largely through the work of Everett Hughes (1897–1983), who took up an appointment specifically to teach fieldwork at the university. As Herbert Gans, a doctoral student at the time, recalls:

> just after World War II, no one talked much about participant-observation; we just did it. Like many of my fellow sociology students, I enrolled in Everett Hughes's course 'Introduction to Field Work' and like them, I found it a traumatic introduction; we were sent to a census tract in nearby Hide Park and asked to do a small participant-observation study. Everett Hughes gave us some words of introduction and of instruction, but good father that he was, he quickly pushed us out of the nest and told us to fly on our own. (1968: 301)

Hughes was convinced that participant observation was a method to collect data which enabled objectivation of the activities and experiences of certain actors. Participation was in this sense ancillary to observation, although it was its complement for the correct production of theoretical material.

Interactionism

The participant observation method was given a privileged role and specific theoretical importance by interactionism, an approach developed between the 1930s and 1950s by Herbert Blumer (1900–1987). He believed that social research must adopt a 'naturalistic' approach and rely on fieldwork in order to grasp the perspective of social actors and see reality from their point of view. Blumer thus furnished the theoretical–methodological bases for a research practice which the first Chicago School had commendably introduced but had confusedly used. The methodological principles of interactionism have been well summarized by Denzin (1970: 7–19) and Silverman (1993: 48, table 3.2). Stated extremely briefly, they are:

1　relating symbols and interaction, showing how meanings arise in the context of behaviour;
2　taking the actors' point of view;
3　studying the 'situated' character of interaction;
4　analysing processes instead of structures, avoiding the determinism of predicting behaviour from class, gender, race, and so on;
5　generalizing from descriptions to theories.

'Grounded Theory'

The task of introducing methodological rules and procedural rigour into interactionism fell to two sociologists of medicine: Barney G. Glaser and Anselm Strauss (1916–1996). Their book *The Discovery of Grounded Theory: Strategies for Qualitative Research* (1967) rapidly became the standard methodological reference work. It was the first study to organize ethnographic methodology into its various phases: the gathering of information, its classification, and then its analysis. This was also by virtue of Strauss's wide experience as an ethnographer (see Charmaz and Bryant, this volume).

Structuralist Ethnography

Another fruitful approach that has contributed to the prestige of ethnography is 'structural' analysis. The term denotes an approach less interested in the subjective aspects of action (contrary to interactionism) than in its social context. To use a celebrated phrase from Goffman (a representative of this approach), it is an approach concerned with: 'Not, then, men and their moments. Rather moments and their men' (1967: 3).

A protagonist of structuralist ethnography was William Foote Whyte (1914–2000). Between 1936 and 1940, he conducted ethnography in *North End*, a poor district of Boston (which he renamed *Cornerville*) inhabited by a large number of Italian immigrants. His aim was to study the relationship between everyday life in Boston's juvenile gangs, the formation of their leaderships, and politics in the slums. His monograph, published with the striking title *Street Corner Society* (1943), was the first urban ethnography ever produced. Focusing on the bottom-up growth of political activities and their relations with the politics of the city in general, Whyte observed Cornerville in light of its dependent relation with the broader urban context. In this respect his approach differed from that of the urban studies conducted by the Chicago School, which described the slums as autonomous and isolated spaces.

Whyte's ethnography is not only important on the substantive and structural level; it also has methodological implications. After its publication, *Street Corner Society* had very little impact. But, in 1955, when the publisher was considering whether to bring out a second edition of the book, the idea came to Whyte of giving it greater interest by adding a methodological appendix. For the first time in research, this appendix recounted how ethnographic research had been conducted. Whyte thus introduced what today is termed *reflexivity*: the self-aware analysis of the dynamics between researcher and participants, the critical capacity to make explicit the position assumed by the observer in the field, and the way in which the researcher's positioning impacts on the research process.

Another leading representative of structural ethnography was the Canadian, Erving Goffman (1922–1982). His method of empirical research was almost exclusively ethnographic observation. However, he was not a systematic researcher, and his works (with some exceptions) do not refer to specific settings. His research strategy reflected Hughes' approach, with its unusual comparisons among apparently antithetical categories, behaviours and professions, all mixed together by an unsystematic procedure and an impressionistic style, which, on Goffman's own admission, deliberately emulated Simmel's. To conclude, therefore, methodology was not Goffman's principal concern: as evidenced by the following passage:

> Obviously, many of these data are of doubtful worth, and my interpretations – especially of some of them – may certainly be questionable, but I assume that a loose speculative approach to a fundamental area of conduct is better than a rigorous blindness of it [...] my own experience has been mainly with middle-class conduct in a few regions of America, and it is to this that most of my comments apply. (Goffman 1963: 4–5)

Ethnomethodology

During the 1950s, alongside interactionism and the works of Goffman there arose a new approach developed by Harold Garfinkel (1917–), which he subsequently termed *ethnomethodology*. By this term he meant the study of the means (*methods*) that people (*ethno*) use in their everyday lives to recognize, interpret and classify their own and others' actions. The theoretical core of ethnomethodology drew on the work of various authors: it continued the study of the conditions (trust, normative expectations, etc.) which sustain the *social order* (Talcott Parsons); it examined the properties of the *natural attitude* (Alfred Schutz) represented by commonsense reasoning in the everyday world or *Lebenswelt* (Edmund Husserl); and it criticized the concept of *rule* as a cognitive resource able to determine human actions (Ludwig Wittgenstein). Ethnomethodology mixed these and other ingredients together in an original synthesis whose strength consisted in the radicalism with which theories were applied for the analysis of concrete, everyday activities. In particular, besides his emphasis on 'tacit knowledge', Garfinkel empirically demonstrated the presence of two essential and (in his opinion) intrinsic characteristics of social practices: indexicality and reflexivity.

In the second half of the 1950s, Garfinkel also conducted a series of ethnographic observations in institutional settings: he studied, for example, a courtroom jury (with Saul Mendlovitz) and the psychiatric staff of the UCLA School of Medicine (with Egon Bittner). These ethnographies were not conducted methodically and systematically, probably because they were intended as *demonstrations* of the inescapability of indexicality and reflexivity rather than as empirical *findings*. But they nevertheless opened the way for a new type of process-based ethnography which sought to grasp phenomena as they unfolded. This approach inspired a series of ethnographic studies conducted by Garfinkel's colleagues, assistants and pupils during the 1960s and 1970s in a variety of institutional settings: police departments, newspaper editorial offices, law courts, therapy sessions, hospitals, halfway houses and so on.

Cultural Studies and Reception Ethnography

The approaches described in the previous chapter were current, with alternating fortunes, until the end of the 1970s. Thereafter new approaches arose (reception ethnography, postmodernist ethnography, feminist ethnography, and so on) which critically distanced themselves from the previous ethnographic traditions, although the latter obviously did not disappear and continued to operate in parallel with the new approaches. The ethnographic panorama, consequently, grew highly diversified.

Prior to the 'ethnographic turn', media analysts had attributed enormous power to television in conditioning people's tastes and opinions. This theoretical view derived from a Marxist doctrine (developed in France by the philosopher Louis Althusser, and in Germany by Theodor Adorno and Max Horkheimer of the Frankfurt School) which asserted that communication media were instruments used by the state to propagate the dominant ideology. The scholars working in the area of cultural studies were not entirely opposed to this view, insofar as they acknowledged that television was a powerful means of persuasion, but they criticized the doctrine's 'textual determinism' and its claim that a television programme was able per se (automatically and immediately, as if indeed by simple transfusion) to influence or predetermine its audience's opinions. Instead, according to Stuart Hall, another leading representative of cultural studies, consumers were not at all the passive recipients of meanings: they actively produced their own meanings, and they could even reject those proposed by the televisual text. Watching television was not the isolated activity performed in perfect silence, alone in a darkened room, that the academics imagined it to be (Hobson 1982: 110). Rather, it was an activity undertaken in a broader domestic context which conditioned the reception: television programmes are, for example, watched during dinner while those at the table discuss, intervene in, and thus interrupt the media flow. There is consequently a space between the producer (of the programme) and the final consumer (the viewer) where domestic activities condition the programme's reception, with outcomes not easy to predict.

Ethnography could describe consumption practices 'from the virtual standpoint of actual audiences' (Ang 1991: 165) by delineating the meanings that media consumers attribute to the texts and technologies that they encounter in their everyday lives.

In the last few decades many other approaches have emerged: *feminist ethnography*, *interpretative ethnography* (Denzin 1997), *postmodern ethnography*, *constitutive ethnography* (Mehan 1979), *institutional ethnography* (Smith 1986), *performance ethnography* (McCall 2000), *global ethnography* (Burawoy et al. 2000). Each of them introduced new important features which empowered this methodology (see Gobo 2008).

The 'Observation Society': Towards a Theory of Method

As mentioned in the first section, in the last 15 years there has been a trend (or a fashion) which has made ethnographic methodology so diffuse and well known. Why has this happened? Why does a methodology with more than a hundred years of history blow up only recently? Why now and not before?

Explaining the particular success and diffusion of some research methods in a certain historical period leads to an epistemological issue. As a matter of fact, if we accept that there exists a circular and reflexive relationship between science and society (on how social beliefs have influenced knowledge and scientific theories, and vice versa) or between technology and society (on how the birth of certain artefacts, like the bicycle or the personal computer, must be related to the type of society that has produced them), then even the relationship between society and social research, the interdependence among conventions, social beliefs and research methods, can be analysed with this perspective.

Previously Silverman (1997: 248) pointed out that interview and society were mutually constitutive: on the one hand, survey and in-depth interviewing required a particular type of society for them to come into being and develop; on the other, these research methods strengthen the society which has produced them. In accordance with this position, Gubrium and Holstein (2001: xii) argue that the interview is not a simple technique, a neutral instrument of information gathering, but has become an integral part of contemporary society, which has created the social and cultural conditions for its emergence. Atkinson and Silverman (1997) have stated that we live in an 'interview society', a society in which interviewing has become a fundamental activity, and interviews seem to have become crucial for people to make sense of their lives.

Ethnography is becoming as fashionable as the interview became from the 1920s. If the 'interview society' is still the dominant societal model, the recent sudden increase of ethnography can be explained with the hypothesis that we are entering an 'observation society', a society in which observing (as interviewing) has become a fundamental activity, and watching and scrutinizing are becoming important cognitive modes alongside the others, like listening, feeling, hearing and eavesdropping, typical of the 'interview society'.

The clues that we are living in an 'observation society' are many. Wherever we go there is always a television camera ready to film our actions (unbeknownst to us): camera phones and the current fashion for making video recordings of even the most personal and intimate situations and posting them on the Internet; or logging on to webcams pointed at city streets, monuments, landscapes, plants, bird nests, coffee pots, etc., to observe movements, developments and changes. Then there is the trend of webcams worn by people so that they can lead us virtually through their everyday lives. These are not minor eccentricities but websites visited by millions of people around the world.

Observing and being observed are two important features of contemporary Western societies. Consequently there is an increasing demand in various sectors of society – from marketing to security, television to the fashion industry[1] – for observation and ethnography. All of which suggests that ours is becoming an observation society.

The Added Value of Ethnography

As already noted, ethnographic methodology gives priority to observation as its primary source of information. The overriding concern is always to observe actions as they are performed in concrete settings. From this point of view, community studies are not usually ethnographies since, although the researchers may stay for a relatively long period of time in the environment of the group studied, their analyses are often based mainly on interviews and documents gathered on the spot. As Heritage stresses, if one is interested in action, the statements made by social actors during interviews cannot be treated 'as an appropriate substitute for the observation of actual behavior' (1984: 236). In fact, there is an oft-documented gap between

---

[1]The new demand for ethnography and the increase of professions based on observation are visible in marketing with commercial ethnography (*the mystery shopper and related techniques*), the fashion industry (*the cool-hunter*), management studies, IT, ergonomics and action research, industrial design (*shadowing, flanking, focused ethnography*), journalism (*investigative and gossip journalism*), the natural sciences (*birdwatching*), surveillance of leisure activities (*lifeguards*), police investigation and the politics of security, the politics of destabilization (crime and terrorism), art (photography, films and documentaries), tax investigations, paediatrics, and so on.

attitudes and social actions (La Piere 1934), between what people say and what they do (Gilbert and Mulkay 1983; Buscatto, this volume).

The presence of the researchers in the field enables them to gain better understanding of the conceptual categories of social actors, their points of view (emic), the meanings of their actions and behaviour, and social and political processes. This is the main added value of this methodology compared with other methodologies: observing actions and behaviours instead of opinions and attitudes only (see Buscatto, this volume). The consequences are not only theoretical (finding new or different results) but also practical, because a closer view of the routines and practices of social actors facilitates the crafting of remedies and solutions to social problems. In other words, it is easier to outline proposed social, political or organizational changes after having directly observed participants' actual social actions. This is one of the reasons why market research is changing (from in-depth interview and focus group to ethnography). It also accounts for the new demand for observation in social science (mainly sociology and psychology) and for applied ethnography in various professional sectors of society. A recent case comes from political science, a field still dominated by quantitative methods.

Ethnography in Political Science: a Case Study

The entry of ethnography into political science has been favoured by two cultural and theoretical changes in the discipline: an interest in the 'micro' dimensions of political phenomena, and an openness to the insights of qualitative research.

As in other disciplines, in political science the term *ethnography* has assumed a variety of meanings and it has become synonymous with 'fieldwork'. Locatable within this frame of meaning is the work of Weinstein (2007) on political violence and civil wars, and Wood (2000) on democratic transitions in South Africa and El Salvador. Drawing mainly upon narrative interviews (with the addition of some observations, official statistics and governmental documents) these authors have sought to reach the experiences, the subjective perspectives, the points of view of people involved in violent actions (Weinstein) and democratic transitions (Wood).

Weinstein (2007) tries to uncover specific causal mechanisms (why some rebel groups decide to use indiscriminate violence against civilians) by going beyond traditional quantitative studies, which explain this phenomenon of violence through macro-variables such as income and so on. He analyses the inner dynamics (the recruitment of members and the inner hierarchical structure) of rebel groups in Peru, Mozambique and Uganda. He finds that indiscriminate violence against civilians is committed mainly by rebel groups with external financial resources, such as those deriving from drug trafficking, foreign monetary aid, and so on. Consequently, these groups do not need or seek civilians' involvement in and consensus on their political actions.

Wood's (2000) analysis of the democratic transitions in South Africa and El Salvador suggests that these two countries are very different when structural variables (economic development, race composition, and so on) are considered, but quite similar when the link between the political elite and the economic elite is examined. She also focuses on the bottom-up violent mobilization of workers, pointing out that this produces an increase in costs affecting the whole production system (and consequently the economic elite): strikes, damage, economic uncertainty, a decrease of foreign capital inflows, and so on. In order to resolve the situation, the economic elites push for reform of the authoritarian regime and the economic and productive systems which support this form of government. Wood pinpoints everyday political processes, the impact of social actors' local actions on national politics, and the effects of micro-events on macro-phenomena.

A more extensive ethnography has been carried out by Ashforth (2005) focused on violence and democracy in South Africa. Ashforth, a white American, spent three years as a guest with a family in Soweto, the well-known black township on the outskirts of Johannesburg. During his residence, Ashforth realized that it would be extremely difficult to understand local politics (macro) without considering witchcraft (micro) and its role in interactional relations (micro). Through participation in the everyday life of the community, he acquired the conceptual categories, the constellation of meanings and the culture of the Soweto's residents. He learned that witchcraft beliefs were remedies for the uncertainty and insecurity of everyday life, that envy and jealousy produced the social conditions for the success of witchcraft, and that the latter shaped relations among individuals, social groups and political institutions on issues such as the spread of AIDS, its social consequences, and health policies. He also discovered the effects of the building of democracy on community members, their acceptance of violence, the shape of the concept of social justice, and the affirmation of a modern democratic and liberal state.

As Auyero (2006) and Aronoff (2006) maintain, political ethnography highlights aspects neglected by quantitative analysis, such as the impact of micro-politics on macro-phenomena, the complexity of everyday life, the network of participants' meanings, their motivations, the making of political action, the practices of politics (see also Silverman 2010). Ethnographic methods are useful for the analysis of political phenomena consisting not in macro-structures and fixed roles, but in interactions among participants, families and small groups (Tilly 2006), emancipating enquiry from the ethnocentrism (deriving from a purely etic approach) which still characterizes scientific explanations of political science.

Ethnography and its Enemies

Notwithstanding the acknowledged usefulness of ethnography, it is still subject to the following well-known stereotypes and prejudices.

Is Ethnography a Highly Subjective Method?

It is often argued that ethnography is a *highly* subjective method, in the sense that it is very sensitive to the researcher's attitudes and perceptions. In other words, if different researchers visit the same setting, they will see different things, and their ethnographic notes will record different aspects. Instead, a questionnaire or an in-depth interview, if conducted correctly, is more likely to obtain similar replies (reliability) regardless of who the interviewer is. And yet experience shows that this idea has scant empirical grounding (Gobo 2008).

A while ago, some students of mine conducted ethnography in a bar. Two groups (formed of three students each) visited the same bar a few days from each other. The fact that they had chosen the same bar was absolutely coincidental, in the sense that they had not agreed on it beforehand. Nevertheless, the two groups had a specific research design: to study the rituals, ceremonials and social actions of consumption in bars. They then produced a report. And, reading their reports, I discovered, to my great surprise, that they had observed and discovered practically the same things.

Hence the research design makes a greater contribution to discovery (or construction of data) than do the researchers themselves. Ethnography, therefore, is anything but a *highly* subjective methodology (even if subjectivity is ever present, as in all methodologies).

Behaviours are More Consistent than Attitudes and Opinions

What does the experience just described tell us theoretically? In other words, why did six different observers in the same bar notice practically the same things? Because what an ethnography mainly observes are behaviours (rituals, routines, ceremonials), and these are much more stable over time than are attitudes and opinions (the privileged fields of enquiry for discursive interviews and surveys), as proven by Richard La Piere's well-known experiments in the early 1930s.[2] Those who deal with organizations know very well that altering a behaviour requires more time than altering an attitude, not to mention opinions, which are sometimes so volatile that they change from one day to the next.

---

[2] The pioneering study by La Piere (1934) focused on the consistency between people's attitudes and their behaviour (a topic subsequently much debated in the 1940s and 1950s). La Piere concluded that there was no relation between them: social actors are often inconsistent, unconscious and irrational. A Chinese couple used by La Piere for his experiment travelled around the United States for two years, and on no occasion were they refused service by the proprietors of restaurants and hotels. La Piere then sent a postal questionnaire to the same proprietors that had served or accommodated the Chinese couple and obtained a surprising result: 92% of the proprietors of the cafés and restaurants and 91% of the hoteliers replied that they would refuse to accept Chinese clientele, thus contradicting their previous behaviour.

Can Ethnographic Research be Replicated or Reproduced?

From this it follows that, because behaviours are temporally rather stable, the results of ethnographic research can be repeated and reproduced. This depends upon two factors:

1 the presence of a precise research design which has guided the research;
2 that no significant changes have taken place between one piece of research and the next.

Ethnography and Generalization

A recurrent criticism made of ethnographic methods is that their results are impossible to generalize because they are based on few cases, sometimes on only one. However, there are numerous disciplines which work on a limited number of cases: for instance, palaeontology, archaeology, geology, ethology, biology, astrophysics, history, genetics, anthropology, linguistics, cognitive science, psychology (whose theories are largely based on experiments, and therefore on research conducted on non-probabilistic samples and on few cases). According to Becker (1998), these disciplines are unconcerned about their use of only a handful of cases to draw inferences and generalizations about thousands of people, animals, plants and other objects. Moreover, science studies the individual object/phenomenon not in itself but as a member of a broader class of objects/phenomena with particular characteristics/properties (Williams 2000; Payne and Williams 2005).

For these reasons it is anything but odd to think that the results of ethnographic research can be generalized. As Collins (1988) stated, much of the best work in sociology has been carried out using qualitative methods without statistical tests. This has been true of research areas ranging from organizational and community studies to micro studies of face-to-face interaction and macro studies of the world system.

In addition, if the focus of ethnography is on behaviour, and given that these are stable in time, then it is likely that generalizations are possible. Obviously, precise criteria must be followed in the choice of samples (Gobo 2008). Nevertheless, ethnography is not precluded from making generalizations.

Sampling Cases or Instances?

It will by now be clear that the term *case* is used ambiguously in ethnographic research. In surveys and discursive interviews, the cases correspond to the number of persons to interview (the sample), and who are usually interviewed only once. Indeed, it is rather rare for several interviews to be conducted with the same person (during a single piece of research). Hence statistical calculations and analyses of the interview texts are performed on cases.

Ethnographic research is very different. What is usually referred to as the 'case' (the organization or the group studied) is in fact the setting. The cases are instead the hundreds of occurrences or instances (pertaining to rituals, ceremonials and routines) that the researchers observe, or the dozens of individuals that they meet *dozens of times* during their presence in the field. The researcher is not interested in the organization (or the group) per se, but rather in the behaviours which take place within it. Consequently, in order not to create confusion with the other methodologies, it would be better in ethnographic research to abandon the term 'case' and replace it with that of 'occurrence' or 'instance' or 'sequence' (Silverman 2007).

The Future of Ethnography

Until recently, ethnography was a method largely confined to academic research. Moreover, although it has been used for at least a hundred years (since its invention by Malinowski and Radcliffe-Brown), it has always been a marginal method in the social sciences (with the exception of anthropology).

Nevertheless, it has recently acquired new popularity as an interpretive method, sponsored by epistemological approaches such as constructivism, postmodernism, feminism and relativism.

This happened not only in academe but also in the world of marketing, civil society and work. New professions based on some type of observational technique have arisen, and some of those born in the 'interview society' are changing to an observational perspective. The reason why ethnography is now becoming so fashionable probably concerns not its inner features (that is because it better captures the social actors' points of view, perspectives, meanings, motivations and emotions) but the socio-historical period in which we live. Ethnography and society are mutually constitutive and we are probably entering the 'observation society' (Gobo 2008), a social formation in which watching and scrutinizing are becoming the dominant cognitive modes alongside the others, like listening, feeling, hearing and eavesdropping, typical of the 'interview society' whence survey methodology comes.

This phenomenon accounts for the increasing demand in various sectors of society for observation and ethnography. The future seems likely to increase the importance of ethnography.

The case of advertising is a good example of how pervasiveness observation has become. For example, in February 2009 highly distinctive advertising panels were installed in the corridors of the Etoile metro station of Paris (as an experiment).

Sensors in the panels observed the behaviour of passers-by who stopped in front of the advertisements. They recorded how many people paused to look at an advertisement and for how long. Besides measuring the audience of the commercials, thus constituting a formidable tool for advertising agencies and their clients, they are also able to send text messages to the onlookers boasting the merits of a detergent, a film, or any other product. By autumn 2009 more than 1200 of these panels had been installed.

The world of literature has also rediscovered ethnographic observation. I use the prefix 're' because writers like Émile Zola, considered the creator of the naturalist genre, had since 1870 used a narrative style which described the problems of French society in vivid, analytical and participative ways. Indeed, Robert Park, one of the founders of the Chicago School, urged his students and colleagues to do in sociology what Zola had done in literature.

Today we are witnessing the return of a realist narrative which supersedes the postmodern genre represented by Don DeLillo, Thomas Pynchon and Kurt Vonnegut. It uses participant observation to investigate phenomena of which we have only indistinct impressions. Writers and journalists convey powerful social images which arouse our indignation much more than so many political pamphlets and sociological analyses are able to do, reviving the tradition of urban studies which began with the Chicago School.

For example, the journalist and writer Robert Neuwirth, in *Shadow Cities: A Billion Squatters, A New Urban World* (2005), describes his experiences when living in four squatter communities in large cities (Rio de Janeiro, Nairobi, Mumbai and Istanbul), for several months in each. Another journalist and writer, Marc Cooper, in *The Last Honest Place in America* (2005), conducts a fascinating analysis of the city of Las Vegas (where he lived for six months), considered to be the best place to understand the true soul of the contemporary United States. Or, to conclude this brief survey, a book by the journalist Adrian Nicole LeBlanc (*Random Family: Love, Drugs, Trouble, and Coming of Age in the Bronx*, 2004) recounts her 10-year residence in that notorious New York ghetto.

All these are signals, some very recent, that strong demand for observation and ethnography is emerging from different social worlds. And I have tried to explain this phenomenon on the hypothesis that we are entering the observation society. Nevertheless, this is no more than a hypothesis: only the future will tell how well founded it is.

Summary

- Ethnography is a methodology based on direct observation. Other sources of information (such as interviews with participants or documents) are ancillary.

- We are entering an 'observation society', a society in which observing has become a fundamental activity, and watching and scrutinizing are becoming important cognitive modes.

Future Prospects

Due to the added value of ethnography (the presence of the researchers in the field, which enables them to gain better understanding of the meanings of the social actions of social actors), this methodology has the potential to become a prominent approach in applied research.

Questions

- In terms of research practices, what is the difference in doing research based on observation and on interviews?
- What are the five main characteristics of participant observation?
- Why is ethnography becoming so fashionable?

Recommended Reading

Emerson, R.M., Fretz, R.I. and Shaw, L.L. (1995), *Writing Ethnographic Fieldnotes*, Chicago: University of Chicago Press.

Gobo, G. (2008), *Doing Ethnography*, London: Sage.

Silverman, D. (2007), 'Instances or sequences?'. In D. Silverman, *A Very Short, Fairly Interesting, Quite Cheap Book about Qualitative Research*, London: Sage, 61–84.

Internet Links

Ethnobase:

www.lse.ac.uk/collections/ethnobase/

Ethnographic Database Project:

www.ucl.ac.uk/~ucsalfo/EDP/Welcome.html

Visualising Ethnography:

www.lboro.ac.uk/departments/ss/visualising_ethnography/

(Continued)

(Continued)

INCITE – Incubator for Critical Inquiry into Technology and Ethnography
Goldsmiths College, University of London (UK):
www.studioincite.com/
Interaction Design Centre
Middlesex University, London (UK):
www.cs.mdx.ac.uk/research/idc/
Work, Interaction and Technology Research Group
King's College, London (UK):
www.umds.ac.uk/schools/sspp/rngmt/research/wit/

References

Ang, I. (1991), *Desperately Seeking the Audience*, London: Routledge.

Aronoff, M.J. (2006), 'Forty years as a political ethnographer'. *Ab Imperio*, 4: 1–15.

Ashforth, A. (2005), *Witchcraft, Violence and Democracy in South Africa*, Chicago: Chicago University Press.

Atkinson, P. and Hammersley, M. (1994), 'Ethnography and participant observation'. In N.K. Denzin and Y.S. Lincoln (eds), *Handbook of Qualitative Research*, Thousand Oaks, CA: Sage, 248–261.

Atkinson, P. and Silverman, D. (1997), 'Kundera's *Immortality*: the interview society and the invention of self'. *Qualitative Inquiry*, 3 (3): 324–345.

Auyero, J. (2006), 'Introductory note on politics under the microscope. Special issue on political ethnography I'. *Qualitative Sociology*, 29: 257–259.

Becker, H.S. (1998), *Trick of the Trade*, Chicago and London: University of Chicago Press.

Bulmer, M. (1984), *The Chicago School of Sociology: Institutionalization, Diversity, and the Rise of Sociological Research*, Chicago, University of Chicago Press.

Burawoy, M., Blum, J.A., George, S., Gille, Z., Gowan, T., Haney, L., Klawiter, M., Lopez, S.H., Riain, S.O. and Thayer, M. (2000), *Global Ethnography*, Berkeley: University of California Press.

Collins, R. (1988), *Theoretical Sociology*, San Diego: Harcourt, Brace, Jovanovich.

Denzin, N.K. (1970), *The Research Act*, New York: McGraw-Hill.

Denzin, N.K. (1997), *Interpretive Ethnography: Ethnographic Practices for the 21st Century*, Thousand Oaks, CA: Sage.

Gans, H.J. (1968), 'The participant-observer as a human being: observations on the personal aspects of fieldwork'. In H.S. Becker, B. Geer, D. Riesman and R.S. Weiss (eds), *Institutions and the Person*. Chicago: Aldine, 300–317.

Gilbert, N. and Mulkay, M. (1983), 'In search of the action'. In N. Gilbert and P. Abell (eds), *Accounts and Action*, Aldershot: Gower.

Gobo, G. (2008), *Doing Ethnography*, London: Sage.

Goffman, E. (1963), *Behavior in Public Places. Notes on the Social Organization of Gatherings*, Glencoe, IL: Free Press.

Goffman, E. (1967), *Interaction Ritual,* New York: Doubleday Anchor.

Gubrium, J.F. and Holstein, J. (eds) (2001), *Handbook of Interview Research,* Thousand Oaks, CA: Sage.

Hammersley, M. (1989), *The Dilemma of Qualitative Method,* London: Routledge.

Heritage, J. (1984), *Garfinkel and Ethnomethodology*, Cambridge: Polity.

Hobson, D. (1982), *'Crossroads': the Drama of Soap Opera*, London: Methuen.

La Piere, R.T. (1934), 'Attitudes vs. action'. *Social Force*, 12: 230–237.

Lofland, L.H. (1980), 'Reminiscences of classic Chicago: "The Blumer-Hughes Talk"'. *Urban Life*, 9 (3): 251–281.

Madge, J. (1962), *The Origins of Scientific Sociology*, New York: The Free Press of Glencoe.

McCall, M. (2000), 'Performance ethnography'. In N. Denzin and Y. Lincoln (eds), *Handbook of Qualitative Research* (2nd Edition), London: Sage.

Mehan, H. (1979), *Learning Lessons*, Cambridge, MA: Harvard University Press.

Payne, G. and Williams, M. (2005), 'Generalization in qualitative research'. *Sociology*, 39 (2): 295–314.

Platt, J. (1983), 'The development of the "participant observation" method in sociology: origin, myth and history'. *Journal of the History of the Behavioural Sciences*, 19 (4): 379–393.

Platt, J. (1992), '"Case Study" in American methodological thought'. *Current Sociology*, 40 (1): 17–48.

Radcliffe-Brown, A.R. (1948), *A Natural Science of Society*, New York: Free Press.

Silverman, D. (1993), *Interpreting Qualitative Data*, London: Sage.

Silverman, D. (1997), *Qualitative Research: Theory, Method and Practice*, London, Sage.

Silverman, D. (2007), 'Instances or sequences?'. In D. Silverman, *A Very Short, Fairly Interesting, Quite Cheap Book about Qualitative Research*, London: Sage, 61–84.

Silverman, D. (2010), 'Putting society together: what qualitative research can and cannot say about identities'. In P. Baert, G. Procacci and S. Koniordos (eds), *Conflict, Citizenship and Civil Society* (ESA book series), London: Routledge.

Smith, D.E. (1986), 'Institutional ethnography: a feminist method'. *Resource for Feminist Research*, 15: 6–13.

Tilly, C. (2006), 'Political ethnography as art and science'. *Qualitative Sociology*, 29: 409–412.

Weinstein, J. (2007), *Inside Rebellion: The Politics of Insurgent Violence,* New York: Cambridge University Press.

Whyte, W.F. (1943), *Street Corner Society*, Chicago: Chicago University Press.

Williams, M. (2000), 'Interpretativism and generalization'. *Sociology*, 34 (2): 209–224.

Wood, E.J. (2000), *Forging Democracy from Below: Insurgent Transitions in South Africa and El Salvador,* New York: Cambridge University Press.

Using Ethnography to Study Gender ⬤3

Marie Buscatto

Abstract

In the last 40 years, women in Western countries have moved onto the job market *en masse*. They also began working in what were traditionally male occupations, such as doctors, drivers, engineers or lawyers. However, differences in the situations of the two sexes persist: 'inequality regimes' remain operative, though in new ways. The sociological research done to explain these gender-based differentiations combines many different types of materials: statistics, questionnaires, direct observation, interviews, analysis of legal and regulatory texts, photographs, press coverage and other documents. The aim of this chapter is to describe and explain the specific contributions of the ethnographic method for analysis of gender differences in work settings or situations. Using precise empirical examples, it presents the specific contributions that the ethnographic method makes to the study of gendered social relations at work, i.e., enabling researchers to spot disparaging gender stereotypes, describe 'male' occupational networks, and identify gendered norms and conventions.

> **Keywords**:
>
> ethnography, methodology, gender, occupation, work, music, unions.

Introduction

In the last 40 years, women in Western countries have joined the labor market *en masse* (Padavic and Reskin 2002). They also began working in traditionally male fields and occupations (doctors, drivers, engineers, lawyers). Yet the differences between the sexes in the workplace and in work situations persist: 'inequality regimes' remain operative, though in new areas (Acker 2006). 'Horizontal segregation' 'naturally' distributes women around 'female' jobs (secretary, nurse, elementary school teacher) and men around 'male' jobs (police officer, manual worker, mechanic) (Maruani 2005). Men are better paid than women, in part for structural reasons, in part because of discrimination. 'Vertical segregation,' meanwhile, works to limit women's access to the highest social positions and most prestigious occupations (Buscatto and Marry 2009).

The number of research studies presenting and seeking to explain these gender-based differentiations continues to rise, and the first synthetic overviews of men and women at work have now been published (Padavic and Reskin 2002; Maruani 2005) – signs of the relative maturity of this new research field. Sociological research, some substantiated with historical data, combines a variety of materials (statistics, questionnaires, direct observation, interviews, analysis of legal and regulatory texts, photographs, press coverage and other documents) for the purpose of studying the social processes by which gender differences in work settings or situations are produced, legitimated or infringed.

It is in this empirical and theoretical context that the ethnographic method, based on the direct, prolonged in situ observation by the researcher[1] comes to enrich analysis of gender differences in the workplace or in work situations. I present here the specific contributions that the ethnographic method makes to the study of gendered social relations at work.

Mainly based on my empirical research on women jazz singers and musicians (Buscatto 2007a, 2007b) and women unionists in companies (Buscatto 2009), this chapter is organized in four parts:

1. A demonstration of how this method enriches analysis of gender relations in work settings or situations by making 'the arrangement between the sexes' the entry point for analysis.
2. The particular contributions of ethnographic practice in this area as they pertain to identifying degrading or denigrating gender stereotypes.
3. A consideration of the development of 'male' occupational networks.
4. A demonstration of how to identify gender norms and conventions.

---

[1]Atkinson and Hammersley's definition of ethnography is helpful here: 'In its most characteristic forms, it involves the ethnographer participating, overtly or covertly, in people's daily lives for an extended period of time, watching what happens, listening to what is said, asking questions – in fact collecting whatever data are available to throw light on the issues that are the focus of the research' (1995 [1983]: 1). For discussions about definitions of ethnography, see Gobo's chapter in this book.

The 'Arrangement Between the Sexes' as an Entry Point for Analysis

'Doing Gender'

The concept of gender accounts for the principles and modes of constructing, legitimating and circumventing or infringing socially established distinctions between female and male, and it does so by way of an open, dynamic process. To cite Goffman's expression, in studying gender we are studying the ways in which 'the arrangement between the sexes' is produced, contradicted and legitimated (1997 [1977]). Relations between the behaviors of situated men and women are observed in order to get an idea of the specific dynamic of gendered social relations in their particular context. As Salzinger puts it: 'the distinction between a feminine and masculine pair can endlessly be subdivided, as each side of the line can always be subsequently repartitioned internally into its own relative masculine and feminine components' (2004: 16).

Ethnography enriches identification and analysis of gender in work settings or situations precisely by inducing the researcher to focus on 'doing gender' (West and Zimmerman 1987). It is in daily interaction that 'sex-class makes itself felt, here in the organization of face-to-face interaction, for here understanding about sex-based dominance can be employed as a means of deciding who decides, who leads, and who follows' (Goffman 1997: 208). Observing gender in situ leads us to identify social processes of gender segregation that are not so visible in interviews, questionnaires or press coverage, and thereby to supplement what those other sources indicate about occupational trajectories and gender norms, representations and characteristics.

Consider the example of my research on women unionists and the original way of problematizing this subject made possible by my use of ethnography as the primary method – together with the complementary methods of interviewing and document analysis.

Being a Union Representative in a Company: Such a Male Activity

An ethnographic study based on direct observation of union activity was conducted at the Ganesh[2] Company.[3] It brought to light two kinds of gender differentiation

---

[2]A fake name.

[3]My investigation methods combined an ethnographic approach – observing men and women employees and unionists at different hierarchical levels in the workplace and in 'union' situations – with the more classic method of in-depth qualitative interviews and analysis of formal documents (Buscatto 2009).

operative in the six important union organizations that were present in the company. Despite discourse in favor of male–female parity, I observed that there were few women representatives in the company's unions, and that the higher up in the union hierarchy one goes, the fewer women there are. Local union representatives are likely to be men while national-level representatives are extremely likely to be men, and this holds regardless of union structure. Moreover, with few exceptions, the trajectories of the women unionists I observed and spoke with are more fragile than those of men, and those women specialize in less prestigious 'women's' areas (Buscatto 2009).

Ethnographic study brought to light three major social processes that combine over time and work together to produce and legitimate the marginalization of women employees in union structures, especially at relatively high levels in the union hierarchy:

- The non-official model of the 'union career,' which requires having a great deal of time and personal energy to devote to the activity, turns out to be strongly 'male.' The internal process of union promotion corresponds to a role that has been socially constructed as 'male': total commitment to an external activity and delegation of household tasks to the spouse. This means that it is harder for women to attain and remain in these positions.
- It turned out that union activism is a way of 'changing occupations' for men (but not for women) who wish to devote themselves fully to an activity and are unable to do so in their current occupational activity due to a lack of educational, social or occupational resources.
- The 'maleness' of union activity – as reflected in areas of interest, networks, behavioral norms – makes it fairly unattractive to most women. This also means that women who get into such activity 'anyway' are likely to be judged less favorably than men, to appear less legitimate in the eyes of their peers and the people they mix with, regardless of the level at which they practice that activity (I return to this process in the last part of the chapter, in connection with ethnography).

Ethnography defined the way I problematized my research topic, thus enabling me to identify these three processes. My analysis focused on union activity in itself and the role it plays in socializing unionists and determining whether or not they gain access to new responsibilities or important positions in union organizations. The rare studies of this question focus either on union activists at the time of specific labor conflicts or on their activities and careers within one or another union federation (Buscatto 2009). Ethnography, on the other hand, moved me to focus first and foremost on the work context in which union activity takes place, as this is where union representatives are most active and where the occasional hierarchical union career develops. Above and beyond focus on successful unionists, this method identified all the men and women who do not participate in union activity or who do so only occasionally or at certain moments in their occupational trajectory, and all those who are (or were) excluded from the possibility of advancement early on in their union involvement.

Direct observation of union activity repeatedly brought to light the way unionists behave, whether or not those ways are well thought of, the social relations unionists engage in to keep their places and get promoted, the judgment criteria used to decide who is a 'good' and who a 'bad' union activist, and the way tasks and responsibilities are distributed. It is *in situ* observation of union activity that can identify how unionists invest themselves in union activity (and how they are not permitted to). The behavior of the individuals I met and the ways they are viewed by their peers demonstrate the gender differences that appear in informal moments, union meetings, processes of handling union matters, and informal friendly socializing.

Whether one is talking about union career or internal social norms, gender segregation came to seem not so much a reproduction of external social relations as the result of actors' and union organizations' own choices within the work context. It was also an expression of the broader gender differences on which socialization modes are based, both domestic roles and social behavior norms. Gender segregation, a complex, dynamic phenomenon operative at different points in the social order, is actually enacted by actors in the work situation.

To deepen and illustrate this initial conclusion on the uses of ethnography, I now describe the three specific contributions that ethnography can make to the study of gender in work situations, thanks to the way it allows one to identify three social processes of gender differentiation.

'Feminine' Social Stereotypes and the Devaluing of Women's Professional Abilities

Direct observation proves extremely effective for identifying not only existing social stereotypes but also how they are constructed, how they operate in work situations and help produce negative and positive professional legitimacy. As an example, I present my study of jazz singers; I then analyze in greater depth how ethnography was able to reveal these phenomena.

Seductive Power, Femininity, and the Invisibility of Jazz Singers' Stage Work

My ethnographic study of French women jazz singers, based on participant observation and interviews, revealed a twofold gender differentiation.[4] Whereas French

---

[4]This first ethnographic study of the French jazz world was conducted from June 1998 to June 2002. I combined and compared data obtained through extended observation, interviews (done in 2001) and systematic reading of the specialized press (Buscatto 2007a, 2007b).

jazz is a man's world (more than 90% of French jazz musicians are men), most jazz singers (65%) are women. Above all, though some French women jazz singers are well known to colleagues and critics, they are not well known to the public and never earn their living primarily from their art. Three social processes occur and legitimate this hierarchical 'gender' structure (Buscatto 2007a, 2007b). Here I show how ethnography enabled me to identify a female stereotype – the force of women singers' seductive power – that works (along with other processes I could not present here) to devalue their professional abilities.

Singing requires a specific kind of stage work. Singers are the only performers to establish a constant relation with the audience, communicating with it by means of their eyes and the song lyrics, spinning stories for it, working on their physical position on stage so as to appear relaxed and involved (the way they hold the microphone, how they move on stage, facial expressions, clothes).

Moreover, in contrast to instrumentalists, whose attention is focused on the musical act itself, women jazz singers make an effort to be physically pleasing to audiences, programmers and critics. The French singers I met with work on their figure, the way they dress, the kind of gestures and movements they make, their facial expressions, and they do so according to the rules of 'femininity.' Women singers' faces are carefully made up; their hair is carefully arranged; their dress is designed to be attractive; they smile and otherwise vary their expressions in accordance with different emotions; they move their bodies in studied ways meant to have particular effects on spectators – in sum, women singers act so as to appear consummately 'womanly.' Two figures of 'female' seductive power, two 'feminine stereotypes' (Goffman 1976), came to light in the course of my observation: the 'active womanly woman' and the 'innermost womanly woman' (Buscatto 2007a). The 'innermost womanly woman' figure is characterized by a low, warm, expressive and suave voice. Scenic performances and clothes are elegant, low key and sober. Singers do not address the audience much, some even play their instrument all the time. Their energy is restrained, sometimes even intimate. Among current famous jazz singers, one may think of Diane Krall, Cassandra Wilson or Susanne Abbuehl. A second feminine figure is the 'active womanly woman.' She is more of a virtuoso singer, her voice warm, flowing, melodic. If the voice remains low, it goes up and down elegantly. The performances of these singers are active; they interact with instrumentalists and the audience quite openly. Among current famous jazz singers, one may think of Dianne Reeves or Dee Dee Bridgewater.[5]

Neither instrumentalists nor singers define the 'expressing' they do on stage as full-fledged work. It is instead understood to express the singer's personality and her 'natural' physical seductive power. Women jazz singers' strong seductive power

---

[5]Those two expressions were strongly inspired by Goffman's analysis of feminine stereotypes in commercial advertisements (Goffman 1976). If other seductive feminine figures may be found in jazz singing, those two appeared as the main ones on the French jazz scene.

thus proves a sort of paradoxical constraint that relegates them to work whose professional nature is not recognized and may even be denigrated. Either they do not meet the implicit expectations of their environment and are therefore unlikely to get hired, or they *do* meet those expectations and the real professional skills they used to do so are simply denied. The other possibility is that they are criticized for fitting the 'female' stereotype too closely, e.g., they are judged 'too' seductive, their low necklines are considered too 'provocative.'

Direct observation was essential to establishing the tie between singers' 'natural' seductive power and the fact that their stage work is not recognized and even denigrated. Analyzing press photos or singers' own remarks about how hard it is to meet programmers' demands did of course make me sensitive to the role of seductiveness in the jazz singer profession and the images of seduction operative in jazz, at least in the press. But ethnographic observation enriched those initial analyses in several ways.

First, repeated observation over time of women singers on stage systematically brought to the fore (above and beyond the superficial observation that women jazz singers have strong seductive power) the specific types of womanliness – bodily and vocal – that those singers construct, centered around one or the other of the two main female stereotypes mentioned above: the 'active womanly woman' and the 'innermost womanly woman.'

Second, observation brought to light the many efforts singers make to construct an on-stage presence that will be judged favorably. They take acting courses, discuss the matter with peers, learn make-up techniques, regularly practice in front of a mirror. Significantly, this work was either forgotten in the singers' own interview responses or mentioned off-handedly or critically in our exchanges as an unavoidable constraint. Moreover, singers are likely to present this work as part of a personal quest (rather than legitimate stage work deserving of specific professional recognition).

Lastly, observation brought to light the strength of the erotic imaginary associated with the jazz singer, here an incarnation of 'the eternal feminine' (Beauvoir 2000 [1949]), and its direct effects on how women jazz singers are devalued professionally (Buscatto 2007a, 2007b). In becoming objects of desire for the audience, peers and programmers, women jazz singers lose recognition of their professional and musical value, in a way similar to the women manual workers studied by Salzinger (2002).

Ethnography Establishes the Link Between Social Stereotypes and Devaluing of Professional Abilities

Various gender stereotypes make it hard for women to enter male occupational worlds and to gain recognition for their 'feminine' professionality in 'mixed' or 'female' worlds. Those stereotypes imply the legitimating of gender differentiations that are unfavorable to women, e.g., it is more difficult for women to accede to prestigious positions; their working and employment conditions are poorer; their pay lower; and they are more likely to be stigmatized in work settings.

On the one hand, when women move in male worlds, they are necessarily implicated in the 'images of the female' that they evoke in the eyes of others. Their strong seductive power (Salzinger 2002), the difficulty they have gaining recognition for female authority practices (Cassell 1998), and their traditional role of mother (Roth 2006) all prove particularly unsettling female stereotypes for women seeking to construct legitimate occupational positions in traditionally male roles or behavior, e.g., authority, technical prowess, self-assertion, ambition, physical strength, creativity.

On the other hand, in orienting themselves toward 'female' professions or areas of specialization (or in moving into such areas because they are 'easier' to get into), women are likely to be considered less professional than men working in 'male' areas of specialization, deemed more 'noble.' Women practicing a 'woman's job' (Perrot 1987) – singer, nurse, teacher, 'script girl,' cosmetician – tend to be perceived as merely extending their natural bodily or domestic qualities – seductiveness, relational capabilities, ability to listen, manual dexterity, patience, availability, caregiving – to their jobs. These qualities are understood to require no specific learning, complex knowledge or professional recognition.

Many existing 'female' (and 'male') stereotypes vary by the type of behavior in question, e.g. behavior involved in motherhood, appearance, flirting, life in a couple, social behavior or professional activity. They are also expressed in various ways, and their effects vary from one occupational world to another. It is necessary to study stereotypes closely, so as to be able to identify the exact content of gender stereotypes in the field under study and to reveal the specific effects it has when it comes to denigrating occupational or professional abilities or skills. By focusing analysis on daily interaction, ethnography produces this tie between the identification of specific stereotypes and effects on men's and women's professional or occupational reputations. This is shown in Joan Cassell's recent study of American women surgeons (1998), Leslie Salzinger's study of Mexican women manual workers (2002) and Geneviève Pruvost's study of women in the French police force (2007).

The Saliency of 'Male' Social Networks

Studies of business managers (Acker 2006) or television and film screenwriters (Bielby and Bielby 1999) show how social networks that are predominantly 'male' make it extremely difficult for women to enter and remain in male worlds.

The Difficulty of Gaining Access to Male Instrumentalists' Social Networks

Ethnography is useful here not only in identifying the difficulty women have getting into and remaining part of male social networks, but also and above all in spotting the social 'reasons' for this, as shown in my study of women jazz instrumentalists (2007a).[6] Social networks are crucial when it comes to keeping one's place in fluid, open art worlds and constructing a relatively good reputation in them (Becker 1982). I was able to show that French women jazz players over 30 cannot make a living primarily from jazz, partly because they have such a hard time getting into stable, open social networks; in this regard they are extremely dependent on their male jazz musician (programmer, agent or producer) husbands or partners.

French jazz networks are constructed around the relatively impermeable stylistic divisions between traditional jazz, modern jazz and improvisational music. Within each of these major styles, informal groups of individuals who regularly work together may be identified. These groups form freely on the basis of personal affinity. They may of course include occasional encounters or experiences among 'members', but most importantly they constitute the core of an individual's professional activity for at least a few years. Over time, of course, there may be break-ups, changes and reorganizations, some of which may be difficult. Jazz musicians' regular relations are of course played out on stage – during concerts, rehearsals, professional traveling – but also in gatherings of families and friends in the framework of leisure activities.

Women instrumentalists do not belong to solid, stable informal networks; their presence and contributions do not remain in the minds and memories of male colleagues when the latter are developing their professional projects. When I asked men how they had hired musicians for their latest projects (or when, in most cases, I reconstructed those 'hiring' modes by means of my observations), I noted that the people they hired were men with whom they had already worked around different musical projects, or else men who had been recommended to them by well-known musicians. Women jazz players – even women known to these men – do not at all come to mind as potential collaborators in any independent way. Women do not share in the above-described type of on-going work relations with any men other than their husbands or partners, who, as mentioned, are often jazz musicians themselves. And when they do work with other men, it is on the women's own initiative. Conversely, if jazz women absent themselves from the jazz scene for six months (to work steadily on a project in another musical world or for personal reasons such

---

[6]My second ethnographic study was an extension of the first study, focused on women jazz singers. Here I combined observation over an extended time period, interviews and systematic reading of the specialized press (Buscatto 2007a, 2010).

as having a child, living abroad temporarily, temporarily stopping their musical activity), they are likely to 'disappear' from the list of 'hirable' colleagues. Male musicians who could logically be thought of as close partners simply stop calling them.

Invisible, Taboo or 'Natural' Realities

It was by comparing my observations to statements from these men and women collected in interviews and informal situations that I realized that, except for friendly moments spent with their husbands' or partners' friends, these women instrumentalists are not likely to have any prolonged friendships with male jazz musicians. They work with such musicians, go on tour with them, have drinks with them after concerts or rehearsals, but they are unlikely to develop more informal friendships; they never become 'pals.' This means that the network – or more exactly the informal group that a woman jazz player moves in – is usually her husband's or partner's network (as mentioned, he is also very likely to be a jazz professional). Women jazz players participate in their partner's network, *not* in a shared network. If and when their love relationship comes to an end (as I observed to happen several times), the network 'vanishes' for the female musician and she has to start from scratch both personally and professionally. However, when the love relationship is just getting underway or blossoming, the number of projects on which the woman is asked to collaborate multiplies, on the basis of her jazzman partner's network.[7]

But for women jazz players, the 'need' to belong to their partner's network may also work to limit their careers. First, even though they experience this collaboration as a positive situation at the moment they choose it, it can become difficult over time. Several women find or have found it difficult to develop fully or progress alongside their partner. The jazz career of others is seriously damaged when they break up with their partner (a frequent occurrence in this art world). Some women may deliberately decide to limit their own career in order to promote their partner's. Meanwhile, the minority of women jazz musicians who do not have a professional jazzman partner have great difficulty remaining in the world of jazz.

Reconstituting the professional networks of jazz musicians of both sexes required combining and comparing the specific responses collected in interviews to the significant mass of ethnographic data I had noted over time. This was so because the information thus reconstituted – male partner's role in woman's career, social cooptation, professional difficulties – is taboo. But it is also because it is difficult for individuals to retrace their social relations. The disparaging attitude associated with a woman's career that has been facilitated by her musician partner also made the matter difficult to study. Both male and female respondents minimize the importance of

---

[7]This observation also holds for women jazz singers (Buscatto 2007a).

such help, 'forget' the material that constituted it, keep mum about difficulties – at least in exchanges with a person from outside the group. The 'naturalness' of the relations constructed in the couple or with friends also inclines respondents to deny – collectively and in some cases unconsciously – the role played by their partner and by friendships.

Furthermore, to understand how jazz women become socially marginalized also required using observations made after concerts and during work sessions and courses, friendly gatherings, and impromptu jam sessions. It was in such contexts that I was able to observe the fact that women have difficulty interacting informally with men who are not their husbands, partners, or close friends of their husband or partner. Thanks to my prolonged observation, it became clear that informal, regular friendships between jazz men and jazz women were unlikely to develop. The fact that men and women have different tastes and areas of interest also surely works to exclude women from closed networks. Furthermore, the reputation some of these women have of having 'too big a mouth' to be liked by male jazz musicians explains why older jazz women are unlikely to be appreciated by their male colleagues. The fact that it is next to impossible for women to participate in a solid informal network outside of their jazzman partner's network can also be attributed in large degree to these women's 'dangerous' seductive power.

My observations thus enabled me to realize the significance of women jazz instrumentalists' seductive power, power that works on the audience of course but also on their male colleagues, whose responsiveness to that power in turn forces women musicians to 'turn off the seduction' and be careful not to get involved in overly close relations with male colleagues. But women jazz instrumentalists' ability to 'turn off the seduction' then means they are less likely to be perceived as close colleagues, easy to live with or emotionally close.

Ethnographic study allows us to describe social networks that are not very visible in interviews, and to discover 'reasons' that may be invisible to the actors themselves (reasons for the fact that women are less likely to have access to elective affinity networks, i.e., their 'dangerous' seductive power and the fact that self-assertive women are rejected, etc). Collecting real data on long-term work relations makes it possible to reconstruct in detail how the social networks on which women and men rely – and in some cases are unable to rely – are constructed, while identifying the social workings that explain why it is so hard for women to gain access to work networks.

Identifying Implicit 'Male' Norms

Women may become 'fed up' with working in male milieux that they consider unlikely to include them professionally or where they find it difficult to gain recognition for their professional abilities. This difficulty is explained in part by the maleness of work norms, which make it harder for women than men to participate. Here again, ethnography helps in identifying these gender norms and their possible effect on the construction of occupational work positions.

Union Activism and Friendly Socializing

If we return to the example of women unionists in the Ganesh Company (Buscatto 2009) that I presented at length at the beginning of this chapter, it is clear that, as women in a 'male' world, women unionists are likely to have to behave 'like men' in order to be recognized and respected. The very way that union activity operates still seems strongly marked by conventions that are socially constructed as 'male' and that shape these women's relations with unionists at the same or higher levels as their own and with employees and managers. All this makes it difficult for women to gain a toehold in union worlds.

On the one hand, the kind of friendly socializing that goes on in the workplace plays a major role in getting male and female employees to join unions at Ganesh. Moreover, such socializing develops more fully as the person assumes greater responsibilities in the union. And while having social relations outside work is not fundamental at the time a person joins the union, they become increasingly important as a person's involvement in the union deepens.

The union is defined by all as an intense workgroup in which union and private-life components are combined. Union members engage in union activities and actions, of course, but they also celebrate private-life events together, have parties, *have a good time* – they spend time together outside the company or union. During my prolonged observation, I not only saw 'birthday parties' and gatherings at cafés after a labor negotiation or the working day, but also often heard how union members plan to spend leisure time together over the weekend, in the evenings and during holidays.

The fact is that such moments seem very 'male,' first of all in terms of the subjects of conversation. At 'traditional' union X, whose members are relatively advanced in age, people talk about soccer, cycling or hunting, whereas the younger and more 'modern' members of union Y talk about photography, current political events or movies. While the few women present do not share these interests, their silence or laughter makes it clear that they accept this type of conversation. On the other hand, women not present on these occasions seem to have little interest for a world that is not interested in more 'female' subjects, namely those I heard these women discuss throughout my observation of them at work: the family, grocery shopping, specific television programs and reading material, interior decorating, etc. Moreover, men tend to joke and make teasing or sharp remarks (though once again, this varies by union), though some of the women present were obviously quite comfortable in this type of exchange, capable of repartee – they have adopted a very self-assertive, 'male' style.

Extremely 'Male' Union Operation

If we consider union activity in the strict sense of the term, union operation as I observed it seems to promote 'male' behavior. Initial union actions are public and require exposing oneself both verbally and physically: speaking out in public, distributing tracts, going to see the 'boss' to obtain explanations or defend an employee. Men often say they began as unionists by engaging in spectacular actions (active strikes) or small actions focused on others (distributing tracts, speaking with co-workers in order to sensitize them) and that they were then requested to assume greater responsibilities by colleagues who saw them as 'smart' or 'resourceful.' They often spoke with pride during our interviews of these 'battle feats,' which were what led them to more intense commitment to union activity.

The few women union activists I met with were likely to have been asked to join the union incidentally, during a union action. They never say that moments of union public speaking marked their entrance into the union world. One mentioned the fact that her family had a history of union involvement; this was known to her colleagues, who came to ask her to join on that basis. Another had been hired as a secretary in the union organization before becoming directly implicated in union action. The third had become as assertive in her behavior as her male colleagues. This was due to her past as a militant feminist, and it was on this basis that it was accepted. Her case was exceptional, found in only one of the six unions I studied, the only one to have taken in a few women who behave, dress and speak in a 'male' fashion. Such socially 'exceptional' women do not seem at all eager to open the way for other women who have been socialized in the more 'usual' way. Lastly, during my observations, I did not see any women speak out publicly at the local level. That activity seems reserved almost entirely for men, who prize that type of action.

Union activity at the regional or national level is more routine and hidden (dealing with files, participating in hearings or meetings, managing the budget), and this leaves more room for 'female' behavior – women are less inclined to speak in public. But once again, my observation of national-level labor negotiations and internal union meetings confirmed that men have a greater propensity to behave in 'male' fashion during negotiations or among peers, i.e., to state their opinions loud and clear, speak out, joke, leave the room if they disagree. And if we take seriously the approving comments made in response to these 'male' types of behavior, we can only conclude that such behavior works to legitimate unionists' actions and improves their ability to attain high positions.

Women who attain high levels in the union hierarchy are said to know how to maintain a steady grip on union matters, how to assert their point of view, how to be combative, but they are also said to keep a low profile in union action and to be more serious than men when it comes to handling technical matters. These statements agree with my observations: the few women unionists I spoke with and observed first take a position on technical aspects of the issues in question and how to manage discussion time, whereas men, while not rejecting these aspects of discussion, are more focused on making opening declarations, asserting their opposition in style, and threatening management representatives.

As this example clearly shows, it is by comparing data collected in interviews – concerning areas of interest, modes of acceding to union positions, ideas about union activity – to data collected through observation – union member gatherings, social behavior, the mutual inviting that union members do – that the researcher can spot which social norms are valued and/or activated by sex and what their gender-related effects are on unionists' trajectories. Unionism is a 'male' activity, and as such it is less likely to attract women than men. When it does attract them 'anyway,' it affords them a place that they are then hard pressed to construct in a 'normal' way. These observations are similar to those presented in studies of women surgeons (Cassel 1998), women jazz musicians (Buscatto 2007a) and senior business executives (Acker 2006).

Summary

I have presented several ways that ethnography enriches analysis of gender relations at work by situating the observer at the heart of 'the arrangement between the sexes' (Goffman 1997 [1977]). Ethnography of gender – either alone or together with other methods such as document analysis, interviews, questionnaires, statistics – leads the researcher to take into account the fact that gendered social relations are a dynamic, contextual process. This enables him or her to spot and identify operative social stereotypes, social networks and social gender norms in a particularly efficient way. It also allows us to demonstrate the subtle influence of such stereotypes on how women get marginalized in 'male' spheres or how they get confined in 'mixed' or 'female' spheres to 'female' positions that are less valued in professional terms than male positions.

Future Prospects

Once 'male' or 'female' norms, stereotypes or social networks have been understood and described ethnographically, those norms, stereotypes and social networks can in turn become the focus of more codified studies. But while inquiry through questionnaires or interviews enables us to identify these practices, in situ observation is more effective when it comes to seeing how diverse they are and spotting the complex, contradictory, implicit 'reasons' behind them and the collective production, legitimation and subversion of gender differences 'in action.'

Grasping the situations of men and women at work does not imply making exclusive, imperialist use of ethnography but rather smoothly combining different methods. The decisions that individual women and men make then appear the result of a series of conscious or unconscious choices, successes or failures, orientations and reorientations that evolve over time and are subject to the combined influence of numerous social processes, internal and external to the specific occupational world under study. Future research on gender in work settings or situations can only be enriched by researchers' conscious, masterful combining of methods appropriate to the objects being studied and the questions raised.

Lastly, like any method, be it qualitative or quantitative, ethnography and its use does not preclude producing 'artefacts' (Silverman 2007), ideological interpretations or biased views. It should therefore be used in connection with constant 'reflexivity,' as this is the best way of ensuring its scientificity (Burawoy 2003; Taylor 2002). Given that the observer gets drawn into the world he or she intends to study and given that what makes the ethnographic method fully meaningful is its flexibility, fluidity and unpredictability, researchers are well advised to unceasingly question the way they reach and interpret their observations (Buscatto 2008).

Questions

- What are the three main gender differences operative in work settings or situations?
- Give a precise definition of ethnography.
- What are ethnography's three main contributions to the study of gender in work settings or situations?

Acknowledgements

This chapter was translated by Amy Jacobs.

Recommended Reading

Acker, Joan. 2006. Inequality regimes: gender, class and race in organizations. *Gender and Society* 20, no. 4: 441–464.

(Continued)

(Continued)

Atkinson, Paul and Martyn Hammersley. 1983 [1995]. *Ethnography: principles in practice.* New York: Routledge.

Bruni, Attila, Silvia Gherardi and Barbara Poggio. 2005. *Gender and entrepreneurship: an ethnographical approach.* London/New York: Routledge.

Buscatto, Marie. 2007. Contributions of ethnography to gendered sociology: the French jazz world. *Qualitative Sociology Review* III, no. 3: 46–58.

Cassell, Joan. 1998. *The woman in the surgeon's body.* Cambridge, MA: Harvard University Press.

Goffman, Erving. 1977. The arrangement between the sexes. *Theory and Society* 4, no. 3: 301–333.

Padavic, Irene and Barbara Reskin. 2002. *Women and men at work* (2nd ed.). Thousand Oaks, CA: Pine Forge Press.

Salzinger, Leslie. 2003. *Genders in production: making workers in Mexico's global factories.* Berkeley: University of California Press.

Taylor, Stephanie, ed. 2002. *Ethnographic research: a reader.* London: Sage.

Warren, Carol A. B. and Jennifer Kay Hackney. 2000. *Gender issues in ethnography.* Thousand Oaks, CA: Sage.

West, Candace and Don Zimmerman. 1987. Doing gender. *Gender & Society* 1, no. 2: 125–151.

Internet Links

Gender & Society journal:
http://gas.sagepub.com/
Gender, Work & Organization journal:
www.wiley.com/bw/journal.asp?ref=0968-6673
Erving Goffman's short biography:
http://people.brandeis.edu/~teuber/goffmanbio.html
Gender Issues in Ethnography journal:
www.sagepub.com/booksProdDesc.nav?prodId=Book9381

(Continued)

(Continued)

A basic definition of gender:

http://en.wikipedia.org/wiki/Gender

'Ethnographies of artistic work', *Qualitative Sociology Review* special issue:
www.qualitativesociologyreview.org/ENG/volume8.php

Journal of Contemporary Ethnography:
http://jce.sagepub.com

Ethnography journal:
www.uk.sagepub.com/journalsProdDesc.nav?prodId=Journal200906

References

Acker, Joan. 2006. Inequality regimes: gender, class and race in organizations. *Gender & Society* 20, no. 4: 441–464.

Atkinson, Paul and Martyn Hammersley. 1995 [1983]. *Ethnography: principles in practice*. New York: Routledge.

Beauvoir, Simone de. 2000 [1949]. *Le deuxième sexe*. Paris: Gallimard, Folio.

Becker, Howard S. 1982. *Art worlds*. Berkeley: University of California Press.

Bielby, Denise D. and William T. Bielby. 1999. Organizational mediation of project-based labor markets: talent agencies and the careers of screenwriters. *American Sociological Review* 64, no. 1: 64–85.

Burawoy, Michael. 2003. Revisits: an outline of a theory of reflexive ethnography. *American Sociological Review* 68, no. 5: 645–678.

Buscatto, Marie and Catherine Marry. 2009. Le "plafond de verre" dans tous ses éclats: la féminisation des professions supérieures au XXᵉ siècle (introduction to special issue). *Sociologie du travail* 51, no. 2: 170–182.

Buscatto, Marie. 2010. Trying to get in, getting in, staying in: the three challenges for women jazz musicians. *Bourdieu in question. Recent developments in French sociology of art*, ed. Jeffrey Halley and Daglind Sonolet, to be published.

Buscatto, Marie. 2009. Syndicaliste en entreprise: une activité si masculine.... In *Le sexe du militantisme*, ed. Patricia Roux and Olivier Filleule, Paris: Presses de Science p. 75–91.

Buscatto, Marie. 2008. Reflexivity as quality: 'overt' organizational ethnography as an emblematic example. *Qualitative Sociology Review* IV no. 3: 29–48.

Buscatto, Marie. 2007a. *Femmes du jazz: musicalités, féminités, marginalisations*. Paris: CNRS Editions.

Buscatto, Marie. 2007b. Contributions of ethnography to gendered sociology: the French jazz world. *Qualitative Sociology Review* III, no. 3: 46–58.

Cassell, Joan. 1998. *The woman in the surgeon's body*. Cambridge, MA: Harvard University Press.

Goffman, Erving. 1997. Frame analysis of gender. In *The Goffman reader*, ed. C. Lemert and A. Branaman. Malden, MA: Blackwell. First published in 1977 as 'The arrangement between the sexes,' *Theory and Society* 4, no. 3: 301–333.

Goffman, Erving. 1976. *Gender advertisements*. New York: Harper and Row.

Maruani, Margaret, ed. 2005. *Femmes, genre et sociétés: l'état des savoirs*. Paris: La Découverte.

Padavic, Irene and Barbara Reskin. 2002. *Women and men at work* (2nd ed.). Thousand Oaks, CA: Pine Forge Press.

Perrot, Michelle. 1987. Qu'est-ce qu'un métier de femme? *Le mouvement social* 140: 3–8.

Pruvost, Geneviève. 2007. *Profession: policier, sexe: féminin*. Paris: Editions de la Maison des Sciences de l'Homme.

Roth, Louise-Marie. 2006. *Selling women short: gender inequality on Wall Street*. Princeton, NJ: Princeton University Press.

Salzinger, Leslie. 2004. Revealing the unmarked: finding masculinity in a global factory. *Ethnography* 5, no. 1: 5–24.

Salzinger, Leslie. 2002. Manufacturing sexual subjects: 'harassment,' desire and discipline on a Maquiladora shopfloor. In *Ethnographic research, a reader*, ed. Stephanie Taylor. London: Sage.

Silverman, David. 2007. Art and artefact in qualitative research. Unpublished paper delivered at the conference entitled 'Improving the quality of qualitative research' held by the European Science Foundation, Kristiansand, Norway, June 25–27.

Taylor, Stephanie, ed. 2002. *Ethnographic research, a reader*. London: Sage.

West, Candace and Don Zimmerman. 1987. Doing gender. *Gender & Society* 1, no. 2: 125–151.

Organizational Ethnography

4

Thomas S. Eberle and Christoph Maeder

Abstract

Organizational ethnography means doing ethnography in and of organizations. Ethnography is a multi-method approach, whose essential feature is that it is primarily based on direct observation. We discuss the characteristics which distinguish organizational ethnography from general ethnography, and consider how it relates to (organizational) theory. We suggest sorting the great multiplicity of theoretical and methodological approaches in organizational studies along a continuum between theory- and data-guided poles, and present some important sociological approaches of organizational ethnography. We then discuss practical considerations in doing organizational ethnography such as field access and participation, data collection and data analysis, informant and field relations, reporting back, ethical questions, and finally writing up.

Keywords:

organization, ethnography, organizational theory, research methods.

Ethnographic research in and of organizations or, more generally, of organizing processes, is nowadays often called "organizational ethnography". Work in this field significantly predates these designations,[1] but has markedly expanded in recent years, alongside an increased focus on qualitative methods and ethnography more generally. The fact that *organizational ethnography* constitutes a topic of its own may,

---

[1]For its history see Schwartzman (1993).

however, still come as a surprise. Indeed, the field has become very complex. On the one hand, modern societies consist of a multitude of different types of organizations, and new forms of organization and of organizing processes are emerging continuously, like virtual organizations or all sorts of networking. On the other hand, the variety of theoretical and methodological approaches is ever increasing, which makes it difficult to give a "proper" account of the field.

The aim of this chapter is to introduce the field of organizational ethnography and to outline its central features and issues. In particular, we will focus on the following areas:

- What counts as organizational *ethnography* and what does not?
- What is *organizational* ethnography? What are the special characteristics of the field?
- What are the main theoretical and methodological approaches of organizational ethnography?
- Practical issues of doing organizational ethnography

What Counts as Organizational *Ethnography* and What Does Not?

Doing ethnography means using multiple methods of data gathering, like observation, interviews, collection of documents, pictures, audio-visual materials as well as representations of artefacts. The main difference from other ways of investigating the social world is that the researcher does "fieldwork" and collects data him- or herself through physical presence. In contrast to survey research, ethnographic research cannot be done solely from a desk (see Gobo and Buscatto, this volume). An ethnographer enters a field with all of his or her senses, and takes into account the architecture, the furniture, the spatial arrangements, the ways people work and interact, the documents they produce and use, the contents of their communication, the time frame of social processes, and so on. Organizational ethnography, like cultural studies, has contributed to the significant expansion of the meaning of "ethnography" since the 1980s. In organizational studies, quantitative methods became dominant in the 1950s and 1960s, as in the social sciences in general, and have remained widespread up to the present day. Qualitative methods re-emerged against this backdrop, and "organizational ethnography" became, for many, a common denominator of non-quantitative organizational studies using any type of qualitative method, be it in-depth or narrative interviews, qualitative content analysis of documents, pictures and audio-visual data, or non-quantitative case studies.

Such a stretched meaning of the term, however, destroys the very characteristic and potential of ethnography: that its research is based primarily on *observational data* about how actors work, act and interact in their natural environment as they go about their daily activities. Such research does not rely solely on what people say about their lives in an interview or on what is reported in documents – rather such data are treated with caution. Of course, ethnographers also talk to people, read documents and consider all kinds of artefacts, but they do so only in the context of an observational study.[2]

What is *Organizational* Ethnography?

Organizational ethnography predominantly involves research into organizations in modern societies. As globalization changed the world society, it also changed tribal life, and cultural anthropology lost its traditional object. In recent decades anthropologists therefore began researching modern societies too. The conventional distinction between the two disciplines in terms of their different object – tribal vs. modern societies – no longer holds true. Both anthropologists and sociologists do organizational ethnography now. Any differences are rather found in their theoretical concepts and perspectives, their disciplinary discourses and traditions. However, they also share many commonalities and influence and shape each other (cf. Gellner and Hirsch 2001). Of course, researching "the native's view" in modern organizations and comparing tribal life with corporate life sounds rather metaphorical when studying modern organizations. Other theoretical categories, however, became the common ground of many approaches for analysing the symbolic representations of actors' meanings, like "narratives, discourses, stories, metaphors, myths, slogans, jargon, jokes, gossip, rumours, and anecdotes found in everyday talk and text (symbolic language); rites and rituals, practices, customs, routines (symbolic acts); or built spaces, architectural design, clothing, and other physical artefacts (symbolic objects)" (Ybema et al. 2009: 8). All of these categories can obviously be used to analyse remote tribes as well as modern organizations. Is there any difference at all between the ethnography of tribal societies and the ethnography of modern organizations?

Indeed, most of what is written on the methodology of organizational ethnography is valid for any sort of ethnography. This can be well illustrated by the guidebook on how to become an organizational ethnographer by Daniel Neyland (2008). As it is impossible to formulate a fixed set of instructions, rules and procedures on how to do ethnography (Atkinson 1990), Neyland discusses the crucial issues in the form of "sensibilities". Sensibilities do not have the same status as recipes or instructions but are not vague or incoherent either. They provide information and background, questions and a range of answers, and the tricks of the trade available for ethnographic consideration (Becker 1998: 11). The author describes 10 sensibilities (which make up his book):

---

[2]On the importance of naturally occurring data, see Silverman (2007: Chapter 2).

1   Developing an ethnographic strategy in tandem with the situation, making initial choices about the type of group or activity, the place, material object or a very specific question, but keeping it fluid and flexible.

2   Choosing among the three principal approaches to knowledge: a realist ethnography that strives for objective representation; a narrative ethnography which accepts that different interpretations and accounts are possible; and a reflexive ethnography that reflects on how the processes of collecting, organizing and analysing the data produce the outcome.

3   Choosing locations and negotiating access.

4   Establishing field relations by close involvement to key informants and gatekeepers or even by becoming a group member. Establishing trust but not getting too close.

5   The time frame of an ethnographic study or of field access may lead the research towards producing either thick or quick descriptions.

6   Observational skills and writing well-organized field notes are important, as well as keeping a kind of strangeness in order to see the ordinary.

7   Making choices about supplementing observations by interviews, audio-visual recordings and studying other technologies, like the virtual world of computers.

8   Choosing the form of writing, either for a broad (organizational) audience or for scholarly pursuit.

9   Ethical considerations should feature which areas are studied, who is incorporated into the research and how, what will be done with the observational data and if the researched have access to them (e.g. to the field notes or to recordings).

10 Exits should be considered at an early stage of ethnography and in relation to the time frame of the study, the phenomenon and field access.

All these sensibilities are crucial for doing ethnography – not just for organizational but for any kind of ethnography. The same applies to the reader *Organizational Ethnography* of Ybema et al. that aims at "problematizing the practice of organizational ethnography and tackling key challenges and problematics that arise in the doing and writing of organizational ethnography" (2009: 2). The merits of both books lie in their discussion of the basic principles, sensibilities, methodical and methodological choices in doing ethnography in the context of research in and of organizations. It is the specific contextualizations that make the difference. Neyland (2008) illustrates each sensibility through a range of examples from ethnographic fieldwork in organizations that give insight into practical tasks involved in doing organizational ethnography (and which are worthwhile reading).

A fundamental difference between "ethnographying" (Tota 2004) modern organizations vs. tribal societies seems to be the geographical and cultural distance. To research an exotic tribe implied that an anthropological ethnographer would travel far from home, stay for two years, immerse him- or herself in an unfamiliar culture, learn a foreign language and live with a number of hardships. An organizational ethnographer does not need a toothbrush when leaving home (Bate 1997: 1150), as he or she usually returns for the night. Ethnographers can work regular hours and enjoy multiple leisure time activities in between as the other members of the organization do. It is even possible – and common practice – to enter the field only sporadically, to move in for short periods and to move out again.

There are a number of practicalities that are specific to doing *organizational* ethnography, which we will discuss at greater length later. However, the significance of the cultural difference between an ethnographer and the researched can vary a great deal in modern societies and therefore depends on the specific field. The more familiar a setting is, the more difficult it is to keep up sufficient distance and strangeness to recognize the regular and ordinary features of daily routines. But ethnographers have found cultural milieux in modern societies that differ greatly from "regular" life-styles and take ample time to investigate. In a similar vein, sophisticated work settings with high-tech equipment, such as for example scientific laboratories or surveillance and control rooms, require plenty of fieldwork in order to make adequate sense of what is going on (Knorr-Cetina 1999; Latour and Woolgar 1979; Knoblauch et al. 2000).

What are the Main Theoretical and Methodological Approaches of Organizational Ethnography?

Organization as a First- and Second-order Construct

A crucial question remains unanswered so far: what is the difference between *organizational* and other kinds of settings? Which concepts of *organization* or *organizing* are in use in organizational ethnography? In addressing this question, it may be helpful to use Alfred Schutz's (1964) distinction between first- and second-order constructs. First-order constructs are common-sense concepts that people use when accomplishing their daily affairs. We all have some notion of what "organizing" and "organization" mean. We are aware that the term "organization" refers sometimes to the process of ordering activities that are often pursued collaboratively, and sometimes to institutions, like corporations, state agencies or associations. We all agree that "organization" always implies features of an "order"; we would never use the term to designate a wholly chaotic phenomenon or one which was, in other words, "out of order". In this sense any social phenomenon – a state of affairs as well as a process – that has orderly features can be called an "organization" or being "organized".

Organizational ethnographers have to decide if they treat "organization" and "organizing" as a first- or second-order construct. They can, like ethnomethodology, consider "organization" and "organizing" as members' glosses and treat them as members' categories; their subject then is "organizing work" (Silverman and Jones 1976) or the members' activities by which accountable features of social order get produced. Or they can do ethnography *in* organizations, leave this undefined and use any kind of theoretical approach to study their particular phenomenon, like discourses, identities, narratives, etc. Or they can link the ethnographic research directly to organizational theory, as is often done in management research.

The Paradigmatic Diversity of Organizational Studies

A great deal of ethnographic research is linked to organizational studies. When these researchers define their field they refer to what the scientific community generally accepts as constituting the field of organizational studies. This is clearly demonstrated by Kostera (2007) who makes direct references to organizational theory. It is also illustrated by Yanow and Geuijen's (2009) attempt to generate a bibliography of relevant publications which necessarily involved the identification of characteristics with which to determine what to count as *organizational* ethnography:

> we decided to use as criteria those research topics that feature in organizational studies scholarship, ranging from structure to processes of organizing, from human relations to politics, from culture to economics (…), involving various organizational levels, from shop floor workers to middle managers to chief executives, but also including external relations with clients and/or customers, governmental regulators, and other organizations, across a range of organizational types, from government agencies to corporations, health care to education, and so forth. If studies of work were situated in organizational contexts and engaged organizational studies topics such as these, we included them [otherwise not]. (2009: 255)

The field of organizational studies has become rather unclear. An early and often cited attempt to construct an overview was undertaken by Burrell and Morgan (1979). They placed all major existing approaches within a grid divided along the two dimensions of subjective vs. objective approaches and sociology of regulation vs. sociology of radical change, and grouped them into four basic paradigms: (1) functionalist sociology (objective–regulation); (2) interpretive sociology (subjective–regulation); (3) radical structuralism (objective–change); and (4) radical humanism (subjective–change). The first two are descriptive, the latter two are critical (and demonstrate the prevalence of critical theory at the time).

Although any ordering of an academic landscape along two dimensions has its obvious shortcomings, this book prepared the ground for the pending pluralism in organization theory by stating that the paradigms are incommensurable. Since organization theorists sought their inspiration in poststructuralist and postmodern ideas from French philosophers like Lyotard, Baudrillard, Foucault, Derrida or Barthes in the 1980s and 1990s, this diversity has greatly increased. Some authors still bemoan the theoretical pluralism of this paradigmatic jungle and call for more unity, some even attempting to develop a synthesis and an integrative theory. However, by doing this they invariably end up adding another approach and further increasing the diversity. The present state of variety is well documented in *Contemporary Organization Theory* by Jones and Munro (2005), and many organization theorists explicitly welcome it (e.g. Czarniawska 1998).[3]

As organizational ethnographers must interpret their data in relation to a theoretical framework, they face the practical problem of how to come to terms with this variety. Gareth Morgan ([1986] 2006) proposed a solution to this problem which is still relevant today. He suggested understanding the theoretical landscape as a collection of multiple images. Each theory represents an image that has its strengths and weaknesses. Each works like a metaphor, making some aspects of a phenomenon visible and having blind spots in regard to others. If you consider organizations as machines, you will see all their mechanistic aspects and overlook the non-mechanistic properties or treat them as disturbances or threats. The mechanistic image emphasizes technical precision, efficiency and rationality and is appropriate for constructing conveyer belts or analysing the rule-like, bureaucratic side of an organization, but it has difficulty taking account of the "human factor". Taylor's *Scientific Management* (1947) is an illustrative example of such a view. If, however, you choose a different image and regard organizations as holographic brains, for example, you will instead think in terms of information processes, cybernetic feedback loops, network designs, redundancies and variety, self-reference and self-organization. Each approach makes you ask different types of questions about how organizations learn, how they learn to learn, how processes of self-organization emerge, and so on. Similarly, one can consider organizations as organizms, as political systems, as psychic prisons, as instruments of domination or – as cultures. These metaphors create ways of seeing and shaping organizational life. Taking different perspectives when analysing an organizational problem, suggests Morgan, aids the identification of innovative solutions.

Methodological Choices: More Theory or Data Guided?

How theory bound an ethnography is depends on methodological choices. Using the terminology of Harvey Sacks (1992), we can imagine a continuum between the poles of *theory-guided* approaches and *data-guided* approaches. Each ethnography must position itself somewhere in this spectrum: is it more theory guided or more data guided? A great number of organizational studies are theory guided, as we have pointed out, using highly abstract concepts of postmodern and poststructuralist

---

[3]For an illuminating discussion of paradigmatic developments in organization theories see Steyaert and Dey (2007).

philosophy that are difficult to relate to concrete empirical data. Ethnographers usually prefer theoretical concepts that are "closer" to empirical reality than abstract theories, although most do not take such a radically "data-guided" approach as ethnomethodology. The purpose of organizational ethnography is, writes Van Maanen (1979: 540), "to uncover and explicate the ways in which people in particular work settings come to understand, account for, take action, and otherwise manage their day-to-day situation". It claims to provide, in contrast to abstract theories of organization, "a fuller, more grounded, practice-based understanding of organizational life" (Ybema et al. 2009: 2), "a more holistic kind of knowledge" (Kostera 2007: 31) that "relates to the perspective of social actors" and to the "the social world in all its dynamics and complexity" (p. 27) which helps in "creative problem-solving" (p. 32). Nevertheless, there is significant variation in the extent to which different ethnographies are data guided. And many sociological ethnographers do not use what in organizational studies is viewed as "organizational theory".

Selected Sociological Approaches of Organizational Ethnography

It would be futile attempting to account for all the diverse approaches of organizational ethnography. But this does not discharge us from at least mentioning some perceivable branches in organizational ethnographic research. We have a preference for approaches that have a theoretical affinity to "social constructivism": the idea that social reality is inextricably produced in everyday life and its routines of action and interaction (Berger and Luckmann 1966; Goffman 1983). Although such a list is always somewhat arbitrary and necessarily cannot include everything that counts, it can help to orient the student reader about the possible range and some focal points of such research.

Reference to organization theory and/or topics therein is but one way to try to dissect the characteristics of organizational ethnography. Another and widely used approach in organizational ethnography is to focus on selected important aspects of life *within* an organization and to weaken deliberately the project of trying to connect observation with particular strands of organization theories. Instead the formal and the functional side of the organization are treated like a context, or a background in order to observe the social production of essential societal aspects of life within a particular type of organization. This concept is usually called "the social organization of X ", where X can be a first- or a second-order construct (see the beginning of this section). Sudnow's *Passing On* (1967), Zerubavel's *Patterns of Time in Hospital Life* (1979), Gubrium's *Oldtimers and Alzheimer's* (1986), are but a few classic examples of this strategy in the realm of medical organizations. These studies – like most others in this tradition – raise and illuminate important issues and their features, which we almost exclusively can find embedded in particular organizations. But sometimes, when very general sociological topics like for instance identity get linked to different organizational settings, then we can also have it the other way around: a general feature of the social is tracked along different organizations. Nice examples for this approach are the ethnographic studies (there are also non-ethnographic studies in the book) collected in the reader on institutional selves by Gubrium and Holstein (2001).

Jelinek et al. (1983) first outlined *organizational culture* as another possibly defining topic for organizational ethnography in a particularly significant special issue of the *Administrative Science Quarterly* (ASQ), an American journal for organizational science broadly conceived. Work in this tradition popularized the metaphor of "organizational culture" and introduced the idea of considering this as a research topic of its own. Understanding organizational reality through the observation of language use in a semiological research perspective in consequence became another salient way of doing organizational ethnography. Linguistic concepts like metaphors, stories, narratives, forms of talk, and others became employed by the researchers in order to represent and analyse reality construction in organizations and "Organizations as shared meaning" (Smircich 1983) became available for social research, be it in a bank (Weeks 2004) or a cat shelter (Alger and Alger 2003).

Another approach towards the phenomenon of organization stems from the *science and laboratory studies*. Introduced by Latour and Woolgar (1979), the ethnographic view on organization in the sense of the classical social science was twisted towards the scrupulous reconstruction of how, under the organizational conditions of a lab, scientific facts become constructed. Taking ethnomethodological concepts like sensemaking in interaction and organization as a joint production of accomplishments by scientists as a starting point, this approach led to the more general topic of epistemic cultures and the production of scientific knowledge in general (Knorr-Cetina 1999). Directly related to and intertwined with this line of research are the workplace studies, where work and organization are conceptualized as related accomplishments of actors interacting in a given context (see Knoblauch et al. 2000). The science and the workplace studies both show how work or "the work of organizing the organization" is being accomplished through talk and interaction and is only loosely, if at all, coupled to what in more conventional social science is called structure. But the question of the link between sense-making local interaction and the macro-concept of social structure persists and inspires innovative efforts to bridge the gap like – as an example – Psathas (1999) demonstrated under the title of "Studying the organization in action: membership categorization and interaction analysis".

The *grounded theory approach*, as developed chiefly by Barney Glaser and Anselm Strauss (1967), also contributed to the field of organizational ethnography. They introduced many concepts often still used today, such as the ideas of trajectories of chains of linked interactions and processes, going concerns of the members of an organization or a profession, awareness contexts for doing things, etc. (see Charmaz and Bryant, this volume). Perhaps one of the most influential proposals from this approach is the idea of looking at the negotiating that goes on nearly permanently in every social setting. While not everything is negotiable in a given situation, an astonishing lot of judgements on properties at stake are. The idea of negotiating as a fundamental property of human communication fed what is known today as a "negotiated order approach" (Strauss 1978; Fine 1984; Maines 1985; Nadai and Maeder 2008) and continues to inspire ethnographic organizational research.

There are ethnographic studies, which do the research "on the ground" and in one or more organizations, but relate the findings with *overarching organizational schemes or even discourses*. We can see this exemplarily in the work of Beach and Carlson (2004) where the impact of a reorganization of the adult education system by the introduction of markets as a means of coordination is analysed by the use of ethnographic case studies. In their work they carefully look at the impacts of an ideology upon local practices contained in organizations. A similar and even more general analysis of the connection between educational policies and the effects in school organizations, classrooms, etc. is provided by Hammersley (1999) and Troman et al. (2006). And finally we do not want to close the list without pointing at least to all the *ethnographic work on emotion and organization*. A useful start into this realm of organization, work and ethnography can be found in Schweingruber and Berns's (2005) text on the emotion management of young salespeople and Garot's (2004) research on emotions and bureaucracy.

Practical Issues of Doing Organizational Ethnography

Doing organizational ethnography is a difficult analytic task. We must find our way through different theoretical and methodological approaches and their underlying assumptions. This is best done *before* one begins to study a concrete organization. Choosing a suitable and manageable approach helps to reduce and channel the overwhelming flood of information potentially embedded in every organization, or even in a single social setting. Of course, there remains the ethnographer's myth of "nosing around" in order to find the interesting practices, the shared meanings, the sequential order in communication, or whatever there is that is reportable and researchable. But it is one thing to explain how people make sense in interaction, like ethnomethodologists would do, and quite another to describe and understand an organizational culture as a complex system of meaning guiding everyday routines in a work setting, as more conventional ethnographers would choose to do.

So from one perspective "hanging around" in the field might only be necessary for a short time[4] while others may believe that a long time in the field is a prerequisite

---

[4]Short field visits in combination with the intensive use of audio-visual technologies for data collection and data analysis are called "focused ethnography" (Knoblauch 2005). This is not to be confused with "quick and dirty ethnography", which is used to gain a quick general picture of a setting.

if the job is to be done well. But besides these necessary scientific choices, every ethnographer is also confronted with many mundane tasks before, during and after organizational ethnography. In this section of our chapter, we want to highlight and discuss some of the important aspects of the exercise called "organizational ethnography", and we do this from a naturalistic point of view. Some of the information and arguments given here apply to sociological ethnography in general (see Gobo, this volume), but we try to be as specific as possible with reference to ethnography in organizations.

Research in "live settings" or *in vivo* within an organization by the use of physical co-presence of the researcher and the researched involves typically, and at a minimum, the following tasks: (1) gaining access to the organization and finding an appropriate social role; (2) setting up a useful data collection process and defining an analytical framework for the data analysis; (3) establishing a working relation with at least some members of the organization; (4) finding a style of writing for the ethnographic text; (5) reporting findings and analyses back to the field while staying ethically alert and honest towards the people and their organization. These tasks should not be seen in linear order, but rather as constant elements of the exercise of "muddling through" during the process of research in organizational ethnography. It is for this reason that ethnographers sometimes ironically refer to their work as doing "dirty fieldwork".[5]

Field Access and Participation

Organizations usually regulate membership and access carefully. This can make them difficult sites for ethnographic research and sometimes even renders it impossible. Think, for example, of the ethnography of the secret service or a nuclear submarine. Even after the researcher has identified the organization he or she wants to study, a good reason is required for the local authorities to grant permission to enter, stay and to collect data.

This is why some ethnographers choose to do what is called participant observation by complete immersion in the field. This means the ethnographer tries to become a full member of the organization with a full job and duties against which he or she will be scrutinized. In such a case the ethnographer undertakes all entry routines into an organization as with the other members and he or she attains full membership status.

An example of this strategy of complete immersion into a field is Gary Alan Fine's text on the culture of work in restaurant kitchens (1996). He worked in four different

---

[5]The day-to-day practice of doing ethnography often differs from its ideal–typical representation in scientific publications. Cf. "Ten lies of ethnography", in Fine (1993) and Fine and Shulman (2009).

restaurants as a kitchen helper. While not hiding his research interest, he fully participated in the work and became a true member for a limited amount of time. Such an approach offers the unique chance of gathering first-hand knowledge on the hidden or backroom side of organizations. This can reveal informal aspects of social relations and gives the ethnographer the chance to experience personally some less apparent aspects of the organization such as, for instance, pride in the work or economic exploitation.

But this ideal type of "being there" does not work in every case. The same author used another more common approach in organizational research when he was doing ethnography on meteorologists: he participated as an observer without taking on any working responsibilities (Fine 2007). The more specialized and professionally infused the work within organizations becomes, the more likely the researcher will have to use this second approach. The danger is that we end up with what is called "quick and dirty" ethnography. In particular in the business field and the related realm of management studies, where time is money, this poses a sombre threat. It poses a risk to the reputation of more serious ethnographic studies, because such "quick and dirty" studies pretend to be ethnographic, but in fact they are only sketchy impressions without any theoretical ambitions. Like every serious business, organizational ethnography as a method and a scientific endeavour needs thorough training and lots of time. Only this allows us to advance to the "thick description" (Geertz 1973), the reconstruction of the polyphony of emic (participants') views and their relation to the practical social order in the field of research.

Of course, in many cases we can also find a public, accessible and open side of organizations. And these accesses can be used as research sites and topics too, as the French ethnographers Dubois (1999) and Weller (1999) demonstrated in their studies of the state bureaucracy "at the counter window". But such a coincidence of research question and accessibility to the setting is a rather rare exemption. If for instance Paul Atkinson (2006) in his seminal work on the opera or Buscatto (this volume) in her research on female jazz singers had restricted themselves simply to presentation of the public part of the performance, we would have missed the most insightful points they made. And sometimes the ethnographer even has to accept real danger to life as the price of gaining field access. A very nice example of this can be found in Van Maanen's report (1988: 109–115) on his participation in police patrol work, where he ended up with his wish "don't shoot the fieldworker" (p. 112).

Another important question besides the degree of involvement possible and/or needed refers to what is called "researching up" or "researching down". Depending on where in the organizational hierarchy the ethnographer gains access to the field, his or her opportunities for learning can become restricted. As an example, think of doing research in a huge multinational company, structured into functional divisions and with long chains of hierarchy dispersed over different national boundaries. Even if the ethnographer's freedom to move around is not hindered at all by the organization itself, the sheer size makes it impossible to get something like "the whole picture".[6] And although people in the organization usually get rapidly adapted to the fact of one or more ethnographers being around, they observe the ethnographers too. The higher the ranks, the more they might take care of the image of their organization and therefore sometimes try to control the knowledge available to and distributed by the researchers. Howard Becker's (1967) famous dictum, "Whose side are we on?", arises. And there is no easy answer to that question once you are in the field, since most of the members of an organization want the ethnographer to be on their side (Dalton 1959).

Looking at an organization from the top down creates another set of data, shows other structures of relevance, and displays different practices than doing research "at the bottom". The last strategy is called "researching up". At first sight it might look more sympathetic than "being with the chiefs". But sympathy is not the point here, since ethnography as a form of description always distances the researcher from the researched to a certain degree. Even a study like Adler and Adler's book on hotel work (2004), the ethnography of luxury resorts in which they "research up" from the labourer's perspective, puts a remarkable distance between the researchers and the researched. And, as Melville Dalton's classic study *Men Who Manage* (1959) brilliantly documents, research within the upper echelons shows interesting and important features of organizations too. So, in the context of power structure, the organizational ethnographer must be aware that different hierarchical and functional positions within an organization evoke different systems of meaning, different practices, different perspectives and voices. But which strategy to choose depends on the research questions and the contacts available for field access.

Data Collection and Data Analysis

Even if you restrict yourself to work with only field notes and the documents in use in the researched organization, and you abandon the use of more complex data like sound or video recordings, the amount of information collected can easily overwhelm the researcher. The risk of producing heaps of useless data but missing the essential material is very real in organizational ethnography if, for instance, you are going to try to describe and deconstruct the culture of an organization. Of course, sound and video data allow more fine-grained analysis and do have the advantage of

---

[6]On the question of scope, of the broad and the narrow in organizational ethnography, see Bergman (2003).

intersubjective control, something field notes cannot provide.[7] On the other hand they pose tricky challenges insofar as the ethnographer needs the organization's permission to use this technology. This is not always obtainable because the people in an organization can also distinguish between bulletproof evidence of a technically recorded and infinitely reproducible strip of data and a researcher's memory. In particular, if you touch on sensitive issues like informal networks, unprofessional practices and so on, this tension will apply.

So it is advisable to have such a project and its potential empirical focus discussed with colleagues *before and as* you enter the field. This does not mean that the researcher cannot adapt to unanticipated but emerging and particularly interesting features of the field. Indeed this usually happens and is regarded here as one of the strengths of organizational ethnography. The authors' own research on human resources management serves as a useful example. We found a multinational company with a very belligerent wording when it came to the description of its staff: "war for talents", "high performance as a goal for everyone", etc. So we expected a hire and fire culture with a lot of people being dismissed. But, to our surprise, the observable practices were very different. The company offered a lot of training, help and care for those who were not complying with the performance management goals and it generally took a very long time (up to four years) before somebody was discharged. This was a surprising and interesting contradiction between the official language in use and the observable practice (Nadai and Maeder 2008).

Data analysis is the next difficult job in such a project. Which concepts get employed and are useful is closely linked to the kind of ethnography one intends to do. For instance, while in grounded theory (see Charmaz and Bryant, this volume) the analysis will yield codes and categories in relation to trajectories, going concerns or conditional matrices, a more ethnomethodologically oriented project like a membership categorization analysis (MCD analysis, Silverman 2001: 139–152) will emphasize the properties and functioning of particular focused elements (e.g. the CEO) of organizations. There are many more ways to analyse field notes, documents and other data (semiotics, discourse analytic approaches, socio-linguistics, etc.) in organizational ethnography and we often find them combined. There is more than

---

[7]One of the long-standing challenges of doing participant observation in organizational ethnography by the sole use of field notes is summed up in the question of why others should believe the ethnographer when he or she reports. Would another researcher not reach different findings if he or she were to visit the same place and make his or her own field notes? While we do not think that the knowledge gained in the process of serious fieldwork is as arbitrary or sketchy as this question suggests, the advantages of having audio or video recordings in order to check and recheck an interpretation are convincing. The possibility to control and negotiate an interpretation by the use of data and the critical support (comments, objections, etc.) of scientific peers is addressed by the term intersubjective control.

one way to properly design and conduct this kind of research, but the approach should be carefully and knowingly chosen.

Informant and Field Relations; Reporting Back and Ethical Questions

As already mentioned, organizations do have boundaries and usually control access. The student of an organization therefore needs to find a way to cross these barriers. The usual way is to find a person who is a member of the organization and can provide access to it. Such persons are called "informants" from the ethnographic point of view and "members" from the organizational perspective. Whenever such a member becomes an informant for the ethnographer, he or she takes a certain degree of risk. The risk arises because informants are unlikely to be familiar with what the research person does and informants typically do not want to risk their position in the organization as a consequence of providing information to the ethnographer. This is particularly the case when ethnographers reconstruct informal habits, tacit knowledge, routine methods of working around official rules or any other aspect of an organization which belongs backstage and is regularly hidden from the public. Although such knowledge can be very important for the understanding of the everyday functioning of an organization, it is delicate to report. Furthermore, an ethnographer and the informant will sometimes develop close ties due to time spent together. So keeping good field relations becomes a subtle and often ambivalent task in organizational ethnography. As a consequence we strongly recommend that the student ethnographer of organizations consider informants not solely as data sources, but as special sorts of transient professional friends that deserve friendly treatment in many respects (see Ryen, this volume).

Another challenge in building and maintaining contact with informants is the fact that most of them are interested in the outcome of the ethnographic research. But ethnographic texts and analyses regularly put a distance between the researcher and the researched.[8] Although the informants will recognize their organization in such a description, they might not agree, for example, with the importance ascribed by the ethnographer to certain features of the organization. Given the theoretical assumption that there can be many voices and viewpoints within an organization itself, the ethnographer's voice is surely allowed to differ. But sometimes the "polyphony of the field" (the fact that there is seldom just one valid perspective) can

---

[8]To illustrate the point, think of someone doing ethnographic research on you! Most of your daily routines would be described, a lot of your backstage behaviour would be documented, etc. And these descriptions would be compiled into a text, which you could only partially understand due to its reliance on a theoretical background not known to you.

make it necessary to write additional texts targeted at the members of the researched organization itself in addition to scientific publications.

Writing Ethnography

In a broad sense, organizational ethnography is the description of the culture and the everyday life people in organizations share. So the term ethnography indicates the challenge of writing and using a method in order to get a textual representation of that culture. Writing an organizational ethnography hence does not differ from writing any other sociological ethnography and the general categories to differentiate the writing styles in ethnography apply. According to Van Maanen's (1988, 1995: 4–23) well-received proposition, we distinguish the genres of "ethnographic realism", "confessional ethnography", "dramatic ethnography", "critical ethnographies" and "self-" or "auto-ethnography". We do not elaborate these genres here (but see Marvasti, this volume), but want to bring our readers' attention to the fact that writing organizational ethnographies is not only a scientific, but to a certain degree also a literary challenge. While writing, we have to choose an audience, to select a thesis and to adapt a writing style. Of course, this rough description of the writing process does not tell it all. But it provides some structure and should make the student of organizations aware of the storytelling character nearly every organizational ethnography has. The only exception is the study of "institutional talk", informed by conversation analysis (Heritage, this volume), where the writing takes on a more "scientific" format since it is based on the rigorous analysis of audio and video recordings.

Concluding Remarks

Given that modern societies show an unparalleled degree of organization and that most aspects of modern life are handled by, and regulated through, organizations, we are surely likely to see increased attention to organizational ethnography in the future. Ethnographic texts have enriched the description and expanded the understanding of this organizational world in which we live. In this sense organizational ethnography today is already much more than just "tales from the trails". From the interaction-oriented ethnomethodology, to organizations as shared meanings and cultures, right through to the idea of the negotiated order, there emerges a wide array of future possibilities for theoretical underpinnings and empirical observation. The ethnographic approach serves to expand, enrich, and sometimes even overcome, the narrow focus on "objective" data in the more traditional or management-oriented organizational research.

Organizational ethnography will surely always remain empirically local, stay embedded in certain contexts in time and space, be limited in scope, and hardly ever be useful for quick fixes due to its methodological foundation (and slowness) in discovering the social aspects of organizations. The idea that any social order is produced and constructed by the actions and practices of people in a given context is the starting and the end point of such an endeavour.

Summary

Organizational ethnography is a multi-method approach (observation, interviewing, document analysis, examination of the use of artefacts) whose pivotal feature is participant observation. The term organization can refer to the everyday practices and routines of action going on within such a social structure ("ethnography in organization"), or the term and observations in the field can be linked to social theory of organization ("ethnography of organization").

When you do organizational ethnography, you must consider:

- the diversity of organizational theory in the social sciences;
- the difference between what people in organizations call "organization" and the social science concepts of organizations;
- the different strands of organizational ethnography;
- the cluster of practical questions arising in such research when it comes to field access, informant relations, research ethics, data collection and writing ethnography;
- the relative slowness of such research, because the researcher him- or herself has to be socialized in the field.

Questions

1 What is the difference between organization as a first- and second-order construct?
2 Explain how ethnography relates to theory, and list three major strands of organizational ethnography.
3 What are the key factors that will influence your field role in organizational ethnography?
4 Why do you have to be aware that the individual subjects of your ethnographic research may not share your view on the organization under investigation?

Recommended Reading

Besides the organizational ethnographies cited in the text, we recommend the prospective researcher to have a look at the contents of the following books:

Kostera, M. (2007) *Organizational Ethnography. Methods and Inspirations*. Lund: Studentlitteratur AB.

Neyland, D. (2008) *Organizational Ethnography*. London: Sage.

Ybema, S., Yanov, D., Wels, H. and Kamsteeg, F. (2009) *Organizational Ethnography: Studying the Complexities of Everyday Life*. London: Sage.

Internet Links

Journal of Contemporary Ethnography:
http://jce.sagepub.com/
Forum: Qualitative Social Research:
www.qualitative-research.net/
Qualitative Inquiry:
http://qix.sagepub.com/
Qualitative Research:
http://qrj.sagepub.com/
Ethnography and Education:
www.tandf.co.uk/journals/titles/17457823.asp
Qualitative Sociology Review:
www.qualitativesociologyreview.org

References

Adler, P.A., & Adler, P. (2004) *Paradise Laborers: Hotel Work in the Global Economy*. Ithaca, NY: ILR Press.

Alger, J.M., & Alger, S. (2003) *Cat Culture. The Social World of a Cat Shelter*. Philadelphia: Temple University Press.

Atkinson, P. (1990) *The Ethnographic Imagination: Textual Constructions of Reality*. London: Routledge.

Atkinson, P. (2006) *Everyday Arias: An Operatic Ethnography*. Lanham, MD: Altamira Press.

Bate, S. (1997) Whatever happened to organizational anthropology? A review of the field of organizational ethnography and anthropological studies. *Human Relations*, 50 (9): 1147–1176.

Beach, D., & Carlson, M. (2004) Adult education goes to market: an ethnographic case study of the restructuring and reculturing of adult education. *European Educational Research Journal*, 3 (3), 673–691.

Becker, H.S. (1967) Whose side are we on? *Social Problems*, 14 (3), 239–247.

Becker, H.S. (1998) *Tricks of the Trade*. Chicago: Chicago University Press.

Berger, P., & Luckmann, T. (1966) *The Social Construction of Reality. A Treatise in the Sociology of Knowledge*. London, New York: Penguin Books.

Bergman, M.M. (2003) The broad and the narrow in ethnography on organizations. *Forum: Qualitative Social Research (FQS)*, 4 (1), Art. 23, Jan. (Conference Essay).

Burrell, G., & Morgan, G. (1979) *Sociological Paradigms and Organizational Analysis*. London: Heinemann.

Czarniawska, B. (1998) Who is afraid of incommensurability? *Organization*, 5 (2), 273–275.

Dalton, M. (1959) *Men Who Manage: Fusions of Feeling and Theory in Administration*. New York: Wiley.

Dubois, V. (1999) *La vie au guichet. Relation administrative et traitement de la misère*. Paris: Economica.

Fine, G.A. (1984) Negotiated orders and organizational cultures. *Annual Review of Sociology*, 10, 239–262.

Fine, G.A. (1993) Ten lies of ethnography: moral dilemmas of field research. *Journal of Contemporary Ethnography*, 22: 267–294.

Fine, G.A. (1996) *Kitchens. The Culture of Restaurant Work*. Berkeley: University of California Press.

Fine, G.A. (2007) *Authors of the Storm. Meteorologists and the Culture of Prediction*. Chicago: University of Chicago Press.

Fine, G.A., & Shulman, D. (2009) Lies from the field: ethical issues in organizational ethnography. In S. Ybema et al., *Organizational Ethnography: Studying the Complexities of Everyday life*. London: Sage, 177–195.

Garot, R. (2004) "You're Not a Stone": emotional sensitivity in a bureaucratic setting. *Journal of Contemporary Ethnography*, 33, 735–766.

Geertz, C. (1973) *The Interpretation of Culture*. New York: Basic Books.

Gellner, D.N., & Hirsch, E. (2001) *Inside Organizations. Anthropologists at Work*. Oxford, New York: Berg.

Glaser, B.G., & Strauss, A.L. (1967) *The Discovery of Grounded Theory: Strategies for Qualitative Research*. Chicago: Aldine.

Goffman, E. (1983) The interaction order. *American Sociological Review*, 48: 1–17.

Gubrium, J.F. (1986) *Oldtimers and Alzheimer's: The Descriptive Organization of Senility*. Greenwich, CT: JAI Press.

Gubrium, J.F., & Holstein, J.A. (2001) *Institutional Selves. Troubled Identities in a Postmodern World*. New York, Oxford: Oxford University Press.

Hammersley, M. (Ed.) (1999) *Researching School Experience: Ethnographic Studies of Teaching and Learning*. London: Routledge.

Jelinek, M., Smircich, L. & Hirsch, P. (1983) Introduction: a code of many colors. *Administrative Science Quarterly*, 28 (3), 331–338.

Jones, C., & Munro, R. (Eds) (2005) *Contemporary Organization Theory*. Malden, MA, Oxford: Blackwell.

Knoblauch, H. (2005) Focused ethnography. *Forum: Qualitative Social Research (FQS)*, 6 (3), Art. 44, Sept.

Knoblauch, H., Heath, C., & Luff, P. (2000) Technology and social interaction: the emergence of 'workplace studies'. *British Journal of Sociology*, 51 (2): 299–320.

Knorr-Cetina, K. (1999) *Epistemic Cultures. How the Sciences Make Knowledge*. Cambridge, MA: Harvard University Press.

Kostera, M. (2007) *Organizational Ethnography. Methods and Inspirations*. Lund: Studentlitteratur AB.

Latour, B., & Woolgar, S. (1979) *Laboratory Life. The Social Construction of Scientific Facts*. Beverly Hills, CA, London: Sage.

Maines, D.R. (1985) Social organization and social structure in symbolic interactionist thought. *Annual Review of Sociology*, 3, 235–259.

Morgan, G. ([1986] 2006) *Images of Organizations*. Updated Edn. Thousand Oaks, CA: Sage.

Nadai, E., & Maeder, C. (2008) Negotiations at all points? Interaction and organization. *Forum Qualitative Research*, 9 (1), 32 paragraphs: http://nbn-resolving.de/urn:nbn:de:0114-fqs0801327.

Neyland, D. (2008) *Organizational Ethnography*. London: Sage.

Psathas, G. (1999) Studying the organization in action: membership categorization and interaction analysis. *Human Studies*, 22: 139–162.

Sacks, H. (1992) *Lectures on Conversations*. Vols 1 & 2. Oxford: Blackwell.

Schutz, A. (1964) Common-sense and scientific interpretation of human action. In A., Schutz *Collected Papers Vol. 2: Studies in Social Theory*, The Hague: Nijhoff, 3–47.

Schwartzman, H.B. (1993) *Ethnography in Organizations*. Newbury Park, CA: Sage.

Schweingruber, D., & Berns, N. (2005) Shaping the selves of young salespeople through emotion management. *Journal of Contemporary Ethnography*, 34, 679–706.

Silverman, D. (2001) *Interpreting Qualitative Data. Methods for Analysing Talk, Text and Interaction*. London: Sage.

Silverman, D. (2007) *A Very Short, Fairly Interesting, Quite Cheap Book about Qualitative Research*. London: Sage.

Silverman, D., & Jones, J. (1976) *Organizational Work*. London: Collier Macmillan.

Smircich, L. (1983) Organizations as shared meanings. In L.R. Pondy, P.J. Frost, G. Morgan & T.C. Dandridge (Eds), *Organizational Symbolism*. Greenwich, CT, London: JAI Press, 55–65.

Steyaert, C., & Dey, P. (2007) Post-Weickian organization theory. In T.S. Eberle, S. Hoidn & K. Sikavica (Eds), *Fokus Organization. Sozialwissenschaftliche Perspektiven und Analysen*. Konstanz: UVK, 40–62.

Strauss, A.L. (1978) *Negotiations. Varieties, Contexts, Processes, and Social Order*. San Francisco: Jossey-Bass.

Sudnow, D. (1967) *Passing On: The Social Organization of Dying.* Englewood Cliffs, NJ: Prentice Hall.

Taylor, F. (1947) *Scientific Management.* New York: Harper.

Tota, A.L. (2004) Ethnographying public memory: the commemorative genre for the victims of terrorism in Italy. *Qualitative Research,* 4: 131–159.

Troman, G., Jeffrey, B. & Beach, D. (2006) *Researching Education Policy: Ethnographic Experiences.* London: Tufnell Press.

Van Maanen, J. (1979) The fact of fiction in organizational ethnography. *Administrative Science Quarterly,* 24 (4): 539–550.

Van Maanen, J. (1988) *Tales of the Field. On Writing Ethnography.* Chicago, London: University of Chicago Press.

Van Maanen, J. (1995) An end to innocence: the ethnography of ethnography. In J.V. Maanen (Ed.), *Representation in Ethnography.* Thousand Oaks, CA: Sage, 1–35.

Weeks, J. (2004) *Unpopular Culture. The Ritual of Complaint in a British Bank.* Chicago, London: University of Chicago Press.

Weller, J.-M. (1999) *L'état au guichet. Sociologie cognitive du travail et modernisation administrative des services publics.* Paris: Desclée de Brouwer.

Yanow, D., & Geuijen, K. (2009) Defining 'organizational ethnography': Selection criteria. In S. Ybema et al., *Organizational Ethnography: Studying the Complexities of Everyday Life.* London: Sage, 253–259.

Ybema, S., Yanov, D., Wels, H. and Kamsteeg, F. (2009) *Organizational Ethnography: Studying the Complexities of Everyday Life.* London: Sage.

Zerubavel, E. (1979) *Patterns of Time in Hospital Life. A Sociological Perspective.* Chicago, London: University of Chicago Press.

PART III
TEXTS

Analysing Documentary Realities ⬤ 5

Paul Atkinson and Amanda Coffey

Abstract

This chapter – which complements that by Lindsay Prior – discusses a particular sort of documentary analysis. Recognising that organisations in contemporary society are major producers of documentary materials, the chapter urges qualitative researchers to pay proper attention to the forms and functions of such documents. Documents are not neutral, transparent reflections of organisational or occupational life. They actively construct the very organisations they purport to describe. Analysis therefore needs to focus on *how* organisational realities are (re)produced through textual conventions. The chapter is illustrated with extracts of documents relating to the UK Research Assessment Exercise (RAE), whereby higher education institutions were tasked with representing themselves through the construction of various texts. Readers are reminded that there are many documentary sources like the RAE that are in the public domain (often accessible electronically) and that lend themselves to this sort of documentary analysis.

Keywords:

documents, organisations, genre, register, intertextuality.

Introduction: Documentary Realities

A significant amount of contemporary ethnographic fieldwork takes place in literate societies, in organisational or other settings in which documents are written, read, stored and circulated. Ethnographic fieldwork was historically conceived and developed for research in essentially oral settings. Not only in non-literate societies, often studied by social anthropologists, but also in essentially oral cultures in more advanced literate societies. In contrast, contemporary fieldwork is often conducted in settings that are themselves documented by indigenous social actors. While such documentary work is rarely 'ethnographic' in itself, it is important to recognise the extent to which many social settings are self-documenting. In this chapter we consider the methodological opportunities of studying 'documentary' cultures, and indicate some of the ways in which qualitative researchers can set about the study of documentary realities. Many qualitative researchers continue to produce ethnographic accounts of complex, literate social worlds as if they were entirely without documents or texts. Many published studies of, for example, occupational, professional, organisational and even educational settings are implicitly represented as devoid of written documents and other forms of textual recording. Such accounts do not, therefore, always do justice to the settings they purport to describe.

In this chapter we focus on just one aspect of documentary work and analysis. We look at how organisations represent themselves collectively to themselves and to others through the construction of documents. Consider an ideal–typical organisation. It goes virtually without saying that this quintessentially modern kind of social formation is thoroughly dependent on documents. Administrators, accountants, lawyers, civil servants, managers and other specialist functionaries are all routinely, often extensively, involved in the production and consumption of written records and other kinds of document. If we wish to understand how organisations work and how people work with/in them, then we cannot afford to ignore their various activities as readers and writers.

In addition to familiar record-keeping tasks, organisations also produce significant documents of other kinds, including materials concerned with their self-presentation. These might involve reports, prospectuses, financial accounts and the like. Many, though by no means all of those documents, are produced for external, even public, consumption. They may be among the methods whereby organisations publicise themselves, compete with others in the same marketplace or justify themselves to clients, shareholders, boards of governors or employees.

In the contemporary world, we should also include electronic and digital resources among the ways in which documentary realities are produced and consumed. organisations produce websites, promotional videos and similar artefacts. These are all among the techniques and resources that are employed to create organisational versions of reality. Over and above these institutional-level documents there are also textual records that embody individual actions, interactions and encounters. People-processing professions, for example, routinely compile documents of professional–client interactions. These written records can be used to inform future action, and are themselves drawn upon in the more formal recording (and documentary) mechanisms of official statistics, performance indicators, efficiency league-tables and similar constructs.

The purpose of these introductory paragraphs is not simply to list a few indicative types of documents or to outline their functions. Rather, it is to remind readers of the pervasive significance of documentary records, written and otherwise, in contemporary social settings. What follows logically from such an observation is that qualitative field research should pay careful attention to the collection and analysis of documentary realities. Such enquiry is not confined to the inspection of documents themselves (important though a close scrutiny may be). It must also incorporate a clear understanding of how documents are produced, circulated, read, stored and used.

The production and consumption of documentary data has formed a part of qualitative analyses of a range of settings. Classic examples include work that has incorporated analyses of school reports (Woods 1979), medical records (Rees 1981), classifications of causes of death (Prior 1985), and health visitors' case records (Dingwall 1977). Indeed there are many research questions and settings that cannot be investigated adequately without reference to the production and use of documentary materials. It would be fruitless to study the everyday work and occupational culture of a profession such as actuaries without addressing the construction and interpretation of artefacts such as the life-table (cf. Prior and Bloor 1993). As Bloomfield and Vurdabakis (1994) point out, textual communicative practices are a vital way in which organisations constitute 'reality' and the forms of knowledge appropriate to it.

In paying attention to such materials, however, one must be quite clear about what they can and cannot be used for. Documents are 'social facts', in that they are produced, shared and used in socially organised ways. They are not, however, transparent representations of organisational routines, decision-making processes, or professional practices. Documents construct particular kinds of representations using literary conventions. Documentary sources are not surrogates for other kinds of data. We cannot, for instance, learn through written records alone how an organisation actually operates day by day. Equally, we cannot treat records – however 'official' – as firm evidence of what they report. This observation has been made repeatedly about data from official sources, such as statistics on crime, suicide, health, death and educational outcomes (Cicourel and Kitsuse 1963; Sudnow 1968; Atkinson 1978; Roberts 1990; Maguire 1994; see also Macdonald 2008). This recognition or reservation does not mean that we should ignore documentary data. On the contrary, our recognition of their existence as social facts (or constructs) alerts us to the necessity to treat them very seriously indeed (Prior 2008). We have to approach documents for what they are and what they are used to accomplish. We should examine their place in organisational settings, the cultural values attached to them, their distinctive types and forms. The analysis of such evidence should therefore be an important part of ethnographic studies of everyday organisational life and work. Of course documentary work may be the main method for qualitative research in its own right (Prior 2003). In either event it is important to establish a methodological framework for documentary analysis. In the remainder of this chapter we outline complementary strategies for approaching this kind of qualitative analysis. This is not intended as a comprehensive review of all relevant analytical strategies. Rather our intention is to introduce some practical approaches to the systematic analysis of documentary data and the contexts of their use.

It is important to note in what follows that we are not trying to use documents to support or validate other data. It is tempting, when undertaking qualitative research, to treat observational and oral data (such as may be derived from interviews or recorded interaction) as the primary data, and any documentary materials as secondary. If used at all, then the latter are often drawn on to cross-check the oral accounts, or to provide some kind of context. Our view here, on the contrary, is that such attitudes to documentary data are inappropriate and unhelpful. We would urge that documentary materials should be regarded as data in their own right. They often enshrine a distinctively documentary version of social reality. They have their own conventions that inform their production and circulation. They are associated with distinct social occasions and organised activities. This does not mean that there is a documentary level of reality that is divorced from other levels, such as the interactional order. Documents are used and exchanged as part of social interaction, for instance. Nevertheless, it is vital to give documentary data due weight and appropriate analytic attention. There are many ways in which such documentary data can be analysed and it is not our intention to try to describe these in detail (see Silverman 2006). Rather, we introduce and exemplify a series of related themes that can be brought to bear on documentary sources. Our perspective is informed by a broadly ethnographic interest, while our specific analytic approaches perhaps derive more from a semiotic perspective. By that we mean an analytic perspective that examines how documents can be treated as systems of signs and modes of representation (cf. Feldman 1995). Through illustrating such an approach we consider how one needs to take account of the *form* of textual materials, the distinctive uses of language they may display, the relationships between texts and the conventions of genre.

Documentary Language and Form

Documentary constructions of social reality depend upon particular uses of language. Certain document types constitute – to use a literary analogy – *genres*, with specific styles and conventions. These are often marked by quite distinctive uses of linguistic *registers* – that is, the specialised use of language associated with particular domains of everyday life. Occupations often have distinctive registers, as do particular kinds of organisation or cultural activity. One can often recognise what *sort* of document one is dealing with simply from its distinctive use of language. You can, for example, probably recognise the register of, say, a theatre review, or a wine appreciation, without seeing more than a random extract from it (see Lehrer 1983). You can tell a managerial document and distinguish it from a personal diary-entry from their characteristic styles.

At a common-sense level we can recognise that official documents and reports are couched in language that differs from everyday language use. Indeed this is one sort of device that is used to construct the distinctive and special mode of documentary representation. It is usually unhelpful to approach the analysis of documentary materials from an initially critical or evaluative stance. It is more helpful to adopt a more interpretative standpoint. The initial task is to pay close attention to the question of *how* documents are constructed as distinctive kinds of products. It is therefore appropriate to pay close attention to the textual organisation of documentary sources. As we have emphasised, the important analytic question is: *What kind of reality is this document creating, and how does it do it?*

Our illustration here derives from the UK's Research Assessment Exercise (RAE). In this national evaluation of research performance (to be replaced by the somewhat similar Research Excellence Framework from 2013), each university was required to prepare a submission relating to each 'Unit of Assessment'. The latter term corresponds roughly to an academic 'discipline', which may or not be coterminous with an administrative division, such as a 'department'. A key part of each submission is a narrative account of the unit's research strengths and achievements, intended to provide a context for the peer review of selected 'outputs' (publications) and other indicators, such as research grants and doctoral students. Each university has a certain amount of leeway in constructing its submissions, but it is in the nature of exercises like this that there is a high degree of predictability in the style and content of submissions.

We have chosen to illustrate our argument with reference to brief extracts from Cardiff University's submission to the Sociology Panel. These documents are now in the public domain (see http://www.rae.ac.uk/), and can be examined from a textual–analytic point of view. The particular extract we have selected for our purposes here is about intellectual matters close to the subject matter of this volume; the promotion of methodological scholarship. The Cardiff sociology RAE narrative was constructed in part through a series of thematic sections. The research of over 60 individuals was summarised in terms of seven themes, one of which was 'innovations in social research', an extract of which is reproduced below.

Innovations in Social Research

This theme represents a significant and cross-cutting research focus at Cardiff, influencing all staff and research students. Cardiff's established strengths in qualitative methods and the ethnographic approaches pioneered by Atkinson, Delamont and Coffey are internationally recognised. They have been considerably strengthened during the review period by a number of key appointments, including Henwood (qualitative longitudinal analysis), Sampson (dangerous fieldwork) and M. Williams (digital qualitative methods).

The establishment of Qualitative Research Methods in the Social Sciences: Innovation, Integration and Impact (Qualiti) […] as a node of the ESRC's National Centre for Research Methods (NCRM) both reflected these strengths and provided a basis for further development. Under the direction of Coffey and Taylor, the Qualiti team has conducted methodologically-driven projects which explore issues such as multi-modality (building on previous ESRC-funded projects on hypermedia and digital technologies); participatory methods; and the role of qualitative methods in policy formation. International collaboration in this area was furthered by the establishment of EUROQUAL, the Qualitative Research in Social Sciences in Europe programme. Funded by the European Science Foundation and chaired by Atkinson, this is a network of 14 member states devoted to promoting innovations and new techniques in qualitative research across Europe.

Before we consider this particular extract, we should note a larger function of the RAE text itself. The diversity of university departments, research groups, individual scholars and so on is translated into a particular kind of uniformity by the process itself. Each field of research, or discipline, is translated into a 'unit of assessment', of which there is a prescribed, limited list of categories. The entire system is predicated on a classificatory system – so that, for instance, there were separate units of assessment of sociology, social policy, social work and social anthropology. Each submission from each university was required to conform to a uniform format (driven by prescribed software). The classifications and boundaries are conventional, though not entirely arbitrary. The semblance of uniformity is a creation of the exercise itself. It is, moreover, a textual achievement. A 'unit' corresponds to a single text. The representation of research reflects not just the practical arrangements of everyday work 'on the ground', but also the organisational formats through which it is reported. This is, in turn, a common feature of bureaucratic texts.

Work in modern bureaucracies and other complex organisations would be impossible without the creation of these kinds of documentary reality. Indeed, the development of modern methods of accountancy, marketing, trading and so on has depended completely on the construction of standardised categories and types – largely managed through the creation of standard documentary forms. (The congruence of meaning of the term 'forms' is revealing here – referring as it does both to types and the paper or electronic means through which a typical case is constructed.) Documentary reportage is closely related to the existence of official classificatory systems, such as the international classification of diseases (see Bowker and Starr 1999). It is important to remember that such official categories and classificatory systems do not simply describe classes and systems – they are active in creating and shaping them.

Organisational reality is partly created through the use of distinctive (but not unique) textual conventions. Readers who are familiar with contemporary higher education – particular in the UK – will be familiar with the sort of language embodied in the RAE. It is a sort of dialect of English. The style associated with these and similar documents prepared for the assessment of quality and quality assurance in universities has been dubbed 'Quahili' (a pun on the African language Swahili). The extract reproduced above shares some of those features, as well as displaying more generic bureaucratic conventions. You will notice some of the distinctive features of bureaucratic language. Although the RAE text reports what we did at Cardiff, it is written in a very impersonal manner. The use of the passive voice and similar constructions removes personal agency in favour of impersonal institutional realities: 'pioneered by Atkinson, Delamont and Coffey are internationally recognised'; 'the establishment of ... reflected these strengths and provided a basis for ...'; 'international collaboration in this area was furthered by the establishment of ...'. Likewise, one can recognise that the text deploys 'buzzwords' that help to establish its overall tone: 'a significant and cross-cutting research focus' is actually poorly constructed as a metaphor (can a focus be cross-cutting?) but it helps to convey the 'right' sort of message, in that contemporary research cultures are conventionally described in terms not only of themes but also of cross-cutting themes (that therefore provide a degree of integration and coherence). In the same vein, 'established strengths' that were 'pioneered' by members of academic staff are among the sorts of features that one would expect to find in a successful research environment (and the very notion of a 'research environment' is itself part of the research assessment culture). So too is 'international collaboration': one expects to find research described as collaborative, as this implies networks of mutual influence and co-operation that normally and typically characterise high-level academic research. When such networks (a buzzword in its own right) are international, then that is all to the good. Note too how the text implies a degree of strategic planning. 'Established strength' is added to and strengthened yet further (and so must be very strong indeed). Likewise, the establishment of Qualiti provided a basis for 'further development'. So in this text at least, things have not just happened: they have a direction that implies planned progress. The text itself constructs a process of strategic planning. It goes without saying, of course, that a fair amount of what we might call institutionalised boasting is an expected feature of such a document.

When we look at such a document, therefore, we can ask ourselves questions about the use of language. As we have already suggested, documents like the one we have discussed display a distinctive *register*. That is, a distinctive and specialised use of language associated with a special context or *domain*. It might be associated with a particular occupation, a distinctive kind of intellectual field, or an esoteric pursuit. It implies a general feature of language in social life: distinctive uses of language (written and spoken) are associated with, and indeed are constitutive of, specialised social contexts.

We can go beyond the 'style' of documentary realities. When confronted by a document like our RAE submission, we can also ask ourselves about the functions of the text. In other words, we can ask ourselves what the text is *doing*. One way of approaching that is to think in terms of what the linguistic philosopher Austin described in his analysis of *speech acts*. This refers to the fact that language does not merely describe events or states of affairs. It also creates or performs them. When you make a promise or utter a threat, you are not using language to describe something else; you are using the language to accomplish the act itself. Of course, you do not always have to say 'I promise that …', or 'I threaten that …', or 'I warn you that …' in so many words in order to accomplish those particular actions. (Verbs like those are called performatives and they vividly illustrate the nature of speech acts in general, but they are not necessary for their actual performance.)

The RAE document is performing some special work, then. It is making a series of *claims*, and *performing* a certain sort of licensed boasting. In doing so, it deploys the discursive devices we identified earlier in order to create a *plausible* account of sociology at Cardiff University. In other words, such a document is inescapably rhetorical. Rhetoric does not imply anything bogus here. Any and every act of persuasion, or reality-construction, depends on rhetorical devices. This applies equally to the most sober of 'factual' accounts (such as scientific papers) as to the most overtly of interested documents (such as political manifestos). Documents describe, they also justify and explain. They may apportion blame and responsibility. They may claim merit and achievement. These all have to be achieved, in the sense that they always depend on textual conventions.

The social actors who write such documents and the social actors who read (and evaluate) them bring to bear their knowledge – often tacit – of the conventions that go into their production and reception. We do not have to assume that they are unduly cynical, or that they act in bad faith, to recognise that they understand the conventions they are using. Writers develop a working knowledge of the register(s) of their own professions or organisational role. Readers bring to bear the same repertoire of conventional understanding in making sense of such documents. The phrase 'making sense' is especially apposite when we think of the socially organised activity of interpreting documents. Their interpretation is always an active one. We know already that documentary sources do not transparently describe or reveal states of affairs. They help to construct them. But that construction requires the participation of readers as well as writers. Reading documents and making sense of their contents requires readers to bring their own background assumptions to bear. Our example from the RAE is relevant here. First, the writer(s) were *au fait* with the relevant register and the rhetorical devices. Second, they wrote the document with an audience in mind. The document in question was what we call *recipient designed*: constructed with an actual or implied reader in mind. Third, the primary readers, charged with peer review, shared the same occupational culture and therefore brought to bear the same conventional, cultural knowledge. (Since the document is now in the public domain, one cannot assume that all subsequent readers share the same cultural competence.)

The culturally competent reader 'knows' how to use documentary sources to create the organisational reality they purport to describe. They will know how such organisations are managed and organised, and something about their general cultural features. Consequently, they use what Mannheim called – appropriately – the 'documentary method'. That is, the text is used to furnish indications or traces of what the reader interprets as the 'underlying' social reality. He or she reads into the text what might reasonably be assumed to be the case, given a shared stock of knowledge about how organisations typically function. Typical cases are interpreted in terms of their typical manifestations and their typical rhetorical representations.

In conducting analyses of this sort one can take various more specific perspectives. We have chosen to focus here on the organisational functions that texts can perform, and some of the sorts of textual features that contribute to those effects. It is also possible to take a more explicitly *ethnomethodological* view of how records and documents work. Garfinkel's commentary on the analysis of hospital records is a case in point (Garfinkel 1967). His starting-point was the use made of clinical records by researchers, who appeared to be able to make practical use of clinical records as data in making sense of how clinics work. But Garfinkel went beyond that to argue that the researchers were only able to make sense of those records by 'reading into' them what they already understood about clinics as organisations. The records themselves were messy, but competent readers – clinicians, administrators or researchers – were able to *make* sense of them by bringing to bear prior background assumptions. In just the same way, we can see that competent readers of the RAE documents or their equivalent can make something of them by virtue of their background knowledge – of how universities work, of how university research is organised, and how such documents are read. They presuppose a community of readers and writers who share a common stock of knowledge and taken-for-granted assumptions. Our analysis can therefore examine those cultural and organisational features that are implicitly invoked when records and documents are produced and used. This general approach to documentary reality is also to be seen in Green's analysis of official documents, again from an explicitly ethnomethodological perspective. In his analysis of policy documents about poverty, he also demonstrates how texts depend upon background assumptions, so that they can convey more than they say 'in so many words', because readers and writers alike bring to bear a variety of social and cultural assumptions (Green 1983). One of the classic examples of this approach is by McHoul (1982), who examines what competent readers need to do in order actively to make sense of a range of different texts. This approach – by no means coincidentally – explores what is called the 'documentary method'. That does not mean that it is restricted to documents in the conventional sense, or in the sense dealt with in this chapter. Rather, it describes a general method that everyday, practical social actors use in order to interpret appearances, shreds of evidence, partial understandings, or representations: they use those to infer underlying patterns or states of affairs, and to fill in those 'texts' with their common-sense knowledge. Hence readers of our RAE document will have to work at it – to 'read between the lines' if you like – in order to reconstruct a picture of the academic department that is being described. In order to do so they draw on what they know about typical departments, typical academic staff members, typical research projects.

Intertextuality

Documents do not construct systems or domains of documentary reality as individual, separate activities. Documents refer – however tangentially – to other realities and domains. They also refer to *other* documents. This is especially, though not exclusively, true of organisational settings and their systems of accountability. The analysis of documentary reality must, therefore, look beyond separate texts, and ask how they are related. It is important to recognise that, like any system of signs and messages, documents make sense because they have relationships with other documents. It is useful here to return to the theme of audit, of which the RAE might be considered an example within UK higher education. If we consider the mechanics of audit, then it starts to become quite easy to grasp the point of systematic relations between documents. One of the root metaphors of an audit is that of the *audit trail*. Conventionally defined audits of firms and organisations carried out by accountants place great emphasis on this audit trail. Audit trails relate each document in the organisational accounts to other documents contained in the audit file (the preparation of papers for an audit). There is an inbuilt assumption that reference can and should be made to other documents. An auditor's task is to establish the extent of these relationships and intertextualities.

Academic auditors follow similar procedures. Such investigative procedures are predicated on the assumption that there are and should be regular, identifiable relationships between documentary records. These relationships are based on elementary – but significant – principles. They include principles of *sequence* and *hierarchy*. These in turn are part of the constitutive machinery whereby organisations produce and reproduce themselves. From a general analytic perspective, therefore, we can see that the realm of documentary reality does not rely on particular documents mirroring and reflecting a social reality. Rather, we can think of a semi-autonomous domain of documentary reality, in which documents reflect and refer (often implicitly) to other documents.

In simple terms, that means following an organisational decision, an innovation or a problem through a sequence of documents. Such a trail might, for instance, examine the minutes of departmental meetings in order to trace the progress of an item from one meeting to the next and so on. Such organisational records have distinctive characteristics. Again, we can note that such documents have specific, stylised formats. They also have particular functions. Minutes of meetings, for instance, do not record everything that was said and done in a meeting. Indeed, in a sense they precisely are not intended to record what was actually said. They record what was *decided*. In a sense, indeed, they constitute what was decided. Unless challenged and corrected with the agreement of the members, the written record takes precedence over members' own recollections and intentions. Moreover, such documents are written in order to refer to other, equivalent documents. They are constructed and read precisely as part of a documentary domain of interlinked documents. If we pursue the hypothetical example of our academic audit, we can see that an audit trail would pick up on documents such as minutes of staff–student meetings, meetings of the academic staff (or sub-groups of them). We can analyse such documentary realities in various ways. We have already referred to the notion of *intertextuality*. This term is derived from contemporary literary criticism, in which context it is used to refer to that fact that literary texts (such as novels) are not free-standing, and that they do not refer just to a fictional world. Rather, they refer, however implicitly, to other texts. They include other texts of the same genre, or other kinds of textual product (such as journalism, biography, movies). We can therefore analyse texts in terms of these intertextual relationships, tracing the dimensions of similarity and difference.

In analysing the documentary realities of an organisational setting, therefore, we can explore the intertextual relationships. We can examine how conventional formats are shared between texts, and thus how they construct a uniform, bureaucratic style. We can note how they are linked as sequences of documents. Minutes of meetings refer to previous minutes and things like 'matters arising'. Minutes of different meetings will look remarkably similar in construction, language and tone. They thus construct rational sequences of decisions and their consequences, distributed regularly over time, and reported in uniform formats. Thus, we can also examine how documentary realities have *temporal* dimensions built into them. Note that this is organisational or documentary time; it does not describe the passage of time as experienced as an everyday phenomenon by the individual actors concerned. In another sense, documentary sources *suppress* time, by lifting events out of the flow of lived experience, and recording them in the de-contextualised language and formats of official records. Intertextuality thus alerts us to the fact that organisational documents are part of wider systems of distribution and exchange. Documents circulate through social networks which in turn help to identify and delineate divisions of labour and official positions. One important analytic theme here is the observation that the systematic relationships between documents actively *construct* the rationality and organisation that they purport transparently to record.

Documents can circulate and be exchanged partly because they are used to de-contextualise events. We transform things by incorporating them into texts. By writing something into a documentary format, we translate events from the specific and the local, and make of them 'facts' and 'records' which take on an independent existence. Some texts become 'official' and can become 'proof' of events and roles. This point is made in relation to the production of scientific facts and findings by Latour and Woolgar (1986), who write about the production of scientific papers, and suggest that they achieve an independence of their original site of production – the research group, the laboratory – and take on an independent existence. The accountants' audit of a business organisation takes on a similar existence. The audit report *becomes* the documentary reality, superseding other files, records and memories. Similar observations could be made about the RAE submissions where units of assessments become 'real' and the documentary reality that is presented supersedes other accounts.

Documents are also written and read with reference to other occasions of use. They can be referred to in order to warrant or challenge subsequent actions and decisions – possibly long after they were first constructed. They can also inscribe positions of hierarchy. Documents report discussions, decisions and events to people or bodies that are superior to the originators. The right to (re)construct a document, to challenge, receive and act on it (or not), is part of the formal division of labour within many social settings. One cannot 'read off' such organisational realities from documentary sources, and to attempt to do so would be based on a fundamental misunderstanding. Documentary realities, based on complex interlinkages between documents, *create* their own versions of hierarchy and legitimate authority. Indeed, the issue of authority raises too the closely related issue of authorship.

Authorship and Readership

The kinds of documents we have been discussing may have identifiable, individual authors or they may be anonymous, even collective, products. They may be addressed to specific audiences or they may appear to address an impersonal world at large. In any event it is important to address authorship (actual or implied) and readership (actual or implied) if one is to understand the overall system of production, exchange and consumption of documentary materials. Documents, like all texts and utterances, are 'recipient designed'. That is, they reflect implicit assumptions about who will be the reader. The implied reader does not have to be an actual individual person. The implied recipient can correspond to what George Herbert Mead referred to as the 'generalized other'. It is a basic tenet of interactionist social analysis that social actors monitor and shape their actions in the light of generalised others' imputed responses and evaluations. So when we create a document, we do so in the light of the kind of readership we are expecting or writing for.

In the case of the RAE submissions, for example, the readers are both specific and generalised. The membership of the panels of experts reviewing submissions is known to those constructing the submission, as this is public knowledge. But the bureaucratic formats and other conventions governing the preparation of the documents precludes a highly personalised appeal to particular readers. So even if the head of an academic department knows the chair of the expert panel of reviewers, he or she cannot construct the submission as a personal appeal to that specific individual. It has to be couched in the appropriate register, suited to the institutional demands and expectations of the exercise itself. Indeed, it is part of the skill in constructing such documents in administrative contexts that one should be able to use the right kinds of phrases, deploy the right kinds of arguments, and generally convey the right sort of tone. In audit exercises like the RAE, this includes the use of distinctive terms and ideas that are intended to reflect the coherence of a department's research strategic thinking and the cogency of its research plans. While the self-assessment part of the document is intended to convey a picture of the research activities of the academic department, in an important sense it *creates* the reality it reports. This report is normally not a highly individual picture, but a highly predictable version, suited to the intentions and the readership created by the exercise itself.

While it is self-evident that a person or a group must actually author documents (since they do not write themselves), that does not always imply a social recognition of 'authorship'. Indeed, it is part of the facticity of many organisational documents that they are not identifiably the work of an individual author. Anonymity itself is part of the official production of documentary reality. There may be an implied 'ownership' of a document – such as the originating administrator or department – but official materials do not normally have visible human agencies expressing opinions, beliefs and so on. We can therefore inspect texts for indications of authorship, or its absence. In that sense, too, we can look for how they claim whatever *authority* may be attributed to them.

Summary

- Documentary reality does not consist of descriptions of the social world that can be used directly as evidence about it. One cannot assume that documentary accounts are 'accurate' portrayals in that sense. Rather, they construct their own kinds of reality. It is, therefore, important to approach them as *texts*.
- Texts are constructed according to conventions that are themselves part of a documentary reality. Hence, rather than ask whether an account is true, or whether it can be used as 'valid' evidence about a research setting, it is more fruitful to ask ourselves questions about the form and function of texts themselves.
- Texts can be examined for their formal properties. One can look at the characteristic language used and in their *rhetorical* features. Rhetoric is, fundamentally, about how texts *persuade* their readers.
- It is important to think about documents in relation to their production (authorship) and their consumption (readership), but one should note that in textual terms these are not coterminous with the particular individual social actors who write and read. We need to pay close attention to the implied readers and to the implied claims of authorship
- Texts do not refer transparently to the social world. Their referential value is often in their *intertextuality* – their relation to other texts. In literate, bureaucratised settings in particular, one may identify a semi-autonomous domain of texts and documents that refer primarily to one another. A dense network of cross-referencing, and shared textual formats, can create a powerful version of social reality.

Future Prospects

Our focus in this chapter has been on the documentary realities of organisations and other research settings. Implicitly we have restricted our discussion to written texts (mainly words) and to formal and quasi-formal documents. However, it should be noted that the analysis of 'documents' can be developed in many different ways, offering the potential for the application of innovative qualitative research practice. Documents can, of course, incorporate visual materials, and there are established ways of analysing visual data. Moreover, in the digital age, there is scope to develop our understandings of research settings, through scholarly analysis of new forms of documents – including the World Wide Web, electronic communication and social networking sites.

Questions

- What does the term intertextuality mean, and how might it be applied to the study of documents in organisations?
- Why might it be analytically productive to focus on the form and function of documents?

Recommended Reading

Macdonald, K. (2008) Using documents, in N. Gilbert (ed) *Researching Social Life*. London: Sage

Prior, L. (2003) *Using Documents in Social Research*. London: Sage

Prior, L. (2004) Documents, in C. Seale, G. Gobo, J.F. Gubrium and D. Silverman (eds) *Qualitative Research Practice*. London: Sage

Plummer, K. (2001) *Documents of Life 2*. London: Sage

Scott, J. (1990) *A Matter of Record*. Cambridge: Polity Press

Scott, J. P. (ed) (2006) *Documentary Research* (4 volumes), London: Sage

Internet Links

www.archives.gov/education/lessons/worksheets/

www.rae.ac.uk/

http://chnm.gmu.edu/worldhistorysources/whmdocuments.html

References

Atkinson, J.M. (1978) *Discovering Suicide: Studies in the Social Organization of Sudden Death*. London: Macmillan.

Bloomfield, B.P. and Vurdabakis, T. (1994) Re-presenting technology: IT consultancy reports as textual reality constructions, *Sociology*, 28, 2: 455–478.

Bowker, G.C. and Star, S.L. (1999) *Sorting Things Out: Classification and its Consequences*. Cambridge, MA: MIT Press.

Cicourel, A. and Kitsuse, J. (1963) *The Educational Decision-Makers*. New York: Bobbs-Merrill.

Dingwall, R. (1977) *The Social Organization of Health Visitor Training*. London: Croom Helm.

Feldman, M.S. (1995) *Strategies for Interpreting Qualitative Data*. Thousand Oaks, CA: Sage.

Garfinkel, H. (1967) *Studies in Ethnomethodology*. Englewood Cliffs, NJ: Prentice Hall.

Green, B. (1983) *Knowing the Poor: A Case-Study in Textual Reality Construction*. London: Routledge & Kegan Paul.

Latour, B. and Woolgar, S. (1986) *Laboratory Life*. Princeton, NJ: Princeton University Press.

Lehrer, A. (1983) *Wine and Conversation*. Bloomington: Indiana University Press.

Macdonald, K. (2008) Using documents, in N. Gilbert (ed) *Researching Social Life*. London: Sage.

Maguire, M. (1994) Crime statistics, patterns and trends, in M. Maguire, R. Morgan and R. Reiner (eds) *Oxford Handbook of Criminology*. Oxford: Oxford University Press.

McHoul, A.W. (1982) *Telling How Texts Talk: Essays on Reading and Ethnomethodology*. London: Routledge & Kegan Paul.

Prior, L. (1985) Making sense of mortality, *Sociology of Health and Illness*, 7 (2): 167–90.

Prior, L. (2003) *Using Documents in Social Research*. London: Sage.

Prior, L. (2008) Documents and action, in P. Alastuutari, L. Bickman and J. Brannen, (eds) *The Sage Handbook of Social Research Methods*. London: Sage.

Prior, L. and Bloor, M. (1993) Why people die: social representations of death and its causes, *Science as Culture*, 3, 3: 346–374.

Rees, C. (1981) Records and hospital routine, in P. Atkinson and C. Heath (eds) *Medical Work: Realities and Routines*. Farnborough: Gower.

Roberts, H. (1990) *Women's Health Counts*. London: Routledge.

Silverman, D. (2006) *Interpreting Qualitative Data*. 3rd Edition. London: Sage.

Sudnow, D. (1968) *Passing On*. Englewood Cliffs, NJ: Prentice Hall.

Woods, P. (1979) *The Divided School*. London: Routledge & Kegan Paul.

Using Documents in Social Research ⬤ 6

Lindsay Prior

Abstract

This chapter focuses on the different ways in which documents enter 'the field'. Four distinct social scientific modes in which data about documents might be collected and analysed are identified. The respective modes involve studying documents as 'resource', as 'topic', in use, and in action. It is argued that there has hitherto been an undue emphasis placed on the first of these modes and a relative neglect of the last of the modes. As a result, the study of document content has tended to dominate relevant research methods. The author consequently seeks to broaden the range of data that ought to be collected in relation to research on documents, and his various claims and suggestions are illustrated throughout by reference to data derived from his own research projects.

> **Keywords:**
>
> content analysis, documents, discourse, documents as actors, semantic webs.

Doing Things with Documents

here I sit and govern [Scotland] with my pen: I write and it is done. (King James VI (Scotland) James I (England))[1]

---

[1]Cited in, Lee, M. (1980) *Government by Pen. Scotland under James VI and I*. Urbana: University of Illinois Press. p. vii.

This is an instructive quotation. It demonstrates, above all, how people do things with documents – in particular, how writing connects to action. And as social researchers we could choose to concentrate on any number of features associated with James and his writing. We could, for example, focus on the thoughts of the man, and the meaning that James attached to the words on pages that he dispatched from London to Edinburgh. Or we might choose to focus on the meaning of those who read the words (including ourselves, as well as long-dead subordinates). Indeed, we could set aside an interest in meaning altogether and focus, instead, on how the words (and documents that contained them) were recruited and used in episodes of social interaction.

Any study of documents should probably encompass all of the above features, yet it is notable that in most forms of social research documents tend to enter the 'field' in only one of the aforementioned dimensions. Indeed, when documents are put forward for consideration in fieldwork they tend to be approached solely in terms of what they contain. Yet despite this, it is quite clear that each and every document enters into human projects in a dual relation. First, and as with James' royal commands, they enter the field as a receptacle (of instructions, obligations, contracts, wishes, reports, etc.). Second, they enter the field as agents in their own right. Indeed, as agents documents have effects long after their human creators are dead and buried (wills provide a readily available example of such effects). And as agents, documents are always open to manipulation by others; as allies, as resources for further action, as opponents to be destroyed, or suppressed. (We should not forget that people burn, ban and hide documents as well as read them.) It is the examination of this dual role that forms the intellectual backbone of the current chapter.

In what follows I shall talk of documentation as if it is equivalent to text – though that is clearly not so. Indeed, architectural drawings, books, paintings, X-ray images, film, World Wide Web pages, CD-ROM discs, bus tickets, shopping lists, tapestries and sequences of DNA can all be considered as 'documents' – depending on the use that is made of such artefacts in specific circumstances (Prior, 2003). For heuristic purposes, however, I will ignore non-textual forms of data and proceed as if the terms text and documentation were synonymous.

Four Approaches to the Study of Documentation

In one of the most influential texts on social scientific research methods produced during the second half of the twentieth century, Glaser and Strauss (1967: 163) argued that, in matters of sociological investigation, documents ought to be regarded as akin 'to an anthropologist's informant or a sociologist's interviewee'. The authors subsequently devoted an entire chapter to how the principles of grounded theory could and should be deployed on inert text. A focus on documents merely as

TABLE 6.1   *Approaches to the study of documents*

Focus of research approach	Document as Resource	Document as Topic
Content	(1) Approaches that focus almost entirely on what is 'in' the document	(2) 'Archaeological' approaches that focus on how document content comes into being
Use and function	(3) Approaches that focus on how documents are used as a resource by human actors for purposeful ends	(4) Approaches that focus on how documents function in and impact on schemes of social interaction, and social organization

Source: Prior (2008a)

containers of data had, of course, been well established in social science from the earlier part of the twentieth century. And as a key source of data, it is nowadays recommended that document content be screened, counted and 'coded' for appropriate evidence in support or refutation of relevant hypotheses (Krippendorf, 2004; Weber, 1990). Indeed, an understanding of documents as inert carriers of content is normally well reflected in most of the textbook discussions on research methods and often associated with the idea that the study of documents should be allied to the use of 'unobtrusive' methods (see, for example, Bryman, 2004). So it will probably be as well for me to outline at this stage some alternative approaches that might be adopted for the study of documents. I shall begin by referring to the contents of Table. 6.1.

This table is aimed at offering some understanding of the various ways in which documents have been dealt with by social researchers. Thus, approaches that fit into Cell 1 have been dominant in the history of sociology and of social science generally. Therein documents (especially as text) have been scoured and coded for what they contain in the way of descriptions, reports, images, representations and accounts. In short, they have been scoured for evidence. Data analysis strategies concentrate almost entirely on what is in the 'text' (via various forms of content analysis, thematic analysis, or even grounded theory). This emphasis on content is carried over into Cell 2 types of approaches with the key difference that analysis is concerned with how document content comes into being. The attention here is usually on the conceptual architecture and socio-technical procedures by means of which written reports, descriptions, statistical data and so forth are generated. Various kinds of discourse analysis have been used to unravel the conceptual issues, whilst a focus on socio-technical and rule-based procedures by means of which clinical, police, and other forms of record and reports are constructed has been well represented in the work of ethnomethodologists. In contrast, and in Cell 3, the research focus is on the ways in which documents are used as a resource by various and different kinds of 'reader'. Here, a concern with document content or how a document has come into being are marginal, and the analysis concentrates on the relationship between specific documents and their use or recruitment by identifiable human actors for purposeful ends. Thus, in the field of medical sociology for example, there are various studies that focus on how medical professionals call upon and use X-rays, charts, notes, files, images, and so forth, in routine clinical settings (see Prior 2003). Finally, the approaches that fit into Cell 4 also position content as secondary. The emphasis here is on how documents as 'things' function in schemes of social activity, and with how such things can drive, rather than be driven by, human actors – that is, the spotlight is on the *vita activa* of documentation (see, for example, Prior 2008a). In the following sections I shall outline some examples of work in each of the four frames.

Document as Resource

Most organizations – especially bureaucratic ones – are awash with documentation. Forms, memos, monthly, quarterly and annual reports, procedure manuals, spreadsheets and records, as well as policy and mission statements, are just a few examples of the documentation that can be found routinely in organizational settings. In most instances researchers focus on the content of these documents, and use the data as a resource that 'tell us about what is going on' in the organization. To illustrate one way in which we can analyse such material I am going to focus on some UK (Scottish) government health policy documents. However, one of my key aims here is to demonstrate how an interest solely in document content is rarely sufficient to 'understand' what is, indeed, 'going on', and that it is always necessary to make some kind of connection between what might be called the 'word' and the 'world' if we are to capture essential elements of organizational culture.

Governments tend to produce policy statements in abundance. For example, I estimate that the UK government published some 228 health policy and guidance documents on its website during 2007 alone. Fortunately, the content of such documents can often be dealt with in a relatively straightforward manner. The most direct way is to begin with a concordance or index of all the words in a text together with a count of the number of times each word appears. A concordance can often highlight what is important in a document and it can also serve to highlight what is absent from any given document. And at a slightly more complex level it is possible to move beyond the presence or absence of words and look at (and enumerate) phrases, concepts, ideas and even 'themes' that are contained in or that emerge from

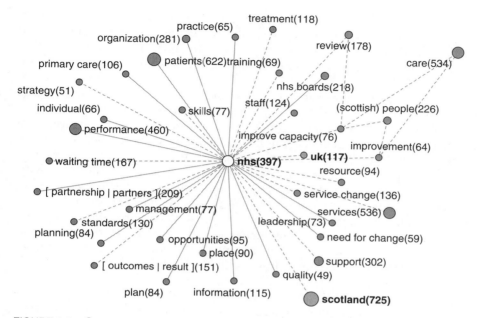

FIGURE 6.1   *Concept cluster for NHS in four Scottish policy documents*
Line thickness proportional to the strength of the similarity coefficient. Size of nodes reflects relative frequency of concept and (numbers) refer to the frequency of concept. Solid lines indicate relationships between terms within the same cluster and dashed lines indicate relationships between terms in different clusters.

the documentation. Normally such themes and concepts are 'coded' as appropriate. Take the following example: it is based on an analysis of some health policy documents published between 2001 and 2007 in Scotland.

I have analysed the documents using text-mining techniques (SPSS, 2007). One product of such text mining is the material in Figure 6.1; it illustrates what we might call a semantic web. The web is based, in part, on all the words contained in the Scottish policy documents just referred to, and it is possible to see the number of times selected terms have appeared in the data set – 'Scotland', for example, appears some 725 times. The more times a word has appeared, the larger is the 'node' for that particular term. However, the figure also shows how the words in the document are associated or co-occur. In this particular case our key node is towards the centre of the diagram (NHS or National Health Service with 397 citations), and we can see that it is strongly associated with such concepts as 'improvement', 'change' and 'performance'. (The thickness of the various lines connecting the nodes is proportional to the strength of the co-occurrence in the data set.)

In the context of qualitative research, of course, this kind of (quantitative-based) analysis constitutes just one of many possible entry points into what might be called a policy discourse – and it is just an entry point. To understand how the words in the documents connect to the world beyond the text – to the actions of the politicians and policy-makers who produced the document as well as to the audience for whom the documents were intended – we would need to use other sources of data (such as interview data) and other sources of text (such as political speeches).

One framework in which we might do that would be to invoke the concept of a narrative (Czarniawska, 2004) and, in particular, the concept of a policy narrative (Fischer, 2003). Virtually all health documents in all countries contain policy narratives and although such documents can relate to vastly different areas of activity, they tend to contain a similar storyline. Roughly speaking, this storyline argues that what has gone on until now is bad; that the existing state of affairs is bolstered only by people with narrow and sectional interests at heart; that there is a consequent need to transform, modernize, change and improve services; that the current government is going to achieve that by listening to; by empowering; by working in partnership with the voters. And this is exactly the kind of story that is told in the Scottish documents.

It is in the frame of such a narrative – a narrative that is contained in political speeches, party political documentation, newspaper stories and other media – that the terms and concepts that appear in Figure 6.1 are melded together. One thing that is interesting about the semantic web is that it is connected every bit as much to nation building (Scotland and the Scottish people) as with improving the national health. Indeed, in all of the smaller countries of the UK and in contrast to England, health policy statements often take a distinctively nationalist turn, and tend to function to underpin a sense of national identity, as much as they serve to describe a set of health actions. A straightforward content analysis could of course reveal such themes in part, but in order to understand fully why 'Scotland' and the 'Scottish people' have such a prominent role in documentation about health services we have to connect the publications to that wider narrative to which I have just referred, and especially to the political and social infrastructure that exist outside of the text. In short, even when focusing on content, documents have to be studied as components in networks of action rather than as independent and inert 'things' that can be approached 'unobtrusively'.

Documents as Topic

A second way in which documents may be approached in a research frame is as 'topic'. That is to say, instead of accepting the content of documentation as

TABLE 6.2   *Prevalence of psychiatric disorders in private households by gender. Rates per thousand of population in past week (GB 1995)*

Nature of disorder	Females	Males
Mixed Anxiety & Depressive Disorder (MADD)	99	54
Generalized Anxiety Disorder (GAD)	34	28
Depressive episode	25	17
All phobias	14	7
Obsessive–Compulsive Disorder (OCD)	15	9
Panic disorder	9	8
Functional psychoses*	4	4
Alcohol dependence*	21	75
Drug dependence*	15	29

* Rates per thousand of population in past 12 months.

Source: Meltzer, Gill, Petticrew and Hinds (1995)

'evidence', as data to be drawn down and used as fact, we can ask questions about how the content came to assume the form that it did. Following the ideas of Michel Foucault (1972), I have previously referred to this kind of orientation as an 'archaeology of documentation' (Prior, 2007). The virtues of the approach are best displayed by reference to the analysis of statistical reports – on crime, education, deprivation, illness, mortality and the like – though, in fact, any document can be analysed in the archaeological frame. Let us take an example.

I am looking at a table of research results (Table 6.2). It tells us about the community prevalence rates in Great Britain of certain types of what are sometimes called 'neurotic' disorders, together with some estimates for the 'functional psychoses'. The table represents 'facts' about mental illness. It is intended to be used, together with others related to it, as a resource for researchers. Thus, we can, for example, refer to Table 6.2 as evidence for our statement that during the 1990s, in Great Britain, about 16 per cent of people in any one week showed symptoms of a neurotic disorder. But how were this and other facts arrived at? How was the report put together? And what would an answer to such questions tell us about fundamental social processes?

The study of the manner in which social data, such as are found in Table 6.2, are produced has a good sociological pedigree. Some early markers in this particular history are available in the works of Cicourel (1964, 1976), Douglas (1967) and Garfinkel (1967) who tended to focus on crime and suicide statistics. As with the manufacture of crime or suicide or any other form of statistics, the production of psychiatric statistics depends on the existence of at least two mechanisms. The first of these concerns the existence of a conceptual or theoretical scheme, while the second concerns a set of rules and technical instructions by means of which events and occurrences can be allocated to categories. Now, the conceptual scheme in terms of which mental illness is routinely comprehended is that contained in the *Diagnostic and Statistical Manual of the American Psychiatric Association* (such as the DSM IV, 2000, for example). The latter contains a series of categories relating to the various psychiatric maladies that people might be said to suffer from, and it also contains diagnostic criteria for recognizing the distinct disorders. Some of the disorders are listed in Table 6.2. The DSM is in itself a document of some interest and demonstrates one of the ways in which we 'sort things out' in Western culture (Bowker and Star, 1999). As such it is always worthwhile examining how psychiatric disorders appear and disappear from the DSM nosology. Thus, Multiple Personality Disorder, for example, is a category that once was present in the DSM and which is no longer present, while Post Traumatic Stress Disorder was once absent and is now present. For now, however, let us focus on how the figures in Table 6.2 were obtained, rather than on the DSM.

The data in the table are derived from answers to a survey conducted in over 10,000 private households, some members of whom were asked to respond to a specific questionnaire (see Meltzer et al., 1995). In this particular case the questionnaire or instrument was called the Clinical Interview Schedule (Revised) or CIS-R. The CIS-R is one of a variety of 'instruments' that produce clinical and other phenomena (see, for example, Bowling, 1997). In many respects documents such as the CIS-R are like machine tools – tools for producing 'facts'. Indeed, phenomena such as 'disability', types of psychiatric illness and 'quality of life' are conditions routinely manufactured by instruments of the kind referred to here. In the case of the CIS-R the tool operates through a system of questions and answers. For example, one such question asks, 'During the past month, have you felt that you've been lacking in energy?' Another question asks, 'Have you any sort of ache or pain in the past month?' Respondents are required to answer 'Yes' or 'No'. Normally these responses are coded into a machine-readable form. So a 'Yes' might be coded as, say, a one and a 'No' as a zero. The ones and zeros are then added so that for each respondent in the sample it is possible to determine at least two things: a total score for the individual concerned, and a very precise indication of which section of the questionnaire the scores came from. Should an individual score a total of 12 or more points on the CIS-R then they are usually regarded as a 'case' of psychiatric disorder. In that sense 12 is said to function as the cut-off point for 'caseness'. Whether a person is then to be allocated to the category of 'depression', 'functional psychoses' or 'compulsive disorder' is dependent on the distribution of scores ('Yes's and 'No's) within the instrument. No mention of any diagnostic condition is made in the interview schedule itself and at no point were subjects asked whether they suffered from Obsessive Compulsive Disorder or Depression or whatever – the diagnosis is achieved via the deployment of machine-driven algorithms.

So what does all of this suggest about our concept of psychiatric disorder? And what would happen if someone decided to set the cut-off point on the schedule to 10 or 18 rather than 12? Such questions are in many ways related. It is possible, for example, to select a different cut-off point. Moving the point to, say, 10 would increase the prevalence of mental illness in the community. Moving the point to 18 would decrease it. So there is a sense in which we can have as much or as little mental illness in the community as we want. The acceptance of '12' as a cut-off point is merely a (useful) convention. In the same way, if we altered the rules by means of which the different illnesses take precedence one over the other then our entire picture of the prevalence of the different disorders would change. So the 'facts' about psychiatric disorder in the community are in a sense malleable, and the same thing is true of the 'facts' about economic activity, crime, obesity, mortality and other events and activities. (I have demonstrated how 'facts' about mortality can be studied as topic in Prior, 2003.)

Naturally, most social researchers prefer to use data of the kind just discussed as 'resource' or evidence. However, what the above analysis suggests is that it is always worthwhile investigating such data as 'topic' (on this distinction, see Zimmerman and Pollner, 1971). That is to say, it is forever beneficial to ask how documents are produced; who, exactly, produced them; and how the production process was socially organized.

Studying Documents in Use

Text and documentation are not only produced, but also, in turn, productive. For example, in his discussion of a psychiatric record, Hak (1992) provides an illustration of how a professional psychiatrist translates items of patient talk and observed behaviour into a written record. In so doing the psychiatrist – as note taker – highlights the essential details of a patient's conversation, codes them into professional language (of delusions, hallucinations, diagnostic terms, etc.) and makes suggestions for future action (entry into a psychiatric unit or whatever). In Figure 6.2, we can see similar processes at work. Figure 6.2 is a facsimile of a page of nursing assessment notes that I came across in a psychiatric hospital in the late 1980s. It is clear from the notes that the members of the nursing staff were concerned to categorize their patients in a variety of ways. The latter included a one-word diagnosis of the patient's condition, an assessment of 'activities of daily living' (ADL) skills, brief notes concerning the level of co-operation and hygiene exhibited by the patient and so forth. These assessments were based on conversations and interchanges between nurses and patients and among nurses alone. It is important to recall that the patients/clients – as with all human beings – commonly indulged in a wide array of activities and behaviours. Yet of such a myriad array of activity only

Patient	Admissions	Diagnosis	Problems/Constraints	Medication	Plans	Assets
Name: Dob 11/12/36 Admin area: East Dr: Yellow Ward: Blue	No. of adm. = 1 Date of last adm. 17/06/1962	Schizophrenia	Long time in hospital Temper tantrums & bad language Activities of daily living poor Recently quarrelsome with ASB	Gavison tabs bd Trifluoperazine 2mg bd Vit BPc 1 tab mane	Maintain	
Name: Dob 23/02/53 North Dr: Green Ward: Blue	No. of adm. = 5 Date of last adm. 29/09/1987	Paranoid Schizophrenia	Loner. Poor motivation Wishes to stay in hospital Failed RA (stay in residential accommodation) Injury to right hip	Piroxican 30 mg nocte Ranitidine 150 mg nocte Vit BPC am	Move to community	ADL skills good
Name: Dob 3/07/58 West Dr: Green Ward: Blue	No. of adm. = 3 Date of last adm. 17/05/1988	Schizophrenia Low IQ	Poverty of thought Withdrawn ADL skills limited Childish and naive in manner Mother has encouraged dependence over the years but is now opting out Poor road safety	Benxtropine 2 mg mane Thioridizine 75mg tid Senna 2 tabs nocte	ADL activities	Pleasant & co-operative Hygiene good
Name: Dob 10/08/60 West Dr: Green Ward: Blue	No. of adm. = 6 Date of last adm. 10/03/1988	Dependent Personality	Multiple Somatic complaints Resistant to suggestions Poor compliance tends to opt out Poor response to antidepressant therapy Poor attendance at OT unit Poor Hearing	Thyroxine 0.1 mg mane Nifedipine 10 mg bd Thioridizine 50 mg bd	Maintain	ADL good

FIGURE 6.2 Facsimile of a ward-based nursing assessment record (UK psychiatric hospital 1989)

a few activities are ever highlighted. Thus, in the case of the first-named patient, it is their 'schizophrenia', their poor ADL skills, their temper tantrums and quarrelsome behaviour that are highlighted. This selectivity of focus would become even more evident were one to examine other kinds of patient records. Thus, in the hospital to which I am currently referring there were also psychiatric records (called 'charts') and social work records kept on each patient. The former were maintained by the medically trained psychiatrists and contained other kinds of information, such as data on whether the patients exhibited any 'first rank symptoms' (of schizophrenia), their medication and its effects, their 'history', items about family life, patient delusions and so forth. In fact the psychiatric records looked very much like those alluded to and reported upon by Hak (1992) and Barrett (1996). Social work records were also made up for each of the patients. These paid relatively little attention to medical diagnoses and the effects of medication and referred more often to the stability and maturity of the patient vis-à-vis relationships with others, the nature and level of their state benefits and the like. Considerable reference to the whereabouts, behaviours and opinions of other family members was also made within social work files. Access to such records and the 'right' to make entries in such records were more or less restricted to the members of the individual professional groupings. In that respect the 'script' in each document served, in part, to mark out the realm and expertise of the various parties. Social work 'talk' belonged in social work records, psychiatric talk belonged in medical records, and nurse talk belonged in nursing records.

Recorded observations on patients/clients are, then, highly selective. In the case of public service agency files, such records often define the human beings that they refer to in specific and particular ways. In so doing they call upon and activate a whole series of membership categorization devices or MCDs (Silverman, 1998). How a particular device comes to be associated with any individual and how that categorization might be used and called upon to account for and explain an individual's behaviour in specific circumstances can form the occasion for important and fundamental sociological research.

In a similar fashion, Zerubavel (1979: 45) has indicated how notes written up by medical and nursing professionals were 'among the main criteria used by their supervisors to evaluate their clinical competence', as well as forming the primary mechanism through which continuous supervision of patients were maintained. In fact Zerubavel's study highlights the centrality of charts, graphs and records of all kinds in underpinning the routine social organization of hospital life. Thus, printed schedules are used to organize the patient/staff day; printouts of various kinds are routinely used to monitor patients; and notes are written so as indicate how the 'hospital' cares for its clients. (In US hospitals, of course, patient records are also used as a hook on which to hang financial costs and transactions.)

This capacity of medical records to mediate social relationships of all kinds has been further researched by Berg (1996, 1997) who points out how hospital patients are both structured through records and accessed through records. One important feature of patient existence that is emphasized by Berg is the manner in which medical records are used so as to keep the case (and the patient) 'on track'. Such structuring of patient trajectories through records is achieved in numerous ways, planning and monitoring being two of them. In this respect it is of interest to note the column headed 'Plans' in Figure 6.2. In the context of these records the most important plans concerned whether or not the patient was ready for life in the community. (My own hospital study was executed at that rather important cusp where psychiatric patients were being moved out of hospitals and into 'the community'.) In most cases, the patients were to be 'maintained' (kept in the hospital ward). The detail hardly concerns us here. What is important to note is that records of this type always contain some rules for action. Other rules for action are contained in the column relating to medication. Latour (1987) has used the term 'action at a distance' to indicate how decisions written down in one context and setting can carry implications for action in future settings. And it is indeed the case that records often contain instructions for future organizational activity. King James' claim that opened this chapter provides an excellent example of the process.

Patient 'careers' are not, of course, the only things that are kept 'on track' by the use of records; patient identities are also constructed through documentation – Barrett (1996), for example, argues that patients are constituted through their psychiatric notes. Nor are such processes of monitoring, tracking and identifying limited to hospitals and medical organizations; rather they are ubiquitous in areas as diverse as educational and welfare organizations, prisons and factories, and as such are always open to study.

Studying Documents in Action

I have argued elsewhere (Prior, 2008a) that, as well as looking at how documents are used by human actors for everyday purposes, it can also be useful to look at how documents can in turn drive and fashion episodes of human interaction. A key argument here is that rather than see relationships of hierarchy and determinism between human and non-human agents, we should view the potential of all agents as equivalent, and subsequently open our eyes to the various ways in which 'things' can structure human interaction. In what follows I am going to draw once again on an example from my own work. My aim is to illustrate how documentation can form the occasion for talk and interaction; how documentation is routinely drawn into interaction; and how documentation exerts an effect on the entire interactive sequence – in short, how text can display agency (Cooren, 2004). The data are provided in Box 6.1.

Box 6.1   Documents as actors in episodes of interaction

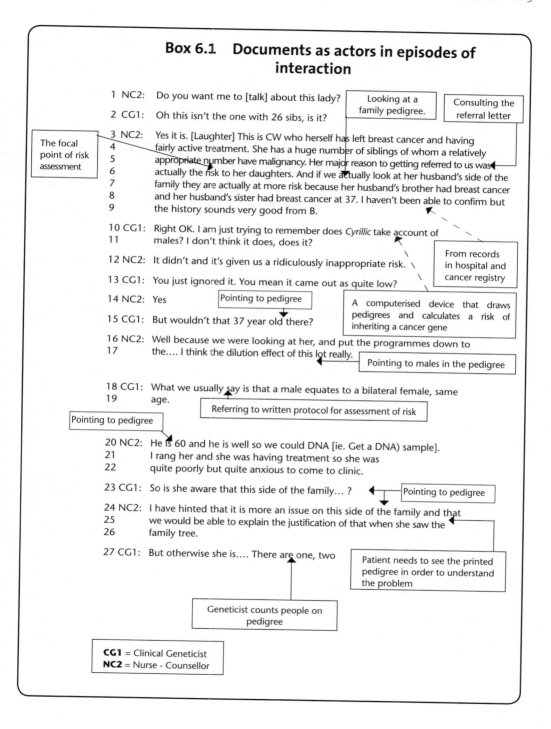

1 NC2:   Do you want me to [talk] about this lady?

2 CG1:   Oh this isn't the one with 26 sibs, is it?

Looking at a family pedigree.

Consulting the referral letter

3 NC2:   Yes it is. [Laughter] This is CW who herself has left breast cancer and having
4   fairly active treatment. She has a huge number of siblings of whom a relatively
5   appropriate number have malignancy. Her major reason to getting referred to us was
6   actually the risk to her daughters. And if we actually look at her husband's side of the
7   family they are actually at more risk because her husband's brother had breast cancer
8   and her husband's sister had breast cancer at 37. I haven't been able to confirm but
9   the history sounds very good from B.

The focal point of risk assessment

10 CG1: Right OK. I am just trying to remember does *Cyrillic* take account of
11   males? I don't think it does, does it?

From records in hospital and cancer registry

12 NC2: It didn't and it's given us a ridiculously inappropriate risk.

13 CG1: You just ignored it. You mean it came out as quite low?

14 NC2: Yes

Pointing to pedigree

A computerised device that draws pedigrees and calculates a risk of inheriting a cancer gene

15 CG1: But wouldn't that 37 year old there?

16 NC2: Well because we were looking at her, and put the programmes down to
17   the.... I think the dilution effect of this lot really.

Pointing to males in the pedigree

18 CG1: What we usually say is that a male equates to a bilateral female, same
19   age.

Referring to written protocol for assessment of risk

Pointing to pedigree

20 NC2: He is 60 and he is well so we could DNA [ie. Get a DNA) sample].
21   I rang her and she was having treatment so she was
22   quite poorly but quite anxious to come to clinic.

23 CG1: So is she aware that this side of the family... ?

Pointing to pedigree

24 NC2: I have hinted that it is more an issue on this side of the family and that
25   we would be able to explain the justification of that when she saw the
26   family tree.

27 CG1: But otherwise she is.... There are one, two

Patient needs to see the printed pedigree in order to understand the problem

Geneticist counts people on pedigree

CG1 = Clinical Geneticist
NC2 = Nurse - Counsellor

The talk was gathered from a study of work in a cancer genetics clinic. In this instance a clinical geneticist (designated CG) and nurse counsellor (designated NC2) are discussing their understanding of the degree to which a given patient is at risk of inheriting a certain type of cancer mutation. The episode more or less opens with NC2 reading a letter (lines 3–9) of referral to the clinic. The letter frames the ensuing discussion. A second document enters into the frame at line 6 – it's a family history, or 'pedigree' as it is called in clinical genetics. The pedigree traces the ancestry of the patient who is the focus of the discussion, and it does so in a drawing that contains symbols for males and females and lines linking those who are related (see lines 17 and 20 of the data extract). In this case, the drawing has been composed by what Latour (1987) would refer to as an 'inscription device' (known here as 'Cyrillic'). Cyrillic has also calculated the numerical risk (lines 10–12) of inheritance. By following the turn-taking sequence, we can see how the documents (notes, records, pedigrees) are central to the manner in which the interaction is patterned and structured. Thus some documents (notes) are read; some documents (the Cyrillic printout) are used as the occasion for the talk; some (the pedigrees) are (frequently) pointed at (lines 15, 17, 20, 23, 24) and used to develop good arguments and justifications. What is more, the documents are linked to the speakers in distinct ways and in clear sequences, and among other things serve to underline the ways in which the division of labour (between 'doctors' and 'nurses') is underpinned in routine interaction.

Whichever way we read this sequence, it is clear that the issue of documentation cannot be adequately dealt with by focusing on document content. Rather the entire complex of events deserves study, and in that structure the documents function as props, allies, rule-makers, calculators, decision-makers, experts and illustrators. In short, they appear as what might justifiably called 'hybrids' (Callon and Rip, 1992), and some might argue that they function as actors. Though, whichever way we approach the data, it is clear that documents play an active (and a far from passive) role in the configuration of the clinical encounter of which the extract forms a part. Unfortunately, the examination of documents in this kind of dynamic frame is rarely seen, for, as I have said throughout this chapter, the mainstream emphasis is on what is 'in' documents rather than with how documents can function to shape social relationships.

Summary

- In the history of the social sciences there has been an undue emphasis on conceptualizing documents as inert objects that need only to be studied for their content.

- Document content is important and deserves systematic analysis, but we also need to focus on how documents are assembled, how they are used, and how they can function in episodes of interaction.
- In terms of fieldwork, it is essential to remember that each and every document stands in a dual relation to fields of action. Namely, as a receptacle (of instructions, commands, wishes, reports, descriptions, etc.), and as an agent that is open to manipulation and/or use as an ally to be mobilized for further action.
- As a general rule it is best to contextualize the study of documents by thinking in terms of networks of influence – visualizing such networks has an important role to play in social research (see Prior, 2008b), and it is in terms of such visualizations that important advances have still to be made.

Future Prospects

Despite my plea for the research effort to focus on the ways in which documents are produced, 'consumed' or used, and how they circulate in schemes of social action, rather than on document content, I suspect that immediate advances in the study of documentation will most likely be linked to the development of text-mining procedures. The latter encourages a sophisticated form of content analysis using computer-based algorithms that recognize synonyms and similarities among both words and concepts. The consequent links and relationships are often visualized in the form of semantic and conceptual networks, thereby emphasizing the ways in which text both is a form of web and at the same time reflects webs or networks in the social relations in which they are based.

Questions

- What are the key differences entailed in studying documents as (a) topic and (b) resource?
- How exactly might one analyse the content of a document?
- What is implied by arguing that documents should be considered as 'hybrids'?

Recommended Reading

Prior, L. (2003) *Using Documents in Social Research*. London: Sage.

Prior, L. (2007) Documents and action. In P. Alasuutari, L. Bickman & J. Brannen (Eds), *Handbook of Social Research Methods*. London: Sage, 479–492.

Prior, L. (2008) Repositioning documents in social research. *Sociology* (Special Issue on Research Methods), 42: 821–836.

Prior, L. (2008) Researching documents. In P. Leavy & S. Hesse-Biber (Eds), *Handbook of Emergent Methods*. New York: Guilford, 111–126.

Internet Links

- For information on a variety of digital archives and text mining:

  www.jisc.ac.uk/

- For a database of newspaper stories across the globe, the LexisNexis database (available via most university libraries) is indispensible. See also:

  http://academic.lexisnexis.com/

- For a gateway into a wide variety of WWW resources such as diaries, letters, images and other documents, go to:

  www.intute.ac.uk/socialsciences/

References

American Psychiatric Association. (2000) *Diagnostic and Statistical Manual of Mental Disorders. DSM-IV-TR*. Washington, DC: American Psychiatric Association.

Barrett, R. (1996) *The Psychiatric Team and the Social Definition of Schizophrenia. An Anthropological Study of Person and Illness*. Cambridge: Cambridge University Press.

Berg, M. (1996) Practices of reading and writing: The constitutive role of the patient record in medical work. *Sociology of Health and Illness*, 18 (4): 499–524.

Berg, M. (1997) *Rationalizing Medical Work. Decision-support Techniques and Medical Practices*. Cambridge, MA: MIT Press.

Bowker, G.C. and Star, S.L. (1999) *Sorting Things Out. Classification and Its Consequences*. Cambridge, MA: MIT Press.

Bowling, A. (1997) *Measuring Health. A Review of Quality of Life Measurement Scales*. 2nd Edition. Buckingham: Open University Press.

Bryman, A. (2004) *Social Research Methods*. Oxford: Oxford University Press.

Callon, M. and Rip, A. (1992) Humains et non-humains: morale d'une coexistence. In J. Theys and B. Kalaora (Eds), *La Terre outragée*. Paris: Autrement, 140–156.

Cicourel, A.V. (1964) *Method and Measurement in Sociology*. New York: The Free Press.

Cicourel, A.V. (1976) *The Social Organisation of Juvenile Justice*. London: Heinemann.

Cooren, F. (2004) Textual agency: how texts do things in organizational settings. *Organization*, 11 (3): 373–393.

Czarniawska, B. (2004) *Narratives in Social Science Research*. London: Sage.

Douglas, J.D. (1967) *The Social Meanings of Suicide*. Princeton, NJ: Princeton University Press.

Fischer, F. (2003) *Reframing Public Policy: Discursive Politics and Deliberative Practices*. Oxford: Oxford University Press.

Foucault, M. (1972) *The Archaeology of Knowledge*. Tr. A. Sheridan. New York: Pantheon.

Garfinkel, H. (1967) *Studies in Ethnomethodology*. Englewood Cliffs, NJ: Prentice Hall.

Glaser, B.G. and Strauss, A.L. (1967) *The Discovery of Grounded Theory. Strategies for Qualitative Research*. New York: Aldine De Gruyter.

Hak, T. (1992) Psychiatric records as transformations of other texts. In G. Watson and R.M. Seiler (Eds), *Text in Context. Contributions to Ethnomethodology*. London: Sage, 138–155.

Krippendorf, K. (2004) *Content Analysis. An Introduction to its Methodology*. 2nd Edition. London: Sage.

Latour, B. (1987) *Science in Action. How to Follow Engineers and Scientists through Society*. Buckingham: Open University Press.

Meltzer, H., Gill, B., Petticrew, M. and Hinds, K. (1995) *The Prevalence of Psychiatric Morbidity among Adults Living in Private Households. OPCS Surveys of Psychiatric Morbidity in Great Britain*. Report 1. London: HMSO.

Prior, L. (2003) *Using Documents in Social Research*. London: Sage.

Prior, L. (2007) Documents and action. In P. Alasuutari, L. Bickman & J. Brannen (Eds), *Handbook of Social Research Methods*. London: Sage, 479–492.

Prior, L. (2008a) Repositioning documents in social research. *Sociology* (Special Issue on Research Methods), 42: 821–836.

Prior, L. (2008b) Researching documents. In P. Leavy & S. Hesse-Biber (Eds), *Handbook of Emergent Methods*. New York: Guilford, 111–126.

Silverman, D. (1998) *Harvey Sacks. Social Science and Conversation Analysis*. Cambridge: Polity Press.

SPSS (2007) *Text Mining for Clementine*. 12.0 User's Guide. Chicago: SPSS.

Weber, R.P. (1990) *Basic Content Analysis*. London: Sage.

Zerubavel, E. (1979) *Patterns of Time in Hospital Life: A Sociological Perspective*. London: University of Chicago Press.

Zimmerman, D.H. and Pollner, M. (1971) The everyday world as a phenomenon. In J.D. Douglas, *Understanding Everyday Life*. London: Routledge & Kegan Paul, 80–103.

Internet Research 7

Annette N. Markham

Abstract

This chapter reviews salient characteristics of the internet to illustrate some of the ways internet-based media can influence the shape, scope, and direction of a study. This chapter suggests that substantial benefit can be gained by considering the methodological implications of these characteristics, whether one is using the internet as a tool for non-internet-related topics, studying social phenomena directly implicated by the internet, or studying the internet itself. Ethical considerations of internet research are also discussed.

Keywords:

internet research ethics, geographic dispersion, anonymity, internet media, networked identity.

The internet is a social phenomenon, a tool, and also a field site for qualitative research. Depending on the role the internet plays in the qualitative research project or how it is conceptualized by the researcher, different epistemological, logistical, and ethical considerations will come into play. The term 'Internet' originally described a network of computers that made possible the decentralized transmission of information. Now, the term serves as an umbrella for innumerable technologies, capacities, uses, and social spaces. Because the types of social interaction made possible by the internet vary so widely, qualitative researchers find it necessary to define the concept more narrowly within individual studies. This is complicated by the fact that the study of the internet cuts across all academic disciplines. There are no central methodological or theoretical guidelines and research findings are widely distributed and decentralized.

As the internet becomes more and more ubiquitous, it saturates literally every part of our civic, social, and professional lives, whether or not we even use the technologies themselves. In terms of qualitative inquiry, the internet does not simply provide new tools or venues for conducting social research, it challenges taken-for-granted frameworks for how identities, relationships, cultures, and social structures are constructed. Likewise, it challenges how we understand and conduct qualitative inquiry in an epoch of media convergence, mediated identities, redefinitions of social boundaries, and the transcendence of geographical boundaries (Baym & Markham, 2009).

Core methodological principles do not change, however, and this chapter maintains that successful navigation of these challenges by qualitative researchers relies on their ability not only to ask reflexive questions at critical junctures throughout the project, but also to 'remain grounded as the research contexts, technologies, and the very nature of their social worlds seem to change, converge, collide, or collapse' (Baym & Markham, 2009, p. ix).

The internet tends to be studied in one or more of the following ways:

The study of any social phenomenon using internet-based tools for collecting, sorting, storing, and/or analyzing information gathered:

Inquiry related to any topic might utilize various capacities and interfaces available via the internet to augment or replace traditional qualitative methods of collecting, storing, sorting, and analyzing information. The internet is also associated with the use of data analysis software, albeit inaccurately, as the internet is not strictly necessary to enable the functioning of such analytical tools.

The study of sociocultural phenomena that are mediated by, interwoven with, or rely on the internet for their composition or function:

Inquiry might focus on the way people use or experience various aspects of the internet, or on the cultural formations emerging from or made possible through the internet. Methods drawn from a wide range of disciplines can be adapted to studying internet use or internet-mediated environments.

The study of the internet or aspects of it as phenomena in themselves:

Inquiry might focus on the network, technologies, or capacities of the internet. This research scenario is distinguished from the previous one because of a greater focus on various features and implications of this globe spanning network of connectivity, rather than those social phenomena resulting from internet use.

These categorizations of inquiry are not necessarily mutually exclusive. Researchers studying an online community may conceptualize the internet simultaneously as a tool for collecting information, the fieldsite, and also an object of analysis. A researcher mapping the way text messages flow through networks may use the internet as a tool for collecting data or measuring speed of transmission. At the same time, the researcher might explore the social impact of this mapping or examine the social life of the messages themselves as they travel beyond the individual.

As with any framework, these three frameworks guide and naturally restrict the researcher's general approach as well as specific practices. As the purpose of research is identified and the study unfolds, certain characteristics of the internet will become more meaningful than others. For example, Researcher 1, studying how breast cancer survivors frame their experiences, might conceptualize the internet as a tool, using various internet media to contact participants, schedule interviews, distribute open-ended question lists, collect research diaries, organize and sort data, and so forth. Researcher 2, studying how women feel about being members of a virtual breast cancer group, may conceptualize the internet as a field site, observing interaction practices and group norms among participants. Researcher 3, studying how frames of meaning surrounding breast cancer are negotiated and reproduced, might focus on the networked features of blogging, studying the hyperlinks between websites, mapping the network of connections created by repeated elements across multiple sites. In the first case, the information processing and transmitting features of the internet are salient, but only inasmuch as these tools function effectively. It is essential to consider how these tools are operating, but the internet itself or the internet-mediated aspects of sensemaking are not the subjects of study. In the second case, the internet-mediated characteristics of the group become salient if one is attempting to study the uniqueness of a 'virtual' community (as opposed to those that are physically based). In the third case, the networks of connections constitute the phenomenon; links between users are the primary focus.

These cases are oversimplified to demonstrate that one's definitional and conceptual framework for the internet will shift depending on one's ontological and epistemological premises, research goals, and the specific form of the research question. Rigorously analyzing the connections between one's questions, the subjects of inquiry, and the possible methods of collection, analysis, and interpretation is an essential part of all qualitative inquiry. In qualitative internet studies, reflecting on various characteristics of the internet is a crucial part of this iterative process. It helps the researcher create more internal theoretical consistency and also narrows the monumental range of choices for previous studies that might guide the current research project.

Below, I review some basic characteristics of the internet that might be salient to one's project. This list is not exhaustive but general, intended heuristically. These are characteristics that tend to cause problems for qualitative researchers, raise challenging questions about research methods, or create new opportunities for researchers. Reflecting on these characteristics with a specific case study in mind can help researchers make wise choices as they investigate potentially unfamiliar forms of mediation, new technologies, or unique research environments. These characteristics can apply to almost any internet-mediated research context, regardless of the specific technologies involved.

Salient Characteristics of the Internet

The Internet as a Medium of Communication

As a medium for communication, the internet provides multiple means of interaction and performance of identity and community. Conceptualizing the internet as a medium allows us to see it in such ways as a conduit for the transmission of information from one place and person to another; a range of language aids for interacting with others; a tool for bundling up bits of information into a package that makes sense. The internet provides the means for creating, displaying, and framing the objects of study and the boundaries for experience. It is also a method for reaching out to participants or information.

Although composed of vast networks of connections between computers, the internet is more associated with the tangible capacities afforded by these instantaneous connections. Users focus less on the actual networks of connections than the communities made possible by these networks or the texts, still and moving images, and sounds facilitated by these networks. People use the internet in ways that parallel but depart from or extend earlier media for communication, such as letter writing, telephone, Post-it notes, bulletin boards, and so forth. People can use multiple media simultaneously, connecting to vast and complicated social and informational networks. One's use of the media can be asynchronous or synchronous; one-to-one, one-to-many, or many–many; anonymous or not. The presentation of self may be represented in writing, sound, moving and still images, live or pre-recorded video, avatars, various displayed artifacts, and so forth.

One should neither get bogged down in this nor dismiss it as commonplace, but reflect on what is being created when one uses the internet as a medium for communication, or when one is studying those sociocultural phenomena constituted via the internet. Use of a particular form of internet media may appear homogeneous at the surface level of behaviour when, in fact, there are as many motives and purposes as there are conversations. For example, the seemingly simple practice of sending text messages could be conceptualized variously as: a conversation continuer, a marker of presence, a sign of status, an opportunity to represent oneself authentically, a move of resistance, an opportunity to wear a mask, a location device, or a signal for unified action.

If used as a tool for research, the internet and it capabilities should be matched to the goals, topics, or participants of the project. Because internet technologies are defined and adapted in distinctive ways by different users and groups, this is often an inductive process. Collecting life histories via email may be satisfactory, but allowing participants to create ongoing life history accounts on websites that they can design with color and images may yield richly textured results. Using photo or video blogging would yield yet a different outcome for analysis. For an interview study, real-time text-based interfaces may provide anonymous participation and spontaneous conversation, but that may be inadequate for certain participants or research questions. Interviewing via videoconferencing may be preferred by some participants, but others might provide more information if they also had an instant messaging window open; sometimes people can not vocalize something face to face, but can and will express it in text. Email interviews may be better suited to participants who have busy schedules or desire time to consider their responses, but may be unsuitable for users more familiar with shorter snippet forms of interaction.

It is essential to consider the various ways in which people use and make sense of the internet as a communication medium, because sensemaking practices differ widely. One might make sense of it as a tool, focusing on the ability of the internet to make information seeking and retrieval more efficient and effective. Another might perceive the internet as a place, focusing on the cultural boundaries created by interactions rather than on the channel for communication. These different perceptions can influence greatly the way people utilize and talk about the internet. One must also consider the skill of participants: obviously, certain media are second nature to some users while for others these tools are completely foreign. This does not mean a researcher should adopt or dismiss certain media without due consideration of the value of the tool in relation to the research questions and the goal of research.

A final point to consider in this section is the extent to which the researcher's own perceptions about what the internet is will influence the way he or she observes and interprets in internet-based contexts. Being aware of the distinctions can help one better understand and adapt. One key is making a conscious analysis in order to best match the media of communication to the context, the user's preferences, and the research question. Another key is ascertaining, to the extent possible, how the subjects themselves frame their communicative behaviors.

Internet as Geographically Dispersed

Internet interfaces disregard location and distance, enabling the instantaneous and inexpensive transmission of information between people and databases. This capacity of the internet is generally taken for granted in everyday communication with others. Logistically, the distance-collapsing capacity of the internet allows researchers to connect to participants around the globe. This increases and/or alters the available pool of participants and can enable questions and comparisons that were previously less available.

Research can be designed around questions of interaction and social behavior unbound from the restrictions of proximity or geography. Participants can be selected on the basis of their appropriate fit within the research questions rather than their physical location or convenience to the researcher. Hine (2000) argues that the ethnographer's notion of cultural boundary must be reconsidered given this capacity of the internet. Rather than relying on traditional, geographically based means of encapsulating the culture under study, such as national boundaries or town limits, ethnographers might find more accuracy in using discourse patterns to find boundaries.

It is suggested that qualitative researchers carefully consider the ways in which unlimited reach complicates the research project, particularly regarding the size of one's data sets and cross-cultural issues. Internet researchers have found themselves daunted by enormous data sets, collected simply because internet technologies make archiving easy. This can frustrate researchers who find it impossible to analyze from any traditional qualitative methods. Although computer-aided analytical tools have grown in sophistication, their use should be balanced against the premise that qualitative approaches are uniquely developed and best suited to inductive, close analysis and depth of understanding. This is often at odds with the broad view encouraged by large pools of data. In addition, globally situated subjects reveal multitudes of cultural differences in assumptions, approaches, and sensemaking practices. Qualitative researchers have long grappled with cultural differences, but the fact that internet technologies bring the data to us – rather than the other way around – tends to hide what might have been much more obvious to scholars situated in cultures foreign to themselves.

Finally, geographic dispersion should not be equated with global reach or global research. Although the term 'global' might imply a planet-wide field site for research or the application of universal principles in the interpretation of social behavior, social problems and interactions themselves always occur at the local level. This is where qualitative research remains strongest. The term 'global' gains more usability when applied as a guide for one's sensibilities, rather than for one's scope (Markham, 2009, p. 39). This is particularly meaningful when one realizes that even if geographic dispersion is made possible by the internet, it does not mean our pool is equally dispersed; our research sites and subjects are in all likelihood still determined by our own networks.

Internet as Anonymous

Certain interaction environments facilitate actual or perceived anonymity. This has obvious advantages for certain topics or methods of qualitative inquiry. Part of this perception is facilitated by the internet's disconnection from geographic markers, which means that one's participation in interaction with other people is not necessarily linked to one's physical proximity to others, as would be the case in all face-to-face contexts.

As well as the natural – though not necessary – separation between people interacting via internet-mediated communication, certain interfaces are designed to promote and protect anonymity. These anonymous interaction environments may allow participants to speak more freely without restraints brought about by social norms, mores, and conventions. This feature is useful in studies of risky or deviant behaviors or socially unacceptable attitudes.

Johnson (2003) explores the way the 'pro-anorexia' movement was born and evolved online. Rather than talking face to face with participants, she examined their discursive practices in websites they had created. The infrastructure of the internet allows pro-anorexics to express their ideas and values without censure and without connection to their actual identities. They may have provided this information to the researcher in focus groups or in interviews, but because of the stigmatized nature of this eating disorder, Johnson's task as a researcher would have been much more difficult; in this case, she was able to access over 500 sites.

Bromseth (2002) studied the sensemaking practices of Norwegians exploring lesbianism and bisexuality. Again, although she could have obtained this data in face-to-face settings, it was unlikely that she would have obtained such a rich and diverse sample. The population of Norway is very small and therefore residents may feel less anonymous in general (Bromseth, 2002). Within a culture of heterosexual normativity, the likelihood of involving face-to-face participants in the manner Bromseth achieved via the internet is unlikely.

Anonymity and geographic distance both complicate and ease ethical considerations. In meeting the ethical requirements for conducting research involving human subjects in most countries, it is required, among other things, to gain informed consent. It is difficult if not impossible in an anonymous environment to ascertain if the user is capable of granting informed consent. The physical and legal markers traditionally available to qualitative researchers in the field are obviously absent if the participant wishes to remain bodiless, nameless, and faceless in an online context. This has raised the question of whether our regulations associated with informed consent are appropriately designed to protect human subjects. Using the internet as a method of interacting with participants may actually facilitate protection of human subjects; the participant has many outlets to withdraw from the study and certain interaction environments can improve the likelihood of maintaining confidentiality.

Viewed from another perspective, however, anonymity is not guaranteed in any internet context, which makes this a double-edged sword for the researcher. Even if one is ostensibly studying publicly accessible texts, the potential harm to real people should be considered carefully and thoroughly. Any study of social interaction via internet technologies involves real people, whose privacy concerns may be quite different from what the researcher presumes. Not only should researchers understand internet research ethics guidelines and principles by keeping up with current trends and debates, but they should also make their own ethical decision-making clear in the research report. This topic has been addressed in many arenas and there are no simple answers or formulas to follow. Recommended readings are provided at the end of this chapter.

As an interpretive rather than legalistic issue, anonymity can be discomfiting for researchers who may not know who the participant is, at least in any embodied, tangible way. This raises concerns about 'authenticity,' which has been a sticking point for many internet researchers and remains a dubious concept in general. On one hand, interacting with participants in anonymous environments results in the loss of many of the interactional qualities taken for granted in face-to-face interviews and observations. This may constitute a meaningful gap of information for the researcher who relies on these qualities as a way of knowing. On the other hand, authenticity is questionable in any setting, online or offline. Identical gaps of information occur in more traditional research and interaction environments, but are generally considered to be more a problem of interpretive clarity than a natural condition of doing research with unfamiliar participants. Solutions to these research situations, if one insists on searching for authenticity, require pragmatic sensitivity to all the details of the situation in which one is conducting research. In internet-mediated environments, however, the concept may not be meaningful at all, in that the researcher is attending to the textuality of individuals.

Internet as Chrono Malleable

As well as collapsing distance, internet technologies can disrupt the traditional uses and concepts of time in interaction. Because internet technologies accommodate both asynchronous and synchronous communication between individuals and groups, the use of time can be more individually determined. In real-time conversations, users can see their messages before they are sent. Backspacing and editing are made possible by stopping time in this way. In text-based environments, pauses and gaps are expected. Users may be participating in multiple conversations or tasks at once. Users may experience different speeds of connection or interruptions in service. In asynchronous media such as email, forum discussions, social media updates or blog postings, these pauses can be quite long, perhaps even weeks or months. In synchronous audio/visual contexts as well, users not only work around but also expect disjunctive and fragmented interactions.

The chrono-malleable features of internet-mediated communication can assist researchers in conducting interviews, for example. Complications regarding venue, commuting, and scheduling conflicts are less restrictive when interactions occur on the internet.

The elasticity of time can be associated with greater perceived control over the communication process. Because of the time-stop nature of most online media as well as the knowledge that connections sometimes fail, users have the opportunity to reflect on and revise their utterances and actions. In the midst of a conversation, synchronous or asynchronous, users can reflect on a comment or message before responding and review their own messages before sending. In the research setting, these taken-for-granted capabilities can significantly enhance both the scope of a study and the collection of information from participants. Several years ago, as I was conducting interviews online, it became clear that the questions asked could be carefully considered and rewritten during the interview. In one interview, I began to write, 'Would you describe yourself as an internet addict?' Realizing that the outcome of this question was limited by its format, I erased this question and modified it to read: 'How would you define an internet addict?' Whether the latter was an excellent choice is of less importance to this discussion than the fact that it is a better question than the first, which was both leading and close-ended. Even in a synchronous environment, I had the opportunity to reconsider my message and reformat my query. Designing research to take advantage of these capabilities can significantly enhance both the scope of a study and the collection of information from participants. Not only is it useful to consider the way that time can be utilized as a malleable construct in qualitative inquiry, but also it is necessary to consider that as modes of interaction continue to merge, the technologies for communication increasingly saturate our everyday lives (Gergen, 1991). If we take seriously the collapse of time–space distinctions (Giddens, 1991) in the 'knowledge age,' these become not simply pragmatic but ontological considerations.

Internet as Multi-modal

Communication via the internet occurs in multiple modes, alternately or simultaneously. Whether sponsored by software and hardware, a person's individual use, or the emergence of dyadic or group norms over time, these multiple modes operate on the sense making practices of users. Consequently, the issue of the internet as multi-modal becomes meaningful when designing or capturing interactions in the research context.

Users generally employ more than one internet-based modality at once; a user might be sending status updates to his or her social network, playing interactive games with friends, downloading music, updating his or her blog, and watching streaming video. When instant messages pop up on the screen, he or she is prompted to type a reply within a new or continued conversation.

Much more than mere technical accomplishments, these activities can be seen as adaptive, evolving means of constituting and maintaining networked identities in a media-saturated environment. These can be studied as phenomena or used as tools to augment the ways that researchers engage and communicate with participants. For example, researchers can use one channel with a group and different 'back channels' with individuals to interact privately while the larger group activity is occurring. These non-disruptive 'whispers' can add valuable data that might not otherwise be captured in the moment.

Certain environments are set up to facilitate multiple simultaneous modes of interaction, such as interactive gaming, virtual classrooms, and other social networking systems. Even in straightforward information transmission environments, which were not designed to facilitate a sense of presence, programs can evolve into shared spaces as the meanings, relationships, and communities created by the interactions transcend the limitations of the programs in which people are interacting.

During an online focus group discussion conducted by the author, participants used multiple technologies simultaneously in ways that complicated data collection but facilitated in-depth participation levels. The environment allowed for pseudonymous real-time participation among the group. Each person's comment would be posted as soon as he or she clicked the send or enter button. Messages scrolled up the screen as the conversation progressed. In one session, two participants who had previously been active contributors were not talking as actively as others were. Because of the programmed environment we were using, I was able to send one of them a request to talk privately, which, when accepted, opened a new screen that appeared only on our two desktops, in which we chatted privately. The participant told me that she and the other non-talkative participant had actually been chatting, as we were, in a private room, discussing one of the group's earlier issues in depth.

My discussion with this participant was similar to whispering during a group conversation, except that exchanges in the larger group were not disrupted. Her private chat with another participant was also an extended side conversation, one that added valuable data and could not have occurred unobtrusively in a physically present focus group setting. Of course, the data must be captured and archived, which requires that participants be well informed enough to realize this and tell the researcher that they are producing valuable information when they engage in these whispered – and private from the researcher – conversations.

In another instance, when a participant appeared to stop participating, I found out, using this same technique, that the participant had been offended by an earlier comment made by another participant. He stated that he was no longer certain that his contributions to the conversation were desired, and that perhaps he should withdraw from the study. By talking with him about this in a private, online discussion, I was able to convince him that the offending comment was not directed at him, and that his contributions were valuable. Certainly, this could have happened in the course of a physically located focus group, but our private sideline conversation defused the situation, eased the participant's misgivings, and allowed the larger group conversation to continue while we were sorting this out. The participant re-entered the conversation and later told me he talked about the offending comment with the person who wrote it, with positive results. These examples illustrate how a researcher can take advantage of multi-modal features of internet media, using a wide range of technologies.

Whether the technology provides the multiple modes or the users adapt technologies to a multi-modal way of thinking is less important than the fact that these characteristics can influence the way users perceive contexts and interact with one another. For researchers, this has great potential for augmenting traditional approaches and creating previously impossible methods of interacting with participants.

Internet as a Context of Social Construction

As I write this chapter, various programs on my computer and my smart phone collaborate to present a snapshot of not only my world, but also my understanding of *the* world. I filter news, I follow links sent by friends, and I follow random or not-so-random paths of information to build my knowledge of the world. I scan and contribute to various social networks. Each context is unique, each post authored by a slightly different version of 'me' and targeted to slightly different audiences. I am a cook posting new recipes. I am a photographer. I could be a methodologist, but I could also be a birdwatcher, a player of multiplayer online games, a dominatrix in an avatar-based social space, or a microcelebrity, known for my acerbic reviews of YouTube viral videos or my roles in amateur porn video. I could have a team of ghostwriters enacting my identity through Twitter if I were important enough.

For many, this is everyday life in the twenty-first century. Of course, the saturated, multiphrenic self (Gergen, 1991) emerged well before the internet. But the extent to which our identities are saturated with media, networked with others, and intermingled with information and communication technologies is a recent phenomenon, one worthy of study and reflection. This is not just a sociological issue, but a methodological issue, as 'the sociological subject is powerful, shifting, and in terms of qualitative research design, confusing. Our research models do not fit the multiphrenic subject very well' (Baym & Markham, 2009, p. x).

The internet comprises discursive forms of presentation and interaction that can be observed immediately and archived. This capacity facilitates the researcher's ability to witness and analyze the structure of talk, the negotiation of meaning and identity, the development of relationships and communities, and the construction of social structures as these occur discursively. Linguistic and social structures emerging through social interaction via the internet provide the opportunity for researchers to track and analyze how language builds and sustains social reality.

The internet is not novel in that individual use, habitual practice across groups, and technical capacities constitute patterns of temporal interactions, building social structures that may become concrete realities. These processes describe any language system. The internet is unique, however, in that it leaves visible traces of these processes. Internet technologies allow the researcher to see the visible artifacts of this negotiation process in forms divorced from both the source and the intended or actual audience. This can give researchers a means of studying the way social realities are displayed or how these might be negotiated over time.

Ethical Considerations in the Post-Google Era

The internet is often chosen as a method of collecting information because of the ease with which researchers can gain access to groups, download texts, capture conversations, observe individual and group behaviors, or interact with participants in the field. The ethics associated with internet research are complicated and, because researchers come from all disciplines and norms for research practices, hotly contested. It is crucial to be aware of the basic ethical issues involved in internet research, to make ethical decisions throughout the project, and to articulate one's ethical choices in written reports, so future generations of scholars can learn from one's decisions and so that reviewers and readers can be assured that ethical practices were followed.

Although all issues cannot be covered in this chapter, ethical challenges and controversy tend to arise in the following circumstances:

- Many users perceive publicly accessible discourse sites as private. For example, although many online discussion groups appear to be public, members may perceive their interaction to be private and can be surprised or angered by intruding researchers. Other groups know their communication is public but nonetheless do not want to be studied. Researchers must be aware of not only the obvious parameters of the site, but also the non-obvious perceptions and attitudes of the participants in these sites. This has proven to be very complicated for many researchers (for extensive discussion of these issues, see Gajjala, 2002; Markham & Baym, 2009; Sveningsson, 2004).
- Anonymity is difficult to guarantee. For example, some users have a writing style that is readily identifiable in their online community, so that the researcher's use of a pseudonym does not guarantee anonymity. Also, search engines are often capable of finding statements used in published qualitative research reports. The potential harm to individuals, relationships, families, and careers is not to be dismissed lightly. Many researchers have come up with innovative solutions to this dilemma (see Ess and the AoIR Ethics Working Committee, 2002).

- Online discussion sites can be highly transient. For example, researchers gaining access permission in June may not be studying the same population in July. Therefore, while a researcher may have gained consent from a group at one moment, this consent may not apply at later points in time.
- Vulnerable persons are difficult to identify in certain online environments. For example, age is difficult if not impossible to verify in certain online environments (see for example Stern, 2003, for more discussion of studying youth online).

Ethical guidelines and stances vary by person, institution, and country. It should be noted that many current regulations were not designed for internet research scenarios and therefore remain inadequate. For example, while 'informed consent' is an often required protection for human subjects, it is not always possible or warranted to obtain in the way intended by regulators. What if the participant is adamant that they use only his or her online identity? It is then impossible to determine if the participant is capable of giving informed consent (incapable typically refers to underage or mentally challenged). As another example, internet texts are often defined by researchers as public texts, not human subjects. Yet if the author of those texts believes they constitute an extension of the self or an independent online identity, are they subject to the same ethical protection as physical human subjects?

These are not easily answered questions. Given the variations in ethical stances as well as the diversity of methodological choices, each researcher must explore and define research within his or her own integral frameworks while also following 'best practice' guidelines. This is a task best accomplished by being well versed in contemporary ethical issues and debates. Comprehending and critically evaluating the broader discussions about ethics is essential, not only those discussions within internet studies or within disciplines, but those within communities of qualitative researchers. An extensive reaching list of case studies, arguments, and best practice documents is recommended at the end of this chapter.

Asking the Right Questions

Research environments utilizing various internet media must undergo careful evaluation, as each decision one makes throughout the course of a research project makes a difference. Testing various mediated environments and reflecting on the associated characteristics can help one discern which might be most suitable for the particular participants or research questions. Evaluating the research environment is not just a matter of looking at the tools and technologies but also reflexively interrogating the self as a researcher, to understand one's own assumptions and habitual practices.

Reflection and adaptation are necessary as one integrates internet communication technologies into qualitative research design. Adapting to the internet is one level of reflexivity; as we use new media for communication, the interactional challenges and opportunities can teach us about how to use these methods. Adjusting to the individual is another level; as in face-to-face contexts, a skilled researcher will pay close attention to participant conceptualization and utilization of the medium for communication. Without having access to physically embodied non-verbal features of interaction, the researcher conducting internet-based interviews may want to address deliberately these concerns with the participants so they may aid in the interpretation of discourse. Remaining methodologically agile is yet another level of reflexivity, particularly as our networked selves and social forms do not appear to be getting any less complex.

It is best to remain context sensitive, constantly engaged in self-reflexive analysis, and open to adaptation. If researchers cannot adjust to the particular features and capacities of internet technologies, they may miss the opportunity to understand these phenomena as they operate in context. As Gergen (1991) notes, if we are to survive, flexible adaptation and improvisation will become our norm. The shape of this improvisation varies with each project and scholar, yet the basic principles remain the same: to manage the dizzying array of contingencies in ever-changing internet contexts is to remain solidly grounded in the core practices and principles of social inquiry. Good qualitative research takes time, trial, and error, regardless of how easy and swift the technologies seem or how quickly research papers seem to flood the market after the release of some new technology. In internet related research environments, when everything may seem up for grabs, quality derives from asking the right questions, a process that begins by asking a lot of questions.

Summary and Future Prospects

Qualitative study of the internet is likely to continue to shift and change as new technologies and capacities tempt researchers to explore or reinvent methodological approaches to internet-related interactions. Although innovation is encouraged where necessary, the underlying foundations of qualitative research remain. An adroit researcher will deal with the seemingly constant changes in technologies by remaining grounded and inductive. This chapter offers an overview of characteristics associated with the internet-mediated social contexts as a guide to this end. Focusing on these or other salient characteristics can help the researcher focus on associated ethical and practical issues and can also help guide a researcher's search into previous studies for crucial grounding.

Research in this arena is often considered to be on the 'cutting edge' because it involves research of novel capacities for communication. Researchers from all disciplines flock to this area of research, bringing myriad theories, methods, and techniques. As technologies continue to converge, we will find that research practices related to internet technologies influence not only internet researchers, but also the entire academic community. In this hyped environment of novelty, mixed methods, and varying levels of quality, it is evermore crucial to remain solidly grounded and knowledgeable in a range of qualitative approaches.

Questions

- Given each of the salient characteristics of the internet described above, what might be some key concerns for different types of qualitative methods, such as ethnography? Discourse analysis? Case study research?
- How might qualitative internet researchers have to deal with ethical issues at a different level from journalists? Why would there be a difference?
- In what ways are internet-based contexts advantageous to physical contexts? In what way are they disadvantageous?

Recommended Reading

For overviews of ethical issues in internet studies, the following resources are recommended: Ess and The Association of Internet Researchers' 'Ethical decision-making and Internet research' (2002); Frankel and Siang's 'Ethical and legal aspects of human subjects research on the Internet' (1999); Elizabeth Buchanan's edited collection *Readings in Virtual Research Ethics* (2004); May Thorseth's *Applied Ethics in Internet Research* (2003); and McKee & Porter's *The Ethics of Internet Research* (2009). Also strongly recommended is the Internet Research Ethics Commons, a web resource that not only provides resources and overviews of trends and codes of practice, but access to blogs and discussion forums devoted to the discussion of specific cases and issues: http://www.internetresearchethics.org/

For in depth information on various methodological issues and strategies relating to qualitative internet research, the following edited collections are recommended: Mark Johns et. al., *Online Social Research: Methods, Issues, and Ethics* (2004); Christine Hine's *Virtual Methods* (2005); and Annette Markham & Nancy Baym's *Internet inquiry: Dialogue among Scholars* (2009).

For book-length qualitative analyses of the internet from a range of perspectives, the following titles are recommended: Nancy Baym's *Tune In, Log On* (2000); Lori Kendall's *Hanging Out in the Virtual Pub* (2002); Christine Hine's *Virtual Ethnography* (2000); Annette Markham's *Life Online* (1998); Miller and Slater's *The Internet: An Ethnographic Approach* (2000); and Shani Orgad's *Storytelling Online* (2005).

References

Baym, N. (2000). *Tune In, Log On. Soaps, Fandom, and Online Community*. Thousand Oaks, CA: Sage.

Baym, N. & Markham, A. (2009). Introduction: making smart choices on shifting ground. In Markham, A. & Baym, N. (Eds.) *Internet Inquiry: Dialogue among Scholars* (pp. vii–xix). Thousand Oaks, CA: Sage.

Bromseth, J. (2002). Public places…private activities? In Morrison, A. (Ed.) *Researching ICTs in Context* (pp. 44–72). Oslo: Intermedia Report 3/2002. Unipub forlag. Retrieved December 1, 2002, from http://www.intermedia.uio.no/publikasjoner/rapport_3/.

Buchanen, E. (Ed.) (2004). *Readings in Virtual Research Ethics: Issues and Controversies*. Hershey, PA: Idea Group.

Ess, C. & the AoIR Ethics Working Committee. (2002). Ethical decision-making and Internet research: Recommendations from the AoIR Ethics Working Committee. Retrieved January 1, 2003 from http://www.aoir.org/reports/ethics.pdf.

Frankel, M. & Siang, S. (1999). Ethical and legal aspects of human subjects research on the Internet: A report of a workshop. American Association for the Advancement of Science. Retrieved February 1, 2002, from http://www.aaas.org/spp/dspp/sfrl/projects/intres/main.htm.

Gajjala, R. (2002). An interrupted postcolonial/feminist cyberethnography: Complicity and resistance in the "Cyberfield." *Feminist Media Studies, 2* (2), 177–193.

Gergen, K. (1991). *The Saturated Self*. New York: Basic Books.

Giddens, A. (1991). *Modernity and Self-identity: Self and Society in the Late Modern Age*. Cambridge: Polity.

Hine, C. (2000). *Virtual Ethnography*. London: Sage.

Hine, C. (Ed.) (2005). *Virtual Methods: Issues in Social Research on the Internet*. Oxford: Berg.

Johns, M.D., Chen, S.L.S. & Hall, J.G. (Eds.) (2004). *Online Social Research: Methods, Issues, and Ethics*. New York: Peter Lang.

Johnson, C. (2003). Social interaction and meaning construction among community websites. Unpublished Master of Arts thesis. University of Illinois at Chicago.

Kendall, L. (2002). *Hanging Out in the Virtual Pub: Masculinities and Relationships Online*. Berkeley, CA: University of California Press.

Markham, A. (1998). *Life Online: Researching Real Experience in Virtual Space*. Walnut Creek, CA: AltaMira Press.

Markham, A. (2009). How can qualitative researchers produce work that is meaningful across time, space, and culture? In Markham, A. & Baym, N. (Eds.) *Internet Inquiry: Dialogue among Scholars*. (pp. 131–164). Thousand Oaks, CA: Sage.

Markham, A. & Baym, N. (Eds.) (2009). *Internet Inquiry: Dialogue among Scholars*. Thousand Oaks, CA: Sage.

McKee, H. & Porter, J. (2009). *The Ethics of Internet Research: A Rhetorical, Case-based Process*. New York: Peter Lang.

Miller, D. & Slater, D. (2000). *The Internet: An Ethnographic Approach*. Oxford: Berg.

Orgad, S. (2005). *Storytelling Online: Talking Breast Cancer on the Internet*. New York: Peter Lang.

Stern, S. (2003). Encountering distressing information in online research: A consideration of legal and ethical responsibilities. *New Media and Society, 5,* 249–266.

Sveningsson, M. (2004). Ethics in Internet ethnography. In Buchanan, Elizabeth A. (Ed). *Virtual Research Ethics: Issues and Controversies* (pp. 45–61). Hershey, PA: Idea Group.

Thorseth, M. (Ed.) (2003). *Applied Ethics in Internet research.* (Programme for Applied Ethics, Publication Series No. 1.) Trondheim: Norwegian University of Science and Technology.

PART IV

INTERVIEWS AND FOCUS GROUPS

The "Inside" and the "Outside": Finding Realities in Interviews

8

Jody Miller and Barry Glassner

Abstract

In this chapter, we argue that in-depth interview accounts provide a meaningful opportunity to study and theorize about the social world. We reject the objectivist–constructivist divide, and show how the narrative accounts produced through in-depth interviews provide us with access to realities. Specifically, we suggest that interviews reveal evidence of the nature of the phenomena under investigation, including the contexts and situations in which it emerges, as well as insights into the cultural frames people use to make sense of these experiences and their social worlds. We illustrate by discussing two projects completed by one of the authors.

Keywords:

in-depth interviewing, symbolic interactionism, narrative accounts, social worlds.

In his *Interpreting Qualitative Data*, Silverman (2001) highlights the dilemmas facing interview researchers concerning what to make of their data. On the one hand, positivists have as a goal the creation of the "pure" interview – enacted in a sterilized context, in such a way that it comes as close as possible to providing a "mirror reflection" of the reality that exists in the social world. This position has been thoroughly critiqued over the years in terms of both its feasibility and its desirability. On the other hand, emotionalists suggest that unstructured, open-ended interviewing can and does elicit "authentic accounts of subjective experience." While, as Silverman points out, this approach is "seductive," a significant problem lies in the question of whether these "authentic accounts" are actually, instead, the repetition of familiar cultural tales. Finally, radical social constructionists suggest that no knowledge about a reality that is "out there" in the social world can be obtained from the interview, because the interview is obviously and exclusively an interaction between the interviewer and interview subject in which both participants create and construct narrative versions of the social world. The problem with looking at these narratives as representative of some "truth" in the world, according to these scholars, is that they are context specific, invented if you will, to fit the demands of the interactive context of the interview, and representative of nothing more or less.

For those of us who hope to learn about the social world, and, in particular, hope to contribute knowledge that can be beneficial in expanding understanding and useful for fostering social change, the proposition that our interviews are meaningless beyond the context in which they occur is a daunting one. This is not to say that we accept the positivist view of the possibility of untouched data available through standardized interviewing, nor that we take a romanticized view of seamless authenticity emerging from narrative accounts. Instead, it is to suggest that we are not willing to discount entirely the possibility of learning about the social world beyond the interview in our analyses of interview data.

In this chapter, we try to identify a position that is outside of this objectivist–constructivist continuum yet takes seriously the goals and critiques of researchers at both of its poles. We will argue that information about social worlds is achievable through in-depth interviewing. The position we are attempting to put forward is inspired by authors such as Harding (e.g., 1987) and Latour (e.g., 1993), who posit explicitly anti-dualistic options for methodological and theorizing practices in media studies and science studies – options which recognize that both emulation and rejection of dominant discourses such as positivism miss something critically important. Dominant discourses are totalizing only for those who view them as such; they are replete with fissures and uncolonized spaces within which people engage in highly satisfying and even resistant practices of knowledge making.

We concur with Sanders that while

> [w]e would do well to heed the cautions offered by postmodern ethnographers . . . [t]here is a considerable difference between being skeptical about the bases of truth claims while carefully examining the grounds upon with these claims are founded (a conventional interactionist enterprise) and denying that truth – as a utilitarian and liberating orientation – exists at all. (1995: 93, 97)

Narratives and Worlds

As Silverman notes, for interviewers in the interactionist tradition, interview subjects construct not just narratives, but social worlds. For researchers in this tradition, "the primary issue is to generate data which give an authentic insight into people's experiences" (Silverman, 2001: xx). While interactionists do not suggest that there is

> "a singular objective or absolute world out-there" . . . [they] do recognize "objectified worlds." Indeed, they contend that some objectification is essential if human conduct is to be accomplished. Objectivity exists, thus, not as an absolute or inherently meaningful condition to which humans react but as an accomplished aspect of human lived experience. (Dawson and Prus, 1995: 113)

Research cannot provide the mirror reflection of the social world that positivists strive for, but it may provide access to the meanings people attribute to their experiences and social worlds. While the interview is itself a symbolic interaction, this does not discount the possibility that knowledge of the social world beyond the interaction can be obtained. In fact, it is only in the context of non-positivistic interviews, which recognize and build on their interactive components (rather than trying to control and reduce them), that "intersubjective depth" and "deep mutual understanding" can be achieved (and, with these, the achievement of knowledge of social worlds).

Those of us who aim to understand and document others' understandings choose qualitative interviewing because it provides us with a means for exploring the points of view of our research subjects, while granting these points of view the culturally honored status of reality. As Charmaz explains:

> We start with the experiencing person and try to share his or her subjective view. Our task is objective in the sense that we try to describe it with depth and detail. In doing so, we try to represent the person's view fairly and to portray it as consistent with his or her meanings. (1995: 54)

Silverman and others accurately suggest that this portrayal of what we do is in some ways romanticized. We will address below some of the problems that make this the case. But the proposition that romanticizing negates, in itself, the objectivity Charmaz defines, or the subjectivities with which we work, does not follow.

We have no trouble acknowledging, for instance, that interviewees sometimes respond to interviewers through the use of familiar narrative constructs, rather than by providing meaningful insights into their subjective view. Indeed, as Denzin notes:

> The subject is more than can be contained in a text, and a text is only a reproduction of what the subject has told us. What the subject tells us is itself something that has been shaped by prior cultural understandings. Most important, language, which is our window into the subject's world (and our world), plays tricks. It displaces the very thing it is supposed to represent, so that what is always given is a trace of other things, not the thing – lived experience – itself. (1991: 68)

In addition to this displacing, the language of interviewing (like all other telling) fractures the stories being told. This occurs inevitably within a storyteller's narrative, which must be partial because it cannot be infinite in length, and all the more partial if it is not to be unbearably boring. In the qualitative interview process, the research commits further fractures as well. The coding, categorization and typologizing of stories result in telling only parts of stories, rather than presenting them in their "wholeness" (Charmaz, 1995: 60). Numerous levels of representation occur from the moment of "primary experience" to the reading of researchers' textual presentation of findings, including the level of attending to the experience, telling it to the researcher, transcribing and analyzing what is told, and the reading.

Qualitative interviewers recognize these fissures from the ideal text (i.e., interviewees' subjective view as experienced by the interviewees themselves). Interviewers note, for example, that "[t]he story is being told to particular people; it might have taken a different form if someone else were the listener" (Riessman, 1993: 11). The issue of how interviewees respond to us based on who we are – in their lives, as well as the social categories to which we belong, such as age, gender, class and race – is a practical concern as well as an epistemological or theoretical one. The issue may be exacerbated, for example, when we study groups with whom we do not share membership. Particularly as a result of social distances, interviewees may not trust us, they may not understand our questions, or they may purposely mislead us in their responses. Likewise, given a lack of membership in their primary groups, we may not know enough about the phenomenon under study to ask the right questions.

Studying adolescents, as we have done in our own research, presents unique concerns along these lines. On the one hand, the meaning systems of adolescents are different from those of adults, and adult researchers must exercise caution in assuming they have an understanding of adolescent cultures because they have "been there". On the other hand, adolescents are in a transitional period of life, becoming increasingly oriented to adult worlds, though with "rough edges" (Fine and Sandstrom, 1988: 60). As a consequence, "age begins to decrease in importance as a means of differentiating oneself, and other dimensions of cultural differentiation, such as gender and class [and race], become more crucial" (Fine and Sandstrom, 1988: 66). These dimensions are thus of critical importance in establishing research relationships, rapport and trust, and in evaluating both the information obtained and the interaction that occurs within in-depth interviews.

To treat a young person's age as the determinant or predictor of his or her experiences or ways of talking is to neglect another key point about age ordering as well:

> The idea of an ending of childhood is predicated upon a normative system wherein childhood itself is taken for granted. But childhood may also be "ended" by narratives of personal or societal "deviance" or by new stories reconstituting the modelling of childhood itself. (Rogers and Rogers, 1992: 153)

PlusBus

Adds urban bus travel to your train ticket.

www.plusbus.info

Endorsements:

Anytime Day Single

Date of travel
08-MAY-21

Valid for one journey
from Liverpool Stations
to   St Michaels

Adult Standard Class

Refundable and exchanseable for a fee

07757-2719-9712-21-05-00

In our experience, much of what adolescents talk about in open-ended interviews is precisely how their acts seem wayward, delinquent, premature or otherwise not befitting proper youthful behavior. Their discourse toward and with us (and for themselves) is much about where and who they are. It is about trying out social locations and identities:

> Our approach is to treat the adolescents' reports as situated elements in social worlds. On the one hand they are ways of making sense to oneself and to another (cf. Mills, 1940). One cannot read the transcripts and fail to recognize that much of what goes on is two persons trying to understand topics that neither would consider in quite this manner or detail except in such special circumstances. The interviewees typically seem to enjoy the chance to "think aloud" about such matters, and often they say this to the interviewer. Much of that thinking is directed at a major project of their present lives – figuring out what type of person they are and what type they want to be. The interview offers an opportunity to try out various possibilities on this older student who is asking questions, and with reference to how it fits with one's self-image or might work out if directed at other audiences. On the other hand, these ways of viewing self and world come from and build into the social world itself. Ways of thinking and talking derive from daily experiences and are also used in these. (Glassner and Loughlin, 1987: 34–35)

Life Outside the Interview

Interactionist research starts from a belief that people create and maintain meaningful worlds. As interactionist research with adolescents illustrates, this belief can be accepted "without assuming the existence of a single, encompassing obdurate reality" (Charmaz, 1995: 62). To assume that realities beyond the interview context cannot be tapped into and explored is to grant narrative omnipotence. The roots of these realities are "more fundamental and pervasive" (Dawson and Prus, 1995: 121; see also Dawson and Prus, 1993; Schmitt, 1993) than such a view can account for. A vivid illustration of this is to be found in Charmaz's work on the chronically ill, who, she notes, experience sickness regardless of whether they participate in her interviews (1995: 50). We note that the adolescents in our studies experience their age-, gender- and ethnic-based identities and fluidity of identity whether or not we interview them – and within our interviews with them.

Language shapes meanings but also permits intersubjectivity and the ability of willful persons to create and maintain meaningful worlds (Dawson and Prus, 1993: 166). Recognizing this, we cannot accept the proposition that interviews do not yield information about social worlds. Rather, "we take it that two persons can communicate their perceptions to one another. Knowing full well that there are both structures and pollutants in any discussion, we choose to study what is said in that discussion" (Glassner and Loughlin, 1987: 33). While certainly "there is no way to stuff a real-live person between the two covers of a text", as Denzin (in Schmitt, 1993: 130) puts it, we can describe, truthfully, delimited segments of real-live persons' lives. Indeed, in so delimiting, we may get closer to people's lived experience. As Charmaz (1995) notes, many people do not want themselves revealed in their totality. Recognizing this and responding accordingly may result in deeper, fuller conceptualizations of those aspects of our subjects' lives we are most interested in understanding.

Much the same deserves to be said about the interactionist researcher concerning the place and fullness of his or her life within the interview context. On the one hand, scholarship should preserve "in it the presence, concerns, and the experience of the [researcher] as knower and discoverer" (Smith, 1987: 92; see also Harding, 1987) so that the subjectivity that exists in all social research will be a visible part of the project, and thus available to the reader for examination. As Harding (1987: 9) notes, when "the researcher appears to us not as an invisible, anonymous voice of authority, but as a real, historical individual with concrete, specific desires and interests", the research process can be scrutinized. Yet on the other hand, these dictates do not necessitate, as some excessively revealing authors have taken them to mean, engaging in confessionals either with one's interviewees or with one's readers, or boring them with excessive details about oneself. It is precisely the "concrete, specific desires and interests" that merit airing, not everything that might be aired.

In addition, it is important to consider that being a "good listener" – while a necessary quality to produce rich interview accounts – does not end the attention we should pay to how our positionality affects the production of qualitative interview data. We recognize that the interview itself is a particular kind of interaction. Interviews are "instances of social action – speech-acts or events with common properties, recurrent structures, cultural conventions, and recognizable genres" (Atkinson, 2005: 6). Moreover, we accept that what stories interviewees share with us, and how they tell their stories, may be shaped not just by the rapport established, but also by social similarities and distances between us and those we interview. Yet, rather than argue that this creates "bias" or makes the data of limited utility, we suggest that attention to how our social positioning affects the interview exchange offers an important site for social inquiry (see Grenz, 2005; Miller, 2010; Presser, 2005).

In our experience, interviewees will tell us, if given the chance, which of our interests and formulations make sense and non-sense to them. Glassner and Loughlin (1987: 36) describe instances in their study in which the interviewer brought up a topic that was seen by the subject as irrelevant or misinterpretation, and they offered correction. Moreover, as Charmaz points out, "creating these observations at all assumes that we share enough experience with our subjects and our readers to define things similarly" (1995: 64).

Of paramount importance regarding how (and how much) we present ourselves is the influence this presentation has on interviewees' ability and willingness to tell various sorts of stories. Richardson notes, "People organise their personal biographies and understand them through the stories they create to explain and justify their life experiences" (1990: 23; see also Lempert, 1994; Mishler, 1986; Riessman, 1993). We believe a strength of qualitative interviewing is precisely its capacity to access self-reflexivity among interview subjects, leading to the telling of stories that allow us to understand and theorize the social world:

> Respondents may reveal feelings, beliefs, and private doubts that contradict or conflict with "what everyone thinks," including sentiments that break the dominant feeling rules. ... In other cases, interviewers will discover the anxiety, ambivalence, and uncertainty that lie behind respondents' conformity. (Kleinman et al., 1994: 43)

In-depth interviewing is a particularly useful method for examining the social world from the points of view of research participants. As Orbuch (1997: 455) explains, interview accounts offer a means of identifying "culturally embedded normative explanations [of events and behaviors, because they] represent ways in which people organize views of themselves, of others, and of their social worlds." Yet, we argue here that they do more than provide information on cultural and subjective meanings. Rigorous analysis of accounts provides two intertwined sets of findings: evidence of the nature of the phenomenon under investigation, including the contexts and situations in which it emerges, as well as insights into the cultural frames people use to make sense of these experiences. Combined, they offer important insights for theoretical understanding.

Two Illustrations

We have suggested that narratives which emerge in interview contexts are situated in social worlds; they come out of worlds that exist outside of the interview itself. We argue not only for the existence of these worlds, but also for our ability as researchers to capture elements of these worlds in our scholarship. To illustrate some of the interactionist strategies for achieving that access we turn to two research efforts one of us has recently completed (Miller, 2001; 2008).

One of the Guys: Studying Gender Inequality and Gender Ideologies in Youth Gangs

When analyzing in-depth interviews in a study of young women's experiences in gangs, Miller was faced with an important discrepancy that required address. While most young women were adamant that they were "equals" with the boys in their gangs, they simultaneously described systematic gender inequalities within these groups, which they themselves often upheld through their own attitudes about other girls. Thus, her analysis required her to make sense of the disconnect between girls' claims that they were "one of the guys" (a cultural frame they used to situate themselves in the gang) and their descriptions of inequality (experiences situated in the gang context).

Successful interviewing involves the interviewee feeling comfortable and competent enough in the interaction to "talk back" (Blumer, 1969: 22) – to label particular topics irrelevant, point out misinterpretations and offer corrections. When respondents talk back they provide insights into the narratives they use to describe the meanings of their social worlds and into their experience of the worlds of which they are a part. One way Miller's interviewees talked back – both to her and to the audiences for her works about them – was in their resistance to her efforts to get them to articulate how gender inequality shaped their experiences in the gang. In doing so, they situated their personal narratives into larger cultural stories about girls in gangs, both by vigilantly challenging these stories and by embracing them in their discussions of "other" girls.

A dominant theme in Miller's interviews with young women was their insistence that their gangs were a space of gender equality, where males and females were treated as equals. As one explained, "they give every last one of us respect the way they give the males." Another was visibly frustrated with her line of questions about gender, and repeatedly cut her off in response:

JM:	You said before that the gang was about half girls and half guys? Can you tell me more about that? Like you said you don't think there are any differences in terms of what –
Interviewee:	There isn't!
JM:	Ok, can you tell me more –
Interviewee:	Like what? There isn't, there isn't like, there's nothing – boy, girl, white, black, Mexican, Chinese.

Such exchanges were a direct challenge to one sort of cultural story about girls in gangs. A longstanding cultural stereotype of girls' roles in gangs is that they are peripheral or auxiliary members whose primary function is as a sexual outlet for male members (see Campbell, 1984, for a discussion). For the young women in Miller's study, claiming a normative space of equality was an important means of rejecting this interpretation of their experiences.

Despite this prevailing discursive construction of gender equality, the young women's descriptions of the activities and behaviors of gang members markedly contradicted these statements. Instead, without exception, young women described a distinct gender hierarchy within mixed-gender gangs that included male leadership, a sexual double standard with regard to sexual activity, the sexual exploitation of some young women, perceptions of girls as "weak" and boys as "strong," and most girls' exclusion from serious gang crime – specifically, those acts that built status and reputation within their groups (Miller, 2001).

It would be easy to simply discount girls' claims of gender equality as wrong or misguided. Instead, making sense of such contradictions provides an important basis for building theoretical insight. Miller's task, then, was to explain the basis on which girls made claims to gender equality and the functions that such claims served. First, she looked carefully at *how* girls made the case that they were treated as equals. Examining their accounts closely, it became apparent that the means by which this was accomplished was not to make broad claims that all women should be treated as equals, but to differentiate themselves from *other* girls – and in the process, uphold the masculine status norms of their groups. As one explained:

> A lot of girls get scared. Don't wanna break their nails and stuff like that. So, ain't no need for them to try to be in no gang. And the ones that's in it, most of the girls that's in act like boys. That's why they in, 'cause they like to fight and stuff. They know how to fight and they use guns and stuff.

In addition, because the young women Miller interviewed also described a range of gender inequalities in their gangs, they also had to account for these descriptions of girls' mistreatment, and do so in ways that were consistent with their central belief in the norm of gender equality. Again, this required her to look at not only *what* they said about girls' mistreatment, but *how* they made sense of it. Closely analyzing their accounts, Miller discovered that young women drew on two types of frames: first, they individualized acts they recognized as involving the mistreatment of females, describing them as unique or exceptional cases. When this was not possible – for instance, when the mistreatment was recurring or routine – they sought ways to hold young women accountable for their mistreatment. They did so both by justifying particular acts as deserved because of the behaviors of the young women in question, and by characterizing *other* young women as possessing particular negative "female" traits – having "big mouths," being "troublemakers," or being "'ho's" or "wrecks."[1]

The other piece of the puzzle that required explanation was *why* young women both insisted on their equality and strongly differentiated themselves from other girls. Answering this question was key to providing an analytic framework that could

---

[1]Wreck was a slang term used by young women to refer to girls who were seen as sexually promiscuous.

link the structures of gender inequality in gangs to the processes by which they were reproduced and maintained. Miller did so by situating their gang participation in the broader contexts of their environments and life experiences, concluding that the over-arching gender hierarchy in girls' gangs was not unique, but was embedded within a broader social environment in which gender inequalities were entrenched.[2]

Thus, to the extent that there *was* normative space within gangs for "gender equality" – however narrowly defined – gang participation actually provided individual young women with a means of empowerment and self-definition not available in other contexts. But this required them to accept a "patriarchal bargain" (Kandiyoti, 1988) by which *they* could lay claim to being "one of the guys" only by supporting and justifying the mistreatment of *other* girls. Identifying with dominant beliefs about women, and rejecting such images for themselves, allowed them to construct a space of gender equality *for themselves*, and draw particular advantages from their gangs that were less available in other social spaces in their lives (see Miller, 2001: chapter 8, for a more detailed account of the analysis).

In addition, another challenge Miller faced was that her findings were counter to previous research on young women in gangs, which tended to uncover bonds of solidarity among young women. This also required an explanation. She began by looking closely at what differences might exist between the gangs previous researchers had studied and those represented in her sample, and what she noticed was that the gender composition of many of the gangs from which her sample was drawn were "skewed" groups, in which the preponderance of members was male. In contrast, other studies reported findings on gangs that appeared to be either gender-balanced, or were all female. This led her to examine the role of group proportion in shaping gender dynamics in gangs.

To test this hypothesis, she employed a constant comparative method within her data, whereby the researcher "always attempt[s] to find another case through which to test out a provisional hypothesis" (Silverman, 2006: 296). She carefully sought instances in her data in which girls strongly articulated their position as "one of the guys," as well as instances in which girls were critical of gender inequalities and espoused more close and supportive relationships with other girls. What she discovered supported her hypothesis – the handful of girls in her study who were in gender-balanced or all-female gangs did not match the pattern she had previously uncovered. Her distinct findings about "one of the guys" were shaped by the gendered organizational structure of their groups,[3] and this pattern was revealed through the use of a constant comparative method in the analytic process.

---

[2]This insight emerged from stories young women told that were peripheral to the research project, as well as from recognizing how these stories fit with what other research had uncovered.

[3]In fact, in subsequent research, Miller and her colleagues tested these hypotheses using quantitative data with continued meaningful results concerning the role of group structures in gangs.

Running Trains: Gaining Insight through Attention to the Interview as a Joint Accomplishment

Some scholars have argued that researchers should be members of the groups they study, in order to have the subjective knowledge necessary to truly understand their life experiences. For example, Collins argues that in order to make legitimate knowledge claims, researchers should "have lived or experienced their material in some fashion" (1990: 232). Likewise, with regard to adolescents specifically, Taylor et al. (1995: 36) point out that "[a]dolescents may choose a form of political resistance – that is, choose not to speak about what they know and feel – to people they see as representing or aligning with unresponsive institutions and authorities." However, we would also suggest that the existence of social differences between the interviewer and interviewees does not mean that the interviews are devoid of information about social worlds. In fact, the interviews can be accomplished in ways that put social differences and similarities to use for providing information about social worlds.

We illustrate by drawing on interview data from Miller's (2008) recent project on violence against African American young women in urban neighborhoods. The interviews were conducted by several interviewers, with divergent positions of similarity and difference from the interviewees. Miller's research uncovered a common practice, as described in interviews with young men, of "running trains" on girls: a sexual encounter that involved two or more young men engaging in penetrative sexual acts with a single young woman. Nearly half of the young men interviewed described engaging in such behaviors. And while researchers routinely classify such incidents as gang rape, and young women interviewed for the project described their experiences in this way as well, the young men defined girls' participation in trains as consensual. Thus, it was important to examine how young men understood running trains, and, especially, how they came to perceive these behaviors as consensual.

In this case, interviews conducted by two different research assistants – one a white European man (Dennis), the other an African American woman who grew up in the same community as the research participants (Toya) – revealed two sets of findings about boys' constructions of running trains. These offered different types of accounts of the behavior, each of which revealed different dimensions of the meaning and enactment of running trains.

An especially striking feature of the accounts provided in Dennis's interviews was the adamancy with which boys claimed that girls were willing, even eager, participants. Moreover, their descriptions were particularly graphic, focusing specific attention to the details of their sexual performances. Consider the following examples:

I mean, one be in front, one be in back. You know sometimes, you know like, say, you getting in her ass and she might be sucking the other dude dick. Then you probably get her, you probably get her to suck your dick while he get her in the ass. Or he probably, either I'll watch, and so she sucking your dick, or while you fuck her in the ass. It, I mean, it's a lot of ways you can do it.

There's this one girl, she a real, real freak…She wanted me and my friend to run a train on her… [Beforehand], we was at the park, hopping and talking about it and everything. I was like, "man, dawg, I ain't hitting her from the back." Like, "she gonna mess up my dick."…He like, "oh, I got her from the back dude." So we went up there… [and] she like, "which one you all hitting me from the back?" [I'm] like, "there he go, right there. I got the front." She's like, "okay." And then he took off her clothes, pulled his pants down. I didn't, just unzipped mine 'cause I was getting head. She got to slurping me. I'm like, my partner back there 'cause we was in the dark so I ain't see nuttin'. He was back, I just heard her [making noises]. I'm like, "damn girl, what's wrong with you?" [More noises] [I'm like], "you hitting her from the back?" He's like, "yeah, I'm hitting it."

Both accounts, which emerged in the interviews conducted by a white male interviewer, emphasized young men's performance and were extremely sexually graphic. Research on gang rape suggests that group processes play a central role: its enactment increases solidarity among groups of young men, and the victim is treated as an object (Franklin, 2004). Just as performance played a central role in young men's accounts of these incidents, their accounts were themselves a particular sort of masculine performance in the context of their interview exchange.

In contrast, when young men were interviewed about their participation in "running trains" by Toya – the African American female interviewer – two different features emerged. First, they were much less sexually graphic in their accounts. Second, due in part to Toya's sensitivity to issues of consent, she followed up with questions that undermined young men's construction of the events as consensual, while also revealing how they accomplished this construct. The following conversation with Terrance is illustrative:

Terence:	It was some girl that my friend had knew for a minute, and he, I guess he just came to her and asked her, "is you gon' do everybody?" or whatever and she said "yeah." So he went first and then, I think my other partna went, then I went, then it was like two other dudes behind me … It was at [my friend's] crib.
Toya:	Were you all like there for a get together or party or something?
Terence:	It was specifically for that for real, 'cause he had already let us know that she was gon' do that, so.
Toya:	So it was five boys and just her?

Terence:	Yeah.
...Toya:	And so he asked her first, and then he told you all to come over that day?
Terence:	We had already came over. 'Cause I guess he knew she was already gon' say yeah or whatever. We was already there when she got there.
Toya:	Did you know the girl?
Terence:	Naw, I ain't know her, know her like for real know her. But I knew her name or whatever. I had seen her before. That was it though.
...Toya:	So when you all got there, she was in the room already?
Terence:	Naw, when we got there, she hadn't even got there yet. And when she came, she went in the room with my friend, the one she had already knew. And then after they was in there for a minute, he came out and let us know that she was 'gon, you know, run a train or whatever. So after that, we just went one by one.

By Terence's own account – but due to the sensitivity with which Toya probed – the young woman arrived at a boy's house that she knew and may have been interested in. Waiting for her on her arrival were four additional young men whom she did not know or know well. And they had come in advance specifically for the purpose of running a train on her. While he described the incident as consensual, because his friend said "she was down," his description of what transpired provided evidence that the young woman had not freely consented.[4]

Likewise, Tyrell described running a train on a girl, and also described it as consensual. Toya's question about the details of the event revealed contradictory evidence, so she asked him whether he thought the girl felt bad about what happened. Tyrell replied:

Tyrell:	I can't even say. I don't even know her like that. I really can't say. She do that kinda stuff all the time.
Toya:	She does?
Tyrell:	No. I'm just saying. I don't know. If she don't she probably did feel bad, but if she do she probably wouldn't feel bad ... But if she didn't really wanna do it, she shouldn't have did it.

---

[4] This description was in keeping with young women's accounts of having trains run on them, which they described as non-consensual.

Tyrell slipped easily into noting that "she do that kinda stuff all the time," but when pressed, conceded that he had no basis on which to draw such a conclusion.

That these nuances emerged had much to do with Toya's skills as an interviewer and her sensitization to the topic. Nonetheless, the role that social similarities and differences between the interviewers and interviewees played in producing these disparate accounts of the same phenomenon also cannot be discounted. Both revealed facets of the nature of "running trains." Dennis's interviews demonstrated its function as masculine performance. In fact, young men's acts of *telling* Dennis about the events were also masculine performances, constructed in response to *whom* they were doing the telling. In contrast, Toya's interviews revealed evidence of the processes by which young men construct their interpretations of girls' consent, and reveal the various ways in which they do so by discounting the points of view of their female victims (see King, 2003). This example suggests that it is both necessary and useful to pay close attention to how the interview context shapes accounts. Doing so can reveal multifaceted features of behaviors and their meanings. Moreover, it reveals the benefits for data analysis that can emerge by utilizing diverse research teams, and using this diversity itself as a means of furthering the analysis.

Finding Realities in Interviews

We have suggested that a strength of qualitative interviewing is the opportunity it provides to collect and rigorously examine narrative accounts of social worlds. In Miller's illustrations, several facets of the interviews – including the disjuncture between the cultural frames adopted and description of experiences, and the different types of accounts that emerge from interviews with different interviewers – provide important insights into how young people understand their place in gangs, their participation in troubling behaviors, and the broader social worlds in which they live. We have suggested that it is possible to find realities within interviews – stories that reveal "culturally embedded normative explanations" (Orbuch, 1997: 455) are a significant aspect of this reality, but so are accounts of events and activities that are ultimately contradictory to these stories. By juxtaposing gang girls' stories of equality with incongruous descriptions of gender *inequality*, Miller (2001) built her theoretical discussion around the contradictory operation of gender within gangs. Likewise, comparing young men's descriptions of "running trains" as they were told to different interviewers – one who shared their gender but not their race, and another who shared their race but not gender – provided multiple insights into the role of masculinity in this behavior, how such events played out, and the ways that young men constructed them as consensual.

Summary

Silverman argues in *Interpreting Qualitative Data* that "while 'open-ended' interviews can be useful, we need to justify departing from the naturally occurring data that surrounds us and to be cautious about the 'romantic' impulse which identifies 'experience' with 'authenticity'" (2001: xx). We agree, but with different words in scare quotes.

On the one hand, we have tried to suggest in this chapter some strategies by which interviews can be less than problematically open-ended, and that interviewers need not resort to romanticism, or to identifying experience with authenticity, in order to call upon interviewees' experiences and produce authentic accounts of social worlds. On the other hand, we would put in scare quotes "naturally occurring data," because we question the grounds for any neat distinction between the natural and cultural, in sociological data as elsewhere (cf. Douglas, 1986). In making such claims, it is not the case that we are "not too sure whether interviews are purely local events or express underlying external realities," as Silverman (2001: xx) has suggested. Instead, we argue against the dualistic imperative to classify them as one or the other.

Future Prospects

Qualitative interviewing produces accounts that offer researchers a means of examining intertwined sets of findings: evidence of the nature of the phenomenon under investigation, including the contexts and situations in which it emerges, as well as insights into the cultural frames people use to make sense of these experiences. Combined, they offer important insights for theoretical understanding. Two approaches to data collection and analysis point to future directions for research using this methodological approach. The use of comparative samples is one. This strategy allows for some specification of similarities and variations in social process and meaning systems across groups, settings and/or over time. Second, interview-based research can be enhanced when it includes diverse research teams, and this diversity is taken into account in data analysis. Both strategies can strengthen internal validity by allowing for more refined analysis and greater contextual specification.

All we sociologists have are stories. Some come from other people, some from us, some from our interactions with others. What matters is to understand how and where the stories are produced, which sort of stories they are, and how we can put them to honest and intelligent use in theorizing about social life.

Questions

- How does the constructionist position of the authors differ from positivism, emotionalism and radical social constructionism?
- How do the authors make the case that interviews provide evidence of both the nature of social worlds and individuals' culturally embedded understanding of social worlds?
- How do the authors argue that contradictory evidence in narrative accounts can lead to theoretical insights?
- How do the authors argue that social distance and social similarity can be put to use in theorizing about social worlds?

Recommended Reading

Charmaz, Kathy (2006) *Constructing Grounded Theory: A Practical Guide Through Qualitative Analysis*. Thousand Oaks, CA: Sage.

Holstein, James A. and Gubrium, Jaber F. (1995) *The Active Interview*. Thousand Oaks, CA: Sage.

Miller, Jody (2010) "The impact of gender when studying 'offenders on offending.'" In *Offenders on Offending: Learning about Crime from Criminals,* edited by Wim Bernasco and Michael Tonry. London: Willan Press.

Spradley, James P. (1979) *The Ethnographic Interview*. Fort Worth, TX: Harcourt Brace Jovanovich.

Internet Links

www.qualitative-research.net/fqs/fqs-eng.htm

Click "search" then type "interview" in the search box.

References

Atkinson, P. (2005) "Qualitative research – unity and diversity," *Forum: Qualitative Social Research,* 6: Article 26 (www.qualitative-research.net/fqs/).

Blumer, H. (1969) *Symbolic Interactionism: Perspective and Method*. Berkeley: University of California Press.

Campbell, A. (1984) *The Girls in the Gang*. New York: Basil Blackwell.

Charmaz, K. (1995) "Between positivism and postmodernism: implications for methods," *Studies in Symbolic Interaction*, 17: 43–72.

Collins, P.H. (1990) *Black Feminist Thought*. Boston, MA: Unwin Hyman.

Dawson, L.L. and Prus, R.C. (1995) "Postmodernism and linguistic reality versus symbolic interactionism and obdurate reality," *Studies in Symbolic Interaction*, 17: 105–124.

Dawson, L.L. and Prus, R.C. (1993) "Interactionist ethnography and postmodern discourse: affinities and disjunctures in approaching human lived experience," *Studies in Symbolic Interaction*, 15: 147–177.

Denzin, N.K. (1991) "Representing lived experiences in ethnographic texts," *Studies in Symbolic Interaction*, 12: 59–70.

Douglas, M. (1986) *Risk Acceptability According to the Social Sciences*. New York: Russell Sage Foundation.

Fine, G.A. and Sandstrom, K.L. (1988) *Knowing Children: Participant Observation with Minors*. Newbury Park, CA: Sage.

Franklin, K. (2004) "Enacting masculinity: antigay violence and group rape as participatory theater," *Sexuality Research & Social Policy*, 1: 25–40.

Glassner, B. and Loughlin, J. (1987) *Drugs in Adolescent Worlds: Burnouts to Straights*. New York: St. Martin's Press.

Grenz, S. (2005) "Intersections of sex and power in research on prostitution: a female researcher interviewing male heterosexual clients," *Signs*, 30: 2092–2113.

Harding, S. (1987) *Feminism and Methodology*. Bloomington: Indiana University Press.

Kandiyoti, D. (1988) "Bargaining with patriarchy," *Gender & Society*, 2: 274–290.

King, N. (2003) "Knowing women: straight men and sexual certainty," *Gender & Society*, 17: 861–877.

Kleinman, S., Stenross, B. and McMahon, M. (1994) "Privileging fieldwork over interviews: consequences for identity and practice," *Symbolic Interaction*, 17 (1): 37–50.

Latour, B. (1993) *We Have Never Been Modern*. Cambridge, MA: Harvard University Press.

Lempert, L.B. (1994) "A narrative analysis of abuse: connecting the personal, the rhetorical, and the structural," *Journal of Contemporary Ethnography*, 22 (4): 411–441.

Miller, J. (2010) 'The impact of gender when studying "Offenders on Offending."' In W. Bernasco and M. Tonry (eds.), *Offenders on Offending: Learning about Crime from Criminals*. London: Willan Press.

Miller, J. (2008) *Getting Played: African American Girls, Urban Inequality, and Gendered Violence*. New York: New York University Press.

Miller, J. (2001) *One of the Guys: Girls, Gangs and Gender*. New York: Oxford University Press.

Mills, C.W. (1940) "Situated actions and vocabularies of motives," *American Sociological Review*, 5: 904–913.

Mishler, E.G. (1986) *Research Interviewing: Context and Narrative*. Cambridge, MA: Harvard University Press.

Orbuch, T.L. (1997) "People's accounts count: the sociology of accounts," *Annual Review of Sociology*, 23: 455–478.

Presser, L. (2005) "Negotiating power and narrative in research: implications for feminist methodology," *Signs*, 30: 2067–2090.

Richardson, L. (1990) *Writing Strategies: Reaching Diverse Audiences*. Newbury Park, CA: Sage.

Riessman, C.K. (1993) *Narrative Analysis*. Newbury Park, CA: Sage.

Rogers, R.S. and Rogers, W.S. (1992) *Stories of Childhood*. Toronto: University of Toronto Press.

Sanders, C.R. (1995) "Stranger than fiction: insights and pitfalls in post-modern ethnography," *Studies in Symbolic Interaction*, 17: 89–104.

Schmitt, R.L. (1993) "Cornerville as obdurate reality: retooling the research act through postmodernism," *Studies in Symbolic Interaction*, 15: 121–145.

Silverman, D. (2006) *Interpreting Qualitative Data: Methods for Analyzing Talk, Text, and Interaction*, 3rd edition. Thousand Oaks, CA: Sage.

Silverman, D. (2001) *Interpreting Qualitative Data: Methods for Analysing Talk, Text and Interaction*. London: Sage.

Smith, D.E. (1987) "Women's perspective as a radical critique of sociology". In S. Harding (ed.), *Feminism and Methodology*. Bloomington: Indiana University Press, 84–96.

Taylor, J.M., Gilligan, C. and Sullivan, A.M. (1995) *Between Voice and Silence: Women and Girls, Race and Relationship*. Cambridge, MA: Harvard University Press.

Animating Interview Narratives ⑨

James A. Holstein and Jaber F. Gubrium

Abstract

This chapter discusses the implications of viewing the interview as an actively constructed conversation through which narrative data are produced. It explores the ramifications of framing the interview and resulting data as by-products of interpretive practice – the *whats* and *hows* of an animated process involving active subjects behind interview participants. Matters of reliability, validity, bias, and rigor are considered.

Keywords:

active interview, participant agency, animating the interview, interview narratives, interview interaction, bias, rigor.

Interviewing is more popular than ever as a means of generating information for both scholarly and professional purposes. In our 'interview society' (see Gubrium and Holstein 2002a; Silverman 1993), the mass media, human service providers, employers, and researchers increasingly conduct interviews. When done well, the interview may be viewed as a dispassionate, passive instrument for obtaining information. Interviewers ask unbiased questions. Respondents provide pertinent answers. The interview process is merely a neutral conduit between the two. The standard version of the interview keeps the interviewer's involvement to a minimum. The interviewer should be disinterested and inconspicuous, like the proverbial fly on the wall. The cooperative and open respondent provides pertinent information.

This chapter presents a contrasting perspective that highlights the interview process as interactionally active. We argue that *all* interviews are active, regardless of how neutral the interviewers and how cooperative the respondents. No matter how hard interviewers try to restrain their presence in the interview exchange and no matter how forthright interviewees are in offering their views, these are interactional accomplishments rather than neutral communicative grounds. It takes work to accomplish the passivity and ostensible forthrightness of interview participation. Accordingly, we refer to the *active interview* to distinguish this perspective from the more conventional model. The term does not apply to a distinctive type of interview, differentiating it from, say, the standardized survey interview or the minimally directive life story interview. Instead, we use the term to highlight the inherent interpretive activity of the process as a hallmark of all interviews. This chapter stresses how this recognition leads to an animated analytic view of interview narratives.

From Distortion to Interpretive Practice

It has been estimated that 90 percent of all social science investigations involve interviews (Briggs 1986). Interviewing spans academic disciplines as well as myriad professions, providing so-called 'windows on the world' (Gubrium and Holstein 2002a). As an information-gathering form of conversation, interviews vary from highly structured, standardized, quantitatively oriented survey interviews, to semi-formal guided conversations, to free-flowing informational exchanges. Being international across the variety, they collaboratively produce narratives of people's lives and circumstances. These narratives may be as truncated as forced-choice survey answers or as elaborate as oral life histories, but they are all conversations incited and shaped by the interview process.

While most researchers acknowledge the interactional bases of interviewing (see Conrad and Schober 2008; Warren and Karner 2005), the technical literature stresses the need to keep conversational 'bias' in check. Guides to interviewing – especially those oriented to standardized surveys – are primarily concerned with maximizing the flow of valid, reliable information while minimizing distortions of what the respondent knows (Fowler and Mangione 1990; Gorden 1987). If the interview conversation is framed as a potential source of bias, error, misunderstanding, or misdirection, it is a persistent set of problems that must be minimized. The corrective is simple: if the interviewer asks questions properly and the interview situation is propitious, the respondent will convey undistorted information. In this view, the interview conversation is a pipeline for transporting truthful knowledge.

Recently, a heightened sensitivity to everyday representational matters (see Gubrium and Holstein 1997, 2002a, 2002b) – characteristic of poststructuralist, postmodernist, constructionist, and ethnomethodological inquiry – has raised questions about the very possibility of collecting knowledge within the traditional model. Attention has focused on the in situ activeness of interviews (e.g., Hootkoop-Steenstra 2000; Kvale 1996). These perspectives suggest that all meaning is socially constituted; all knowledge is created from the actions undertaken to obtain it (see Cicourel 1964, 1974; Garfinkel 1967). Treating interviewing as a social encounter in which knowledge is actively formed and produced implies that the interview is not so much a neutral conduit or source of distortion, but rather a site of, and occasion for, interpretive practice (see Warren and Karner 2005).

Anthropologist Charles Briggs (1986) argues that the social circumstances of interviews are more than obstacles to respondents' articulation of particular truths. Interviews fundamentally, not incidentally, shape the form and content of what is said. As he and Clara Mantini-Briggs (2003) note, interviews result in stories – some very short, some very long – that offer accounts of opinion, persons, events, and the world at large. Indeed, with considerable foresight, decades earlier Aaron Cicourel (1974) maintained that interviews imposed particular ways of understanding reality upon subjects' responses. The general point is that interview participants are deeply and unavoidably implicated in creating meanings that ostensibly reside within the experiences under consideration. Meaning is not merely directly elicited by apt questioning, nor simply transported through respondent replies; it is assembled in the interview encounter. Participants are not so much elicitors and repositories of experiential knowledge, as they are constructors of experiential information.

Technical attempts to strip interviews of their interactional constituents will be futile (Houtkoop-Steenstra 2000; Maynard et al. 2002). Instead of refining the long list of methodological constraints under which standardized interviews should be conducted, we have suggested that researchers embrace the view that the interview is a process of experiential animation and capitalize upon interviewers' and respondents' constitutive contributions to the production of interview data. This entails conscientiously attending to the interview process as a form of interpretive practice that not only produces results, but also points to the constructive work and auspices operating in varied interview encounters (Gubrium and Holstein 2009).

This means that researchers need to pay explicit attention to both the practical *hows* and the substantive *whats* of interviewing, taking care to give them equal status in both the research process and in reporting results (see Gubrium and Holstein 1997, 2009). Understanding *how* the narrative process unfolds in the interview is as critical as apprehending *what* is substantively said. The *whats* always reflect the circumstances and practices conditioning the interview. A dual interest in the *hows* and *whats* of interview narratives makes visible the animated parameters of the interview process.

This appreciation derives from ethnomethodologically informed, social constructionist sensibilities (cf. Berger and Luckmann 1967; Blumer 1969; Garfinkel 1967; Holstein and Gubrium 2008). The approach also resonates with methodological critiques and formulations offered by feminist scholars (see DeVault 1990; Harding 1987; Smith 1987).

Ethnomethodology, constructionism, poststructuralism, postmodernism, and some versions of feminism all are attuned to subjectivity, complexity, perspective, and meaning construction. In one way or another, all cast an analytic eye on interpretive practice. If their concerns and debates have often related to the epistemological status of interview data, they do not lose sight of the everyday facets of experience. At the same time, while the perspective we describe here has postmodern sensibilities, it does not abide the view that interviews are just another realm of swirling signifiers. Rather, animated as they might be, interview narratives reflect both socially grounded interpretive practices and subject matter with which the practices are concerned.

Key Points

- A common view of the ideal interview is that of a neutral conduit for conveying undistorted knowledge.
- A growing number of researchers has come to recognize the interview as a meaning-making conversation – a site of interpretive practice.
- Interviewing is unavoidably interactional and constructive. In a word, the interview is *actively* productive of its results.

Viewing the Subjects behind Interview Participants

Conventional or otherwise, every vision of the interview is built upon images of the subjects behind interview participants (Holstein and Gubrium 1995). These images provide the basis for theorizing the interview process, as well as for arguing that all interviews are active from start to finish. The images confer varying degrees of epistemological agency upon interview participants, which bears on researchers' understanding of the relative validity of the information that is reported. For example, in conventional approaches, respondents are basically conceived as passive *vessels of answers* to whom interviewers direct their questions. They are repositories of facts, reflections, opinions, and other traces of experience. While we limit most of our comments to the respondent's subjectivity, the purported passivity of the interviewer also comes into question.

Our view extends to interviews conducted for other than research purposes. Studs Terkel, the consummate journalistic interviewer, held to a version of the image. He reports that he simply turned on his tape recorder and asked people to talk. Writing of the interviews he did for his bestselling book titled *Working*, Terkel (1972, p. xxv) notes:

> There were questions, of course. But they were casual in nature ... the kind you would ask while having a drink with someone; the kind he would ask you ... In short, it was a conversation. In time, the sluice gates of dammed up hurts and dreams were open.

As plain-spoken as this may be, Terkel's view of the subject behind the respondent is that of a wellspring of information and emotion.

Interviewing is likened to 'prospecting' for the true facts and feelings residing within the respondent (cf. Kvale 1996). The image of the researcher/prospector casts the interview as a search-and-discovery mission, with the interviewer intent on detecting what is already there inside variably cooperative respondents, undertaken for scientific reasons. The challenge lies in extracting information as directly as possible, without contaminating it. Highly refined interview techniques streamline, systematize, and sanitize the process. Occasionally, researchers acknowledge that it may be difficult to obtain accurate information, but the information is still viewed, in principle, as held undistorted in the subject's vessel of answers. The trick is to formulate questions and provide an atmosphere conducive to open communication between the interviewer and the respondent. Much of the methodological literature on interviewing deals with the nuances of these procedural matters.

In the vessel-of-answers approach, the image of the subject is passive; this subject is not engaged in the production of knowledge. If the interviewing process goes 'by the book' and is non-directive and unbiased, respondents will validly speak of whatever is presumed to reside within – the unadulterated facts of experience. Contamination creeps in from the interview setting, its participants, and their interaction; in principle, the subject is pristinely communicative and, under ideal conditions, his or her respondent serves up authentic reports when beckoned.

What happens, however, if we animate the image of the subject behind the respondent? An animated subject behind the respondent not only holds the facts and details of experience, but, in the very process of offering them up, constructively adds to, takes away from, and transforms them into artefacts of the occasion. The respondent can hardly 'spoil' what he or she is, in effect, subjectively shaping. Because interviews are always dialogical, they are inevitably performances aimed at particular audiences. This alone necessarily animates the *whats* of the matter.

In the conventional view, the objectivity or truth of interview responses is commonly assessed in terms of reliability and validity (Kirk and Miller 1986), criteria which elide performativity. When the interview is viewed as a dynamic, meaning-making occasion, however, different criteria apply. The focus is equally on the way narratives are constructed, the circumstances of construction, and the meaningful linkages that are assembled for the occasion. While interest in the content of answers persists, research coverage extends to both how and what the subjectively animated respondent, in collaboration with an equally subjectively animated interviewer, produces and conveys in the interview process.

Assuming an animated subject, a different sense of the value of interview data applies. With the proper adjustments, this can be put in terms of reliability and validity. As far as reliability is concerned, one cannot expect answers on one occasion to necessarily replicate those on another, because they may emerge from different circumstances of production. Of course, to the extent occasions are similar, we would expect greater reliability. As such, good interview material should be viewed as 'reliable enough,' *under the circumstances*. Similarly, the validity of answers derives not from their one-to-one correspondence to meanings held within the respondent, but from the respondent's ability to convey communicated experiences in terms that are locally comprehensible. (See Gubrium and Holstein (2009) for parallel criteria applicable in relation to the everyday value of stories and storytelling.)

The animated image of the interview comes into full relief when concretely contrasted with approaches undergirded by passive images of participant subjectivity. One widely applied approach – standardized survey interviewing – orients to the rational, factual value of what is communicated. It focuses on the substantive statements, explanations, and reasons with which the respondent articulates experience. Jean Converse and Howard Schuman's (1974) candid book *Conversations at Random* offers a superb vision of the imagined survey respondent.

As Converse and Schuman discuss standardized survey interviewing techniques, they suggest that good interview data are there to be extracted from the repository of knowledge represented by the basically passive subject behind the survey respondent. Respondents harbor information, but they do not construct it, even if they can do a better or worse job of conveying it. While Converse and Schuman grant that survey interviewing involves experiencing the 'pleasure of persons,' they urge interviewers to conform to their clearly designated roles and the rules of standardized interviewing to effectively gain access to the vessel of answers behind the respondent. Their book is replete with anecdotal reminders of what interviewers must learn in order to keep that vessel of answers in view and the respondent on target.

In part, this is a matter of controlling oneself as an interviewer so that one does not interfere with what the passive subject is willing to put forth. The interviewer must shake off self-consciousness, suppress personal opinion, and avoid stereotyping the respondent. Learning the interviewer role is a matter of controlling the interview situation to facilitate the candid expression of opinions and sentiments. The seasoned interviewer learns that the so-called pull of conversation must be managed so that the 'push of inquiry' (Converse and Schuman 1974: 26) is kept in focus.

Another, less known approach – creative interviewing – orients to the purportedly deeper and more authentic domain of the subject's feelings. It emphasizes sentiment and emotion, the ostensible core of human experience. If Jack Douglas's book *Creative Interviewing* (1985) provides a vivid illustration, the approach's romanticist sentiments are longstanding and now increasingly inform qualitative interviewing especially. Despite the numerous contrasts with Converse and Schuman's view of survey interviewing, we see remarkable similarity in their respective images of the subjectivity of interview participants. For Douglas, the term 'creative' applies primarily to the interviewer, not the respondent. He notes that in his many empirical studies, he repeatedly discovered that standard recommendations for interviewing were inadequate for his research purposes. Canons of rational neutrality, such as those Converse and Schuman espouse, failed to capture what Douglas calls his respondents' 'emotional wellsprings.' In response to this shortcoming, Douglas calls for a methodology of deep disclosure.

Douglas's difficulties relate as much to his image of the passive subject as they do to the shortcomings of standardized interviewing technique. Like the image of the subject behind the survey respondent, Douglas imagines his subjects to be repositories of answers, but in his case, they are viewed as well-guarded vessels of feelings. They are 'there,' to be sure; the trick is how to elicit them. His model is of a respondent who authentically communicates from an emotional wellspring, at the behest of an interviewer who knows that mere words or words carefully chosen cannot draw out or convey what experience ultimately is about. Standard survey questions and answers touch only the surface of experience, according to Douglas. He aims deeper by intimately 'getting to know' the real subject behind the respondent.

Creative interviewing is a set of techniques for deeper discovery. To achieve this, the interviewer must establish a climate for mutual disclosure. The interview should be an occasion that displays the interviewer's willingness to share his or her own feelings and deepest thoughts. This is done to assure respondents that they can, in turn, share their own intimate thoughts and feelings. The interviewer's deep disclosure both occasions and legitimizes the respondent's reciprocal revelations. This, Douglas suggests, is thoroughly suppressed by the cultivated neutrality of the standard survey interview.

The wellsprings tapped by creative interviewing are said to be emotional, in distinct contrast to the preferred 'factual' emphasis that permeates Converse and Schuman's book. The subject behind Douglas's respondent nevertheless remains an essentially passive, if expressively emotional, fount of experience, not unlike the respondent who 'opens up' and gushes forth while having a friendly drink with Studs Terkel. Located deeper within the respondent than the subject behind the survey respondent, the subject behind Douglas's image of the respondent remains a relatively static, inert vessel, in this case, of emotional data.

> ## Key Points
>
> - All approaches to interviewing rest on images of the subjects behind the interview participant.
> - Conventional approaches envision the subject behind participants as essentially passive. Interview guidelines actively cultivate a passive subjectivity.
> - Images of subjects behind interview participants have important implications for how the interview process is conducted and interview data are construed.

Animating the Interview

Animating interview subjectivity is part of a broader vision of reality as an ongoing, interpretive accomplishment. From this perspective, interview participants constantly work to discern and designate the recognizable, meaningful, and orderly features of experience. But meaning-making is not merely artful (Garfinkel 1967); meaning is not built out of nothing on each interpretive occasion. Rather, interpretation orients to, and is conditioned by, the substantive resources and local contingencies of interaction. In other words, meaningful reality is constituted at the nexus of the *hows* and the *whats* of the process, by way of 'interpretive practice' – the procedures and resources used to apprehend, organize, and represent everyday life (Holstein 1993; Holstein and Gubrium 2011; Gubrium and Holstein 1997, 2009).

As short or as long as they may be, the responses produced in interviews are actively assembled using the interpretive resources at hand, in light of the situated contingencies of the moment. Meaning is not constantly formulated anew, but reflects relatively enduring and recognizable forms of meaning (Foucault 1979), such as the research topics presented by interviewers, participants' biographical particulars, locally accepted ways of orienting to those topics, institutionalized means of understanding and talking about things, and larger discourses deploying 'what everyone knows' (Gubrium 1988, 1989; Holstein and Gubrium 2000, Holstein and Gubrium 2011). Those resources are astutely and adroitly adapted to the demands of the occasion, so that meaning is neither predetermined nor absolutely unique.

An image of animated subjectivity transforms one's orientation to all kinds of interviewing. The respondent is far from a repository of experiences or a wellspring of emotions, but a productive source of opinions and feelings. The subject behind the interviewer is similarly animated. From the time one identifies a research topic, to respondent selection, questioning, and answering, and, finally, to the interpretation of responses, interviewing itself is a knowledge construction project. In this context, the respondent as much assembles narratives of experience as he or she answers interview questions.

Whats and Hows of the Interview

Some time ago, we distinguished two sets of communicative contingencies that shape the interview's meaning-making activity. One kind involves the *whats* of the interview (see Gubrium and Holstein 1997). The substantive focus and circumstances of the research project provide interpretive signposts and resources for developing interview narratives. The eventual narrative is always already told in the kind of story prompted by the research project through the interviewer. For example, a project might deal with the quality of care and quality of life of nursing home residents (see Gubrium 1993). This might be part of a study related to a national debate about the proper organization of home and institutional care. If active, animated interviewing practices are deployed, participants draw out the substantiality of these topics, narratively linking the topics to biographical particulars in the interview process, producing a subject who responds to, or is affected by, the matters under consideration.

A second communicative contingency of animated interviews centers on the *hows* of the process. The standpoint from which information is offered is continually developed within ongoing interview interaction. In speaking of the quality of care, for example, nursing home residents, as interview respondents, not only offer substantive thoughts and feelings pertinent to the topic in view, but simultaneously and continuously monitor who they are in relation to the person questioning them. Respondents continually work up their roles, from whose narrative standpoints answers are provided. We cannot take for granted, for instance, that 'the' formally selected nursing home resident takes this narrative standpoint throughout an interview, but rather might usefully monitor the *hows* of the matter. How and where respondents experientially locate themselves in the interview helps reveal what they mean by what they choose to say.

Concertedly Putting *Whats* and *Hows* to Work

Interviews are useful tools for systematic social inquiry because of their special capacity to incite the production of narratives that address issues relating to particular research concerns. Animated interviews concertedly put the *whats* and *hows* of interpretive practice to work. In standardized interviewing, the allegedly passive subject actively engages in a 'minimalist' version of interpretive practice – participants concertedly perceive, inquire about, and report experience in the formulaic terms allowed. In contrast, expressly animating the interview strategically invests the subject with a substantial repertoire of interpretive methods and an extensive stock of experiential materials.

On one side, the animated interview eschews the image of the vessel of answers waiting to be tapped in favor of the notion that the respondent's narrative agency is activated, stimulated, and cultivated in relation to an ever-shifting and reflexive stock of knowledge. The interview also is a commonly recognized occasion for systematically prompting the respondent to formulate and talk about experience, opinions, and emotions in particular ways, implicating the interviewer, on the other side. Active interviewers do not coax interviewees into preferred responses to their questions. Rather, they converse with respondents in such a way that emergent forms of response come into play. Interviewers may suggest orientations to, and linkages between, diverse aspects of respondents' experience, hinting at – even inviting – interpretations that make use of specific resources, connections, and outlooks. Interviewers may explore incompletely articulated aspects of experience, encouraging respondents to develop topics in ways relevant to their own experience (DeVault 1990). The objective is not to dictate an interpretive frame, as a minimalist standardized survey approach would do, but to provide an environment conducive to the production of the range and complexity of narratives that might develop.

If the respondent actively constructs and assembles interview narratives, he or she does not simply 'break out' talking. Neither elaborate stories nor one-word replies emerge without incitement. The animated interviewer's role is to stimulate respondents' answers, working up responses to interview questions or comments in the process. Standardized approaches to interviewing attempt to strip the interview of all but the most neutral, impersonal stimuli. An animated sense of interviewing turns us to the narrative positions, resources, orientations, and precedents that engage the process for all participants.

Consider, for example, how diverse aspects of a respondent's knowledge, perspectives, roles, and orientations are implicated in an interview with an adult daughter who is caring for her demented mother at home. The daughter is employed part-time, and shares the household with her employed husband and their two adult sons, one a part-time college student and the other a full-time security guard. The following extract begins when the interviewer (**I**) asks the daughter (**R**) to describe her feelings about having to juggle so many needs and schedules. This relates to a discussion of the so-called 'sandwich generation,' which is said to be caught between raising children and caring for frail elderly parents. Note how, after the interviewer asks the respondent what she means by saying that she has mixed feelings, the respondent makes explicit reference to various ways of thinking about the matter, as if to suggest that there is more than one plot to the story. The respondent displays considerable narrative agency; she not only references possible *whats* of caregiving and family life, but, in the process, informs the interviewer of *how* she could possibly construct her answer, further adding to the meaning of the *whats* in question. Of course, not all interviews present *hows* so vividly; the extract is instructive precisely because it does.

I: We were talking about, you said you were a member of the, what did you call it?

R: They say that I'm in the sandwich generation. You know, like we're sandwiched between having to care for my mother...and my grown kids and my husband. People are living longer now and you've got different generations at home and, I tell ya, it's a mixed blessing.

I: How do you feel about it in your situation?

R: Oh, I don't know. Sometimes I think I'm being a bit selfish because I gripe about having to keep an eye on Mother all the time. If you let down your guard, she wanders off into the back yard or goes out the door and down the street. That's no fun when your hubby wants your attention too. Norm works the second shift and he's home during the day a lot. I manage to get in a few hours of work, but he doesn't like it. I have pretty mixed feelings about it.

I: What do you mean?

R: Well, I'd say that as a daughter, I feel pretty guilty about how I feel sometimes. It can get pretty bad, like wishing that Mother were just gone, you know what I mean? She's been a wonderful mother and I love her very much, but if you ask me how I feel as a wife and mother, that's another matter. I feel like she's [the mother], well, intruding on our lives and just making hell out of raising a family. Sometimes I put myself in my husband's shoes and I just know how he feels. He doesn't say much, but I know that he misses my company, and I miss his of course. [Pause] So how do you answer that?

The interviewer goes on to explain that the respondent should answer in the way she believes best represents her thoughts and feelings. But as the exchange unfolds, it's clear that 'best' misrepresents the nonlinear complexity of the respondent's experience. In the next portion of the interview, notice how the respondent struggles to sort her narrative to accord with categorically distinct identities, which in the context of an agent who recognizes diverse narrative standpoints can produce distinct, even contradictory, accounts. At one point, the respondent explains that she now knows how a wife could and should feel because she gathered from the way her husband and sons acted that 'men don't feel things in the same way.' This response suggests that her own thoughts and feelings are drawn from gendered standpoints. Note, too, how the interviewer actively collaborates with the respondent to define her working identity as a respondent.

R: I try to put myself in their [husband and sons'] shoes, try to look at it from their point of view, you know, from a man's way of thinking. I ask myself how it feels to have a part-time wife and mama. I ask myself how I'd feel. Believe me, I know he [husband] feels pretty rotten about it. Men get that way; they want what they want and the rest of the time, well, they're quiet, like nothing's the matter. I used to think I was going crazy with all the stuff on my mind and having to think about everything all at once and not being able to finish with one thing and get on to the other. You know how it gets – doing one thing and feeling bad about how you did something else and wanting to redo what you did or what you said. The way a woman does, I guess. I think I've learned that about myself. I don't know. It's pretty complicated thinking about it. [Pause] Let's see, how do I really feel?

I: Well, I was just wondering, you mentioned being sandwiched earlier and what a woman feels?

R: Yeah, I guess I wasn't all that sure what women like me feel until I figured out how Norm and the boys felt. I figured pretty quick that men are pretty good at sorting things out and that, well, I just couldn't do it, 'cause, well, men don't feel things the same way. I just wouldn't want to do that way anyway. Wouldn't feel right about it as a woman, you know what I mean? So, like they say, live and let live, I guess.

I: But as a daughter?

R: Yeah, that too. So if you ask me how I feel having Mother under foot all the time, I'd say that I remember not so far back that I was under foot a lot when I was a little girl and Mother never complained, and she'd help Dad out in the store, too. So I guess I could tell you that I'm glad I'm healthy and around to take care of her and, honestly, I'd do it all over again if I had to. I don't know. You've talked to other women about it. What do they say?

I: Well, uh

R: Naw, I don't want to put you on the spot. I was just thinking that maybe if I knew how others in my shoes felt, I might be able to sort things out better than I did for ya.

The respondent's comments about both the subject matter under consideration and how one formulates responses show that the respondent, jointly with the interviewer, mobilizes diverse communicative resources as an integral part of exchanging questions and answers. Viewing the interview as animated, we can acknowledge and appreciate how the interviewer participates with the respondent in shifting positions in the interview so as to explore alternative perspectives and narrative possibilities. The analytic presumption is that narrative reality emerges out of the interplay of narrativity, not simply from within the respondent.

A methodological matter that we will mention but not develop here is the question of procedural guidelines for treating the interview as a thoroughly animated encounter. Just as there are virtual rule books for conducting good standardized interviews, potentially there are sophisticated guidelines for how to conduct and analyze interviews that are treated as animated. Granted, such guidelines do exist, but mostly in the form of unsystematic, seat-of-the-pants advice on how to encourage narrative expansiveness, on how to elicit 'rich' data. In a word, the textbook for animated interviewing has yet to be written, but the idea, if not the realization, does follow from the application of animated subjectivity.

Key Points

- Animated interview participants concertedly engage the work of meaning-making.
- The versions of meaningful experience that emerge from interviews are constituted in the interplay of the *hows* and the *whats* of the process.
- Because all interviews involve the co-construction of experiential reality, the conventional model of the respondent as a passive vessel-of-answers and the interviewer as a neutral interrogator shortchanges how possible responses may be analyzed.
- There is both an analytic and empirical warrant for thinking of responses as narratives, sets of themes, and plotlines. Interview guidelines in this case would provide methods for activating an animated subjectivity.

Animation, Bias, and Rigor

An emphasis on the animated quality of interviewing might suggest that active interviewing merely invites unacceptable bias into the information-gathering process. 'Contamination' seems to lurk everywhere and understandably needs to be controlled. But this criticism only holds if one's point of departure is an image of passive participant subjectivity. Bias is a meaningful concept only if the respondent is viewed as a preformed, purely information-producing commodity that the interview process might somehow distort or defile.

If the substance of responses is seen as a narrative product of the animated *hows* and *whats* of interviewing, they are neither preformed, nor ever pristinely communicated. Any interview situation – no matter how formalized, restricted, or standardized – relies upon interaction between participants who are constantly engaged in interpretive practice. Because interviewing is unavoidably collaborative, it is virtually impossible to free interaction from factors that could be construed as contaminants.

Participants in an interview are inevitably implicated in making-meaning, even if that sometimes takes a highly constricted form.

While naturally occurring talk and interaction may appear to be more spontaneous than what transpires in an interview, this is true only in the sense that such interaction is staged by persons other than an interviewer. Seemingly spontaneous conversations are not necessarily more authentic, bias free, or unstructured. They simply take place in what have been conventionally recognized as non-interview settings. But these settings, too, play a definite role in the production of experiential knowledge – just like interview situations. Still, with the development of the interview society, and the related increasing deprivatization of personal experience (see Gubrium and Holstein 1995), the interview has become more and more commonplace, increasingly making it a naturally occurring occasion in its own right.

Given an orientation to the animated interview, how can one make sense of interview data? Once we acknowledge that all interactional and discursive data are products of interpretive practice, analysis begins to center on the interplay of the *hows* and *whats* of interviewing. This stands in contrast to more traditional naturalistic research, which focuses mainly on the *whats* of the social worlds described in interviews (see Gubrium and Holstein 1997, chapter 2). These interviews are typically analyzed as more or less accurate descriptions of experience, as reports or re-presentations of reality, depending on how postmodern the author's sensibilities. Analysis takes the form of systematically grouping and summarizing the descriptions, and providing a coherent organizing framework that encapsulates and offers an understanding of the social world varied members portray. Respondents' interpretive activity is subordinated to the substance of what they report; the *whats* of experience take precedence over the *hows*.

When researchers consider the constructive activity operating in the interview process, data extend to the *hows* of the matter as they reflexively relate to the *whats*. Respondents' comments are not seen as reality reports delivered from a fixed repository. Instead, they are considered for the ways they narratively construct experiential reality in collaboration with the interviewer. The focus is as much on the assembly *process* as on what is assembled and conveyed.

Interactionally and contextually sensitive forms of narrative and discourse analysis can reveal reality-constructing practices as well as the subjective meanings that are circumstantially in tow (see Gubrium and Holstein 2009; Potter and Hepburn 2008). The goal is to document how interview narratives are produced in the interaction between interviewer and respondent, without losing sight of the meanings produced or the circumstances that mediate the narrative process. The analytic objective is not merely to describe situated narrative construction, but to describe what is being said in relation to the experiences and lives being represented in the circumstances at hand. Viewing the interview as animated means analysis must be every bit as rigorous as the analysis of conventionally construed interview data. Analyzing such interview data requires disciplined, methodical procedures and sensitivity to both process and substance (see Gubrium and Holstein 2009).

Key Points

- The concept of the animated interview casts interview 'bias' in a new light. All participants in an interview are implicated in the construction of narrative reality. They are involved in narrative production, not contamination.
- The guiding question should not be whether interview procedures contaminate data, but how the interview generates the information it does.
- Because interview data are products of interpretive practice, data analysis demands a rigorous sensitivity to both the *hows* and *whats* of the interview process.

Summary and Future Prospects

In conclusion, let us highlight the chapter's key points. First, the active interview is not a particular type of interview, to be distinguished from other forms of interviewing. Rather, we use the term 'active' to underscore the notion that all interviews are unavoidably active communicative enterprises. Active is an ontological reference to the enterprise. Even the standardized survey interview is active, because standardization procedures actively structure the interviewer's input and restrict the respondent's range of responses.

Second, by specifying the vision of an active, animated interview, we are not offering an oblique criticism of standardized interviewing methods. Rather, by calling attention to the constitutive activity inherent in all forms of interviewing, we are pointing to alternative models of the interview, abrogating the perspective that there is a foundational sense of the interview and, equally important, eclipsing the idea that there is a gold standard for interviewing.

Third, at the same time, by animating interview narratives, we are not saying that 'anything goes.' Put into place, every image of the subjectivity of interviews spawns its own operating rules. The concept of the animated interview derives from an ontologically warranted basis for construing the production, collection, and analysis of information in a particular way, and demands its own set of procedural and analytic guidelines.

The view of the narratively animated interview broadens the analytic purview of interview research to consider a wider array of questions than are the bailiwick of more standardized or naturalistic approaches. In the future, researchers will no longer be content simply to catalog what was said in an interview. The challenge of viewing the interview as a thoroughly animated narrative process is to carefully consider what is said in relation to how, where, when, and by whom narratives are conveyed, and to what end. Construing the interview as animated, then, provides us with a much wider, more richly variegated field of inquiry than ever before. This will require the continued development of contextually sensitive forms of narrative analysis (e.g., Baker 2002; DeVault and McCoy 2002; Gubrium and Holstein 2009; Potter and Hepburn 2008) that capture the complexities of narrative realities produced through interviews.

Questions

1 What does the idea of an interview society suggest we consider in doing research on inner lives and social worlds?
2 What view of participant agency does animating interview narratives put into place?
3 Distinguish between the *hows* and *whats* of interpretive practice and how this can be applied to the interview.

Recommended Reading

The Active Interview by James A. Holstein and Jaber F. Gubrium (1995) describes the active interview in greater depth. It provides extensive illustration of the interactional, interpretive activity that is part and parcel of all interviewing.

InterViews by Steinar Kvale (1996) is an introduction to qualitative research interviewing. The book frames the issues in terms of the active view presented here.

The *Handbook of Interview Research* edited by Jaber F. Gubrium and James A. Holstein (2002b) is a both a thematic and encyclopedic collection of state-of-the-art descriptions of different approaches to interviewing. The handbook covers theoretical, technical, analytic, and representation issues relating to interview research.

Analyzing Narrative Reality by Jaber F. Gubrium and James A. Holstein (2009) offers an approach to analyzing actively constructed narratives, including those produced by interviewing.

Internet Links

The Active Interview, Google Books:

http://books.google.com/books?id=LgR3TjzCxf8C&dq=the+active+interview&printsec=frontcover&source=bn&hl=en&ei=iK16S5aAEeP08Qbh2Zm0Cg&sa=X&oi=book_result&ct=result&resnum=4&ved=0CBUQ6AEwAw#v=onepage&q=&f=false

(Continued)

(Continued)

Handbook of Interview Research, Google Books:

http://books.google.com/books?id=uQMUMQJZU4gC&dq=handbook+of+interview+research+context+%26+method&printsec=frontcover&source=bn&hl=en&ei=ubZ6S4XGOsLT8QaGtOnzCQ&sa=X&oi=book_result&ct=result&resnum=4&ved=0CBoQ6AEwAw#v=onepage&q=&f=false

Journal of Contemporary Ethnography:

http://jce.sagepub.com/

Qualitative Inquiry:

http://qix.sag.com/

Qualitative Inquiry, 'The Shaping Effects of the Conversational Interview:

http://qix.sagepub.com/cgi/content/abstract/15/7/1265'

Qualitative Research:

http://qrj.sagepub.com/

Qualitative Sociology Review:

www.qualitativesociologyreview.org

The New Language of Qualitative Method:

www.us.oup.com/us/catalog/general/subject/Sociology/TheoryMethods/?view=usa&ci=9780195099942

References

Baker, Carolyn D. 2002. 'Ethnomethodological Analyses of Interviews.' Pp. 777–795 in *Handbook of Interview Research,* edited by Jaber F. Gubrium and James A. Holstein. Thousand Oaks, CA: Sage.

Berger, Peter L. and Thomas Luckmann. 1967. *The Social Construction of Reality.* New York: Doubleday.

Blumer, Herbert. 1969. *Symbolic Interactionism.* New York: Prentice Hall.

Briggs, Charles L. 1986. *Learning How to Ask: A Sociolinguistic Appraisal of the Role of the Interviewer in Social Science Research.* Cambridge: Cambridge University Press.

Briggs, Charles L. and Clara Mantini-Briggs. 2003. *Stories in the Time of Cholera.* Berkeley: University of California Press.

Cicourel, Aaron V. 1964. *Method and Measurement in Sociology.* New York: Free Press.

Cicourel, Aaron V. 1974. *Theory and Method in a Study of Argentine Fertility.* New York: Wiley.

Conrad, Frederick G. and Michael F. Schober. 2008. 'New Frontiers in Standardized Survey Interviewing.' Pp. 173–188 in *Handbook of Emergent Methods,* edited by S.N. Hesse-Biber and P. Leavey. New York: Guilford Press.

Converse, Jean M. and Howard Schuman. 1974. *Conversations at Random: Survey Research as Interviewers See It*. New York: Wiley.

DeVault, Marjorie. 1990. 'Talking and Listening from Women's Standpoint: Feminist Strategies for Interviewing and Analysis.' *Social Problems* 37: 96–117.

DeVault, Marjorie and Liza McCoy. 2002. 'Institutional Ethnography: Using Interviews to Investigate Ruling Relations.' Pp. 751–776 in *Handbook of Interview Research*, edited by Jaber F. Gubrium and James A. Holstein. Thousand Oaks, CA: Sage.

Douglas, Jack D. 1985. *Creative Interviewing*. Beverly Hills, CA: Sage.

Foucault, Michel. 1979. *Discipline and Punish*. New York: Vintage.

Fowler, Floyd. J. and Thomas W. Mangione. 1990. *Standardized Survey Interviewing*. Newbury Park, CA: Sage.

Garfinkel, Harold. 1967. *Studies in Ethnomethodology*. Englewood Cliffs, NJ: Prentice Hall.

Gorden, Raymond L. 1987. *Interviewing: Strategy, Techniques, and Tactics*. Homewood, IL: Dorsey.

Gubrium, Jaber F. 1988. *Analyzing Field Reality*. Beverly Hills, CA: Sage.

Gubrium, Jaber F. 1989. 'Local Cultures and Service Policy.' Pp. 94–112 in *The Politics of Field Research*, edited by Jaber F. Gubrium and David Silverman. London: Sage.

Gubrium, Jaber F. 1993. *Speaking of Life: Horizons of Meaning for Nursing Home Residents*. Hawthorne, NY: Aldine de Gruyter.

Gubrium, Jaber F. and James A. Holstein. 1995. 'Biographical Work and New Ethnography.' Pp. 45–58 in *The Narrative Study of Lives*, vol. 3, edited by Ruthellen Josselson and Amia Lieblich. Newbury Park, CA: Sage.

Gubrium, Jaber F. and James A. Holstein. 1997. *The New Language of Qualitative Method*. New York: Oxford University Press.

Gubrium, Jaber F. and James A. Holstein. 2002a. 'From the Individual Interview to the Interview Society.' Pp. 3–32 in *Handbook of Interview Research*, edited by Jaber F. Gubrium and James A. Holstein. Thousand Oaks, CA: Sage.

Gubrium, Jaber F. and James A. Holstein (eds.) 2002b. *Handbook of Interview Research*. Thousand Oaks, CA: Sage.

Gubrium, Jaber F. and James A. Holstein. 2009. *Analyzing Narrative Reality*. Thousand Oaks, CA: Sage.

Harding, Sandra (ed.). 1987. *Feminism and Methodology*. Bloomington, IN: Indiana University Press.

Holstein, James A. 1993. *Court-Ordered Insanity: Interpretive Practice and Involuntary Commitment*. Hawthorne, NY: Aldine de Gruyter.

Holstein, James A. and Jaber F. Gubrium. 1995. *The Active Interview*. Newbury Park, CA: Sage.

Holstein, James A. and Jaber F. Gubrium (eds.). 2008. *Handbook of Constructionist Research*. New York: Guilford.

Holstein, James A. and Jaber F. Gubrium. 2000. *The Self We Live By: Narrative Identity in a Postmodern World*. New York: Oxford University Press.

Holstein, James A. and Jaber F. Gubrium. 2011. 'The Constructionist Analytics of Interpretive Practice.' Forthcoming in *Handbook of Qualitative Research*, 4th ed., edited by N. Denzin and Y. Lincoln. Thousand Oaks, CA: Sage.

Hootkoop-Steenstra, Hanneke. 2000. *Interaction and the Standardized Survey Interview.* Cambridge: Cambridge University Press.

Kirk, Jerome, and Marc L. Miller. 1986. *Reliability and Validity in Qualitative Research.* Beverly Hills, CA: Sage.

Kvale, Steinar. 1996. *InterViews.* London: Sage.

Maynard, Douglas W., H. Houtkoop-Steenstra, J. van der Zouwen, and N.C. Schaeffer (eds.). 2002. *Standardization and Tacit Knowledge: Interaction and Practice in the Survey Interview.* New York: Wiley.

Potter, Jonathan and Alexa Hepburn. 2008. 'Discursive Constructionism.' Pp. 275–293 in *Handbook of Consructionist Research,* edited by J. Holstein and J. Gubrium. New York: Guilford Press.

Silverman, David. 1993. *Interpreting Qualitative Data.* London: Sage.

Smith, Dorothy E. 1987. *The Everyday World as Problematic: A Feminist Sociology.* Boston, MA: Northeastern University Press.

Terkel, Studs. 1972. *Working.* New York: Avon.

Warren, Carol A.B. and Tracy Karner. 2005. *Discovering Qualitative Methods.* Los Angeles: Roxbury.

10 Analysing Focus Group Data

Sue Wilkinson

Abstract

This chapter examines two different ways of analysing focus group data: content analysis and ethnographic analysis. It outlines key theoretical and epistemological issues associated with each. It provides an illustrative example of the use of each approach in analysing one segment of a particular focus group, in which women diagnosed with breast cancer talk about the possible causes of their cancer. Finally, it briefly considers when it is appropriate to use focus groups, and ways in which focus group research is likely to develop.

Keywords:

breast cancer, content analysis, conversation analysis, ethnographic analysis, focus groups.

Although the 'invention' of focus groups can be traced back to the 1920s, it was not until the 1990s that they became a popular method of research across a broad range of disciplines, including education, communication and media studies, feminist research, sociology and social psychology (for reviews see Morgan, 1996; Wilkinson, 1998a,1998b,1998c, 1999). The popularity of focus group research continues to rise, with almost 6000 focus group studies published across the social sciences in the last five years, more than a quarter of these in 2009 alone.

Focus group methodology is, at first sight, deceptively simple. It is a way of collecting qualitative data, which usually involves engaging a small number of people in an informal group discussion (or discussions), 'focused' around a particular topic or set of issues. This could be, for example, young women sharing experiences of dieting, single parents evaluating childcare facilities, or fitness instructors comparing and contrasting training regimes. The discussion is usually based on a series of questions (the focus group 'schedule'), and the researcher generally acts as a 'moderator' for the group: posing the questions, keeping the discussion flowing, and enabling group members to participate fully.

Although focus groups are sometimes referred to as 'group interviews', the moderator does *not* ask questions of each focus group participant in turn but, rather, facilitates group discussion, actively encouraging group members to interact with *each other*. This interaction between research participants – and the potential analytic use of such interaction – has been described as the 'hallmark' of focus group research (Morgan, 1988: 12).

Typically, the discussion is recorded, the data transcribed, and then analysed using conventional techniques for qualitative data: most commonly, content or thematic analysis. Focus groups are distinctive, then, primarily for the method of data *collection* (i.e. informal group discussion), rather than for the method of data *analysis*. It is this, perhaps, which leads most accounts of the method to emphasize how to run an effective focus group, rather than how to analyse the resulting data. There is a plethora of advice on the methodological and procedural choices entailed in setting up and conducting a focus group – see, for example, Barbour (2007), Krueger and Casey (2009), Morgan and Krueger (1998), Stewart et al. (2007), Wilkinson (2003, 2008) – but remarkably little on the theoretical and epistemological choices entailed in analysing and interpreting focus group data. I attempt to redress that imbalance in this chapter, drawing upon my own focus group research.

Two Approaches to Data Analysis

There are many ways of analysing focus group data: for example, content, thematic, ethnographic, phenomenological, narrative, experiential, biographical, discourse, or conversation analysis (some of these are discussed in other chapters). Here, I will compare just two of these approaches – content analysis and ethnographic analysis – highlighting what is distinctive about each, what theoretical and epistemological assumptions each includes, and what each has to offer the focus group researcher.

Content analysis produces a relatively systematic and comprehensive summary or overview of the data set as a whole, sometimes incorporating a quantitative element. Ethnographic analysis is more selective, typically addressing the issue of 'what is going on' between the participants in some segment (or segments) of the data, in greater analytic depth and detail. The two different approaches relate, of course, to different types of research question and the 'results' produced by the two types of analysis look very different.

An initial sense of the distinction between them can be gained from a project on heart attack risk factors, which utilizes *both* types of analysis (Morgan and Spanish, 1984). In this project, content analysis is used to address the question of how *often* different risk factors for heart attacks are mentioned, and what these factors *are*, while ethnographic analysis is used to address the question of exactly *how* (and could also perhaps address *why*) risk factor information is introduced and discussed, in the context of these particular focus groups.

Content analysis is based on examination of the data for recurrent instances of some kind; these instances are then systematically identified across the data set, and grouped together by means of a coding system. The researcher has first to decide on the unit of analysis: this could be the whole group, the group dynamics, the individual participants, or (as is most commonly the case) the participants' utterances (Carey and Smith, 1994; Morgan, 1995). The unit of analysis provides the basis for developing a coding system, and the codes are then applied systematically across a transcript (or transcripts). Once the data have been coded, a further issue is whether to quantify them – many qualitative researchers would, of course, argue that the most valuable features of qualitative data are thereby lost. Morgan (1993) argues for the use of simple 'descriptive counts' of codes – that is, stopping short of using inferential statistical tests, whose assumptions are unlikely to be met in focus groups. These counts are an effective way of providing a summary or overview of the data set as a whole.

In contrast to content analysis, ethnographic analysis is rarely systematic or comprehensive, rather it is much more selective and limited in scope. Its main advantage is to permit a detailed – more or less interpretive – account of mundane features of the social world, whether this relates to processes occurring within the focus group itself, or whether (as is more typical) talk within the focus group is seen as a means of access to participants' lives. Ethnographic analysis aims to ground interpretation in the particularities of the situation under study, and in participants' (rather than analysts') perspectives. Data are generally presented as accounts of social phenomena or social practices, substantiated by illustrative quotations from the focus group discussion. Key issues in ethnographic analysis are:

- how to select the material to present;
- how to give due weight to the specific context within which the material was generated, while retaining some sense of the group discussion as a whole;
- how best to prioritize participants' orientations in presenting an interpretive account.

A particular challenge is to address the *interactive* nature of focus group data: a surprising limitation of focus group research is the relative rarity with which group interactions are analysed or reported (Kitzinger, 1994; Wilkinson, 1999). For exceptions see, for example, Duggleby (2005) and Warr (2005).

Content Analysis

The majority of published focus group studies use some type of content analysis. At its most basic, content analysis simply entails inspection of the data for recurrent instances of some kind. This is irrespective of the type of instance (e.g. word, phrase, some larger unit of 'meaning'); the preferred label for such instances (e.g. 'items', 'themes', 'discourses'); whether the instances are subsequently grouped into larger units, also variously labelled (e.g. 'categories', 'organizing themes', 'interpretive repertoires'); and whether the instances – or larger units – are counted or not. In the sense, then, that most analyses of focus group data report recurrent instances of some kind, and do so more or less systematically, they are essentially content analyses.

To illustrate this point, I show (in Box 10.1) two different content analyses – one quantitative, one qualitative – of the *same* piece of focus group data. The 'results' of the quantitative content analysis are presented as frequency counts, while the 'results' of the qualitative content analysis are presented as illustrative quotations. The data are drawn from a segment of a focus group in which three women who share a breast cancer diagnosis are talking about possible causes of the disease (see Wilkinson, 2000, for the larger context). Both analyses take the 'mention' of a cause as the unit of analysis, and organize these 'mentions' using a category scheme derived from Blaxter's (1983) classic study of talk about the causes of health and illness. However, the first analysis systematically records the *number* of 'mentions' within each category (including null categories), summarizing what these 'mentions' are, while the second records the *words* in which these 'mentions' are couched, presenting them as quotations under each category heading (excluding null categories).

BOX 10.1 Content analyses (causes of breast cancer)

(1) QUANTITATIVE VERSION

1. *Infection:* 0 instances
2. *Heredity or familial tendencies*: 2 instances
   family history (×2)
3. *Agents in the environment:*

   (a) *'poisons', working condition, climate:* 3 instances
       aluminium pans; exposure to sun; chemicals in food
   (b) *drugs or the contraceptive pill:* 1 instance
       taking the contraceptive pill

(Continued)

(Continued)

4. *Secondary to other diseases:* 0 instances
5. *Stress, strain and worry:* 0 instances
6. *Caused by childbearing, menopause:* 22 instances
    not breast feeding; late childbearing (×3); having only one child; being single/not having children; hormonal; trouble with breast feeding – unspecified (×4); flattened nipples (×2); inverted nipples (×7); nipple discharge (×2)
7. *Secondary to trauma or to surgery:* 9 instances
    knocks (×4); unspecified injury; air getting inside body (×4)
8. *Neglect, the constraints of poverty:* 0 instances
9. *Inherent susceptibility, individual and not hereditary:* 0 instances
10. *Behaviour, own responsibility:* 1 instance
    mixing specific foods
11. Ageing, natural degeneration: 0 instances
12. *Other:* 5 instances
    'several things'; 'a lot'; 'multi-factorial'; everybody has a 'dormant' cancer; 'anything' could wake a dormant cancer

(2) QUALITITATIVE VERSION
Heredity or familial tendencies

- 'I mean there's no family <u>history</u>'

Agents in the environment:

(a) *'poisons', working condition, climate*

- 'I was once told that if you use them aluminium pans that cause cancer'
- 'Looking years and years ago, I mean, everybody used to sit about sunning themselves on the beach and now all of a sudden you get cancer from sunshine'
- 'I don't know (about) all the chemicals in what you're eating and things these days as well, and how cultivated and everything'

(b) *drugs or the contraceptive pill*

- 'You know, obviously I took the pill at a younger age'

Caused by childbearing, menopause

- 'Inverted nipples, they say that that is one thing that you could be wary of'
- 'Until I came to the point of actually trying to breast feed I didn't realise I had flattened nipples and one of them was nearly inverted or whatever, so I had a lot of trouble breast feeding, and it, and I was several weeks with a breast pump trying to get it right, so that he could suckle on my nipple, I did have that problem'

(Continued)

(Continued)

- 'Over the years, every, I couldn't say it happened monthly or anything like that, it would just start throbbing, this leakage, nothing to put a dressing on or anything like that, but there it was, it was coming from somewhere and it were just kind of gently crust over'
- 'I mean, I don't know whether the age at which you have children makes a difference as well because I had my eight year old relatively <u>late</u>, I was an old mum'
- 'They say that if you've only had <u>one</u> that you're more likely to get it than if you have a <u>big</u> family'

Secondary to trauma or to surgery

- 'Sometimes I've heard that <u>knocks</u> can bring one on'
- 'I then remembered that I'd <u>banged</u> my breast with this ... you know these shopping bags with a wooden rod thing, those big trolley bags?'
- 'I always think that people go into hospital, even for an exploratory, it may be all wrong, but I do think, well the <u>air</u> gets to it, it seems to me that it's not long afterwards before they simply find that there's more to it than they thought, you know, and I often wonder if the <u>air</u> getting to your inside ... brings on cancer in any form'

Behaviour, own responsibility

- 'I was also told that if you eat tomatoes and plums at the same meal'

Other

- 'He told them nurses in his lectures that <u>every</u>body has a cancer, <u>and</u> it's a case of whether it lays dormant'
- 'I don't think it could be one cause, can it? It must be multi-factorial'

These two content analyses, then, *look* very different, although both are derived from the same underlying theoretical framework. The second type, reporting qualitative data, is often described as a 'thematic' analysis (sometimes as a 'discourse' analysis) and may be presented with the quotations integrated into the text, rather than in tabular form (e.g. Braun and Wilkinson, 2003). Note that neither of these analyses has preserved the interactive quality of the focus group data, although it is possible for a thematic analysis to do so (see, for example, Braun and Wilkinson, 2005; Ellis, 2002).

Ethnographic Analysis

So far, we have seen that content analyses which look very *different* (i.e. providing quantitative or qualitative 'results') in fact treat the data in the *same* kind of way (i.e. inspecting the data systematically for recurrent instances). We can further note that these various types of content analysis share a *similar underlying epistemology*, one in which research participants' talk is taken as providing a 'means of access' to something that lies behind or beyond it. In my content analyses of women's talk about the causes of breast cancer, the words of focus group participants are taken to provide a 'transparent' window onto what they understand, think or believe about – say – the role of reproductive factors in the aetiology of breast cancer. Self-report is used to infer the relatively stable 'cognitions' (beliefs, attitudes or opinions) assumed to underlie people's talk (and – at least sometimes – to inform their subsequent behaviour), to which the researcher has no independent access.

A similar epistemological status is commonly given to talk in focus group studies which are designedly *ethnographic* (rather than content analytic) in nature – that is, studies which aim to provide contextual, interpretive accounts of their participants' social worlds. For example, in Lyons et al.'s (1995) study of women with multiple sclerosis, and Agar and MacDonald's (1995) study of ex-users of LSD, research participants' talk is taken to provide a 'transparent' window onto the circumstances of their lives outside the focus group (to which the focus group moderator has no independent access), inferred from self-report. What people say in the context of the focus group discussion is taken as 'revealing', for example, the nature of daily life for people with chronic physical illness, or a as flagging up a 'significant issue' in the life 'territory' of the drug-experienced young. In other words, talk is used as a 'means of access' to something that lies behind or beyond it, rather than treated as of interest in its own right (see Miller and Glassner and Holstein and Gubrium, this volume).

I will contrast this view of talk (i.e. talk as a means of accessing a pre-given social or psychological world) with an alternative: talk as *constituting* the social world on a moment-by-moment basis. This very *different* epistemological status radically effects both the kind of study undertaken and the kind of 'results' obtained. It opens up the possibility of seeing the focus group discussion as a social context *in its own right*, and, further, the possibility of subjecting it to *direct* observation (rather than studying it in order to infer more distal social – or psychological – phenomena). The resulting study will *necessarily* be ethnographic, and will provide a detailed, contextual account of social processes. This is a radical proposal for most focus group researchers, including those working within an ethnographic tradition. Even though (most) ethnography is predicated upon direct observation, few focus group researchers conducting (broadly) ethnographic analysis have turned their attention to observation of 'what is going on' in the focus group itself; still fewer have paid detailed attention to talk as constitutive of social – or psychological – life.

In taking such an approach, I have found the theoretical framework offered by ethnomethodology and conversation analysis (see Heritage and Peräkylä, this volume) particularly valuable. Conversation analysis assumes that it is fundamentally *through interaction* that participants build social context. Central to its framework is the notion of talk as *action* – that is, as designed to *do* particular things within a particular interactional context. Within a focus group we can see how people (for example) tell stories, joke, agree, debate, argue, challenge or attempt to persuade. We can see the ways in which they present particular 'versions' of themselves (and others) for particular interactional purposes: (for example) to impress, flatter, tease, ridicule, complain, castigate or condone. Participants build the context of their talk *in* and *through* that talk itself, on a moment-by-moment basis. The talk itself, in its interactional context, provides the primary data for analysis. Further, it is possible to harness analytic resources intrinsic to the data: by focusing on participants' *own* understanding of the interaction – as displayed *directly* in their talk, through the conversational practices they use. In this way, a conversation analytic approach prioritizes the participants' (rather than the analysts') analysis of the interaction: a broadly ethnographic goal (if not one achieved in all ethnographic analyses).

The traditions of ethnomethodology and conversation analysis rely primarily upon the use of naturally occurring data, i.e. data produced independently of the researcher. These data, however, encompass a range of institutional contexts (e.g. classrooms, courtrooms, doctors' surgeries), in which talk has been shown both to follow the conventions of 'everyday' conversation and systematically to depart from these (Drew and Heritage, 1992). Likewise, data from focus groups range both across 'everyday' social actions (e.g. arguing, joking, teasing, complaining) and actions likely to be specific to the particular (research) context, e.g. asking elaborate questions (Puchta and Potter, 1999) or displaying opinions (Myers, 1998). While it may be useful to consider what goes on in focus group *qua* focus group, analysis need not be limited by the specificity of this particular context: it can also address more generic conversational phenomena (e.g. Schegloff, 1997).

To illustrate this approach, here is a sample ethnographic data analysis, based upon the principles of ethnomethodology and conversation analysis: that is, it seeks to offer a detailed interpretive account of 'what is going on' within the talk which constitutes the focus group; and it theorizes this talk as action oriented, as in pursuit of particular, local interactional goals.

The data extracts for this analysis are presented below in Boxes 10.2 and 10.3. These two extracts are drawn from the *same* segment of the *same* focus group as used in the content analyses above, i.e. the part of the discussion in which the three women are talking about possible causes of breast cancer. Here, I have identified myself ('SW'), as moderator of the focus group, and I have called the participants 'Freda', 'Doreen' and 'Gertie'. The level of detail presented in the transcripts is appropriate to the level of analysis which follows, i.e. somewhere between a simple orthographic rendition and a full 'Jeffersonian' (conversation analytic) transcription.

BOX 10.2 Data extract 1

SW: BCP12 (Causes extracts 1+2)

01	SW:	D'you have any idea what <u>caus</u>ed your breast cancer [pause] any of you.
02	Fre:	No- What <u>does</u> cause breast cancer do you think.
03	SW:	What do you think it <u>might</u> be?
04	Ger:	[cuts in] There's a lot of <u>stor</u>ies going about.=I was once told that
05		if you use them aluminium pans that cause cancer. .hh I was also told
06		that if you- if you eat tomatoes and plums at the same meal that-
07	Dor:	[laughs]
08	Ger:	[to Doreen] Have you heard all these those things?
09	Dor:	[laughs] No
10	Ger:	Now that's what <u>I</u> heard and-
11	Dor:	[laughs] Mm
12	Ger:	Oh there's several things that if you <u>lis</u>ten to people [pause] we::ll-
13	Dor:	Mm
14	SW:	[to Gertie, laughingly] What else have they told you?
15	Ger:	Pardon?
16	SW:	[to Gertie, laughingly] What else have they told you?
17	D/SW:	[laughter]
18	Ger:	I can't think off hand I knew a- I knew a <u>lot</u> that I've heard over the
19		years from people who've passed on 'Oh yeah well that causes cancer'.
20	Dor:	Mm
21	Ger:	But I don't know but-
22	Dor:	[cuts in] I mean uhm-
23	Ger:	Now <u>I've</u> no views on this [To Doreen] have you?

Data extract 1 (Box 10.2) opens with my question (as moderator) about causes, and the responses from Freda and Gertie to this question. A content analysis (of the kind presented earlier) might code Freda's initial response (line 2) as 'I don't know', and Gertie's subsequent response (lines 4–6) as items in the categories 'agents in the environment' (aluminium pans) and 'behaviour, own responsibility' (choosing to eat tomatoes and plums at the same meal). An ethnographic analysis, by contrast, focuses on the immediate interactional context. Talk about causes can be interactionally tricky – particularly when a presumed 'expert' is asking questions, or in settings in which potentially equally knowledgeable others might have different or even conflicting opinions. Conversation analysts (e.g. Sacks, 1992: 340–347) have noted the asymmetry between being the first to express an opinion and being second: going first means you have to put your opinion on the line, whereas going second offers an opportunity either for agreement or for potential challenge. Consequently, speakers often try to avoid first position, and this is precisely what Freda does in response to the moderator's question: she declines to gives an opinion, and bounces the question right back to the moderator, as a 'counter' (Schegloff, 2007: 16–19). It is not simply then, as a content analysis (within an essentialist framework) might suggest, that Freda 'doesn't know' what causes breast cancer: from the perspective of an ethnographic analysis within a social constructionist framework, she is not here reporting a state of mind, but is engaged in a piece of local interactional business.

The moderator (SW) avoids answering Freda's direct question: instead she reformulates it (in the manner typically recommended for interviewers and focus group moderators), making clear she is interested in what the participants themselves 'think it <u>might</u> be' (line 3), rather than in any purported 'actual' (i.e. scientific) causes of breast cancer. It is with this reassurance that Gertie offers some 'stories' (i.e. folk wisdom, labelled as such), thereby putting herself in the vulnerable first speaking position, and attracting just the kind of second-speaker disagreement that Freda's counter enabled her to avoid: Doreen, the third member of the group, *laughs* at Gertie's response.

Note that within most other approaches, Gertie's references to 'stories', and to what she has 'heard over the years', would be taken as transparent reports of the *source* of her ideas about cause, i.e. as indicating a reliance on folk knowledge. Within a social constructionist framework, however, this attribution of ideas about cause to folk knowledge is seen an *interactional device* seeking to protect the speaker from challenge (although, here, it fails to avert ridicule).

Gertie's candidate causes, then, are presented as 'stories'. However, only moments later, even these 'stories' are retracted. By the end of Doreen and Gertie's subsequent exchange (at line 23), Gertie, like Freda before her, is claiming to have 'no views' on the causes of breast cancer.

Again (within this approach to data), this not simply a straightforward report of a cognitive state: it arises out of the interactional sequence within which it is embedded, in the course of which both Doreen and the moderator have implied, through their laughter, that Gertie's candidate causes are rather implausible; indeed, the moderator's probe (line 14) can be heard as 'positioning' (Wilkinson and Kitzinger, 2003) Gertie as the sort of gullible person who believes anything she is told. Gertie responds first by reminding everyone that she is not reporting her own views, but those of others, and then she flatly refuses to offer further candidate answers, explicitly handing the floor to Doreen at (line 23).

BOX 10.3   Data extract 2

SW: BCP12 (Causes extracts 4+5)

65	Ger:	My sister was a <u>nurse</u> [pause] wa:y <u>back</u> in the 1920s she [indistinct].
66		And she-she was at what is Springfield General now.=She did her
67		training there and there was a doctor Patterson at the time .hh who
68		used to lecture to the nurses .hh and he told them <u>nurses</u> in his
69		lectures that <u>every</u>body has a cancer [pause] <u>and</u> [pause] it's a case
70		of whether it lays dormant
71	Fre:	Yes I've heard that
72	Dor:	Mm
73	Ger:	Have you heard that?
74	(F):	Mm
75	Ger:	Well yes that she told us <u>that</u> and that came in her lectures.hh and
76		[pause] according to *him* anything could wake it up
77	Dor:	Mm
78	Ger:	a knock or whatever in the appropriate place.hh and <u>then</u> it would
79		develop but that's what-
80	Dor:	Mm
81	Ger:	that's what <u>she</u> was told
82	Dor:	Mm
83	Ger:	But when I-
84	Fre:	[cuts in] Sometimes I've heard that <u>knocks</u> can bring one on but I've
85		never (had any knocks) [indistinct]
86	Ger:	No
87	Fre:	[cuts in] (I don't think that) [indistinct]
88	Dor:	[cuts in] Well I'd heard <u>that</u> from somebody else and so when I-
89		when obviously this was sus- my lump was suspicious I then- I
90		then remembered I'd *banged* my breast with this .hh uhm [tch] you
91		know these shopping bags with a wooden rod thing .hh those big
92		trolley bags?
93	Fre:	Mm
94	Dor:	I-I-I >don't ask me how I do these stupid things< but I got it <u>wedged</u>
95		between the car door as I was getting out of the <u>car</u> I got it wedged
96		in the car door so it- so this [pause] appropriately sized *rod* that
97		was the size of this <u>lump</u> you know went into my breast and I- and I
98		queried that .hh and Mr Fell [consultant surgeon] said you know
99		'You're always looking for a <u>reason</u>' [laughs] d'you know
100		'You've always got to find something that might be the cause of it'

(Continued)

```
(Continued)
101        you know.hh but I thought 'Well I'd just better mention it' in case
102        it turned out to be.hh you know sort of they'll say-, they then come
103        round to me afterwards and say 'Are you sure you haven't d-
104        done some injury to yourself' >or that sort of thing< 'cos you know,
105        it just sprung to mind. .hh 'Cos I-I'd mentioned it to the GP and
106        she'd sort of said 'No no .hh it's nearly always hormonal' so it'd
107        gone out of my head and an- but- but then she was saying 'No it'll be
108        be a cyst' >whatever< and when it wasn't a cyst then I started to
109        think of another cause you see but- .hh
110  (G):  Mm
111  Dor:  uh:m I-I mean I sup- if-if they knew what the cause was they
112        would- they would be able to treat it wouldn't they.
113  Ger:  Well you know I-
114  Dor:  [cuts in]I don't think it could be one cause can it? It must be multi
115  (G):  Mm
116  Dor:  .hh multi-factorial
117  Ger:  [cuts in] You've heard them say-
118  Dor:  whatever the word is
```

When Gertie re-enters the conversation (at line 65, in data extract 2, Box 10.3), with a subsequent suggestion of a candidate cause (the theory that cancer is 'dormant' until woken), she is still attending to the danger of being laughed at. However, here she deals with the risk of ridicule by using a very different kind of footing (Goffman, 1981): the 'dormant cancer' theory is painstakingly constructed as someone else's opinion – that of a specified medical expert, a Dr Patterson, at Springfield General Hospital (the hospital where most of these women will have received treatment). She carefully monitors the reception of this theory, and even though Freda and Doreen affiliate with this view (at lines 71 and 72), she checks to be sure she has their support (line 73), and continues repeatedly to stress that this theory comes from her sister's nursing training: 'she told us that, and that came in her lectures' (line 75); 'according to him' (line 76); 'that's what she was told' (line 81). The effect of all this footing is to emphasize that these ideas are not her own, and that she is not to be held accountable for believing them.

Again, within a social constructionist framework, the attribution of views to others does not offer a 'transparent' window on what Gertie 'believes', nor does it indicate the 'source' of her information. Gertie is not simply repeating what her sister may or may not have told her Dr Patterson had said – rather, she is using footing as a conversational resource, in order to manage the delicate interactional business of presenting an opinion without sounding ignorant or stupid.

Doreen then rejoins the conversation (at line 88) to offer another candidate cause – a 'bang' on her breast. Her story, elaborated in lines 88–105, is apparently 'touched off' by Gertie's mention of 'a knock or whatever in the appropriate place' causing cancer to develop (line 78), followed by Freda's subsequent acknowledgement of the theory that '*knocks* can bring one on' (line 84). Note that just before Doreen begins her story, Gertie and Freda have both placed considerable distance between themselves and the 'knock' theory: Freda saying it is a theory she has 'sometimes heard', but that she has never had any knocks herself (lines 84–85), and Gertie attributing the theory to her sister's nursing training, some 70 years earlier (lines 65–68 and 78–81). In telling a story about her own knock, then, Doreen can be seen to attend to the risk of aligning herself with a belief in knocks, and thereby possibly attracting scorn or censure (see Potter, 1996: 142–147, for a detailed discussion of distancing, neutrality and alignment; also Potter, this volume).

Doreen never actually says directly that she believes her breast cancer to have been caused by a knock to her breast. She simply 'remembered' (line 90) having banged her breast, and reports feeling it necessary to 'mention it' (line 101) to her surgeon, thereby further displaying to her co-conversationalists that she is a rational person who informed a medical professional of the knock in order to check out all possibilities (she has already shown herself to be aware of a range of other possibilities, in her previous discussion of reproductive factors, not reproduced here). The surgeon's reported response, 'You're always looking for a <u>reason</u>' (line 99), is a generalized formulation that does not dismiss the 'knock' theory *specifically*, but that even-handedly dismisses *any* theory (actually or potentially) offered by Doreen – and, by implication, anyone else. Ventriloquizing the surgeon in this way enables Doreen to present the 'knock' theory as no more *or less* plausible than any other theory (to which the 'always looking for a reason' dismissal is equally applicable).

The surgeon's response, with its implicit suggestion that looking for 'reasons' and 'causes' is futile, also provides evidence for Doreen's later claim that 'they' (doctors) do not know the causes of breast cancer (line 111). If they do not, and if looking for causes is pointless, then the 'knock' theory is as plausible as any other. Likewise, the GP's dismissal of Doreen's theory is also reported in such a way that the 'knock' theory is left open as a possible cause: the competing cause offered by the GP ('it's nearly always hormonal', line 106) is explained as having been offered as a cause for a *cyst*, not cancer. The reported misdiagnosis has the added benefit of pointing to the fallibility of the medical profession (re-emphasized in lines 111–112).

Within a social constructionist framework, the concern is not with whether Doreen 'really' believes the 'knock' theory, or with whether medical professionals 'actually' dismissed her possible explanation. Rather, it is with how Doreen *designs* her talk to illustrate: (a) her own rationality, both in reporting the knock and in assessing its merits and demerits as a theory; (b) her own willingness to listen to the opinions of expert others; (c) the fallibility of the medical profession; and (d) the plausibility of a knock as a cause for breast cancer.

Doreen's final statement – that the causes of breast cancer must be 'multi-factorial' (line 116) – enables her to maintain the possibility that her injury was causally implicated, while not denying the potential relevance of other (more medically approved) causes. In this interaction, then, Doreen designs her talk to display to her co-conversationalists that she is a rational and open-minded person.

Summary and Future Prospects

In this chapter, I have outlined what is involved in analysing focus group data, with particular reference to the theoretical and epistemological issues entailed in two different types of analysis: content analysis and ethnographic analysis. Although I am a keen advocate of focus groups, I would not want to claim that they are always appropriate. Focus groups are a method of choice when the objective of the research is primarily to study *talk*, either conceptualized as a 'window' on participants' lives or their underlying beliefs and opinions, or as constituting a social context in its own right, amenable to direct observation. If, by contrast, the purpose of the research is to categorize or compare types of individuals or social groups, in terms of the lives they lead or the views they hold, then focus groups are less appropriate (although they are not uncommonly used in this way).

Focus group data readily lend themselves to analysis by content analytic or ethnographic methods, as well as by other qualitative techniques; the resulting analyses can be presented in a variety of ways, ranging from numerical tables summarizing a whole data set, through prose accounts containing illustrative quotations, to detailed interpretive accounts of a relatively circumscribed single data extract. Focus groups offer particular opportunities for the study of interaction between research participants, and ethnomethodological and conversation analytic approaches may prove particularly useful for developing sustained analyses of interaction. This is one possible future direction for focus group research. Other ways in which focus group research seems likely to develop include increasing use of the method – appropriately adapted in culturally sensitive ways – in social and community contexts outside Western, developed countries (see Hennink, 2007), and increasing reliance on virtual (i.e. computer-mediated) focus groups (e.g. Fox et al., 2007; Stewart and Williams, 2005).

Questions

1   What are the key differences between 'content analysis' and 'ethnographic analysis' of focus group data?
2   How would you analyse interaction between focus group participants?

Recommended Reading

Wilkinson, S. (1998) Focus group methodology: A review. *International Journal of Social Research Methodology*, 1 (3): 181–203.

Good brief introduction to the method and the ways it has been used in various disciplinary contexts.

Barbour, R. (2007) *Doing Focus Groups*. London: Sage.

A very accessible introduction to using focus groups.

Krueger, R.A. and Casey, M.A. (2009) *Focus Groups: A Practical Guide for Applied Research*. 4th ed. Thousand Oaks, CA: Sage.

One of the best contemporary 'handbooks' on focus group research, comprehensive and practical.

Wilkinson, S. (2000) Women with breast cancer talking causes: Comparing content, biographical and discursive analyses. *Feminism & Psychology*, 10 (4): 431–460.

Useful for more examples of different types of data analysis, and discussion of their implications.

Internet Links

Website for key focus group researcher Richard A. Krueger:

www.tc.umn.edu/~rkrueger/index.html

Section on 'Focus Group Interviewing' includes practical tips, instructional guides, examples and reflections.

Article by Anita Gibbs in Social Research Update:

http://sru.soc.surrey.ac.uk/SRU19.html

A brief overview of focus group methodology.

References

Agar, M. and MacDonald, J. (1995) Focus groups and ethnography. *Human Organization*, 54(1): 78–86.

Barbour, R. (2007) *Doing Focus Groups*. London: Sage.

Blaxter, M. (1983) The causes of disease: Women talking. *Social Science & Medicine*, 17: 59–69.

Braun, V. and Wilkinson, S. (2003) The vagina: Liability or asset? *Psychology of Women Section Review*, 5: 28–42.

Braun, V. and Wilkinson, S. (2005) Vagina equals woman? On genitals and gendered identity. *Women's Studies International Forum*, 28(6): 509–522.

Carey, M.A. and Smith, M.W. (1994) Capturing the group effect in focus groups: A special concern in analysis. *Qualitative Health Research*, 4(1): 123–127.

Drew, P. and Heritage, J. (1992) Analyzing talk at work: An introduction. In P. Drew and J. Heritage (eds) *Talk at Work: Interaction in Institutional Settings*. Cambridge: Cambridge University Press.

Duggleby, W. (2005) What about focus group interaction data? *Qualitative Health Research*, 15: 832–840.

Ellis, S. (2002) Doing being liberal: Implicit prejudice in focus group talk about lesbian and gay human rights issues. *Lesbian and Gay Psychology Review*, 2(2): 43–49.

Fox, F.E., Morris, M. and Rumsey, N. (2007) Doing synchronous online focus groups with young people: Methodological reflections. *Qualitative Health Research*, 17: 539–547.

Goffman, E. (1981) *Forms of Talk*. Oxford: Basil Blackwell.

Hennink, M.M. (2007) *International Focus Group Research: A Handbook for the Health and Social Sciences*. Cambridge: Cambridge University Press.

Kitzinger, J. (1994) The methodology of focus groups: The importance of interaction between research participants. *Sociology of Health and Illness*, 16: 103–121.

Krueger, R.A. and Casey, M.A. (2009) *Focus Groups: A Practical Guide for Applied Research*. 4th ed. Thousand Oaks, CA: Sage.

Lyons, R.F., Sullivan, M.J.L., Ritvo, P.G. with Coyne, J.C. (1995) *Relationships in Chronic Illness and Disability*. Thousand Oaks, CA: Sage.

Morgan, D.L. (1988) *Focus Groups as Qualitative Research*. Newbury Park, CA: Sage.

Morgan, D.L. (ed.) (1993) *Successful Focus Groups: Advancing the State of the Art*. Newbury Park, CA: Sage.

Morgan, D.L. (1995) Why things (sometimes) go wrong in focus groups. *Qualitative Health Research*, 5: 515–522.

Morgan, D.L. (1996) Focus groups. *Annual Review of Sociology*, 22: 129–152.

Morgan, D.L. and Krueger, R.A. (1998) *The Focus Group Kit* (6 vols). Newbury Park, CA: Sage.

Morgan, D.L. and Spanish, M.T. (1984) Focus groups: A new tool for qualitative research. *Qualitative Sociology*, 7(3): 253–270.

Myers, G. (1998) Displaying opinions: Topics and disagreement in focus groups. *Language in Society*, 27: 85–111.

Potter, J. (1996) *Representing Reality: Discourse, Rhetoric and Social Construction*. London: Sage.

Puchta, C. and Potter, J. (1999) Asking elaborate questions: Focus groups and the management of spontaneity. *Journal of Sociolinguistics*, 3: 314–335.

Sacks, H. (1992) *Lectures on Conversation* (ed. G. Jefferson). Oxford: Basil Blackwell.

Schegloff, E.A. (1997) Practices and actions: Boundary cases of other-initiated repair. *Discourse Processes*, 23(3): 499–545.

Schegloff, E.A. (2007) *Sequence Organization in Interaction: A Primer in Conversation Analysis*. Cambridge: Cambridge University Press.

Stewart, D.W., Shamdasani, P.N. and Rook, D.W. (2007) *Focus Groups: Theory and Practice*. 2nd ed. Thousand Oaks, CA: Sage.

Stewart, K. and Williams, M. (2005) Researching online populations: The use of online focus groups for social research. *Qualitative Research*, 5(4): 395–416.

Warr, D.J. (2005) 'It was fun ... but we don't usually talk about these things': Analyzing sociable interaction in focus groups. *Qualitative Inquiry*, 11(2): 200–225.

Wilkinson, S. (1998a) Focus groups in health research: Exploring the meanings of health and illness. *Journal of Health Psychology*, 3(3): 329–348.

Wilkinson, S. (1998b) Focus group methodology: A review. *International Journal of Social Research Methodology*, 1(3): 181–203.

Wilkinson, S. (1998c) Focus groups in feminist research: Power, interaction, and the co-construction of meaning. *Women's Studies International Forum*, 21(1): 111–125.

Wilkinson, S. (1999) Focus groups: A feminist method. *Psychology of Women Quarterly*, 23: 221–244.

Wilkinson, S. (2000) Women with breast cancer talking causes: Comparing content, biographical and discursive analyses. *Feminism & Psychology*, 10(4): 431–460.

Wilkinson, S. (2003) Focus groups. In G.M. Breakwell (ed.) *Doing Social Psychology*. Oxford: Blackwell.

Wilkinson, S. (2008) Focus groups. In J.A. Smith (ed.) *Qualitative Psychology: A Practical Guide to Research Methods*. 2nd ed. London: Sage.

Wilkinson, S. and Kitzinger, C. (2003) Constructing identities: A feminist conversation analytic approach to positioning in action. In R. Harre and F. Moghaddam (eds) *The Self and Others: Positioning Individuals and Groups in Personal, Political and Cultural Contexts*. New York: Prager/Greenwood.

PART V

TALK

Discursive Psychology and the Study of Naturally Occurring Talk ⬤ 11

Jonathan Potter

Abstract

This chapter introduces a style of discourse analysis known as discursive psychology. This is focused on the study of texts and talk as social practices. Basic theoretical and methodological features of discursive psychology are described as well as the kinds of questions that are developed in this style of work. Four features that distinguish discursive psychology from conversation analysis are noted. This schematic overview is followed by an illustration of the logic of analysis which is focused on the attempt to understand why Princess Diana used 'I dunno' twice during her well-known interview with Martin Bashir. This involves considering the way stake and interest become participants' concerns and the way that stake can be managed, or even 'inoculated' against, by using particular discursive constructions. This is further supported by analysing extracts from newspaper reports and relationship counselling sessions.

Keywords:

discursive psychology, discourse analysis, interaction, stake, fact construction.

This chapter will focus on the way discourse analysis can be used to study naturally occurring talk. Discourse analysis as a label can be a source of confusion as different forms of discourse analytic work have developed in the different disciplinary environments of linguistics, cognitive psychology, social psychology, sociolinguistics and post-structuralism (for overviews see Phillips and Jørgensen, 2002; Wooffitt, 2005). This chapter will focus on a strand of discourse research often called discursive psychology (sometimes DP below). This is not just a method; it is a broad approach to social life that combines meta-theoretical assumptions, theoretical ideas, analytic orientations and bodies of work. It is a perspective that draws heavily on conversation analytic work (see Heritage, this volume).

Discursive Psychology

Discursive psychology is characterised by a meta-theoretical emphasis on anti-realism and constructionism. That is, DP emphasises the way versions of the world, of society, events, and inner psychological worlds, are produced in discourse. On the one hand, this leads discursive psychologists to be concerned with participants' constructions and how they are accomplished and undermined; and, on the other, it leads to a recognition of the constructed and contingent nature of researchers' own versions of the world (Potter and Hepburn, 2008). Indeed, it treats realism, whether developed by participants or researchers, as a rhetorical production that can itself be decomposed and studied (Edwards et al., 1995; Gergen, 2009; Potter, 1992).

DP has an analytic commitment to studying discourse as *texts and talk in social practices*. That is, the focus is not on language as an abstract entity such as a lexicon and set of grammatical rules (in linguistics), a system of differences (in structuralism), a set of rules for transforming statements (in Foucauldian genealogies). Instead, it is the medium for interaction; analysis of discourse becomes, then, analysis of what people do. One theme that is particularly emphasised here is the rhetorical or argumentative organisation of talk and texts; claims and versions are constructed to undermine alternatives (Billig, 1991, 1996).

This conception of the focus of DP may make it seem to be pitched at a level of analysis somewhere between studies of individual psychology and studies of structural sociology. On this reading it would be an approach falling squarely within the traditional remit of social psychology or micro-sociology. However, these kinds of distinctions have been made problematic by DP.

On the one hand, DP has eaten away at traditional psychological notions by reformulating them in discursive terms. For example, a classic psychological notion such as a cognitive script can be reworked by considering the sorts of business that people do by 'script formulating' descriptions of their own or others' behaviour (Edwards, 1994). The suggestion is that there is a whole field of discursive study which has hardly been touched in mainstream psychology (Edwards, 1997; Edwards and Potter, 1992, 2005).

On the other hand, the micro–macro distinction has also been made problematic. It has been blurred by three kinds of work. First, there are now a range of conversation analytic studies which are concerned with the way in which the institutionally specific properties of a setting such as a news interview, a doctor–patient consultation or an award ceremony are constituted in talk rather than being structurally determined in any simple way (Drew and Heritage, 1992; see Heritage, this volume). For example, pedagogic interaction certainly happens in school classrooms, and yet much of what happens in classrooms is not pedagogic (playing around, chatting) while much recognisably pedagogic interaction ('test' questions, encouraging discovery) happens over family breakfast tables or with a partner in front of the television. Second, there is work on the way people produce descriptions or stories of social organisation in their talk. For example, Wetherell and Potter (1992) studied the way particular constructions of social groups, processes of conflict and influence, histories and so on were drawn on as practical resources for blaming minority groups for their own disadvantaged social position. That is, social structure becomes part of interaction as it is worked up, invoked and reworked (Potter, 2003a). Third, there is recent work in DP that attempts to highlight the way psychological notions are constructed in and for institutions, and how they can constitute some of the characteristic features of organisations (Edwards, 2008; Potter & Hepburn, 2003).

In contemporary DP the overwhelming analytic focus is on the analysis of naturalistic materials: audio or video recordings of people interacting in everyday or institutional settings. Although much earlier discursive work used open-ended interviews, the virtues of working with naturalistic materials and the shortcomings of interviews have become more and more apparent (see Potter & Hepburn, 2005; Silverman, 2007). DP is overwhelmingly qualitative, although the principled argument is not against quantification per se, but against the way counting and coding often obscure the activities being done with talk and texts (see Heritage, this volume; Peräkylä, this volume; Schegloff, 1993).

Discursive Psychology and Method

In much traditional social research, method is understood as something that can be codified with specific guidelines that, if not guaranteeing good research, are a necessary condition for its conduct. Indeed, research conclusions are often justified by reference to the correct and complete following of procedures such as operationalising variables, getting high levels of inter-rater reliability for codings, and so on. DP is not like this. The analytic procedure used to arrive at claims is often quite different from the way those claims are justified.

Like most research practices in the natural and social sciences, doing discourse analysis has an important element of craft skill; it is sometimes more like sexing a chicken than following the recipe for a mild Chicken Rogan Josh (although, come to think of it, that is rather a craft skill too!). This makes it hard to describe formally and it takes time to learn. But that does not mean that the claims are necessarily hard to evaluate – if you cannot easily say precisely how someone has learned to ride a bike, you do not have so much difficulty saying whether they have fallen off or not. Likewise, there are a range of ways in which the adequacy of discourse analytic studies can be evaluated, including a focus on deviant cases, checking that participants' themselves orient to claimed phenomena, coherence with other discourse analytic studies, and, most importantly, the evaluation that readers themselves can make when they are presented with transcript alongside its analytic interpretations (Potter, 2003b). Nor does it mean that it cannot be learned – it is not merely dependent on intuitions or imagination, but learning the requisite sets of skills.

In traditional stories of method in social research you have a question and then you search for a method to answer that question. For example, you may be interested in the 'factors' that lead to condom use in sexual encounters, and ponder whether to use an experiment with vignettes, some open-ended interviews or discourse analysis to check them out. Adopting DP in this way is a recipe for confusion. Some questions are simply not suited to DP. For example, the kinds of assumptions about factors and outcomes that underpin a lot of thinking in traditional social psychology and sociology do not mesh with its rhetorical and normative logic. Rather than conceiving of a world of discrete variables with discrete effects, in DP there are constructions and versions that may be adopted, responded to or undermined. Thus a categorisation, say, may be undermined by a particularisation; no upshot is guaranteed (Billig, 1991). Norms are *oriented to*: that is, they are not templates for action but provide a way of interpreting deviations. The absence of a return greeting does not disconfirm a regularity, rather it is the basis for inference: the recipient is rude, sad, deaf perhaps (Heritage, 1988). The general point is that the phenomena that DP studies are highly ordered but not determined – the patterning is a product of ordered choices as interaction unfolds in settings.

So what kinds of questions are coherent within DP? Given the general focus is on texts and talk as social practices, there has been a dual focus on the practices themselves and on the resources that are drawn on in those practices. Take gender inequalities for example. Studies have considered both the way in which such inequalities are constructed, made factual and justified in talk, and they have also considered the resources ('interpretative repertoires', identities, category systems, metaphors) that are used to manufacture coherent and persuasive justifications that work to sustain those inequalities (Clarke et al., 2004; Stokoe, 2003; Wetherell et al., 1987).

Naturally Occurring Talk as Topic

I am going to focus here on DP specifically as applied to naturally occurring talk. Naturally occurring talk is spoken language produced entirely independently of the actions of the researcher, whether it is everyday conversation over the telephone, the records of a company board meeting, or the interaction between doctor and patient in a surgery. It is natural in the specific sense that it is not 'got up' by the researcher using an interview schedule, a questionnaire, an experimental protocol or some such social research technology. The appropriate test for whether the talk is naturally occurring is whether the talk would have taken place in much the same way if the researcher had been taken ill that morning. Experiments, focus groups and interviews would have had to be cancelled; recordings of therapy sessions or family mealtimes would have carried on regardless.

It is important to note what is distinctive about the considerable body of earlier discursive psychological work that has used open-ended interviews. When interviews are treated as a machinery for harvesting psychologically and linguistically interesting responses, the research is inevitably focused on those elements of interviews contributed by the participant rather than those from the researcher. However, it is possible to conceptualise interviews as arenas for interaction between two or more parties. That is, we can treat them as a form of natural conversational interaction, by analysing them in the same way that we might a telephone conversation between friends or the cross-examination in a court room.

Widdicombe and Wooffitt (1995) provide one of the most thoroughgoing attempts to use interviews in this way, treating materials originally collected for a study of social identity as examples of unfolding conversational interaction where the sense of social categories is refined and reworked (see also Edwards, 2003).

How Is Discursive Psychology Related to Ethnomethodology and Conversation Analysis?

Contemporary discursive psychology draws heavily on the analytic methods of conversation analysis (CA; see Heritage, this volume). There are, however, at least four areas of divergence.

1 *Construction.* DP is constructionist in the sense that it takes a specific focus on the way versions and descriptions are assembled to perform actions. The construction and use of descriptions is a topic of study. Although ethnomethodologists have been critical of the social constructionist tradition in social science, it is not clear that there is so much tension between this take on construction and that in ethnomethodology or conversation analysis (for some arguments, see Button and Sharrock, 1993; Potter, 1996; Potter and Hepburn, 2008).

2 *Rhetoric.* Whereas conversation analytic work is focused on sequential organisation, discursive psychology is also focused on rhetorical organisation – the way versions are put together to counter alternatives. Often an understanding of sequential organisation is a prerequisite for understanding rhetorical organisation.

3   *Cognition.* Discursive psychology is an alternative to dominant cognitivist perspectives in psychology. It rejects the aim of explaining action by reference to underlying cognitive states. The difficult issue of the status of cognition in ethnomethodology and CA is a source of some disagreement (see papers in te Molder and Potter, 2005). Edwards (1995a) has offered an anti-cognitivist reading of Sacks; Potter (2006) has provided an analysis of cognitivist assumptions in some of Drew's conversation analytic work (e.g. Drew, 2005).

4   *Epistemology.* An important influence on DP has been the sociology of scientific knowledge. This has led to a more sceptical position on issues of truth and knowledge than is common in CA. These differences show themselves most clearly at the level of theory and the justification of research procedures than in the actual procedures themselves.

In the opening parts of the chapter I have addressed a number of background issues for discourse analytic research. There are a range of other concerns to do with transcription, interview conduct, coding, forms of validation, writing up discourse research that there is no space to discuss. For a more detailed coverage of these see Antaki et al. (2003), Hepburn and Potter (2003), Potter and Wetherell (1987), Wetherell et al. (2001a, 2001b), Wiggins and Potter (2008) and Wood and Kroger (2000). For the rest of this chapter I will focus on a particular example, with the aim of illustrating the analytic mentality involved in discourse analytic research on talk.

Discursive Psychology and Naturally Occurring Talk

There are a wide range of different ways of analysing discourse. It is useful to make a distinction between studies that focus on the kinds of resources drawn on in discourse and the practices in which those resources are used. The emphasis here will be on the latter kind of study. What I will do is highlight some of the concerns that analysis works with, and one of the best ways of doing this is to work with some specific materials. It will try to avoid the common goal in writing about method that is to provide justifications to other academics rather than assist in the conduct of analysis itself.

Princess Diana and 'I dunno'

I have chosen to start with a piece of talk that is interesting, and probably familiar, at least in its broad outline, to many readers. It comes from a BBC television interview; the interviewer is Martin Bashir and the interviewee is the late Princess Diana Spencer.

Extract 1

Bashir:	The ↑Quee:n described nineteen ninety tw↓o: (0.2)
	as her (0.2) <u>annus</u> (0.4) <u>horribilis</u>>. (0.5)
Princess:	[((adjusts posture))]
Bashir:	[.Dhh and it was in <u>that</u>] year: that (0.2) Andrew
	Morton's book about you was <u>pub</u>lished.
Princess:	Mhm. ((nods and blinks))
Bashir:	Dhhh <u>did</u> ↑you ever: (0.6) <u>meet</u> ↓Andrew Morton,
	[or <u>per</u>sonally (.) help him with the] book?
Princess:	[((raises eyebrows, shakes head))]
Princess:	I never- (0.3) I [never <u>met</u> him.]
Princess:	[((shakes head))]
	(0.4)
Princess:	No.
	[(1.5)]
Princess:	[((shakes head and purses lips))] (0.8)
Bashir:	Did you ever (0.2) <u>per</u>sonally (0.2) as<u>sist</u>
	him with the writing of his book.
	(0.8)
Princess:	A lot of people .hhh ((clears throat))
	saw the dis<u>tress</u> (0.4) that my life (.) was (.) in. (0.8)
Princess:	And they felt- (0.8) felt it was a supportive thing to <u>h:e</u>lp. (1.0)
Princess:	In the way that they <u>did</u>. [(2.4)]
Princess:	[((purses lips))]
Bashir:	Did you: (0.6) al<u>low</u> your frien:ds, >your
	close friends< to speak to Andrew °Morton°?
Princess:	Yes I did. (1.0)
Princess:	((nodding)) Ye[s I d]id.
Bashir:	[°<u>Why</u>°.] (0.7)
Princess:	Hh I was: [(0.5) at the end of my <u>tether</u>.]
Princess:	[((shaking head))]
	(0.4)

Princess:	I was: [(0.9) <u>des</u>perate.]
Princess:	[((shaking head))]
	(1.5)
Princess:	>I ↑think I was so <u>fe</u>d up with being< (0.2) .h
	see:n (0.3) as someone who was a <u>ba:</u>sket <u>ca</u>se. (0.8)
Princess:	Cos I <u>am </u>a very strong <u>p</u>erson, .h (0.2)
	and I <u>know </u>(0.3) .h that causes <u>compli</u>cations. (0.8)
Princess:	In the <u>sy</u>stem (.) that I (0.4) <u>li</u>ve in.
	[(4.0)]
Princess:	[((smiles then purses lips))]
Bashir:	How would a <u>book </u>(0.7) <u>cha</u>nge that.
Princess:	[↑I dunno. .hh]
Princess:	[((raises eyebrows, looks away))]
	Maybe people have a better under<u>standing</u>, (0.6)
	maybe there's a lot of <u>wo</u>men out there, .h
	who <u>suffer.</u> (0.9)
Princess:	On the same level but in a different en<u>vi</u>ronment? (0.2)
Princess:	Who are unable to: .h (0.2) stand up for them<u>se</u>lves? (0.2)
Princess:	Becau:se (0.3) .h their self-esteem is (0.2)
	c-cut [into two, (0.2) I dun↑no]
Princess:	[((shakes head))]

(from *Panorama*, BBC1, 20 November 1995 – see the
Appendix for transcription conventions)

The first thing to note here is that even a short sequence of interaction of this kind is enormously rich, and could be the startpoint for a wide range of different studies. For example, conversation analysts have considered the way the different interactional roles of interviewer and interviewee are produced, and the way issues such as neutrality and evasiveness are managed (Clayman and Heritage, 2002). I am going to pick up a theme more characteristic of discursive psychology in particular. I am going to focus principally on just the two lines that have been arrowed–the two 'I dunno's'. Why these? There are three reasons, all of which illustrate different facets of doing discursive psychological research.

First, these fragments of talk relate to broader and established analytic concerns with fact construction and the role of descriptions in interaction. The point, then, is that although I have not come to this material with a pre-set hypothesis of the kind that a social psychologist might have when designing an experiment, my way into it is related to a wide range of prior interests, knowledge and concerns. However, there is nothing particularly special about the topic of fact construction; a range of different established interests could be brought to bear on this same material.

Second, these fragments are easily treated as the trivial details of interaction. If we were to make a precis of the interaction we would probably not draw attention to them. On the video they sound almost throwaway. However, one of the features of talk that has been strongly emphasised by Harvey Sacks (1992) and other conversation analysts is that what may seem to be minor details can be highly significant for interactants. Social scientists often treat talk as a conduit for information between speakers: there is a message and it is passed from one person to another. Roy Harris (1981) calls this the 'telementation view of language'. When we use this picture it is easy to imagine that what is important is some basic package of information, and then there is a lot of rather unimportant noise added to the signal: hesitations, pauses, overlaps, choice of specific words and so on. For discursive psychologists this view is fundamentally misguided. Rather than treating these features of talk as simply a blurred edge on the pure message, these features are treated as determining precisely what action is being performed as well as providing a rich resource that both participants and analysts use for understanding what that activity is.

It is for this reason that talk is carefully transcribed as it is delivered rather than being rendered into the conventional 'playscript' that is common in many kinds of qualitative work. Note that it is sometimes complained that such transcription is unnecessary, unhelpful or even – sin of sins – positivistic! However, it is important to remember that the playscript that often passes for transcript is itself highly conventionalised and makes a set of mainly inexplicit assumptions about interaction.

The third reason for focusing on 'I dunno' is that is provides a neat way of contrasting discursive psychology with a cognitive psychological approach to talk. What might a cognitive psychologist make of 'I dunno's'? There are all sorts of possibilities, but one approach that might be taken is to treat such utterances as 'uncertainty tokens'; that is, words or expressions that people use to report states of uncertainty. This would be in line with the general cognitive psychological approach of relating language use to an individual's cognitive processes and representations (Edwards, 1997). Considering 'I dunno's' therefore has the virtue of allowing us to compare and contrast a cognitive and discursive approach to talk.

One of the notable features of discourse research is that the best way start making sense of a set of materials like this may be to consider *other* materials or *other* sorts of findings. At its most basic, a good feel for some of the standard features of everyday and institutional talk is essential for producing high-quality analyses (Hutchby and Wooffit, 2008, provide a basic introduction and overview). In this case, I suggest that one of the ways into Princess Diana's 'I dunno's' is to consider the way issues of stake and interest have been conceptualised in discursive psychology.

Stake as a Participant's Concern

Work in the ethnomethodological and conversation analytic tradition has highlighted the centrality of accountability in interaction. Discursive psychologists dealing with psychological issues have emphasised the significance that participants place on issues of stake and interest (Edwards and Potter, 1992). People treat each other as entities with desires, motives, institutional allegiances and so on, as having a stake in their actions. Referencing stake is one principal way of discounting the significance of an action or reworking its nature. For example, a blaming can be discounted as merely a product of spite; an offer may be discounted as an attempt to influence.

Here is an explicit example where the speaker invokes an interest to undercut a (reported) claim. The extract is from a current affairs programme in which the author Salman Rushdie is being interviewed by David Frost. Frost is asking about the fatwa – the religious death sentence on Rushdie.

Extract 2

Frost: And how could they cancel it now? Can they cancel it – they say they can't.

→ Rushdie: Yeah, but you know, they would, wouldn't they, as somebody once said. The thing is, without going into the kind of arcana of theology, there is no technical problem. The problem is not technical. The problem is that they don't want to.

(Public Broadcasting Service, 26 November 1993 – their transcript)

Rushdie's response to the claim that the fatwa cannot be cancelled is to discount the claim as obviously motivated. The familiar phrase 'they would, wouldn't they' treats the Iranians' claim as something to be expected: it is the sort of thing that people with that background, those interests, that set of attitudes *would* say; and it formulates that predictability as shared knowledge. This extract illustrates the potential for invoking stake and interest to discount claims.

Both discourse and conversation analysts have stressed that where some difficulty or issue is widespread, there are likely to be some well-developed procedures for dealing with it. For example, given the established procedures that exist for managing turn taking we would expect there to be some procedures to exist for terminating conversations, and this is what is found (Levinson, 1983; Schegloff and Sacks, 1973). Or, to take a more discourse analytic example, given that scientists tend to keep separate the inconsistent repertoires of terms they use for justifying their own claims and undermining those of opponents, we would expect that some devices would be developed for dealing with situations where those repertoires come together; and this is what is found (Gilbert and Mulkay, 1984). Following this logic, we might expect to find procedures that people use to resist the kind of discounting seen in Extract 2.

Here is a candidate discursive technique for undermining discounting. It was not the product of a systematic search; rather, I came across it while reading the newspaper and thinking about this issue. It comes from an article in the *Guardian* newspaper headlined 'Psychiatrist reveals the agony and the lunacy of great artists'.

Extract 3

The stereotype of the tortured genius suffering for his art and losing his mind in a sea of depression, sexual problems and drink turns out to be largely true, a psychiatrist says today.

While scientists, philosophers and politicians can all suffer from the odd personality defect, for real mental instability you need to look at writers and painters, says Felix Post.

→   Dr Post was initially sceptical, but having looked at the lives of nearly 300 famous men he believes exceptional creativity and psychiatric problems are intertwined. In some way, mental ill health may fuel some forms of creativity, he concludes.

(*Guardian*, 30 June 1994)

The feature of the article that struck me was: 'Dr Post was initially sceptical'. Following the idea that all features of talk and texts are potentially there to do some kind of business, we can ask why this particular feature is there. What it seems to do is counter the potential criticism that Dr Post is perpetrating stereotypes about madness and creativity. His initial scepticism encourages us to treat his conclusions as factual because they are counter to his original interests. The facts forced him into this view.

I have suggested that such features of discourse can be understood by a medical analogy. People can avoid catching a disease such as tuberculosis by being inoculated against it. Perhaps in the same way conversationalists and writers can limit the ease with which their talk and texts can be undermined by doing a *stake inoculation* (Potter, 1996). Just as you have a jab to prevent the disease, perhaps you can inject a piece of discourse to prevent your talk being undermined.

Let me now stand back and highlight two features of the kind of analytic mentality I am working with. First, in common with conversation analysts, discursive psychologists are concerned to use evidence from the materials as far as possible rather than basing interpretations on their own prior assumptions about people, mind, society or whatever. In this case, note that the idea that there is a stereotype about madness and creativity is not my own – it is introduced in the text itself.

Moreover, the analysis does not depend on this stereotype actually existing, merely that it is invoked as an issue in this text. Second, note the way I have moved in this analysis between conversational and textual material. Discursive psychologists have been much more willing than conversation analysts to combine such materials. Moreover, they have tried to avoid making a priori assumptions about differences between the two. Both talk and texts are treated as oriented to action; *both* orient to issues of stake and may be inoculated against discounting.

'I dunno' as a Stake Inoculation

So far, then, I have emphasised some background considerations that might help us understand what Princess Diana's 'I dunno's' in Extract 1 are doing. One helpful way to continue the analysis is to collect some more examples of a similar kind. More formally, we might think of this as building a corpus for study or even coding of a set of data. Whatever we call it, the goal is to help the analyst see patterns and to highlight different properties of particular constructions. Although some of the initial procedures are superficially similar, the goal is not the content analytic one of providing counts of occurrences of particular kinds of talk within categories.

A search for 'I don't know's' through a set of materials taken from relationship counselling sessions provided Extract 4 below. The extract comes from the start of a long story in which the speaker, Jimmy, is describing a difficult evening in a pub with his wife, Connie. As well as Connie and Jimmy there is a counsellor present. One of the themes in the session is a series of complaints by Jimmy about Connie flirting with other men. At the same time Connie has made a number of suggestions that he is pathologically jealous and prone to seeing harmless sociability as sexual suggestion (Edwards, 1995b).

Extract 4

Jimmy: This ↑one particular night, (0.2)

anyway (0.2) there was uh: (1.2) I didn't-

Connie had made arrangements to ↑meet people.

(1.8)

And I didn't want to. (0.6)

It wasn't any other thing.

(1.6)

A:nd (0.8) we sat in the pub and

we (.) started to discuss=

=>we had a <u>li</u>ttle bit of a <u>row</u>.< (2.0)

In the pub. (0.6)

And <u>arg</u>uing about the time. (0.8)

U:m (.) whe:n these people came in. (.)

>It was:< (.) John and Caroline. (1.0)

And then they <u>had</u>- (.)

this <u>other</u> fella <u>Dave</u>.

^oWith them as well.^o

[6 lines omitted]

they <u>all</u> came in the pub anyway. (1.0)

Well (.) Connie sat beside (0.6) Caroline.

And I sat (further back).

So you was (.) you was split between us.

They <u>sat</u> in- on the <u>o</u>ther side.

(1.0)

[16 lines omitted]

And uh:: (1.0)

1→   Connie had a short skirt on

2→   I don't know. (1.0)

And I kn<u>ew</u> this- (0.6)

uh ah- maybe I <u>had</u> met him. (1.0) Ye:h. (.)

I musta met Da:ve before. (0.8)

But I'd h<u>ear</u>d he was a bit of a la:d ( ).

He <u>didn</u>'t care: (1.0) <u>who</u> he (0.2) chatted up or (.)

<u>who</u> was in Ireland (.) y'know

those were (unavailable) to chat up with.

(1.0)

So <u>C</u>onnie stood up (0.8)

pulled her skirt right up her side (0.6)

and she was looking <u>straight</u> at Da:ve (.)

>^olike that^o< (0.6)

(DE:C2:S1:10–11)

Let us start by considering Jimmy's description of Connie's skirt length (arrow 1). For Jimmy this description does some important business related to why they are here for counselling, and who has the problems that need fixing. The short skirt exemplifies something about Connie's character. It is a building block in the construction of Connie as 'flirty', making this an objective particular rather than just Jimmy's opinion. He is merely reporting something that she chose to wear rather than engaging in psychological judgement. However, the description is an especially delicate one, which means that Jimmy's stake in it is likely to be something to be scrutinised. The problem for Jimmy is that the description could be turned round and used as evidence that he is *precisely* the sort of pathologically jealous guy who obsessively remembers every detail of his partner's skirt length. That is, his description might generate problems for him as much as for Connie. How can he manage this delicacy?

It is immediately after the description of the skirt length that Jimmy says 'I don't know' (arrow 2). Why might he be saying just this just here? Let us consider the possibility that it attempts to head off the potential counter that Jimmy was jealously inspecting Connie's clothing, that he was *already* concerned about it even before the evening was under way? This interpretation is consistent with the detail of the sequence. Jimmy provides a description of Connie's skirt length that is part of his picture of *her* flirtatious behaviour, which, in turn, makes *his* own strong reaction more accountable. At the same time the expression of uncertainty works against the idea that *he* is saying this, noticing this, because *he* is pathologically jealous.

Why not treat the 'I don't know' as Jimmy straightforwardly reporting his uncertainty about this feature of the narrative? This would be in line with the cognitive psychological account of such utterances as 'uncertainty markers'. Can we adjudicate between these different interpretations of 'I don't know'? There are various ways we might go about this. One approach that discourse analysts have found particularly fruitful has been to look for variability between different versions. Variability is to be expected where people are constructing their talk in different ways to perform different actions – variability in and between versions can be an important clue to understanding what action is being done. In this case, for example, we can search the materials for other references to Connie's skirt length. We do not have to look very hard! The very first thing Connie says after Jimmy's long narrative is the following.

Extract 5

Connie: My skirt <u>prob</u>ably went up to about there. ((gestures))

Jimmy: ((gives a sharp intake of breath))

Connie: <u>May</u>be a bit <u>short</u>er. It was <u>done</u> for <u>no</u>- I never <u>look</u>ed at that particular bloke when I did it it was my friend commented

Oh you're <u>show</u>ing o:ff a lot o' leg tonight.

(DE:C2:S1:11)

Two things are particularly worth highlighting here. First, note that despite various dramatic events in Jimmy's long narrative of which this is just a fragment (including a suicide attempt) the very first thing that Connie picks out to contest is the description of her skirt length. In doing this she is displaying a skilled awareness of the relationship of descriptions to moral categories. This is a display that we can use to help support our own understanding of the working of this description.

Second, note that *here* Jimmy does not seem to be in any doubt about the precise length of Connie's skirt. His sharp, highly audible, inbreath is a display of disagreement with Connie's claim about her skirt length that occasions a grudging modification by Connie. The point, then, is that there is no evidence of Jimmy's cloudy memory – there is no 'I dunnoness' here; precision in skirt length now seems to be the order of the day. This variability supports the tentative discursive psychological interpretation of this 'I dunno' as a stake inoculation and it does not fit with the plain vanilla cognitive account in which the speaker merely reports their lack of certainty.

Let us return now to Martin Bashir's interview with Princess Diana Spencer. We are now in a better position to make some systematic suggestions about the 'I dunno's' in this passage of talk. We can start to make sense of their role in the management of stake and interest, and in particular their operation as stake inoculations.

The first thing we need to be confident of is that there is an orientation to issues of stake in this material. It is not hard to find. Bashir opens the sequence by formulating the relation between Andrew Morton's book and a hard year for the Queen (her well-known *annus horribilis*). Bashir then pursues a line of questioning to the Princess about her involvement with this book. He attempts to tease out for the viewing audience how responsible she is for this (negatively constructed) book.

Princess Diana responds to these questions with a series of denials, evasions, accounts and implicit versions of the role of the book (in that order in response to the first three questions). However, having accepted that she had some involvement with the book, if only via her friends, she is now faced with a tricky question about how the book make a positive contribution (how would a book change that?). This question is so tricky because of its potential for suggesting that Princess Diana has acted as a spurned and vindictive ex-wife, getting her revenge for a book that Prince Charles was involved with (mentioned soon after this extract). Given this issue of stake, we can make sense of the placement of the two 'I dunno's'. The uncertainty displayed in the answer to 'how would a book change all of that?' precisely manages the danger she will be seen as calculating and malevolent, a woman who has carefully planned her revenge. The 'I dunno's' help break the connection between her action of helping with the book and the potentially noxious identity implied in this action. Note the coordination of verbal and non-verbal here. Her first 'I dunno' is accompanied by what might be called a display of wondering – she looks into the distance as if never having been asked this before or had to think about it before. It is a lovely exhibition of psychological matters being attended to by both vocal and non-vocal actions.

This is by no means a definitive account of the role of 'I dunno' in Extract 1. And, of course, it does not address the very many other live and relevant features of the extract. However, what I have tried to do is show some of the procedures that can help build an interpretation of a piece of discourse, and the mentality that goes with such analysis. Let me list some of these features

Themes in the Analysis of Discourse

This chapter has attempted to overview some of the issues that arise when analysing discourse. Developing analytic skills is best characterised as developing a particular mentality. Discursive psychology is more inductive than hypothetico-deductive; generally work starts with a setting or particular discursive phenomenon rather than a preformulated hypothesis. The focus is on texts and talk as social practices in their own right. Part of the procedure of discursive psychology may involve the coding of a set of materials, but this is an analytic preliminary used to build a corpus of manageable size rather than a procedure that performs the analysis itself. There is nothing sacred about such codings and extracts are often freely excluded and included in the course of a programme of research.

Discursive psychology follows the conversation analytic assumption that any order of detail in talk and text is potentially consequential for interaction, and for that reason high-quality transcripts are used in conjunction with audio or video recordings. In addition, discursive psychology research generally avoids trading on analysts' prior assumptions about what might be called ethnographic particulars (e.g. participants' status, the nature of the context, the goals of the participants), preferring to see these as things that are worked up, attended to and made relevant in interaction rather than being external determinants.

Discursive psychology does not use talk and texts as a pathway to underlying cognitions; indeed, discursive psychology resolutely steers clear of cognitive reduction, instead treating purportedly cognitive phenomena as parts of social practices. It has focused, for example, on the way participants invoke stake and interest to understand and undercut accounts, and how such undercutting may be resisted by performing actions via accounts that are constructed as factual.

In this chapter I attempted to illustrate these themes by way of a discussion of 'I dunno' and 'I don't know'. I have considered only a small number of examples. However, I hope that the insights are more general (Wooffitt, 2005, takes the analysis further). Let me end with an extract from the US sitcom *Friends*. Even with my minimal, cleaned up transcription I think we can start to see the way the humour in the sequence depends on the sorts of features of 'I don't know' discussed above, and in particular the way each 'I don't know' manages the delivery of a piece of subtle psychological insight that generates trouble for the recipients. The sequence starts with Ross talking to a psychologist, Rodge, about his ex-wife.

Extract 6

Ross: You see that's where you're wrong! Why would
          I marry her if I thought on any level that
          she was a lesbian?

Rodge: I don't know. ((shrugs)) Maybe you wanted your   ←
          marriage to fail. ((laughs))

Ross: Why, why, why would I, why, why, why.

Rodge: I don't know. Maybe... Maybe low self esteem,   ←
          maybe to compensate for overshadowing a sibling.
          Maybe you w-

Monica: W- w- wait. Go back to that sibling thing.

Rodge: I don't know. ((shrugs)) It's conceivable that   ←
          you wanted to sabotage your marriage so the
          sibling would feel less like a failure in the eyes of
          the parents.

Ross: Tchow! That's, that's ridiculous. I don't feel
          guilty for her failures.

> (*The One with the Boobies*, 27 June 1996 – Ross is Monica's brother,
> Rodge is a psychologist boyfriend of Ross and Monica's friend.
> Note, each 'I don't know' is heavily emphasised)

Summary

This chapter overviewed discursive psychology. It described basic theoretical and methodological themes and distinguished discursive psychology from conversation analysis. The analytic approach of discursive psychology was introduced by way of an exploration of the role of 'I dunno' in different kinds of materials. This was interpreted in terms of participants managing their stake in particular delicate actions that they are performing.

Future Prospects

In the past decade discursive psychological work has increasingly focused on building programmes of work on large collections of talk taken from different institutional settings (helplines, neighbour mediation). It has moved beyond making theoretically targeted demonstrations of points to building full-scale studies that accumulate into programmes of work.

At the same time there has been an increasingly close engagement with conversation analysis such that at times the two perspectives overlap or merge. The enormous analytic rigour and system of conversation analysis has been an important influence on the development of discursive psychological work. It is likely that this close engagement will continue bearing analytic fruit as well as interesting debates.

In the past few years discursive psychologists have started to focus on video recordings of face-to-face interaction in family settings, with a particular focus on the coordination of action and how traditionally developmental issues (what can young children do?) become live for the participants. It is likely that work of this kind will continue with a focus on applied questions, for example relating to issues of health.

Questions

- Go through the differences between discursive psychology and conversation analysis. Try to decide which differences are most consequential for their different analytic practices (if any).
- Identify three questions that discursive psychologists might ask and one that they would not ask.
- Go through the *Friends* extract from the end of the chapter and carefully examine each 'I dunno' and consider the way it draws attention to the kinds of stake inoculation that such constructions can perform.

Recommended Reading

Edwards, D. (1997). *Discourse and Cognition.* London and Beverly Hills, CA: Sage.

Highlights the interplay of discursive psychology, ethnomethodology and conversation analysis with a range of analyses of psychological matters. A major work that rewards close study.

Potter, J. & Hepburn, A. (2008). Discursive constructionism. In J.A. Holstein & J.F. Gubrium (Eds). *Handbook of Constructionist Research* (pp. 275–293). New York: Guildford.

This shows how recent analytic work has combined discursive psychology and conversation analysis with the topic of constructionism.

Wiggins, S. & Potter, J. (2008). Discursive psychology. In C. Willig & W. Hollway (Eds). *The SAGE Handbook of Qualitative Research in Psychology* (pp. 72–89). London; Sage.

(Continued)

(Continued)

An overview of the different stages in discursive psychological research.

Wooffitt, R. (2005). *Conversation Analysis and Discourse Analysis: A Comparative and Critical Introduction*. London: Sage.

An excellent critical overview of these two traditions of work.

Internet Links

The Loughborough Discourse and Rhetoric Group website includes an up-to-date bibliography, information about methods, and examples of transcription alongside sound and video files. Many articles can be downloaded directly.

www.lboro.ac.uk/departments/ss/centres/darg/dargindex.htm

The Ethno/CA News site maintained by Paul ten Have contains a wealth of information about interaction research – up and coming meetings, and extensive bibliographies, including one specifically focused on discursive psychology.

www2.fmg.uva.nl/emca/

References

Antaki, C., Billig, M., Edwards, D. & Potter, J. (2003). Discourse analysis means doing analysis: A critique of six analytic shortcomings, *Discourse Analysis Online*, 1: www–staff.lboro.ac.uk/~ssca1/DAOLpaper.pdf

Billig, M. (1991). *Ideologies and Beliefs*. London: Sage.

Billig, M. (1996). *Arguing and Thinking: A Rhetorical Approach to Social Psychology*, 2nd edn. Cambridge: Cambridge University Press.

Button, G. & Sharrock, W. (1993). A disagreement over agreement and consensus in constructionist sociology. *Journal for the Theory of Social Behaviour*, 23 (1), 1–25.

Clarke, V., Kitzinger, C. & Potter, J. (2004). 'Kids are just cruel anyway': Lesbian and gay parents' talk about homophobic bullying. *British Journal of Social Psychology*, 43, 531–550.

Clayman, S.E. & Heritage, J. (2002). *The News Interview: Journalists and Public Figures on the Air*. Cambridge: Cambridge University Press.

Drew, P. (2005). Is confusion a state of mind? In H. te Molder & J. Potter (Eds). *Conversation and Cognition* (pp. 161–183). Cambridge: Cambridge University Press.

Drew, P. & Heritage, J.C. (Eds) (1992). *Talk at Work: Interaction in Institutional Settings*. Cambridge: University of Cambridge Press.

Edwards, D. (1994). Script formulations: A study of event descriptions in conversation. *Journal of Language and Social Psychology, 13* (3), 211–247.

Edwards, D. (1995a). Sacks and psychology. *Theory and Psychology, 5,* 579–596.

Edwards, D. (1995b). Two to tango: Script formulations, dispositions, and rhetorical symmetry in relationship troubles talk. *Research on Language and Social Interaction, 28,* 319–350.

Edwards, D. (1997). *Discourse and Cognition.* London and Beverly Hills, CA: Sage.

Edwards, D. (2003). Analysing racial discourse: The discursive psychology of mind-world relationships. In H. van den Berg, M. Wetherell & H. Houtkoop-Steenstra (Eds). *Analysing Race Talk: Multidisciplinary Approaches to the Interview* (pp. 31–48). Cambridge: Cambridge University Press.

Edwards, D. (2008). Intentionality and *mens rea* in police interrogations: The production of actions as crimes. *Intercultural Pragmatics, 5,* 177–199.

Edwards, D. & Potter, J. (1992). *Discursive Psychology.* London: Sage.

Edwards, D. & Potter, J. (2005). Discursive psychology, mental states and descriptions. In H. te Molder & J. Potter (Eds). *Conversation and cognition* (pp. 241–259). Cambridge: Cambridge University Press.

Edwards, D., Ashmore, M. and Potter, J. (1995). Death and furniture: The rhetoric, politics and theology of bottom line arguments against relativism. *History of the Human Sciences, 8,* 25–49.

Gergen, K.J. (2009). *An Invitation to Social Construction,* 2nd edn. London: Sage.

Gilbert, G.N. & Mulkay, M. (1984). *Opening Pandora's box: A Sociological Analysis of Scientists' Discourse.* Cambridge: Cambridge University Press.

Harris, R. (1981). *The Language Myth.* London: Duckworth.

Hepburn, A. & Potter, J. (2003). Discourse analytic practice. In C. Seale, D. Silverman, J. Gubrium & G. Gobo (Eds). *Qualitative Research Practice* (pp. 180–196). London; Sage.

Heritage, J.C. (1988). Explanations as accounts: A conversation analytic perspective. In C. Antaki (Ed.). *Analysing Everyday Explanation: A Casebook of Methods.* London: Sage.

Hutchby, I. and Wooffitt, R. (2008). *Conversation Analysis,* 2nd edn. Cambridge: Polity Press.

Levinson, S.C. (1983). *Pragmatics.* Cambridge: Cambridge University Press.

Phillips, L.J. & Jørgensen, M.W. (2002). *Discourse Analysis as Theory and Method.* London; Sage.

Potter, J. (1992). Constructing realism: Seven moves (plus or minus a couple). *Theory & Psychology, 2,* 167–173.

Potter, J. (1996). *Representing Reality: Discourse, Rhetoric and Social Construction.* London: Sage.

Potter, J. (2003a). Discursive psychology: Between method and paradigm. *Discourse & Society, 14,* 783–794.

Potter, J. (2003b). Discourse analysis and discursive psychology. In P.M. Camic, J.E. Rhodes & L. Yardley (Eds). *Qualitative Research in Psychology: Expanding Perspectives in Methodology and Design* (pp. 73–94). Washington, DC: American Psychological Association.

Potter, J. (2006). Cognition and conversation. *Discourse Studies, 8,* 131–140.

Potter, J. & Edwards, D. (2001). Discursive social psychology. In W.P. Robinson & H. Giles (Eds). *The New Handbook of Language and Social Psychology* (pp. 103–118). London: John Wiley & Sons.

Potter, J. & Hepburn, A. (2003). I'm a bit concerned: Early actions and psychological constructions in a child protection helpline. *Research on Language and Social Interaction, 36,* 197–240.

Potter, J. & Hepburn, A. (2005). Qualitative interviews in Psychology: Problems and possibilities. *Qualitative Research in Psychology, 2,* 281–307.

Potter, J. & Hepburn, A. (2008). Discursive constructionism. In J.A. Holstein & J.F. Gubrium (Eds). *Handbook of Constructionist Research* (pp. 275–293). New York: Guildford.

Potter, J. and Wetherell, M. (1987). *Discourse and Social Psychology: Beyond Attitudes and Behaviour.* London: Sage.

Sacks, H. (1992). *Lectures on Conversation,* Vols I & II, ed. G. Jefferson. Oxford: Basil Blackwell.

Schegloff, E.A. (1993). Reflections on quantification in the study of conversation. *Research on Language and Social Interaction, 26,* 99–128.

Schegloff, E.A. & Sacks, H. (1973). Opening up closings. *Semiotica, 7,* 289–327.

Silverman, D. (2007). *A Very Short, Fairly Interesting and Reasonably Cheap Book about Qualitative Research.* London: Sage.

Stokoe, E.H. (2003). Mothers, single women and sluts: Gender, morality and membership categorisation in neighbour disputes. *Feminism and Psychology, 13*(3), 317–344.

Te Molder, H. & Potter, J. (Eds) (2005). *Conversation and Cognition.* Cambridge: Cambridge University Press.

Wetherell, M. & Potter, J. (1992). *Mapping the Language of Racism: Discourse and the Legitimation of Exploitation.* London: Harvester, New York: Columbia University Press.

Wetherell, M., Stiven, H. & Potter, J. (1987). Unequal egalitarianism: A preliminary study of discourses concerning gender and employment opportunities. *British Journal of Social Psychology, 26,* 59–71.

Wetherell, M. Taylor, S. & Yates, S. (Eds) (2001a). *Discourse Theory and Practice: A Reader.* London; Sage.

Wetherell, M. Taylor, S. & Yates, S. (Eds) (2001b). *Discourse as Data: A Guide for Analysis.* London; Sage.

Widdicombe, S. & Wooffitt, R. (1995). *The Language of Youth Subcultures: Social Identity in Action.* London: Harvester/Wheatsheaf.

Wiggins, S. & Potter, J. (2008). Discursive psychology. In C. Willig & W. Hollway (Eds). *The SAGE Handbook of Qualitative Research in Psychology* (pp. 72–89). London; Sage.

Wood, L.A. & Kroger, R.O. (2000). *Doing Discourse Analysis: Methods for Studying Action in Talk and Text.* London: Sage.

Wooffitt, R. (2005). *Conversation Analysis and Discourse Analysis: A Comparative and Critical Introduction.* London: Sage.

Conversation Analysis: Practices and Methods

John Heritage

Abstract

This chapter outlines some of the basic procedures involved in the analysis of conversational interaction. It describes three levels of analytic engagement: sequence analysis, identification of conversational practices, and description of the order(s) of conversational organization in which these practices are involved. Focusing on the analysis of practices, it describes three interrelated elements in the analysis of a practice: (i) identifying its distinctive characteristics, (ii) locating it within the context of conversational sequences, and (iii) determining the role and intersubjective meaning of the practice. While the aim of identifying a practice in these ways involves examining it in the broadest range of social contexts to determine the extent to which it is contextually bounded, knowledge of the meaning and use of any practice can be used to shed light on the specific context of relevant conversational interaction. Because conversational practices are context-free, context-sensitive elements of human behavior, knowledge of their functioning can play a valuable role in ethnographic studies of the social world and in quantitative analyses of the causes and consequences of human interaction.

Keywords:

context, sequence, practice, reflexivity, comparison.

In this chapter, my aim is to give an overview of the methods of conversation analysis (CA) with a particular focus on ordinary conversation. To understand these methods, it is helpful to remember that they are designed to deal with fundamental features of human action and interaction. By the 1960s, there was a broad consensus on a number of these features:

1   *Human actions are meaningful and involve meaning-making.* Human actions (whether spoken or otherwise) are meaningful. Unlike the processes of the physical universe, they are goal directed and based on reasoning about the physical and social circumstances that persons find themselves in (Schütz 1962; Blumer 1969). This reasoning involves knowledge, socio-cultural norms and beliefs, and a grasp of the goals and intentions of others. Because goals, intentions, and the 'state of play' in interaction can change rapidly, this knowledge and reasoning is continuously updated during the process of interaction itself (Garfinkel 1967). Social interaction also involves *meaning-making.* Actions, no matter how similar or repetitive, are never identical in meaning (Garfinkel 1967; Blumer 1969). Each of them is singular, if only because it takes place in a new and singular situation. Each action therefore is, in some degree, creative in the meaning it creates and conveys.

2   *Actions achieve meaning through a combination of their content and context.* Self-evidently most spoken actions embody specific language content, describe specific circumstances, and implement specific actions just by virtue of the creative power of language. However, to this creativity of content must be added the creative power of context. The meaning of even the most formulaic of actions (such as 'okay,' 'mm hm' and so on) is in fact differentiated by context. The contextual variation (and specification) of action is a profound feature of human socio-cultural life, and a second major source of creativity and meaning-making in interaction that works in tandem with the creative power of language. Analysis of action cannot avoid this contextual variation without appearing superficial and irrelevant, not least because human beings exploit context in the construction of action. 'Context' is complex and layered. It embraces the immediately preceding action (someone just said or did something you have to respond to), through medial (that someone is an old friend), to distal (she is rather closer to your significant other than to you).

3   *To be socially meaningful, the meaning of actions must be shared.* Human actions are socially meaningful only to the extent that their meaning is shared by the actor, the recipient(s) of the act, and (sometimes) other observers. Absent this and actions will be unintelligible to others and will fail to achieve their desired objectives. The shared meaning of actions is constructed by the common use of methods for analyzing actions-in-context (Garfinkel 1967). This means that there must be procedures for persons to check whether their understandings about the meanings of earlier actions are correct, and of whether their responses are 'on target.' As persons construct interaction in an unfolding

sequence of moves, they will also have to keep score of 'where they are' in the interaction and of the interaction's 'state of play.' Like 'context,' shared (or 'intersubjective') meaning is also layered on a gradient from the most public (I asked you a question and you replied 'No'), to less public but available to some observers (your response betrays the fact that you are not an expert), to more private (your 'No' is rationalizing an unstated anxiety, or reflects a private promise you made to someone else).

4   *Meanings are unique and singular.* Actions function in particular ways to create meanings that are particular.

5   Implicit in the first three principles is the idea that actions and their meanings are highly particularized. At first sight the extraordinary singularity of human action would seem inimical to any sustained achievement of coherent meaning. Yet it works – somehow! A key to this working can be glimpsed in the contrast between the number of colors that are perceptible to the average human (around 7.5 million) and the basic color terms used by the average speaker of a language (between 8 and 11) (Heritage 1984a). Somehow all that particularity is being conveyed by very general descriptive terms (red, yellow, etc.). The key to the process is that most description takes place in plain sight of the colored object ('the guy in the red sweater,' 'the blue humming bird') and the color term can do its job by being amplified and particularized by its context ('that red would work better than that one'). Context elaborates the meanings of utterances. A similar principle applies in interaction: 'Is it serious?' is understood differently in the context of a sprained ankle and a cancer diagnosis. Context specifies meaning.

These four features of action have been discussed within the fields of anthropology and sociology for about 150 years, where they have mainly been considered as potential constraints on, or obstacles to, a natural science of society. Nonetheless these are the characteristics that a conception of interaction must come to terms with. Social participants somehow manage their interactions in daily life while coping with, and in fact actually exploiting, these characteristics of human conduct. Conversation analysis (CA) is a discipline that was developed to come to terms with, and model, these capacities.

Basic Principles of CA

Sequence

The foundational principles of CA tackle these four fundamental facts of human action by exploiting the concept of *sequence* (Schegloff 2007). The basic idea is that the most elementary context in which a turn at talk occurs is the immediately preceding turn at talk. It is a default assumption in human conduct that a current action should be, and normally will be, responsive to the immediately prior one. Indeed persons have to engage in special procedures (e.g., 'Oh by the way…') to show that a next action is *not* responsive to the prior.

The inherent turn-by-turn contextuality of conversation is a vital resource for the construction of understanding in interaction. Since each action will be understood as responsive to the previous one, the understanding that it displays is open for inspection. For example, in the following case, Ann's turn in line 1 is treated as an invitation by a response that 'accepts' it:

(1) Ann: Why don't you come and <u>see</u> me some [times.
     Bar: [I would like to

If, by contrast, Barbara had responded with an apology and an excuse:

(2) Ann: Why don't you come and <u>see</u> me sometimes.
     Bar: I'm sorry. I've been terribly tied up lately.

then it would have been apparent that Barbara had understood Ann's initial utterance as a complaint rather than an invitation (Heritage 1984a).

These two understandings are built into the design of the two different responses. They are apparent to observers but, and this is the important point, they are apparent to the participants: however the sequence plays out, Ann will find from Barbara's response how Barbara understood her and that Barbara has, or has not, understood her correctly.

We can take this analysis a step further by recognizing that at this point Ann knows how Barbara understood her turn, but Barbara does not know whether she understood it correctly. Continuation of the sequence allows Barbara to make this judgment (Schegloff 1992):

(3) Ann: Why don't you come and <u>see</u> me some [times.
     Bar: [I would like to
     Ann: I would like you to.

Ann's 'accepting' response to Barbara's acceptance confirms Barbara in her belief that she understood Ann correctly. But it could have gone otherwise:

(4) Ann: Why don't you come and <u>see</u> me some [times.

    Bar: [I would like to

    Ann: Yes but why <u>don't</u> you

In this second scenario, Barbara would see that her understanding of Ann's first turn at talk as an invitation was mistaken. Ann's response, which renews and indeed escalates her complaint, conveys that her original utterance was in fact intended to have been just that.

The sequential logic inherent in these examples is central to the construction of human interaction as a shared sense-making enterprise, regardless of its social context. Because it is the foundation of courses of conduct that are mutually intelligible, this logic underwrites both the conduct of social interaction and its analysis.

Practices

CA investigates interaction by examining the practices which participants use to construct it. A 'practice' is any feature of the design of a turn in a sequence that (i) has a distinctive character, (ii) has specific locations within a turn or sequence, and (iii) is distinctive in its consequences for the nature or the meaning of the action that the turn implements. Here are three examples of conversational practices:

(a) Turn-initial address terms designed to select a specific next speaker to respond (Lerner 2003):

(5) A: Gene, do you want another piece of cake?

(b) Elements of question design that convey an expectation favoring a 'yes' or a 'no' answer: in this case the word 'any' conveys an expectation tilted toward a 'no.':

(6) Prof: Do you have any questions?

(c) Oh-prefaced responses to questions primarily conveying that the question was inapposite or out of place (Heritage 1998):

(7) Ann: How are you feeling Joyce.=

    Joy: Oh fi:ne.

Organizations

The practices that CA finds in interaction cluster into organized collections that center on fundamental orders of conversational and social organization. Detailing these is beyond the scope of this chapter. Suffice it to say that some are clearly central to the management of interaction itself: these organizations, for example embrace clusters of practices that are associated with taking turns at talk; practices of repair that address systematic problems in speaking, hearing and understanding talk; and practices associated with the management of reference to persons and objects in the world (Schegloff 2006).

Other organizations of practices address more broadly social dimensions of interaction: a substantial number of practices are associated with the management of ties of social solidarity and affiliation between persons, favoring their maintenance and militating against their destruction; yet others are associated with the management of epistemic rights to knowledge between persons which is an important dimension of personal identity (Heritage 2008).

Methods for Studying Practices

CA methods for isolating and studying interactional practices have a good deal in common with the method of analytic induction, and in particular the constant comparative method and the search for deviant cases (Glaser and Strauss 1967). The method, of course, is specified to the interactional subject matter of CA as follows.

Stage 1: Deciding that a Practice is 'Distinctive'

First some practice, or candidate practice, will emerge as 'interesting' or worthy of pursuit. For simplicity, we will exemplify this with a fairly well-researched practice: the oh prefacing of responses to questions and other 'first actions' (Heritage 1984b, 1998, 2002). Initially the practice will likely emerge as 'vague' or 'imprecise' (Schegloff 1997). For example, at first sight, (8) and (9) (see below) look rather similar. In (8) Steve and Lesley are talking about the publishing magnate Robert Maxwell. Steve mentions that Maxwell's parents had suffered at the hands of the Nazis, whereupon Lesley infers that Maxwell is Jewish. Steve confirms this at line 8, beginning his turn with an 'oh' that is intonationally 'run into' the next component of his response as a single unit of talk (a single turn constructional unit; Sacks, Schegloff and Jefferson 1974).

(8) [Field:2:3:9]

```
 1 Ste:       Well he didn't either 'ee had a bad start I mean 'ee had 'iz
 2    1->     (0.3) .t.k.hh father shot by the Nazis 'nd is uh .hh mother
 3            died in: Auschvitz yih kno:w [so
 4 Les:                              [Oh really:?=
 5 Ste:       =So eez [had the: ( ] )-
 6 Les: 2->           [Oh 'z a le:w] is he Je:w?
 7            (.)
 8 Ste: 3->  Oh yeah.
 9            (.)
10 Ste:       He's had k- eez a Czechoslovakian Jew so ...
```

In (9) as part of an arrangements-making sequence, Ivy's question at line 5 is countered by one from Jane (lines 6–7). Ivy responds with 'oh' and subsequently a response to the question. Her 'oh' is intonationally distinct and seems to be its own unit of response, temporally separated from the subsequent answer (lines 8–10). At this point in the investigation, while it is clear that the two responses are distinctive, it is not clear that the distinction makes a difference in terms of the meaning of the actions they are performing.

(9) [Rah:C:1:(16):3]

```
 1 Ivy:       An' then (.) she'll pick you up on the way: down then as
 2            ah said.
 3            (0.3)
 4 Jan:       Well it's a [bit eh in a[h it
 5 Ivy: 1->              [Is         [Is that too early.
 6 Jan: 2->   eh- No: no it's not too early it's jist uh how long is she
 7            gon'to be in Middles[ber. Thi[s's the th[ing.
 8 Ivy: 3->                       [.hhh  [Oh:.   [She's got tuh be
 9            ho:me by .hh i-jis turned half past eleven quartuh tih
10            twelve.
```

So now we have a candidate practice: beginning a turn with the word 'oh'. We do not really know much about its meaning yet, and we do not really know whether 'beginning' means being part of the same unit of the talk that follows, or whether 'free-standing' cases followed by more talk from the same speaker are part of the same practice.

Stage 2: Locating the Practice Sequentially

At the end of stage 1, we have identified our phenomenon: the production of 'oh' at the beginning of a turn. We have located the practice within the turn, but not within particular sequences. As we now search for other instances, these will start to get clearer. Cases like the following start to pile up.

(10) [Heritage:01:18:2]

```
 1  Jan:        .t Okay now that's roas:' chick'n isn'it. Th[at ]=
 2  Ivy:                                              [It-]=
 3  Jan:        =[roasting chick'n<]
 4  Ivy: 1->    =[i t h a s bee:n ] cooked.
 5               (.)
 6  Ivy: 1->    It's been co[oked.
 7  Jan: 2->               [Iz ↑BEEN cooked.=
 8  Ivy: 3->    =Oh yes.
 9  Jan:        Oh well thaz good......
```

(11) [NB:II:2:R:7]

```
 1  Nan:        .....hhh one a'the other girls hadda leave
 2        1->   fer something en there I sit with all these (h)you(h)ng
 3        1->   fellas I fel'like a den [mother.
 4  Emm:                                [°Uh huh°
 5  Nan:        .hhh[hh
 6  Emm: 2->        [Are you th:e ol:dest one the cla:ss?
 7  Nan: 3->    °Oh: w- by fa:r.°
 8  Emm:        ↑Are yih rill[y?↑
 9  Nan: 3->                 [°Oh: ya:h.°
10  Emm:        Didju learn a lo:t'n cla:ss?
```

These cases are strongly consistent with (8). In each case, the first speaker (1->) makes an observation which is the object of a pretty obvious inference by the second (2->), whereupon the first speaker reaffirms it (3->), perhaps conveying that the second speaker was questioning something 'obvious' that did not need to be asked.

A further product of looking at these cases is that (9) starts to look different from the others. In this case a questioner turns out to have made incorrect assumptions about the situation being inquired into (arrow 1). Following the correction (arrow 2), the speaker uses a stand-alone 'oh' (arrow 3) to acknowledge the new understanding (Heritage 1984b) – and by implication her earlier misapprehension – before going on to address the newly revealed circumstances. This difference is reinforced by cases like (12) which concerns a mutual acquaintance who has been looking for a job:

(12) [Rah:II:1]

```
1  Ver:        And she's got the application forms.=
2  Jen: 1->    =Ooh:: so when is her interview did she sa[:y?
3  Ver:                                                 [She
4       2->    didn't (.) Well she's gotta send their fo:rm
5              back. Sh[e doesn't know when the [interview is yet.
6  Jen: 3->       [O h : : .                    [Oh it's just the
7              form,
```

Once again an initial question (1->) turns out to be based on faulty assumptions (2->), and a free-standing 'oh' registers that fact before its speaker goes on display a revised understanding of the situation (3->). We are ready, then, to say that (8) and (12) are distinctive from (9), (10) and (11).

Stage 3: Determining the Distinctive Role or Meaning of the Practice

It is clear enough from the materials to hand that oh-prefaced responses to questions often emerge in contexts where the question asks about something that has already been stated or strongly implied, and the answer to the question is therefore obvious or self-evident. But is there evidence that the participants orient to this role or meaning for the practice?

The clearest evidence emerges when the questioner who got an oh-prefaced response then defends the relevance of the question. This is what happens in (13) and (14):

(13) [TG:10]

```
1  Bee:  .  Dihyuh have any-cl- You have a class with Billy this te:rm?
2  Ava:     Yeh he's in my abnormal class.
3  Bee:     mnYeh [ how-]
4  Ava:           [Abnor]mal psy[ch.
```

5 Bee: 1->   [Still not gettin married,

6 Ava: 2=> .hhh <u>Oh</u> no. <u>De</u>finitely not.[married.]

7 Bee: 3->   [No he's] dicided [defin[itely?]

8 Ava: 4=>   [.hhh [O h] no.

9 Bee: 5-> 'hh Bec'z [las'] time you told me he said no: but he wasn't su:re,

10 Ava: [No.]

11 Ava: n:No definitely not. He, <u>he</u>'n Gail were like on the outs,

12   yihknow,

Here Bee defends her question at line 5, by reference to earlier statements she attributes to Ava about Billy's marital intentions being 'not sure' (3-> and 5->). And in (14) Ann defends her initial question by reference to what somebody else had told her about Joyce's health. As it turns out, Joyce had been unwell, but not very recently (line 5).

(14) [Frankel QC:I:2SO:1]

1 Ann: How are you feeling Joyce.=

2 Joy: Oh fi:ne.

3 Ann: 'Cause- I think Doreen mentioned that you weren't so well?

4   A few [weeks ago:?]

5 Joy: [Yeah,] Couple of weeks ago.

6 Ann: Yeah. And you're alright no:[w?

7 Joy: [Yeah.

In other cases, questioners may register that they already knew the answer, as in (15):

(15) [Frankel:TC:I:1:17]

1 Sus: =Yeh <u>y</u>ou guys er g'nna <u>d</u>rive up aren'tchu,

2 Mar: <u>Oh</u> yea:h.

3 Sus: -> That's what I <u>fi</u>gu[red.

4 Mar: [Yeh,=

Or that they have temporarily forgotten the circumstances that make the question inappropriate, as in (16) lines 4 and 6:

(16) [Frankel TC:1:1:15-16]

1 Sus: .hhh So if you guys want a place tuh <u>sta</u>:y.

2   (0.3)

3 Mar: .t.hhh Oh (w-) <u>th</u>ank you but you we ha- yihknow <u>Vic</u>tor.

4 Sus: ->   ↑O<u>H</u> that's ↑RIGHT.=

5 Mar: =<u>Th</u>at's why we were <u>g</u>oing [(we)

6 Sus: ->   [I FER↑<u>GO</u>:T. Comp<u>le</u>tely.

Or the oh-prefaced response producer may assert that her answer is self-evident. In the following case the issue is whether Nan is prepared to phone a service engineer:

(17) [Holt 1:5:5]

1 Les: .hh Are <u>you</u> going tuh phone i:m?

2   (0.3)

3 Nan: ->   O<u>h</u> no: I-<u>::</u> (.) can't sp<u>e</u>ak tuh <u>any</u>one on the phone <u>as</u> you

4   ->   kn<u>o</u>-:w, .hh but uh-: (0.3) if h<u>e</u> will ca<u>:</u>ll, (0.2) and have

5   a look an' see: if there's a <u>l</u>eak.h up the:re,

Reprise

Our practice – oh-prefacing a response to a question – is now very robust. (i) It has a definite 'shape': the 'oh' must be turn-initial and part of a larger unit of talk, not a separate free-standing element of it. (ii) It is located in a specific sequential position: in response to a question. And (iii) It has a determinate 'meaning' that is reflected in a variety of responses to its production. The position our analysis has arrived at is presented in Table 12.1.

A Context-free Practice

One of the chief objectives of basic CA is to identify bedrock practices of interaction, whose meaning and significance are fundamental and obdurate. To this end, an important test is to make sure that practices operate in a stable way across a wide range of social contexts.

   With this in mind, consider the following example from a broadcast interview with Sir Harold Acton, conducted by the British broadcaster Russell Harty. The topic is Acton's life in China and his work as a teacher of T.S. Eliot's poetry at Beijing University. At this point, Harty ventures to ask him if he speaks Chinese:

TABLE 12.1   *Two types of turn-initial 'oh'*

Type of turn-initial 'oh'	Position	Role or meaning of the practice
Prefacing 'oh'	As a response to a question	Showing that the answer to a question was self-evident and that the question need hardly be asked
Free-standing 'oh' + more talk	As a response to an answer to a question	Registering the answer to the question as informative

(18) [Chat Show: Russell Harty–Sir Harold Acton]

```
 1  Act:      ....hhhh and some of thuh- (0.3) some of my students
 2             translated Eliot into Chine::se. I think thuh very
 3             first.
 4             (0.2)
 5  Har:      Did you learn to speak (.) Chine[:se.
 6  Act:  ->                                 [.hh Oh yes.
 7             (0.7)
 8  Act:      .hhhh You cah::n't live in thuh country without speaking
 9             thuh lang[uage it's impossible .hhhhh=
10  Har: ->            [Not no: cour:se
```

Acton's response (line 6) is oh-prefaced, and plainly treats it as self-evident that he 'speaks Chinese.' And he elaborates it with an observation about how necessary it is to speak the language of a host country (lines 8–9). For his part, Harty acknowledges the self-evident truth of this observation with his *sotto voce* 'Not no: cour:se'. Here then the practice is deployed to very similar effect in a very different social setting – a celebrity interview – than in the cases we have seen so far. News interviews contain very many instances of this type.

Similarly in the following case, a doctor finds himself on the receiving end of this practice – in this case, the patient is quite elderly:

(19) [Routine physical]

```
 1  DOC:      Hi Missis Mar[:ti:n,
 2  PAT:                   [Hi (there)
 3  DOC:      How are you toda:[:y,
 4  PAT:  1->                  [Oh pretty goo:d,
 5             (.)
 6  DOC:      How are you fee:ling.
```

7 DOC: 2-> The l[ast time I saw you you had br<u>o</u>ken that ↑ri:b.↑=

8 PAT: [Oh oka:y,

9 PAT: =Mm hm:,

10 DOC: Are you d<u>o</u>ing a little bit b<u>e</u>tter:,

Similar to (14), the doctor's 'how are you' question (line 3), together with his 'follow-up' 'how are you feeling' (line 6), solicit health 'updates' from the patient (Robinson 2006). Both, however, inherit oh-prefaced responses. By line 7, the doctor defends the relevance of his question by invoking the patient's earlier broken rib as grounds for his inquiry. Here too, in the context of the medical consultation, our practice is robust.

A Context-Sensitive Practice and Exploitations

Robust interactional practices like oh-prefacing have the property of 'reflexivity': they can export the meaning that is anchored in routine exchanges into non-routine situations. Here is an example from the celebrated trial of O.J. Simpson in Los Angeles, as narrated by a journalist:

(20) [Margolick 1995]

She [Marcia Clark] also asked Mr. Kaelin whether the place Mr. Simpson took him to eat earlier that evening was not a McDonald's but a Burger King. It was a clear reference to published reports, heretofore entirely unsubstantiated, that Mr. Simpson and Mr. Kaelin went out in the evening of June 12 not to purchase hamburgers and french fries but drugs. 'Oh no,' Mr. Kaelin replied, almost in wonder that such a question would be asked.

And, transparently exploitative is this reply from one of the police officers on trial for the infamous beating of Rodney King who is asked about the videotaped evidence that was used in the prosecution case:

(21) [Goodwin 1994:618]

1 Pro: You can't look at that video and say that every

2   one of those blows is reasonable can you.

3   (1.0)

4 Powell: -> Oh I <u>can</u> if I put my perceptions in.

As Goodwin (1994) shows, the defense case rested entirely on reinterpreting the apparently incriminating video record, and it is the determination to insist on this reinterpretation which is expressed in Powell's oh-prefaced rebuttal of a prosecutor's question that implied that the record is a self-evident basis for a conviction.

In other contextual exploitations, the practice can be used to resist or otherwise 'blow off' new topic beginnings that are unwanted. Thus in (22), Agnes has an unpleasant psoriasis infection in her toenails. Her sister knows about the infection in one foot, but not the other. Thus the initial question is about the 'known about' foot:

(22) [NB:I:6:13]

```
1 C:      How's yer foot?
2 A: ->   Oh it's healing beautif'lly!
3 C:      Goo[::d.
4 A: =>        [The other one may haftuh come off, on the other
5              toe I've got in that.
```

As it turns out the 'known about' foot is healing well, but the oh-preface to this announcement is managed so as to indicate that this is not 'the foot' that Agnes wants to talk about. As her sister responds to the good news at line 3, Agnes starts to talk about the unasked about, 'other' foot in lies 4–5. Here the practice of oh-prefacing is exploited to index the undesirability of one topic in favor of another.

A similar example is given below. Here a question about the recipient's sister starts to attract an oh-prefaced response (line 2). This response is abandoned as the question is expanded to include the sister's husband:

(23) [JG:6:8:2]

```
1 M:      How's your sister an' [her husband?
2 L: ->                         [Oh t'che
3 L:      Well as a matter of fact uh ih Dawn is alright.
4         She had a very very bad cold the last month.
5     =>  An' Charlie is: had a very serious operation. Surgery on the
6         gal, g'll bladder. But I guess he's alright. But .hhh at
7         his age maybe it's a little roughhh.
8 M:      No more wild game hunting 'uh?
```

Subsequent to this, the oh-prefaced response is abandoned in favor of a brief update about the sister, followed by a shift to the husband, who has had the more serious health problem.

Other very refined context-sensitive exploitations of the practice include usages designed to entrap recipients in troubles-telling environments. In the following

case, Jo deploys an oh-prefaced downgraded response to a 'how are you' question
(Sacks 1975; Jefferson 1980; Heritage 1998):

```
(24) [Lerner:SF:I:2:SO]
  1  Mar:         How you doing.
  2  Jo:   a->    Oh: pretty goo:d
  3              (0.8)
  4  Mar:        .hhhhhh[(          )
  5  Jo:   a'->         [This week, hhhhhhehh heh heh [.hhh
  6  Mar: b->                                         [.tlk Oh this week?
  7  Jo:          =hih hheeh, ˙hhh Yea:h. (˙hh-)
  8              (0.2)
  9  Mar: b->    Why what's goin on this week.
 10  Jo:   c->     Oh nothing. I'm j'st inna: (˙) rilly good mood this ( [ )
 11  Mar:                                                  [Oh: good.
 12              (0.8)
 13  M?:         ˙tlk=
 14  Jo:   d->   I have my highs'n lows . . .
```

There is, of course, nothing redundant or inappropriate about a 'how are you' question at the beginning of a phone call (Schegloff 1986), and a response that treats it
in such a way is patently designed to exploit the practice to draw attention to an
underlying problem. Other elements in Jo's subsequent turns are designed to the
same effect, especially the qualifying 'This week,' (line 5) and her reference to her
'highs'n lows' (line 14).

Intermission

Let us pause to take stock of this examination of methods of CA. We began with
a practice – oh-prefacing – that we started to distinguish from starting a turn
with a free-standing 'oh'. We distinguished environments in which this practice
was used: these clustered around 'redundant' questions that reinvoked or reques-
tioned something that had already been said or strongly implied. We then moved
to show other aspects of the sequence that showed the parties' orientation to the
self-evident nature of what was questioned. Finally, we showed that this meaning

of oh-prefacing could be exploited in contexts where what is being questioned is not at all self-evident or redundant. In these latter contexts, this 'why are you asking' meaning of an oh-prefaced response is used manipulatively.

It is often suggested that CA lacks a sensitivity to 'context' and yet, if my comments about the motivation of CA at the beginning of this chapter have any meaning, this suggestion is quite paradoxical. I would rather suggest that basic CA has exquisitely nuanced orientations to the contextuality of talk, *but that this orientation is deployed in the interest of exploring the limits of the context-free meaning of a practice, as well as its context-sensitive uses*. It is these limits and these uses that we have been examining, albeit briefly, in this chapter.

Ethnographic Context and the Uses of CA

As I suggested at the beginning of this chapter, 'contexts' and 'understandings' have many layers, some of which are clearly outside of any particular interaction. Every defined sequential context has its context in the larger conversation, in the sequence of such conversations that have occurred between these participants, in the enduring social relations between the participants and their biographical and emotional tenor, and in the webs of social relations in which the participants are enmeshed both separately and together. Some of this can be reported by the participants in interviews, or observed in other settings, and some of this may not be so observable. Can CA help in exhibiting the 'traces' of these relationships and structural connections in the concrete details of interactions? In this section, I will illustrate what I take to be the 'ethnographic' value of CA in this kind of a context, using the practice – oh-prefacing – that we have been working with.

Consider this datum in which a patient is asked a series of 'lifestyle' questions. Here a middle-aged woman, the owner–manager of a restaurant with a daughter aged 28, who is hypertensive and on medication, is asked about her alcohol use (line 11). The question is devoid of a verb and is elliptical as between the polar question 'Do you use alcohol?' and the more presupposing 'How much alcohol do you use?' This design allows the clinician to circumvent the 'yes/no' question, while permitting the patient to decide how to frame a response. After a 1 second silence (a substantial period of time in an engaged state of interaction) during which the patient assumed a 'thinking' facial expression, the patient articulates a sound which conveys pensiveness ('hm::'), and then offers an estimate ('m_oderate'), concluding her turn with 'I'd say' which retroactively presents her response as an estimate, albeit a 'considered' one. Though presented as a 'considered opinion,' and in scalar terms, the patient's estimate is unanchored to any objective referent. The scene is now set for a pattern of questioning designed to extract a quantitative estimate from the patient.

(25) [MidWest 3.4:6]

```
 1  DOC:       Are you married?
 2             (.)
 3  PAT:       No.
 4             (.)
 5  DOC:       You're divorced (°cur[rently,°??)
 6  PAT:                       [Mm hm,
 7             (2.2)
 8  DOC:       tch D'you smoke?, h
 9  PAT:       Hm mm.
10             (5.0)
11  DOC: ->    Alcohol use?
12             (1.0)
13  PAT:       Hm:: moderate I'd say.
14             (0.2)
15  DOC:       Can you define that, hhhehh ((laughing outbreath))
16  PAT:       Uh huh hah .hh I don't get off my- (0.2) outa
17             thuh restaurant very much but [(awh:)
18  DOC: ->                                 [Daily do you use
19             alcohol or:=h
20  PAT:       Pardon?
21  DOC: ->    Daily? or[:
22  PAT:  =>            [Oh: huh uh. .hh No: uhm (3.0) probably::
23             I usually go out like once uh week.
```

The physician begins this effort by inviting the patient to 'define' moderate (line 15). As he concludes his turn, he looks up from the chart and gazes, smiling, directly at the patient, and briefly laughs. Laughter in interaction is quite commonly associated with 'misdeeds' of various sorts (Jefferson 1985, Haakana 2001). Because the laughter in this case is not targeted at a single word or phrase (Jefferson 1985) but follows the physician's entire turn, it will, by default, be understood as addressing the entire turn. In this case, it appears designed to mitigate any implied criticism of the patient's turn as insufficient or even self-serving.

In her reply, the patient begins with responsive laughter (Jefferson 1979) but does not continue with a 'definition.' Instead she takes a step back from that to remark 'I don't get...outta thuh restaurant very much but,' but her subsequent development of this line is interdicted by the clinician. While this remark may be on its way to underwriting a subsequent estimate, its proximate significance is to convey the context of her alcohol use, or 'how' she drinks. Specifically this remark purports to indicate that her drinking is 'social': she does not drink alone in her apartment, nor does she drink on the job. In this way, the patient introduces a little of her 'life-world' circumstances into the encounter, conveying that her drinking is 'healthy' or at least not suspect or problematic.

The clinician now pursues a measurable metric for the patient's alcohol use by asking 'D̲aily do you use alcohol or:=h'. The question invites the patient to agree that she uses alcohol on a daily basis, thereby permitting her to take a step in the direction of acknowledging a 'worst case scenario' (Boyd and Heritage 2006) for alcohol use. The movement of the word 'daily' from its natural grammatical position at the end of the sentence to the beginning has the effect of raising its salience, presenting a frequency estimate as the type of answer he is looking for. Finally, the 'or' at the end of the sentence invites some other measure of frequency, and thereby reduces the physician's emphasis on 'daily' as the only possible (or most likely) frequency for the patient to deal with.

At this point, although the physician and patient are no more than 2 feet apart, the patient's response to the question is to ask for its repetition. Drew (1997) observes that these kinds of repeat requests are produced in two contexts: (i) when there is a hearing problem or, alternatively, (ii) when there is a problem in grasping the relevance of the talk to be responded to. A hearing problem is out of the question because of the objective circumstances of the participants, and it is subsequently ruled out by the conduct of both of them. Not so the 'relevance' problem. After all, the patient's remark at lines 9 and 10 (that she didn't get out of the restaurant 'very much') was most likely on its way to suggesting that she didn't have many opportunities to drink. The transition from this implication to an inquiry about whether she drinks on a 'daily' basis may indeed have been somewhat jarring, and difficult to process.

Earlier it was suggested that the parties ruled out a 'hearing problem' as the basis for the patient's request for repetition. The physician rules this out when, rather than fully repeating his previous question, he repeats a reduced form in which only the two most salient words are left: 'daily' and 'or.' Only a full repeat would have been compatible with a belief that his patient had not heard him. A drastically reduced repeat like this one conveys, to the contrary, that he believes she did hear him. For her part, the patient confirms this analysis when she proves fully able to respond to this abbreviated repeat, beginning before it is even concluded. Here then the objective circumstances of the interaction and the actual conduct of the parties is compatible with only one interpretation of the patient's 'Pardon?': that it expressed a difficulty with the relevance of the question.

This same difficulty is expressed in a different way when the patient begins to respond. The response includes 'huh uh,' a casual and minimizing version of 'no' designed to indicate that 'daily?' is far off the mark. It is also oh-prefaced, which as we have seen in this chapter conveys that the question was irrelevant or inapposite. Here we see the patient exploit the practice to assert the fundamental inappropriateness of the physician's question and to exert 'push back' against its terms, effectively dismissing it out of hand.

After she rejects the physician's frequency proposal of 'daily' as an estimate of her alcohol consumption, the patient finally comes up with an estimate of her own: 'once a week.' However, she packages this as an estimate of how frequently she 'goes out.' This framing has two consequences: (i) it estimates her actual drinking in an implicit way, leaving it to the clinician to draw the relevant inference; and (ii) it renews her insistence on the social, and morally acceptable, nature of her drinking, implicitly ruling out, for example, solo drinking at work, or at night after work.

With lines 15–16, physician and patient have arrived at a compromise: the physician has a frequency estimate of the patient's drinking, while the patient has been able to retain her focus on 'how' she drinks. At line 17, the physician turns to the patient's chart and starts to write, subsequently acknowledging the patient's response with a sotto voce 'okay' and terminating the sequence.

The transactions of this sequence will be relatively familiar to most qualitative sociologists studying medicine. Physicians need anchored, and preferably quantitative, information as a basis for clinical judgments; patients are often inclined to give more contextualized descriptions. These different orientations were conceptualized by Elliot Mishler (1984) in terms of the 'voice of medicine' with its technical priorities, and the 'voice of the lifeworld' with its experiential grounding. Mishler portrayed these two orientations as in conflict with one another, and this conflict is apparent in this datum. Yet it is a conflict which is effectively mandated by the positions of clinician and patient. In particular, there may be a special vulnerability for patients who offer quantitative estimates of their drinking too readily or too 'technically', (e.g., 'Twenty units a week.'). Patients who are tempted to respond in this manner may reflect that it could be treated as portraying too great a preoccupation with alcohol consumption, a preoccupation which is itself suspect and may attract further inquiry. Persons do not 'talk this way' about alcohol in everyday life and, even in the doctor's office, too radical a departure from ordinary ways of talking about ordinary concerns may be undesirable (Sacks 1984).

Here then, though it is but one practice of many deployed in this sequence, our findings about the nature of oh-prefaced responses give us an element of solid interpretive anchorage in this sequence. They do so because, as we already know, these findings are highly robust.

Conclusion

In this chapter, we have worked with a practice which is robust, and which has been directly validated, not by surveys or psychological testing, but by direct observation of the conduct of persons in a wide variety of settings. This gives our observations about this practice exceptional validity, and allows it to be reliably used as an interpretive resource in ethnographic interpretations of data, and as a quantitative measure or index, if required (cf. Clayman et al. 2007; Heritage et al. 2007).

This practice is but a small cog in a large organization of practices concerned with the management of epistemic relations between persons. These relations concern who knows what, who has rights to know it, and describe it, who knows better than whom, and with what certainty, recency and authority. Large numbers of practices are devoted to this business and it is not surprising that they are, for personhood and identity are deeply implicated in the ways in which we patrol the boundaries of our knowledge preserves, and defend our sovereign epistemic territories against overzealous incursion by others, or against trampling by invaders who care little for our culture, identity or personhood. In the end, it is the cumulative weight of all these practices that allows interactants to live in a densely organized and meaningful social world, and which gives the world of social interaction, and the institutions instantiated in social interaction, their robustness and nuance. For all these reasons and more these practices matter for CA. CA's wholesale effort to map the whole 'genome' of interactional practices is mandated by their extraordinary significance.

Summary

This chapter has focused on the process of identifying, defining and understanding the meaning of specific interactional practices deployed in ordinary interaction. This process involves extracting the practice from a large variety of contexts in order to establish the extent to which it is context free. Once this is determined, the practice (together with many others) can become the basis for narrowing the range of plausible interpretations of context, intention and meaning in indefinitely many other scenes of interaction. The worked example – oh-prefacing an answer to a question – is presented as a typical example of conversation analytic practice.

Future Prospects

The last 10 years have witnessed a wholesale expansion of CA as a research method in a wide variety of fields, including education, medicine, the study of legal process, human–machine interaction and software engineering. CA is currently practiced in around half the world's countries. Applied and cross-linguistic work is proceeding apace. The time has arrived for more attention to the fundamentals of CA – in particular, the analysis of basic conversational practices – on which applied research ultimately depends.

Questions

- What elements of methodology are shared by CA and ethnography?
- How are these elements specified in CA research?
- How do the methods differ?
- How are practices 'located' in interaction?
- What is meant by the 'reflexive' feature of practices?
- How does CA embody two different ways of approaching the role and significance of 'context' in interaction?

Recommended Reading

Paul ten Have (2007). *Doing Conversation Analysis: A Practical Guide*. Second Edition. London: Sage.

Jack Sidnell (2010). *Conversation Analysis*. Boston, MA: Wiley-Blackwell.

John Heritage and Steven Clayman (2010). *Talk in Action: Interactions, Identities and Institutions*. Boston, MA: Wiley-Blackwell.

Tanya Stivers and Jack Sidnell (eds.) (2011). *The Blackwell Handbook of Conversation Analysis*. Boston, MA: Wiley-Blackwell.

Internet Links

Ethnomethodology and conversation analysis newsletter *Ethno/CA News:*

www2.fmg.uva.nl/emca/

Emanuel A. Schegloff's transcription training module:

www.sscnet.ucla.edu/soc/faculty/schegloff/TranscriptionProject/

Loughborough University CA site:

www-staff.lboro.ac.uk/~ssca1/sitemenu.htm

References

Blumer, Herbert 1969. The methodological position of symbolic interactionism. In Blumer Herbert (ed.) *Symbolic Interactionism: Perspective and method*. Englewood Cliffs, NJ: Prentice Hall, 1–60.

Boyd, Elizabeth and John Heritage 2006. Taking the history: Questioning during comprehensive history taking. In John Heritage and Douglas Maynard (ed.), *Communication in Medical Care: Interactions between Primary Care Physicians and Patients*. Cambridge: Cambridge University Press, 151–184.

Clayman, Steven E., John Heritage, Marc N. Elliott and Laurie McDonald 2007. When does the watchdog bark? Conditions of aggressive questioning in presidential news conferences. *American Sociological Review* 72: 23–41.

Drew, Paul 1997. 'Open' class repair initiators in response to sequential sources of trouble in conversation. *Journal of Pragmatics* 28: 69–101.

Garfinkel, Harold 1967. *Studies in Ethnomethodology*. Englewood Cliffs, NJ: Prentice Hall.

Glaser, Barney G. and Anselm L. Strauss 1967. *The Discovery of Grounded Theory: Strategies for Qualitative Research*. Chicago: Aldine.

Goodwin, Charles 1994. Professional vision. *American Anthropologist* 96(3): 606–633.

Haakana, Markku 2001. Laughter as a patient's resource: Dealing with delicate aspects of medical interaction. *Text* 21(1): 187–219.

Heritage, John 1984a. *Garfinkel and Ethnomethodology*. Cambridge: Polity Press.

Heritage, John 1984b. A change-of-state token and aspects of its sequential placement. In J. Maxwell Atkinson and John Heritage (eds.), *Structures of Social Action*. Cambridge: Cambridge University Press, 299–345.

Heritage, John 1998. Oh-prefaced responses to inquiry. *Language in Society* 27(3): 291–334.

Heritage, John 2002. *Oh*-prefaced responses to assessments: A method of modifying agreement/disagreement. In Ceci Ford, Barbara Fox and Sandra Thompson (eds.), *The Language of Turn and Sequence*. Oxford: Oxford University Press, 196–224.

Heritage, John 2008. Conversation analysis as social theory. In Bryan Turner (ed.), *The New Blackwell Companion to Social Theory*. Oxford: Blackwell.

Heritage, John, Jeffrey D. Robinson, Marc Elliott, Megan Beckett and Michael Wilkes 2007. Reducing patients' unmet concerns: the difference one word can make. *Journal of General Internal Medicine* 22: 1429–1433.

Jefferson, Gail 1979. A technique for inviting laughter and its subsequent acceptance/ declination. In George Psathas (ed.), *Everyday Language: Studies in Ethnomethodology*. New York, Irvington Publishers, 79–96.

Jefferson, Gail 1980. On 'trouble-premonitory' response to inquiry. *Sociological Inquiry* 50: 153–185.

Jefferson, Gail 1985. An exercise in the transcription and analysis of laughter. In Teun A. Dijk (ed.), *Handbook of Discourse Analysis*, Vol. 3. New York: Academic Press, 25–34.

Lerner, Gene 2003. Selecting next speaker: The context sensitive operation of a context-free organization. *Language in Society* 32: 177–201.

Margolick, David 1995. Simpson friend testifies of events before killings. *The New York Times*, March 23, p. A8.

Mishler, Elliot 1984. *The Discourse of Medicine: Dialectics of Medical Interviews*. Norwood, NJ: Ablex.

Robinson, Jeffrey D. 2006. Soliciting patients' presenting concerns. In John Heritage and Douglas Maynard (eds.), *Communication in Medical Care: Interactions between Primary Care Physicians and Patients*. Cambridge: Cambridge University Press, 22–47.

Sacks, Harvey 1975. Everyone has to lie. In M. Sanches and B.G. Blount (eds.), *Sociocultural Dimensions of Language Use*. New York: Academic Press, 57–80.

Sacks, Harvey 1984. On doing 'being ordinary.' In J. Maxwell Atkinson and John Heritage (eds.), *Structures of Social Action*. Cambridge: Cambridge University Press, 413–429.

Sacks, Harvey 1992 [1964–1972]. *Lectures on Conversation*, (2 Vols.). Oxford: Basil Blackwell.

Sacks, Harvey, Emanuel A. Schegloff and Gail Jefferson 1974. A simplest systematics for the organization of turn-taking for conversation. *Language* 50: 696–735.

Schegloff, Emanuel A. 1986. The routine as achievement. *Human Studies* 9: 111–151.

Schegloff, Emanuel A. 1992. Repair after next turn: The last structurally provided defence of intersubjectivity in conversation. *American Journal of Sociology* **95**(5): 1295–1345.

Schegloff, Emanuel A. 1997. Practices and actions: Boundary cases of other-initiated repair. *Discourse Processes* **23**(3): 499–545.

Schegloff, Emanuel A. 2006. Interaction: The infrastructure for social institutions, the natural ecological niche for language and the arena in which culture is enacted. In N.J. Enfield and Stephen C. Levinson (eds.), *The Roots of Human Sociality: Culture, Cognition and Interaction*. New York: Berg, 70–96.

Schegloff, Emanuel A. 2007. *Sequence Organization in Interaction: A Primer in Conversation Analysis*, Vol. 1. Cambridge: Cambridge University Press.

Schütz, Alfred 1962. Commonsense and scientific interpretations of human action. In Maurice Natanson (ed.), *Alfred Schütz Collected Papers*, Vol. 1, *The Problem of Social Reality*. The Hague: Martinus Nijhoff.

PART VI
VISUAL DATA

Conceptualizing Visual Data ⬤ 13

Michael Emmison

Abstract

This chapter presents an innovative way of thinking about visual research which is designed to overcome many of the ambiguities and shortcomings which are currently evident. A number of problems and tensions in current visual research practice are identified which stem from its failure to recognize that its principal currency – photographs – are primarily a means to collect and represent information and that there is no necessary unity in the disparate social and cultural phenomena which photographic images depict. As a consequence, it is argued, there is a great deal of confusion as to what the subject matter and methodological practices of visual research should be. An alternative approach which focuses instead on the visible aspects of social life, and the contexts in which these are observed or encountered, is sketched. The chapter proposes a number of theoretically informed types of visual information or data and offers examples of how visual research could be conducted in each of these conceptually distinct arenas.

Keywords:

image, observation, dimensionality, space, place, interaction.

In the last decade or so, interest in 'the visual' in the social sciences and humanities has grown at such a pace that it is no longer possible to treat visual research as the marginalized specialty that it once was. We have witnessed a burgeoning interest – which shows no signs of abating – in all aspects of visual inquiry. The visual has become not only a focus of concern in its traditional homelands of anthropology and sociology, but something which has engaged the interests of scholars in many disciplines which had previously shown little or no interest in this topic. Many national sociological associations now have their own visual studies research groups. In 2009 the International Sociological Association launched a thematic group on 'Visual Sociology'. The plethora of methodological discussions and original research articles which have recently made their appearance testifies to its legitimacy within the broader field of qualitative research practice.[1]

It is, nevertheless, a field which defies easy summary and can present newcomers with a bewildering variety of topics, theoretical perspectives and methodological approaches. Simply put, there appears to be no single way of doing visual research and beginners must of necessity make strategic choices as to how to proceed. Perhaps the most basic is the decision as to whether they should generate the data they seek to analyse or alternatively confine their attention to the numerous images which are already available. Both of these approaches are widely advocated but they draw upon divergent traditions and demand correspondingly different analytic stances. The taking of still photographs has generally been the preserve of anthropologists, ethnographers and documentary sociologists but they have tended to be used in a largely illustrative fashion where their theoretical significance is unclear. The more recent adoption of video by experimental ethnographers (e.g. Pink, 2007) has provided rich opportunities for the representation and dissemination of research data but it has not significantly clarified the purpose that this material might serve. Moreover, the use of ethnographic video pays scant attention to the contribution this technology has begun to play in a quite separate branch of visual research: the ethnomethodologically influenced analysis of naturally occurring interaction, particularly within workplaces (see Heath, this volume; see also Laurier, 2008). Here the theoretical focus is much clearer: the use of conversation analysis procedures to investigate the complex ways in which sequences of conduct are collaboratively constructed, to shed light on, as Monica Büscher has put it (2005: 1), 'social life in the making'.

Visual research which is carried out on existing images presents yet another set of methodological choices. The analysis of newspaper and magazine photographs and advertisements has been traditionally undertaken using concepts derived from the discipline of semiotics (e.g. Ali, 2004; Rose, 2007: chapter 5). This typically entails the detailed examination of a small number of 'texts' with the aim of uncovering or decoding their hidden cultural codes and messages about such things as gender, race or nationality. However, there are other ways in which photographic material

---

[1]Empirical reports which have relied on visual research can be found in disciplines as diverse as psychology (e.g. Lynn and Lea, 2005), criminology, architecture and design, geography and urban studies, science and museum studies and even labour relations (e.g. Bailey and McAtee, 2003). Of the numerous methodological discussions and secondary commentaries which have appeared in the last few years the most useful or accessible are Banks (2008), Prosser and Loxley (2008) and Rose (2007).

can be investigated. One advantage of working with visual materials drawn from the media is that there are often opportunities to derive large samples which can give a study historical depth. Here the methodology of content analysis, involving the systematic coding and counting of the images according to theoretically relevant categories, is appropriate. Rose (2007: chapter 4) illustrates the use of this approach in her discussion of a study which investigated over 600 photographs which were published in *National Geographic* magazine. However, Rose also offers (2007: chapter 10) a more qualitative way of investigating photographic material which she terms 'an anthropological approach'. In essence this involves treating photographs as objects which have a 'social life'. Such an approach, she suggests, is particularly relevant for researching domestic family photographs. These photographs have a material existence; they are stored, displayed and talked about. They are generally mobile, taken in one location but often sent to family members residing elsewhere. In her own research Rose suggests that the social life of family photographs was typically gendered: almost all the things which were done to, and with, the photographs were carried out by the mothers in the families. It is important to note that Rose also had to rely on interviews – and not just the physical photographs – to arrive at her findings. This point serves to remind us that a significant amount of visual research practice does extend beyond the investigation of the visual image. For example, in the method of 'photo-elicitation' (Schwartz, 1989) the researcher relies upon photographs of family, neighbourhood or local community to generate extensive verbal commentary which might not be otherwise forthcoming during the interview process. Alternatively, subjects can be asked to take their own photographs which can then be the basis of subsequent discussion and analysis by the researcher.

Framing the Visual: Preliminary Considerations

My aim in this chapter is to look in more detail at what an agenda for visual research which goes beyond the photograph might entail. The principal message I want to convey is the need to think of visual inquiry as embracing *more* than the study of images. Consequently I will have little more to say about how photographs might be taken and analysed, but these are issues which are given extensive coverage in the existing visual research literature. There are several strands in the argument I develop. The first, and less contentious, is to think of images not simply as a realm of representation but also as containing information which can be brought to bear on the investigation of social and cultural processes. It is this theme – that the visual is a realm of data, not simply a domain amenable to cultural or interpretive modes of inquiry – which is intended to be conveyed by the chapter title. In part, thinking of the visual as data may require going beyond the reliance on the photograph and to consider the possibilities inherent in other forms of visual material of the kind I will refer to later as two-dimensional. For example, newspaper cartoons or comic strips can tell us a good deal about the wider political, economic and gender systems in which they are embedded. Other forms of two-dimensional visual data such as directional signs, maps and instructional diagrams can be used to explicate the claims of ethnomethodologists about the significance of commonsense reasoning. Here the focus is not so much on the discovery of cultural meanings by the academic analyst but rather the ways in which ordinary actors use or make sense of such visual information and incorporate it into their everyday practical routines (see also Prior, this volume).

But the equating of 'the visual' only with such two-dimensional images is also curiously short-sighted and unduly restrictive. Social life is visual in diverse and counter-intuitive ways. Consequently, I will argue, there are many more forms of visual data than the photograph, the advertisement or the cartoon. Objects, places and locales carry meanings through visual means just like images. Clothing, gesture and body language are significant signs which we use to establish identity and negotiate public situations. Eye contact – Simmel's 'mutual glance' – plays a role in regulating social life among strangers (Macbeth, 1999; Sacks, 1992: Lecture 11, pp. 81–94). The material ecology of the built environment – shopping malls, museums and public spaces more generally – has been argued to exert a determining influence on the movement and mutual coordination of people. Tensions between surveillance, visibility and privacy regulate our uses of such spaces. In all of these areas there are rich supplies of material for the visual researcher. In giving up the idea that visual research is only the study of photographs or advertisements, then a far broader range of data becomes available for investigation. From this vantage point visual inquiry is no longer just the study of the image, but rather the study of the seen and observable. Photographs may be helpful sometimes in recording the seen dimensions of social life. Usually they are not necessary.

My reservations about an image-based visual sociology are grounded in the belief that photographs have been misunderstood as constituting forms of data in their own right when in fact they should be considered in the first instance as means of preserving, storing or representing information. In this sense photographs should be seen as analogous to code-sheets, the responses to interview schedules, ethnographic field notes, tape recordings of verbal interaction or any one of the numerous ways in which the social researchers seek to capture data for subsequent analysis and investigation. The majority of social researchers capture their data with surveys, questionnaires and interviews among other methods; visual researchers have traditionally captured images. But unlike the former, who can readily appreciate the difference between the reality they investigate and their means of apprehending this reality, among the latter this distinction has become confounded.

A typical feature of many of the early works in visual sociology has been to present photographically illustrated research reports on a wide range of disparate topics: deviant sub-cultures, occupational work practices, urban street life and so on. Collecting phenomena such as this together in this way implies they have something in common: that in some way each cumulatively advances our understanding of social life. But this is not the case as the only unifying theme in each of these reports is the reliance on photography as a means of recording and displaying the information to which they refer. The apparent unity such phenomena have as a consequence of being collected is thus entirely spurious. Whatever utility they might have as data for social science does not stem from their appearance in photographs but from their characteristics as objects in their own right.

This point can be further illustrated if we turn to one of the works which is frequently invoked by visual researchers as an exemplar of their craft – Goffman's *Gender Advertisements* (1979). Goffman's book is not 'about' advertising at all, despite the fact that it invariably *has* been treated as a major statement on advertising content (e.g. Belknap and Leonard, 1991; McGregor, 1995). In the book Goffman maintains his focus on the issue which preoccupied almost all his life and his other books: the interaction order and 'the syntactical relations among the acts of different persons mutually present to one another' (1967: 2). In *Gender Advertisements* he turned specifically to consider the characteristic ways in which gender is ritually displayed (i.e. advertised) in everyday interpersonal conduct. Goffman could conceivably have used photographs of 'naturally occurring' gendered interaction for his illustrations. That he did not – choosing to rely instead on fictional advertising images – says something about the ease of availability of such material in our culture. But there is also a sense in which Goffman appears uncomfortable in the book with the label of visual researcher. A number of comments he offers about film and photography as methods in social inquiry reveal the deep suspicions he harbours about the value of these approaches. For example, in a footnote aside on Bateson and Mead's *Balinese Character* – a book universally (and rightly) regarded with admiration by visual researchers – he makes the following pointed observation:

> This book brilliantly pioneered in the use of pictures for study of what can be neatly pictured. The work stimulated a whole generation of anthropologists to take pictures. However, very little analysis was – and perhaps could be – made of what these students collected. Somehow a confusion occurred between human interest and the analytical kind. Dandy movies and stills were brought home of wonderful people and fascinating events, but to little avail. Much respect and affection was shown the natives and little of either for the analytical use that can be made of pictures. (Goffman, 1979: 34, note 10)

It is significant that Goffman studiously ignored photographic visual evidence in his numerous other discussions of face-to-face interaction, relying instead on purely textual renditions of this conduct.

Rethinking the Visual: Space, Place and Dimensionality

In an earlier, more detailed, consideration of these issues (Emmison and Smith, 2000) I introduced the idea of 'dimensionality' as a core organizing principle for thinking about the different forms of visual information. Underpinning this argument is the point that visual is also spatial. That is, spatial considerations both influence the various categories or types of visual data that are available for analysis and enter into the ways we think about the meaning, or the relevance, of these items as data. The objects, people and events, which constitute the raw materials for visual analysis, are not encountered in isolation but rather in specific contexts. For the most part we observe the myriad features of our environment as also having a spatial existence and it is this which serves as the means whereby much of their socio-cultural significance is imparted. Visual data, in short, must be understood as having more than just the two-dimensional component which its representation in the photographic image suggests.

Thinking of visual research in this more inclusive form does not, of course, mean that photographs play no part. Two-dimensional images – a category which of course includes photographs but also billboards, cartoons, advertisements, directional signs, maps, instructional diagrams and so on – are a constituent feature of social life. But rather than imposing a spurious unity upon them – as visual researchers have tended to do – it is necessary to look specifically at how each of these forms operates in everyday life and the differing analytical techniques they demand. The addition of spatial considerations in the conceptualization of visual data, however, opens up new vistas while simultaneously allowing more fruitful theoretical connections to be established.

One of these would be to point to closer affinities between traditional ethnography and 'visual inquiry'. Over 20 years ago Stimson (1986) noted that questions of place and space had been virtually ignored in most qualitative research, to such an extent that even talk of participant *observation* was misleading: most ethnography was about listening rather than looking. Stimson developed his call for a visual ethnography by describing in detail the room in which the General Medical Council (GMC) in the UK holds its disciplinary hearings. Most of us will never have occasion to attend the regulatory activities of professional groups like the GMC but we can readily appreciate from Stimson's description how the room can be viewed, not simply as a place where the hearings are conducted, but as a constituent element of the hearing itself. All aspects of the room – the oak panelling, leather chairs, high ceilings, the glass-fronted bookcases, the spatial arrangements of the tables, the presence of a uniformed commissionaire – he argues, convey the formality and solemnity of the occasion:

> This is a room in which serious matters are discussed: the room has a presence that is forced upon our consciousness. This is a room that, even when unoccupied,

impresses on the visitor a solemn demeanour and subdued speech. When occupied, it retains its solemnity, and speech is now formal, carefully spoken, and a matter for the public record. (Stimson, 1986: 643)

Stimson concludes his discussion of the GMC disciplinary tribunal by rhetorically posing the question of how successful the hearings would be if they were conducted in a radically different architectural space such as a McDonald's restaurant. In contrast to the tradition and permanence of the disciplinary setting everything about the fast-food restaurant signifies transience and informality. Furnishings and equipment are plastic, vinyl and polystyrene; lengthy stays are discouraged through uncomfortable seating, noise and proximity to the kitchen areas. 'Conversation here, for customers, is informal. For staff it is rehearsed and repetitive.... Speech here will not make history. It would be difficult to conduct a disciplinary hearing in this setting' (ibid.: 650).

Stimson's analysis of the medical council room illustrates perfectly how visual inquiry which is not dependent upon the photograph can be conducted. By not including photographs in his article two important consequences have followed. The first is that his work has not been seen as a contribution to 'the field' by self-proclaimed visual researchers. But, second, their absence also eliminates the epistemological confusions over the status of data in visual inquiry referred to earlier. Stimson's data are the actual objects encountered in the room and its overall spatial configuration. It is the inferences that he draws from encountering these as phenomena in their own right, not via their representation in an image which is central to his methodology. In terms of the framework being proposed here, Stimson is analysing both 'three-dimensional' and 'lived' visual data. I look in more detail at these concepts and offer further examples of research that could be conducted on these topics shortly.

Two-dimensional Visual Data

But let us return first to two-dimensional material for there is a need here to think of additional possibilities for investigation. Although visual researchers have paid a great deal of attention to cultural and semiotic analyses of texts such as newspaper and magazine photographs and advertisements, there has been a general neglect of other equally available media material such as cartoons or comic strips. One advantage of these latter materials is that it is generally possible to obtain lengthy historical records which can be mined for evidence of changing social and cultural norms. For example, although they do not explicitly address such questions, cartoons can yield insights into the changing assumptions about the workings of the economy or the relation between the economic and political realms which are not available through the conventional business sections of the media.

Prior to the 1940s there was no idea of 'the economy' as an aggregate entity either linguistically or visually. Cartoons featuring economic messages were confined to an older notion of 'economy' as wise or prudent expenditure. But once the modern conception of 'the economy' appears – a process which is bound up with the Keynesian 'revolution' in economic thinking – cartoons invariably feature the economic system and its constituent components as an entity, thing or even a person. Inflation becomes a 'dragon' to be conquered by the would-be St George treasurer or chancellor. Anthropomorphic representations of sick or ailing units of currency or the entire economy become commonplace. Importantly, even when monetarist economic doctrine gained ascendancy and the role of the government in economic affairs was downgraded, cartoonists still persisted with these 'Keynesian' representational forms, but in turning them to humorous or ironic advantage in their satirical endeavours they inadvertently helped obscure the underlying class relations in the economic system which was often more prominent in the earlier cartoons. The Internet has given rise to a new range of possibilities for accessing visual information about the economy. For example, in her research on online share traders who use a technique called 'technical analysis' Mayall (2006) found that these traders relied almost entirely upon constantly updated visual representations of stock price movements on which to base their trading decisions. Mayall refers to the way in which the traders were able to 'see the market' in the maps and graphs they accessed on their computer screens. Becoming a skilled trader involved the acquisition of a special professional vision (Goodwin, 1994) which entailed the ability to recognize the most opportune time for buying or selling particular stocks.

But the Internet also offers innovative means of exploring the topics which visual researchers have traditionally investigated with the profusion of everyday domestic images which are now available on social networking sites such as Facebook and MySpace. In her discussion of 'the anthropological approach' to researching family photographs, Rose expressed some doubts (2007: 227) as to the suitability of this method to the growing number of digital family websites. Luc Pauwels' (2008) recent research suggests that the increase in public web-based family photography has both reinforced and extended the role of the older private analogue photograph collections. Traditional family albums and web-based public family photography are both used to preserve fond memories, to share experiences with remote family members and to socialize newcomers to the family circle. However, Pauwels also suggests that web-based family albums serve a number of new functions. These include the display of pride in the family ancestry and making contact with same name-bearers to trace family genealogies; the ability to make new friends outside the family circle through mutual interests and hobbies; and even a means of dealing with traumatic events such as the death of a child or partner through establishing a commemorative shrine in cyberspace.

A great deal of the 'two-dimensional' visual data we encounter in everyday life – maps, directional signs, assembly guides, traffic regulations and the like – provide us not simply with information, but with information which is to be incorporated into practical routines. This is material which, unlike texts such as advertisements or cartoons, is specifically designed to be used by actors in the accomplishment of their goals. For these data a different set of theoretical coordinates, those offered by ethnomethodology, provide the most appropriate analytical tools. For example, Sharrock and Anderson (1979) demonstrate the value of this perspective in their examination of directional signs in a medical school complex. Signs in themselves, they declare, are of no sociological interest: rather it is the ways in which they are interpreted and the ways these interpretations occasion practical courses of action which deserve attention. Sharrock and Anderson illustrate their analytic interest in directional signs by showing how 'an ordinary user' of the premises in which they were located might conceivably use these signs in negotiating their way around. They argue that the interpretation of signs is an irremediably practical and local matter. Signs are not observed in isolation but in particular contexts and in particular sequences. Finding our way around a building is, quite literally, a procedural affair. Visitors to the hospital may need to follow the directions of several information signs before arriving at their desired destinations. In this process, although signs are encountered 'one at a time', the sequences in which these occur are equally important in conveying information about places or locales.

One important lesson to be drawn from Sharrock and Anderson's analysis is the tacit 'work' that users of signs must perform in way-finding. Pedestrian signs can never provide every detail of the journey that must be taken but instead rely upon the commonsense reasoning of the sign user to supply the 'missing' information. But it is interesting to compare the format of pedestrian direction signs with those which are erected for motorists. Pedestrians may misinterpret signs and be forced to retrace their steps as matters of course, but it is a different matter to rectify a missed turn when one is at the wheel of a car on a freeway. Pedestrians can readily modify their routes, make abrupt turns, or stop dead in their tracks generally without any fear that such activities will occasion collisions with their fellows, but these are not options which are available to drivers. What we find, then, is that these contrasting 'logics of navigation' – finding one's way around on foot as opposed to finding one's way around by car – are reflected in different sign systems. Whereas pedestrians are given only general outlines of where to proceed and must 'work out' the details en route, motorists are invariably given much more explicit visual information as to how to proceed, presumably with the intention of avoiding the kind of recoverable errors that pedestrians routinely engage in. The result is that key traffic directional signs tend to be iconic in that the physical layout of an up coming road system is reproduced as a constituent feature of the sign itself.

Three-dimensional Visual Data

The ethnomethodological investigation of two-dimensional texts, to the extent that it draws attention to their practical uses in particular environments, has, strictly speaking, foreshadowed one of the analytical possibilities in what I will refer to as 'three-dimensional' visual data. Under this broad heading we can locate the objects of material culture which operate as signifiers in social life. These range from those of everyday life encountered in the home and which carry personal meanings to those in public spaces, such as statues or monuments, which represent official public discourses. Although such forms of data can be analysed in traditional semiotic terms, they are also implicated in human actions. Stimson was making much the same point in his discussion of the GMC room and it is also implicit in Rose's (2007) discussion of photographs as objects which have a material existence, although in both cases these methodological differences are not explicitly made. Barthes, however, does just this in his famous essay on the Citroen DS. We have become so accustomed to the cultural studies' semiotic interpretation of advertising texts that it is easy to forget that the objects or artefacts which figure in these texts also carry meanings. Much of Barthes' achievement was to spell out that mythologies were not only located in the representational practices of advertising campaigns, but actually embodied in objects and activities. In the case of the Citroen DS, Barthes likens the car to 'the great Gothic cathedrals'; he emphasizes the smoothness and shape of the car, and suggests its curvaceous glass contributes to a light, spiritual quality. But Barthes also demonstrates the value in going beyond the object itself to look at the responses that people make when they encounter it in its pristine state:

> In the exhibition halls, the car on show is explored with an intense, amorous studiousness: it is the great tactile phase of discovery… The bodywork, the lines of union are touched, the upholstery palpated, the seats tried, the doors caressed, the cushions fondled; before the wheel, one pretends to drive with one's whole body. The object here is totally prostituted, appropriated. (Barthes, 1973: 90)

Generalizing, we can suggest that one of the primary advantages of objects or artefacts for visual inquiry is that they offer a greater range of possibilities than two-dimensional data for inference making about social and cultural behaviour and processes. There is not a great deal we can learn about 'behaviour' from observing people reading or watching television, but observing what people do with objects is much more promising. Often the twin strategies of 'decoding' and behavioural inference making can be utilized in the same research site. For example, simply noting the placement and the gender, racial or other demographic characteristics of the statues or monuments which are located in the urban environment can tell us something about the values or priorities associated with men and women in the official civic culture or national narratives (Bulbeck, 1992; Inglis, 1987). But observing what people actually do when in the presence of such monuments may give us a clearer idea about the attitudes or values of ordinary people (see, for example, Wagner-Pacifici and Schwartz, 1991). Indicators of the cultural significance of particular monuments can be gauged by the simple task or recording the degree or intensity of contact which people make when encountering these objects. Do they stop to read information plaques, do they discuss the item's aesthetic or historical significance, do they photograph it perhaps even to the point of placing themselves in the frame? Informal research in Brisbane, the state capital of Queensland, suggests that it is not the predominantly masculine politicians, explorers and generals which the official culture recognizes that are of most relevance to visitors to the city, but the assorted animal figures which have been erected.

Object-centred visual inquiry has obvious methodological affinities with an older – and these days somewhat neglected and unfashionable – branch of social research, the use of unobtrusive or non-reactive measures (e.g. Webb et al., 1999). The sheer visibility of many kinds of objects means that it is possible to explore social life covertly. Because respondents are not required for many kinds of object-based research we can circumvent the usual problem of normative responding – providing the researcher with a socially acceptable answer. This may be particularly useful in researching fields such as crime and deviance or urban disorder. There is a well-established branch of unobtrusive research which has utilized visual information in these fields in the form of 'traces' and 'accretions': rubbish, litter, graffiti, visible signs of vandalism and so on. Perhaps the most well known is the 'broken-windows' thesis (Wilson and Kelling, 1982) which argues that signs of public incivilities – such as the existence of unrepaired windows, abandoned cars or drinking in streets – tend to attract further crime because potential offenders assume that police and residents alike do not care about the character of these neighbourhoods. Studies on these topics do not need to be small scale or impressionistic. For example, Sampson and Raudenbush (1999) undertook a study of the sources and consequences of public disorder which involved collecting information from over 23,000 street segments in Chicago. Using what they referred to as the 'method of systematic social observation' and 'taking seriously the idea that visual cues matter' (1999: 605), Sampson and Raudenbush devised a project which involved driving a utility vehicle slowly down every street in 196 Chicago census tracts and video recording the social activities and physical features of each side of the street simultaneously. From this voluminous – and permanent – visual record they were able to devise complicated scales to capture the presence or absence of both physical and social disorder. The items they coded included garbage, graffiti, abandoned cars, condoms, syringes, public intoxication, street fighting or arguing, and drug selling. The theoretical underpinnings and statistical details of the project are not relevant in this context;

it is mentioned only to provide some indication of the enormous potential – both qualitative and quantitative – which can be associated with visual inquiry.[2]

Lived and Living Visual Data

From exploring the possibilities in the use of three-dimensional data it is a short step to the next 'higher' analytical level, which is the places and settings – the actual environments or locales in which humans conduct their lives. Attention here turns to such matters as the patterning of zones and activities and the observable movements of people in time and space. The places where we spend our lives – homes, schools, shopping malls, museums, work places, hospitals parks and so on – are not just functional structures but residues of important cultural values. Opportunities for visual inquiry are plentiful and span both the organization and use of private domestic settings as well as public spaces and locales. Perhaps the most well-known example of a decoding of a domestic dwelling is to be found in Bourdieu's (1990) structuralist investigation of the Kabyle (North African) peasant household but a number of investigations of the changing structure of Western house forms, and the way these reflect prevailing norms and values about gender roles and privacy, have also been undertaken (e.g. Hasell and Peatross, 1990; Heath and Cleaver, 2004). Data for these inquiries typically take the form of sketches of the floor plans which the researcher can produce, but they are generally widely available as architectural drawings in the glossy home or lifestyle magazines. A similar methodological approach can be found in Prior's (1988) investigation into the changing design of hospitals. Prior asserts that 'the spatial divisions which are expressed in buildings can be best understood in relation to the discursive practices which are enclosed in their interiors' (1988: 110). By inspecting hospital architectural plans over a 100-year period he shows that their design can be used to illustrate changing medical theories and discourses in relation to such things as the aetiology of disease, nursing and the child as an object of medical intervention.

A good deal of the contemporary research on the design and use of public spaces has revisited the classic discussions of the *flâneur* – the detached or reflexive urban spectator – first introduced by the French poet Baudelaire, or the writings of Simmel on the blasé attitude through which the metropolitan dweller copes with the sensory overload of urban life. However, this work has also benefited from the inclusion of more contemporary analytical frameworks. Some of the most interesting

---

[2]In this sense Sampson and Raudenbush's research can be seen as a continuation – albeit one with added technical complexity – of an important tradition in visual inquiry which has drawn upon quantitative methods and large-scale samples to make important and often unexpected empirical findings. See for example Richardson and Kroeber (1940) and Robinson (1976).

and innovative research in these fields has been carried out in locales such as museums and art galleries. Museum planners and designers have long been aware of the ability of the physical layout to influence both the flow of traffic and the nature of the learning experience. To date, however, the majority of findings from this research have been relatively 'broad-brush'. For example, other things being equal, people will invariably turn to the right on entering the museum; people spend more time at displays at the start of an exhibition than the end; people generally dislike entering areas without visible exits.

In the last few years a much more 'fine-grained' appreciation of museum visitor behaviour has emerged in the work of researchers drawing upon ethnomethodology and conversation analysis. Using video recordings of naturally occurring visitor behaviour in galleries and museums, vom Lehn et al. (2001; see also Heath et al., 2002) have looked specifically at how exhibits are encountered and experienced and the mutual conduct and collaboration on the part of both companions and strangers which this entails. Such research draws upon the long-standing symbolic interactionist interest in behaviour in public places but it adds the complicating factor of how conduct is inextricably embedded in the immediate ecology and the material realities at hand. The research questions being posed here concern precisely how the objects and artefacts – the exhibits, paintings and installations – are both given sense by people in interaction and how, in turn, such objects reflexively inform the production of intelligible conduct. More recently vom Lehn (2006) has investigated the behaviour of visitors to the controversial, but widely acclaimed, 'Body Worlds' exhibition featuring real human bodies which have undergone preservation through the technical process known as plastination. His investigations show that the exhibition visitors typically draw upon their pre-existing medical knowledge of the body, which is frequently shaped by their own experience of injury or illness, when inspecting the plastinated bodies. In their talk with companions about the bodies, and their gestural appraisal of the details of the exhibits, vom Lehn observes that the visitors display a highly contextualized appreciation of the human body which is strikingly different from the detached clinical gaze of medical professionals. Like a great deal of ethnomethodological inquiry into naturally occurring behaviour, this research defies easy summary and requires, for its full explication, detailed consideration of the actual sequences of behaviour, both verbal and visual, that are recorded.

Conclusion, Summary and Future Prospects

All social science inquiry ultimately aims to advance our knowledge of the cultures, structures and processes which constitute, and are constituted by, human social behaviour. For successful research we need both data which are rigorously collected and theoretical frameworks which can be bought to bear on these empirical materials. My argument in this chapter has been that a great deal of what currently passes as visual research fails to meet these two criteria. Far too much of what is offered up as visual research relies upon a largely unreflexive use of the photographic image. A failure to distinguish between the disparate kinds of information which photographs inevitably contain and the use of photographs as the means by which this information can be disseminated has led to a confusion about the status of visual inquiry and a failure to appreciate its divergent theoretical possibilities. If we move away from the commonsense equation of visual research as a purely image-based activity and embrace the claims being advanced here, then it is possible to regard many aspects of twentieth-century social science, and many of the major figures in these disciplines, as contributing to the development of visual research. Thinking of visual research more as the study of the seen and the observable, rather than as something which can only be conducted through recording technology, can facilitate important conceptual connections to be made between 'the visual' as a domain of inquiry and the work of many classical and contemporary theorists alike who might not otherwise be regarded as contributing to this field. In addition this may well open up visual inquiry to students whose substantive research interests might otherwise lead them to overlook the possibility of visual methodologies.

The use of visual data and visual methods are here to stay but future developments in these fields are not easy to predict and are likely to be uneven. The use of still photographic images will no doubt continue to figure in visual inquiry, both as illustrative ends in themselves and as ingredients of other modes of inquiry such as photo-elicitation in ethnography or interviews, but the prospects here appear relatively stagnant. A major growth area is almost certainly to be in the use of video technology given the affordability of new digital technologies and their widespread adoption outside the academy. But the gulf between the experimental ethnographic use of video and the multimodal analysis of interaction by ethnomethodologists and conversation analysts is one that seems likely to remain. However, only when researchers also come to appreciate the value of direct observation of the social world, harnessed with a powerful theoretical imagination, will visual research come to enjoy the centrality throughout the social and cultural fields which it deserves.

Questions

1 What are some of the problems with basing visual research on the use of photographs?
2 Do you think that Goffman has made a contribution to visual research?
3 Identify an example of two-dimensional visual data (not discussed in the chapter) and suggest how it could be analysed.
4 Repeat this exercise for three-dimensional visual data.

Recommended Reading

Banks, M. (2008) *Using Visual Data in Qualitative Research*. London: Sage.

Emmison, M. and Smith, P. (2000) *Researching the Visual: images, objects, contexts and interactions in social and cultural inquiry*. London: Sage.

Rose, G. (2007) *Visual Methodologies: an introduction to the interpretation of visual materials*, 2nd Edition. London: Sage.

Internet Links

The Visual Sociology Group of the British Sociological Association:

www.visualsociology.org.uk

International Visual Sociology Organization (IVSA):

www.visualsociology.org/

Mass Observation Project:

www.massobs.org.uk/index.htm

References

Ali, S (2004) 'Using Visual Materials', in C. Seale (Ed.) *Researching Culture and Society*, 2nd Edition. London: Sage, pp. 265–278.

Bailey, J. and McAtee, D. (2003) '"Another Way of Telling": the use of visual methods in research', *International Employment Relations Review*, vol 9, 1, 45–60.

Banks, M. (2008) *Using Visual Data in Qualitative Research*. London: Sage.

Barthes, R. (1973) *Mythologies*. St Albans: Paladin.

Belknap, P and Leonard, W.M. (1991) 'A Conceptual Replication and Extension of Erving Goffman's Study of Gender Advertisements', *Sex Roles*, vol 25, 3/4, 103–118.

Bourdieu, P. (1990) 'The Kabyle House or the World Reversed', in P. Bourdieu, *The Logic of Practice*. Cambridge: Polity, pp. 271–319.

Bulbeck, C. (1992) 'Women of Substance: the depiction of women in Australian monuments', *Hecate*, vol 18, 2, 8–22.

Büscher, M. (2005) 'Social Life under the Microscope', *Sociological Research Online*, vol 10, 1, www.socresonline.org.uk/10/1/buscher.html.

Emmison, M. and Smith, P. (2000) *Researching the Visual: images, objects, contexts and interactions in social and cultural inquiry*. London: Sage.

Goffman, E. (1967) *Interaction Ritual: essays on face-to-face behaviour*. New York: Doubleday.

Goffman, E. (1979) *Gender Advertisements*. London and Basingstoke: Macmillan.

Goodwin, C. (1994) 'Professional Vision', *American Anthropologist*, vol 96, 3, 606–633.

Hasell, M. and Peatross, F. (1990) 'Exploring Connections between Women's Changing Roles and House Forms', *Environment and Behaviour*, vol 22, 1, 3–26.

Heath, C., Luff, P., vom Lehn, D., Hindmarsh, J. and Cleverly, J. (2002) 'Crafting Participation: designing ecologies, configuring experience', *Visual Communication*, vol 1, 1, 9–33.

Heath, S. and Cleaver, E. (2004) 'Mapping the Spatial in Shared Household life: a missed opportunity?', in C. Knowles and P. Sweetman (Eds) *Picturing the Social Landscape: visual methods in the sociological imagination*. New York: Routledge.

Inglis, K. (1987) 'Men, Women and War Memorials: Anzac Australia', *Daedalus*, vol 116, 3, 35–58.

Laurier, E. (2008) 'Drinking up Endings: conversational resources of the café', *Language and Communication*, vol 28, 2, 165–181.

Lynn, N. and Lea, S. (2005) 'Through the Looking Glass: considering the challenges visual methodologies raise for qualitative research', *Qualitative Research in Psychology*, vol 2, 2, 213–225.

Macbeth, D. (1999) 'Glances, Trances, and their Relevance for a Visual Sociology', in P. L. Jalbert (Ed.) *Media Studies: ethnomethodological approaches*. Lanham, MD: University Press of America, pp. 135–170.

Mayall, M. (2006) '"Seeing the Market": technical analysis in trading styles', *Journal for the Theory of Social Behaviour*, vol 36, 2, 119–140.

McGregor, G. (1995) 'Gender Advertisements Then and Now', *Studies in Symbolic Interaction*, vol 17, 3–42.

Pauwels, L. (2008) 'A Private Visual Practice Going Public? Social functions and sociological research opportunities of web-based family photography', *Visual Studies*, vol 23, 1, 34–49.

Pink, S. (2007) *Doing Visual Ethnography: images, media and representation in research*, 2nd Edition. London: Sage.

Prior, L. (1988) 'The Architecture of the Hospital: a study of spatial organization and medical knowledge', *British Journal of Sociology*, vol 39, 1, 86–113.

Prosser, J. and Loxley, A. (2008) 'Introducing Visual Methods', ESRC National Centre for Research Methods Review Paper.

Richardson, J. and Kroeber, A.L. (1940) 'Three Centuries of Women's Dress Fashions: a quantitative analysis', *Anthropological Records*, vol 5, 2, 111–153.

Robinson, D. (1976) 'Fashions in Shaving and Trimming of the Beard: the men of The Illustrated London News, 1842–1972', *American Journal of Sociology*, vol 81, 5, 1133–1141.

Rose, G. (2007) *Visual Methodologies: an introduction to the interpretation of visual materials*, 2nd Edition. London: Sage.

Sacks, H. (1992) *Lectures on Conversation*, Vol 1, ed Gail Jefferson with an introduction by Emmanuel Schegloff. Oxford: Blackwell.

Sampson, R. and Raudenbush, S. (1999) 'Systematic Social Observation of Public Spaces: a new look at disorder in urban neighborhoods', *American Journal of Sociology,* vol 105, 3, 603–651.

Schwartz, D. (1989) 'Visual Ethnography: using photography in qualitative research', *Qualitative Sociology,* vol 12, 2, 119–154.

Sharrock, W.W. and Anderson, D.C. (1979) 'Directional Hospital Signs as Sociological Data', *Information Design Journal,* vol 1, 2, 81–94.

Stimson, G. (1986) 'Place and Space in Sociological Fieldwork', *Sociological Review,* vol 34, 641–656.

vom Lehn, D. (2006) 'The Body as Interactive Display: examining bodies in a public exhibition', *Sociology of Health and Illness,* vol 28, 2, 223–251.

vom Lehn, D., Heath, C and Hindmarsh, J. (2001) 'Exhibiting Interaction: conduct and collaboration in museums and galleries', *Symbolic Interaction,* vol 24, 2, 189–216.

Wagner-Pacifici, R. and Schwartz, B. (1991) 'The Vietnam Veterans' Memorial', *American Journal of Sociology,* vol 97, 376–420.

Webb, E.J., Campbell, D.T., Schwartz, R.D. and Sechrest, L. (1999) *Unobtrusive Measures: non-reactive research in the social sciences,* Revised Edition. London: Sage.

Wilson, J. and Kelling, G. (1982) 'Broken Windows', *The Atlantic Monthly,* 249, 3, 29–38.

14 Embodied Action: Video and the Analysis of Social Interaction

Christian Heath

Abstract

Video provides an unprecedented opportunity for research in the social sciences. It offers new and distinctive ways of collecting data and analysing social actions and activities. In this chapter we draw on ethnomethodology and conversation analysis to discuss how we can use video recordings to examine social interaction in organisational settings and the ways in which we can begin to consider how visible conduct as well as talk, embodied action, features in the accomplishment of workplace activities.

Keywords:

video, social interaction, work and organisation.

Introduction

In recent years we have witnessed the emergence of a growing corpus of studies that use video to analyse social action and interaction. These studies have generated a substantial range of insights and findings concerning the social organisation of activities within a broad range of everyday environments including the workplace, the home and more public settings such as museums and galleries. In different ways, these studies have built on and developed the rich and diverse range of research concerned with language use and talk that arose over the last three decades or so and have powerfully demonstrated the ways in which social actions and activities are accomplished though the visible, the material, as well as the spoken. This growing interest in embodied action and multimodal communication is reflected in the growing commitment to using video in naturalistic research throughout a range of disciplines, including sociology, linguistics, education, psychology and management, and to readdressing topics and issues that have long been of concern to the social science, including learning, health care, professional practice, technology, markets and the emotions (see for example Knoblauch et al. 2006, Goldman et al. 2007, Jewitt 2009).

This chapter discusses the ways in which we can use video to explore everyday activities as they arise in ordinary, naturally occurring settings. We focus in particular on the analysis of social interaction and the ways in which social interaction not only informs the accomplishment of everyday activities, but also provides a methodological resource with which to prioritise the participants' perspective. Drawing on ethnomethodology and conversation analysis, the chapter addresses how we can explore the situated production of social action and activity and examine the resources and competencies on which participants rely in accomplishing their own actions and making sense of the actions of others. The chapter suggests that we can develop a distinctive approach to the analysis of embodied action and contribute to our understanding of a range of analytic and substantive issues in the social sciences. Video, audio-visual recordings of naturally occurring activities provide a critical resource in this regard.

Background: The Analysis of 'Elusive Phenomena'

It has long been recognised that the moving image, including film and more recently video, provides unprecedented opportunities for social science research. As early as the 1870s Eadweard Muybridge with the support and encouragement of Leland Stanford (the founder of the university) first developed the possibility of combining images to capture a series of actions (Figure 14.1), developing the technology initially to resolve debates concerning how horses gallop (Prodger 2003). Muybridge recognised the scientific potential of the technology, a technology that could reveal and enable the detailed scrutiny of what he referred to as 'elusive phenomena'. His publications, *Attitudes of Animals in Motion* (1881) and *Animal Locomotion* (1887), reveal unique aspects of the structure of movement and activity, both for human beings as well as for certain species of animal, and had an important impact on a range of initiatives to use photography and film to analyse human activities (see for example Marey 1895, Braune and Fischer 1895). These early initiatives proved less influential on sociology than might be imagined, but within social anthropology instantaneous photography and film gained some importance, with for example A.C. Haddon recording various indigenous rituals and activities as part of the Torres Straits expedition in 1898, Spencer and Gillen (1899) using film as part of a study of Australian Aborigines and Poech (1907) in his field trips to New Guinea.

FIGURE 14.1   *Still pictures from Eadweard Muybridge's* The Body in Motion

As Morphy and Banks (1997) suggest, however, this early enthusiasm for the role of film in field work was not sustained, at least within Europe during the first few decades of the twentieth century, tarred by its association with evolutionary anthropology. Indeed it is interesting to note that as late as the early 1970s, Margaret Mead, who with Gregory Bateson helped pioneer the use of visual media in the social anthropology (1942), bemoaned the 'the criminal neglect of film':

> research project after research project fail to include filming and insist on continuing the hopelessly inadequate note-taking of an earlier age, while the behaviour that film could have caught and preserved for centuries ... (... for illumination of future generations of human scientists) disappears – disappears right in front of everybody's eyes. Why? What has gone wrong? (1995 [1974] pp. 4–5)

Sociology, and surprisingly, perhaps, qualitative sociology, has shown less interest than anthropology in using film and video for social research and it is only in recent years that visual media have begun to feature in empirical research. And yet, video appears to provide just the resources that ethnographic studies require – the opportunity to capture versions of activities as they arise in the natural habitats such as the home, the classroom, the office, the factory, the city square and the like. These records can be subject to detailed scrutiny. They can be repeatedly analysed and provide access to the fine details of conduct and interaction, details that are unavailable to more traditional methods of data collection including for example interviews and participant observation. The recordings can be shown and shared with others, and provide the opportunity to develop an archive of data that can be subject to a range of analytic interests. They can enable others, not only fellow researchers but also participants themselves, to examine the data on which observations are based and judge for themselves the quality and rigour of research findings and insights. Despite the enormous potential of video, greater one suspects than film or photography, the social sciences have been slow in responding to the opportunities it affords.

One suspects that the reticence in using video in qualitative research has derived not so much from a reluctance to exploit the potential of a new technology – consider in contrast the significant impact of software packages for data management – but rather the way in which video as data fails to resonate with many of the key concepts and analytic resources commonly found within ethnographic research. It is important at this stage, as Knoblauch et al. (2006) suggest, to differentiate the wide-ranging interest in the 'visual' in sociology and cognate disciplines (see, for example, Banks 2001, Pink 2006, Rose 2004), from research that uses video recordings to analyse conduct and interaction in 'naturally occurring' day-to-day settings. It is the latter with which we are concerned and it is ethnomethodology and conversation analysis that have primarily provided the analytic and conceptual resources that have enabled researchers from a range of disciplines to use video to address the social and interactional organisation of everyday practical activities.

Emerging Fields of Video-based Research

The flowering of video-based research in recent years has given rise to an impressive range of studies of social interaction within a broad variety of everyday settings and situations including both formal and informal environments. So for example we find studies of driving, children's play, dinner parties, cooking, watching television, visits to museums, computer games, the use of mobile phones, shopping, virtual environments and the like (Asch 2007, Dant 2004, Goldman et al. 2007, Laurier and Philo 2006, Goodwin 2006, Heath and vom Lehn 2008, Hindmarsh et al. 2000, Peräkylä and Ruusuvuori 2006, vom Lehn et al. 2001, Relieu and Licoppe 2007). Perhaps the most significant contribution of video-based research has been to our understanding of work and organisation and the ways in which work is accomplished in and though social interaction. Indeed, over the past couple of decades or so we have witnessed the emergence of what have come to be known as 'workplace studies'. This substantial corpus of research has addressed the ways in which specialised tasks and activities are accomplished through embodied activity, activities that involve the interplay of talk, visible conduct and the use of various objects and artefacts, tools and technologies. This corpus of research includes for example studies of control rooms, operating theatres, street markets, medical consultations, call centres, news rooms, financial trading rooms, architectural practices, construction sites and offices (see for example Engeström and Middleton 1996, Luff et al. 2000, Llwellyn and Hindmarsh 2010, Szymanski forthcoming, Streeck et al. forthcoming, Suchman 2007, Clark and Pinch 1995, Heath and Button 2002, Heath and Luff 2000).

One of the more important contributions of video-based studies of organisations has been to our understanding of the ways in which tools and technologies, ranging from highly complex digital systems to seemingly simple artefacts, such as pen and paper, feature in the collaborative accomplishment of workplace activities. These studies stand in marked contrast to more traditional research on technology and system use found within the social sciences in both sociology and fields such as human–computer interaction (HCI). For example, research has examined the ways in which advanced systems for traffic management and surveillance, for instance in rapid urban transport, rely upon operators' ability to participate in, and coordinate, concurrent activities and to remain 'peripherally aware' of the selective contributions of others, both within the immediate environment and beyond (see for example Suchman 1996, 1997, Goodwin and Goodwin 1996, Fillippi and Thereau 1993, Heath and Luff 2000; and for a discussion of related issues see Hindmarsh and Pilnick 2002, Mondada 2003). It has also examined, for instance, how the use of systems to document and retrieve information in service encounters, emergency dispatch centres and medical consultations is systematically interleaved with the interaction between the client and the professional and the ways in which the system shapes and is shaped by the emergent and contingent contributions of the participants (Whalen 1995, Whalen and Vinkhuyzen 2000, Greatbatch et al. 1993). These video-based studies of technology in action have also addressed how the accomplishment of workplace activities, even in highly complex organisational environments, relies upon the use of mundane artefacts and material resources such sketches, plans, records, flight strips, paper timetables, Post-it notes, markers, pens and pencils, and how these objects and artefacts gain their sense and significance in and through interaction (Büscher 2005, Heath 1986). In other words, these video-based studies have powerfully shown how tools and technologies rely upon a body of socially organised practice and reasoning, practice that emerges within and is sustained through the forms of social interaction that arise within particular organisational settings. As Barley and Kunda (2001) suggest, this growing corpus of research has begun to refocus studies of organisation on work and work's practical accomplishment and demonstrated how the analysis of the fine details of organisational interaction provides a distinctive understanding of contemporary work that builds on and extends the ethnographic traditions (see Hughes 1958, Silverman 1970).

Alongside these academic contributions, there is also growing interest in using video-based research to contribute to policy and practice in particular in work and organisational environments. For example, there is a growing commitment to using video-based research to inform the design and development of advanced technologies. Leading research and industrial laboratories in Europe, North America and the Far East are undertaking fine-grained studies of everyday activities and interaction to inform the requirements for innovative systems. We also increasingly find video-based research informing the development of communication skills training for particular occupational groups, and contributing to such diverse interests as architectural design, developing interactive museum exhibits and understanding consumer behaviour.

There is a growing and diverse range of research that uses video to analyse naturally occurring activities, research that draws distinct analytic traditions and has differing theoretical commitments. In this regard, ethnomethodology and conversation analysis have proved particularly fruitful, not only by virtue of a methodological framework that drives analytic attention towards the interactional and sequential character of mundane activities, but also in the light of the substantial corpus of findings and insights that emerged over some years concerning the organisation of talk and in particular talk in interaction (see for example Sacks 1992, Sacks et al. 1974, Atkinson and Heritage 1984, Drew and Heritage 1992, Heritage and Maynard 2006, ten Have 1999) . Studies of naturally occurring conversation and, over the last couple decades or so, talk at work or institutional interaction have provided both the analytic resources and substantive findings with which to address embodied action and activity. In this regard, there are three principal analytic commitments that have underpinned a substantial corpus of video-based research, commitments that resonate with a range of qualitative research, but have particular significance for ethnomethodology and conversation analysis (see Garfinkel 1967, Sacks 1992, Heritage 1984, ten Have 1999). They are:

- *Social action is situated.* Action is produced with regard to the local context and the meaning or intelligibility of an action or activity is bound to, and inseparable from, the circumstances in which it is produced.
- *Social action is an emerging practical accomplishment.* Participants, in concert and collaboration with others, are ongoingly engaged in the production of action and in making sense of the actions of others.
- *Social action relies upon a methodology.* That is, practice(s), reasoning and commonsense knowledge, in and through which people produce their own actions with regard to the contributions of others.

To explore the ways in which these methodological commitments can inform analysis, it is worthwhile considering a brief extract drawn from a substantial corpus of video recordings of auctions of fine art and antiques, recordings gathered both in the UK and abroad (see for example Heath and Luff 2007).

Analysing the Production of Workplace Activities

Auctions of fine art and antiques consist of repeated episodes of intense forms of interaction with up to 500 lots sold in one day. Each episode rarely lasts more than 30 seconds but within those brief moments the price of goods can rise more than five times the starting figure. At any one time there may be up to a hundred people at an auction, many of whom are potential bidders for any of the objects that come up for sale. There may also be a number of people who have booked telephone lines with the auction house to enable them to bid on particular lots through sales assistants and others who have registered to bid over the internet. The auctioneer has to deploy an organisation that encourages and coordinates the contributions of bidders, bidders who not only are in competition with each other, but may have a very different idea of the value of the goods in question. Basically the auctioneer, in cooperation with bidders, has to implement an organisational arrangement whereby the potential contributions of multiple participants, many of whom might wish to bid if the price is right, are organised through an orderly sequence of turns, where those turns, to corrupt Sacks et al. (1974), are 'valued', literally in this case.

Consider the following fragment, a brief extract from a recent auction of antiquities at a sales room in London. For convenience, we have simplified and abbreviated the transcript and represented bidding by [B bids], numbering particular bidders [B.1 bids] in the order that they first enter the bidding.

Fragment 1

    A: Lot one hundred and Six. There it is lot one hundred and six Eighty <u>Six</u> <u>A</u>: (.)
         Fi<u>ve</u>: <u>hun</u>dred please::.

         .

    A: Eight fifty
         [B.1 bids]

    A: Nine hundred
         [B.2 bids]

    A: Nine fifty ma<u>d</u>am thank you
         [B.1 bids]

    A: A thousand <u>there</u>:
         (0.4) [B.2 bids]

    A: Eleven here
         (.) [B.2 bids]

    A: Twelve hundred
         [B.1 bids]

    A: Thirteen hundred
         [B.2 bids]

    A: Fourteen hundred
         [B.1 bids]

    A: Fifteen hundred

         .

A: Two two:: the standing bidder (0.2) last chance [glances at B.3] (0.2) two
        thousand two hundred pounds:::
      (0.6)
      {knock}

From the transcript we can see that there are various characteristics of the event that
differ markedly from other forms of social interaction whether in the workplace or
any other setting for that matter. There is only one speaker, the auctioneer (A), and
talk consists largely of numbers, namely price increments. Those increments remain
stable at £50 up until £1000 and then change to £100. Once begun, the incremental
structure projects the series of prices at which people bid irrespective of the values
they may have in mind. Moreover, it can be seen that bidding alternates between
two principal protagonists, B.1 and B.2. When B.1 withdraws a little later, at £1800, the
auctioneer finds a new bidder, and alternates the bidding between B.2 and B.3. This
ordering principal is known as the 'run' and is used within almost all auctions of
fine art and antiques. The auctioneer establishes two bidders and no more than two
bidders at any one time.

   It is clear from the transcript that visible conduct plays an important part in the
organisation of the event. First and foremost, 'turns' at bidding are accomplished
through gestures (e.g. a nod or a wave) rather than through talk. The participation of potential buyers is largely limited to agreeing or declining to bid at a price.
Secondly, given that there may be up to a hundred or so people in the sales room,
and a number of people eager to bid, it is clear that the visible conduct of the auctioneer may play an important part in enabling individuals to know when it is their
turn to bid. Thirdly, bidders and all those present need to know when a bid has been
successful and who, at any moment, has bid the highest price. In other words, the
organisation of participation during the event, the distribution of opportunities to
bid and the rapid escalation of price, rests upon the visible conduct of the auctioneer and potential buyers. To explore this further it is worthwhile considering a
section of the run. Take for example the announcement of the increment 'Twelve
hundred'.

   From the images in Figure 14.2, one can see that the auctioneer alternates between
gestures with his right hand and gestures with his left. The gestures are accompanied
by shifts in his visual alignment in which he turns from the bidder on his right (B.1)
to the bidder on his left (B.2). As he begins to announce 'Eleven here' (bid by B.1),
he turns towards B.2. His gaze arrives with the word 'here'. He withdraws his right
hand and starts to raise his left to gesture towards B.2. The moment he looks at and
gestures towards B.2, she nods, agreeing to the projected next increment. The visible
realignment and the gesture, coupled with the announcement, enable the buyer to
know when it is her turn and the price that she is expected to bid. It also enables the
bid to be accomplished through the most minimal of actions – a head nod.

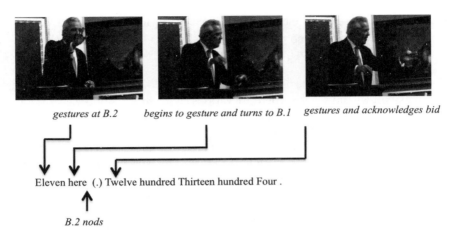

gestures at B.2   begins to gesture and turns to B.1   gestures and acknowledges bid

Eleven here (.) Twelve hundred Thirteen hundred Four .

B.2 nods

FIGURE 14.2   *Fragment 1, Transcript II and images*

The fragment points to a number of analytic consideration that enable us to unpack the very general methodological orientations that were mentioned earlier.

Firstly, we begin to see how visible conduct, like talk, performs social actions and activities. In the case at hand, potential buyers produce turns, that is bids, within the developing course of the interaction, not through talk but rather through visible conduct. The bidder on the right of the auctioneer raises his catalogue, the bidder on the left nods her head. Moreover, the invitation to bid is accomplished not only through the announcement of the current increment, for example 'a thousand there:', but also by virtue of the auctioneer's accompanying bodily conduct, his visual realignment towards the under-bidder and a gesture that offers the opportunity to bid. Visible conduct therefore, both with and without talk, is used to produce specific actions and engender a response from a particular participant.

Secondly, the location or position of the participants' conduct within the developing course of the interaction is critical to its sense and its ability to perform a particular action. For example, a head nod serves to produce a bid of £1200 by virtue of its immediate juxtaposition with the announcement of the increment coupled with the auctioneer's turning and gesturing towards the participant. The head nod is produced as, and is seen as responsive to, the auctioneer's invitation to bid and bid at the projected next increment. Similarly, the announcement of the increment and the gesture with which it is accompanied are intelligible by virtue of the ways in which they stand in contrast to the preceding action of the auctioneer and the conduct of the protagonist. The actions of the participants, whether visible, spoken or a combination of both, are accomplished by virtue of the ways in which they are oriented to the (immediately) preceding action(s) and create opportunities for subsequent action, not infrequently in the next turn.

Thirdly, the actions of the participants are accomplished through sequences of actions and these sequences inform how people produce their conduct and make sense of the actions of others. For example, the run is dependent upon a social and interactional arrangement that selectively places particular participants under the obligation to respond to an invitation to bid. The invitation is produced through the announcement of a figure, an increment, accompanied by the auctioneer's reorienting and gesturing towards a particular individual. The invitation renders relevant, implicates, an action from a potential buyer, to accept or decline to bid, in this case the acceptance, enabling the auctioneer immediately to invite the protagonist to bid the next increment. The participants' actions therefore, and indeed the systematic escalation of price at auction, are accomplished through successive sequences of action, through which particular participants are provided with the opportunity to bid or withdraw. This alternating sequential organisation not only creates successive opportunities for action by particular participants, but also enables an extraordinary economy of behaviour, with turns, bids, accomplished for example through head nods alone, an economy that serves to establish rapidly the value and secure the exchange of goods worth anything from a few pounds to many millions (see Heath and Luff 2007).

Within these rapidly emerging sequences of activity we find evidence of a social organisation that informs the emerging production of each and every action, however minimal or seemingly irrelevant. Consider for example the gesture that accompanies the announcement of the increment, a gesture that on close inspection appears systematically in the course of its production to accomplish at least two actions (Figure 14.3). As B.2 bids in response to the increment and accompanying pointing gesture and bodily realignment, the auctioneer immediately turns away from her and towards B.1, simultaneously announcing the price that she has bid. As she begins to nod in response to the invitation, he transforms his gesture, flipping the hand up and down. The flip of the hand displays acknowledgement of the bid and, as it is raised up and down, the participant turns to one side and ceases her head nod. As the hand flips up and down, the auctioneer begins to turn to the protagonist and announces the current increment, namely 'Twelve hundred'. In turn, we can consider the ways in which visible behaviour, like talk, is systematically shaped, designed, in the course of its production, to accomplish particular actions with regard to the context at hand, a 'context' that is emerging in the light of the concurrent conduct of the co-participant(s).

The way in which people respond to the action or activity can depend on the ways in which they participate during its production and, in the course of producing actions, participants may be encouraged to align and respond to those actions in a particular way. In this regard Goffman (1981) addresses the forms of participation that arise during interaction and introduces the idea of participation framework:

FIGURE 14.3   *Fragment 1: images of gestures*

'Participation framework': when a word is spoken all those who happen to be in perceptual range of the event will have some sort of participation status relative to it. The codification of these various positions and the normative specifications of appropriate conduct with each provide an essential background for interaction analysis – whether (I presume) in our own society or any other. (Goffman 1981 p. 3)

In the case at hand, we can begin to see how auctions rely upon an interactional order that selectively organises both the opportunities to participate and the forms of participation in which people engage within the developing course of the activity. These forms of participation are emergent, accomplished, even within the emerging production of an action, sensitive to the emerging conduct of the co-participant(s). In this way, a particular institutional arrangement is established and maintained in and through the fine-grained interaction of the participants themselves, an interaction that is contingently produced and rests upon the deployment of socially organised practice and procedure.

Analysis of a single fragment of a video recording can provide the resources with which we can begin to examine the social and interactional organisation on which these highly complex events rely. We might then proceed to assemble collections of particular actions or action sequences and compare and contrast their character and organisation.

The analysis of the interactional organisation of social actions and activities provides the resources with which to address the ways in which participants themselves orient to, and display an understanding of, each other's actions. For instance, in considering the auctioneer's announcement of the increment and the accompanying visual alignment and gesture, we can examine how the recipient responds to the action, in this case 'in next turn' in order to consider how the participant herself is treating the auctioneer's conduct. Moreover, by considering how the auctioneer himself, in turn, responds to the bidder's actions, by flipping the hand, announcing the next increment and inviting the protagonist to bid, we can discern how he is treating the head nods of the woman. In other words, the interactional organisation of the participants' actions, their emergent and sequential character, provides a vehicle to analyse the very ways in which participants themselves display an understanding of each other's conduct in subsequent action and activity. The interactional organisation of the activity, in this case an auction, is both a topic and analytic resource (see Sacks et al. 1974, Goodwin 1981, Heath 1986).

Data Collection and Transcription

The analytic standpoint the researcher adopts has important implications for data collection. There are long-standing debates concerning how best to record the visual and audible aspects of human conduct and interaction exemplified in the intense discussion between Margaret Mead and Gregory Bateson where they debate the advantages and disadvantages of fixed and roving cameras (see Brand 1976). With the emphasis on interaction, and exploring the ways in which people respond to and participate in each other's conduct, there are some clear implications for data collection and identifying materials that will serve analytic purposes. First and foremost, it is critical to record the conduct and contribution of all active participants in an activity's accomplishment to enable analysis to address the ways in which particular actions and activities emerge in and through social interaction. Secondly, ordinarily fixed, rather than roaming, cameras are adopted for two principal reasons: in attempting to follow action there is an often a small delay before the camera begins to capture the action in question, thereby missing its onset; and in following the action, people remain highly sensitive, and in some cases orient, to the recording – the researcher becomes an active participant within the scene of action. Thirdly, using a fixed camera position, even if it requires using multiple cameras, enables the researcher to maximise the quality of sound and vision and focus the scene that is best for analysis. In this way, data can be gathered that enables a range of analytic interests to be brought to bear upon the analysis of the material. In the case of auctions we found that in many cases it was necessary to use three cameras simultaneously to record the event. In this way, we were able to access recordings of potential buyers, other participants such as sale assistants and clerks, as well as the auctioneer.

These methodological commitments also point to the importance of transcription and transcription as part of the analytic process rather than simply a means to represent the data in an alternative form. Of particular importance is clarifying the position or location of action in order to examine the ways in which an action is sensitive to the preceding and concurrent contributions of others. In analysing a fragment, an episode or event, we begin by transcribing the talk using the orthography developed by Gail Jefferson, a system that is now widely used within conversation analysis and cognate approaches to the analysis of language use and discourse. We then transpose the transcript of the talk to graph paper or the equivalent and, laying the talk horizontally, systematically map at least the onset and completion of the participants' visible conduct (see Heath et al. 2010). Mapping fragments in this way enables one to identify with some precision the position of particular actions and the components of those actions and to examine the potential relations between the actions of the different participants within the interaction. It also provides a vehicle for scrutinising the original recording and noting the complex details of the participants' actions and interaction. These maps of the action are for analytic purposes and rarely used within presentations or publications, though it is not unusual to provide simplified versions of the original transcripts.

Fieldwork and Video Analysis

The video recording is the principal vehicle for analysis and, with a commitment to demonstrating how participants themselves orient to each other's actions, provides the resources through which we develop evidence for particular observations and warrant our findings and explanations. Fieldwork, however, can prove invaluable both in collecting data, including recorded data, and in subjecting these materials to analysis. The importance of fieldwork in undertaking video-based analysis is perhaps of particular importance to studies of the workplace and complex organisational environments. Fieldwork including observation, interviews, discussions with participants, scrutinising documents and the like, can be invaluable in video-based research in:

- gaining the trust and cooperation of participants themselves to enable recording to take place;
- identifying when it is appropriate to undertake video recording and in deciding how to select, frame, and focus on, activities;
- understanding the complex tasks in which people engage and the organisational constraints that bear upon the production of those tasks;
- becoming familiar with the various tools, technologies, objects and artefacts, on which participants rely in the production and coordination of activities;
- documenting aspects of activities as they arise and noting details of related events that might bear upon the production and coordination of particular actions.

So for example, in our study of auctions, we undertook extensive fieldwork that enabled us not only to resolve certain problems that arose in gathering recorded data, but also to become familiar with some of the techniques and resources on which auctioneers rely in conducting sales. Matters such as why

FIGURE 14.4   *The Station Operations Room at Victoria Station on London Underground*

auctioneers begin the bidding at particular prices, how they structure increments, the information documented on the sales sheets, the ways in which they plan a sale and discriminate certain lots proved invaluable in analysing the recordings. Or, for example, consider the picture in Figure 14.4 of a station supervisor in an operations room on London Underground, a setting in which we have undertaken research for some years (see for example Luff et al. 2008, Heath et al. 2002).

To begin to understand the activities of participants in a domain as complex as the operation rooms it is necessary to become familiar with the resources on which personnel rely. For example, a seemingly simple public announcement to inform passengers and staff that the station is overcrowded and is being temporarily closed will involve the supervisor in scrutinising successive CCTV monitors, reviewing the timing of trains, keying area codes into the public address system, radioing selective station staff and, following the event, entering information into 'the failure and delay' sheets. The supervisor's action and the interaction through which it emerges is dependent upon the 'occasioned' use of these resources and analysis can only proceed by understanding those resources and how they are used within the emerging accomplishment of particular activities.

Video-based studies place particular demands on fieldwork and require a rather different approach than may be commonly used when undertaking more conventional ethnographic research (see Heath et al. 2010). One point that is worthwhile mentioning in this regard is the contribution that can be derived from selectively reviewing recordings with participants or experts in the field. For example, in a recent study of anaesthesia and surgical operations, we found it invaluable to have one of the anaesthetists participate in workshops where we examined the recordings; he was able to explain technical procedures that were being undertaken and the specialist considerations that featured in a particular operation.

Notwithstanding the necessity to undertake fieldwork, the recording, the video record, remains the principal analytic resource and the vehicle through which we can warrant our observations and findings with regard to the actions of the participants themselves. In this way, video recordings do not simply stand as a additional way in which we can gather qualitative data or illustrate events that may be of ethnographic interest, but rather provide a methodological resource that enables us to begin to come to terms with one of the central commitments of qualitative research, that is developing analyses that are sensitive, and demonstrate how participants themselves orient to particular practices or procedures in the production of particular actions and activities.

Summary

Video provides an unprecedented resource for social science research and enables the application of various methodological interests and commitments (see for example Knoblauch et al. 2006). In this chapter, we have discussed a particular use of video, an application that exploits video as an 'investigative technology', a technology that enables us to record activities as they arise in ordinary everyday settings and subject them to detailed scrutiny. Drawing on analytic developments within sociology, namely ethnomethodology and conversation analysis, these recordings can provides us with the resources with which to address the key principles of qualitative research with its commitment to the situated character of practical action, the orientations of the participants themselves and the practices through which they accomplish social actions and activities. Social interaction is critical in this regard, forming both the topic and resource of analysis and enabling us to examine the concerted production of social action and the ways in which people make sense of each other's conduct. It is not surprising therefore that in recent years we have witnessed the emergence of a burgeoning corpus of qualitative research that uses video to examine embodied action, research that provides highly distinctive insights into the social and interactional organisation of everyday activities:

- Video provides unprecedented resources for the analysis of human conduct and social interaction in everyday settings.
- Drawing on ethnomethodology and conversation analysis, video can enable the investigation of embodied action and the ways in which activities are accomplished through the interplay of talk, visible conduct and use of tools and technologies.
- The methodological standpoint that informs the use of video places important constraints on how to collect data and the ways in which these materials can be subject to scrutiny and analysis.
- Video, coupled with an appropriate methodological framework, can serve to provide highly distinctive contributions to analytic and substantive issues within the social sciences.

Questions

- Why is video important for qualitative research?
- How can we use video to analyse the social and interactional accomplishment of everyday activities?
- In what ways does transcription provide resources for analysis?
- Why is it helpful to undertake fieldwork as well record people's actions and activities?

Exercise

Following the recommendations discussed in the chapter undertake a video recording of an everyday activity in the home, workplace or a more public environment. Where relevant seek the permission of the participants prior to recording. Select a brief fragment from the recording, no more than 10 seconds long, transcribe the talk and map the visible aspects of the participants' conduct. What actions arise in the fragment, how do they appear to be related to each other, and how do they inform the accomplishment of the activity in which the participants are engaged.

Recommended Reading

Hubert Knoblauch et al. (2006) provides a wide-ranging exposition of qualitative video analysis built around a series of empirical studies adopting different approaches and techniques.

Ulrike Kissmann (2009) presents a collection of various approaches to the analysis of video, drawing on leading scholars from linguistic anthropology, conversation analysis, ethnography and phenomenology.

Christian Heath, Jon Hindmarsh and Paul Luff (2010) provide an introduction to using video for qualitative research and discuss gaining access and ethics, data collection, the analysis of video recordings of everyday activities, the presentation of data and findings, and future developments.

Internet Links to Ethical Guidelines and Procedures

British Psychological Society (2006):

www.bps.org.uk/the-society/code-of-conduct/code-of-conduct_home.cfm

British Sociological Association: Visual Sociology Statement of Ethical Practice (2006):

www.visualsociology.org.uk/about/ethical_statement.php

Economic & Social Research Council 'Research Ethics Framework' (2005):

www.esrcsocietytoday.ac.uk/ESRCInfoCentre/Images/ESRC_Re_Ethics_Frame_tcm6-11291.pdf

References

Asch, T. (Director) (1975). *The Ax Fight* (Film: Collaborating anthropologist – Napoleon Chagnon). Pennsylvania State University. 30 minutes.

Asch, D. (2007). Using video data to capture discontinuous science meaning making in nonschool settings. In R. Goldman, R. Pea, B. Barron & S.J. Derry (Eds), *Video Research in the Learning Sciences*. London: Routledge.

Atkinson, J. M., & Heritage, J. C. (Eds) (1984). *The Structures of Social Action: Studies in Conversation Analysis*. Cambridge: Cambridge University Press.

Banks, M. (2001). *Visual Methods in Social Research*. London: Sage.

Barley, S. R., & Kunda, G. (2001). Bringing work back in. *Organization Science*, 12(1), 76–95.

Bateson, G., & Mead, M. (1942). *Balinese Character: A Photographic Analysis*. New York: New York Academy of Sciences.

Brand, S. B. (1976). For God's sake, Margaret: conversation with Gregory Bateson and Margaret Mead. *CoEvolutionary Quarterly*, 10, 32–44.

Braune, W., & Fischer, O. (1895). *The Human Gait* (reprinted 1987). Berlin: Springer-Verlag.

Büscher, M. (2005). Social life under the microscope, *Sociological Research Online* (Vol. 10).

Clark, C., and Pinch, T. (1995). *The Hard Sell: The Language and Lessons of Street Wise Marketing*. New York: Harper Collins.

Dant, T. (2004). Recording the 'Habitus'. In C. Pole (Ed.), *Seeing is Believing? Approaches to Visual Methodology*. (Studies in Qualitative Methodology, Vol. 7) (pp. 43–63). Amsterdam: Elsevier.

Drew, P., & Heritage, J. C. (Eds). (1992). *Talk at Work: Interaction in Institutional Settings*. Cambridge: Cambridge University Press.

Engeström, Y., & Middleton, D. (Eds). (1996). *Cognition and Communication at Work*. Cambridge: Cambridge University Press.

Filippi, G., & Theureau, J. (1993). Analyzing cooperative work in an urban traffic control room for the design of a coordinate support system. In *Proceedings of the Third Conference on European Conference on Computer-Supported Cooperative Work* (pp. 171–186). Norwell, MA: Kluwer.

Garfinkel, H. (1967). *Studies in Ethnomethodology*. Englewood Cliffs, NJ: Prentice Hall.

Goffman, E. (1981). *Forms of Talk*. Oxford: Blackwell.

Goldman, R., Pea, R., Barron, B., & Derry, S. J. (Eds). (2007). *Video Research in the Learning Sciences*. London: Routledge.

Goodwin, C. (1981). *Conversational Organisation: Interaction between Speakers and Hearers*. London: Academic Press.

Goodwin, C., & Goodwin, M. H. (1996). Seeing as a situated activity: formulating planes. In Y. Engeström & D. Middleton (Eds), *Cognition and Communication at Work* (pp. 61–95). Cambridge: Cambridge University Press.

Goodwin, M. H. (2006). *The Hidden Life of Girls: Games of Stance, Status and Exclusion*. Oxford: Blackwell.

Greatbatch, D., Luff, P., Heath, C. C., & Campion, P. (1993). Interpersonal communication and human-computer interaction: an examination of the use of computers in medical consultations. *Interacting with Computers*, 5(2), 193–216.

Heath, C. C. (1986). *Body Movement and Speech in Medical Interaction*. Cambridge: Cambridge University Press.

Heath, C. C., & Button, G. (Eds). (2002). Special Issue on Workplace Studies. *British Journal of Sociology* (Vol. 53).

Heath, C. C., & Luff, P. (2000). *Technology in Action*. Cambridge: Cambridge University Press.

Heath, C. C., & Luff, P. (2007). Ordering competition: the interactional accomplishment of the sale of fine art and antiques at auction. *British Journal of Sociology*, 58(1), 63–85.

Heath, C. C., & vom Lehn, D. (2008). Construing interactivity: enhancing engagement with new technologies in science centres and museums. *Social Studies of Science*, 38, 63–96.

Heath, C., Luff, P., & Sanchez Svensson, M. (2002). Overseeing organisations: configuring the environment of action. *British Journal of Sociology*, 53(2), 181–203.

Heath, C. C., Hindmarsh, J., & Luff, P. (2010). *Video in Qualitative Research: Analysing Social Interaction in Everyday Life*. London: Sage.

Heritage, J. C. (1984). *Garfinkel and Ethnomethodology*. Cambridge: Polity Press.

Heritage, J. C., & Maynard, D. (Eds) (2006). *Practising Medicine: Talk and Action in Primary Care Encounters*. Cambridge: Cambridge University Press.

Hindmarsh, J., & Pilnick, A. (2002). The tacit order of teamwork: collaboration and embodied conduct in anaesthesia. *Sociological Quarterly*, 43(2), 139–164.

Hindmarsh, J., Fraser, M., Heath, C., & Benford, S. (2000). Object-focused interaction in collaborative virtual environments. *ACM Transactions on Computer-Human Interaction (ToCHI)*, 7(4), 477–509.

Hughes, E. C. (1958). *Men and their Work*. Glencoe, IL: Free Press.

Jewitt, C. (Ed.) (2009). *Routledge Handbook of Multimodal Analysis*. London: Routledge.

Kissmann, U. T. (Ed.). (2009). *Video Interaction Analysis: Methods and Methodology*. Frankfurt-am-Main: Peter Lang.

Knoblauch, H., Schnettler, B., Raab, J., & Söffner, H.-G. (Eds). (2006). *Video-Analysis: Methodology and Methods Qualitative Audiovisual Data Analysis in Sociology*. Frankfurt am Main: Lang-Verlag.

Laurier, E., & Philo, C. (2006). Natural problems of naturalistic video data. In H. Knoblauch, J. Raab, H.-G. Soefnner & B. Schnettler (Eds), *Video Analysis: Methodology and Methods* (pp. 181–190). Frankfurt: Peter Lang.

Llewellyn, N. & Hindmarsh, J. (Eds) (2010). *Organization, Interaction and Practice: Sudies in Ethnomethodology and Conversation Analysis*. Cambridge: Cambridge University Press.

Luff, P., Hindmarsh, J., & Heath, C. (Eds). (2000). *Workplace Studies: Recovering Work Practice and Informing System Design*. Cambridge: Cambridge University Press.

Luff, P., Heath, C., & Sanchez Svensson, M. (2008). Discriminating conduct: deploying systems to support awareness in organisations. *International Journal of Human Computer Studies*, 24(4), 410–436.

Marey, E.-J. (1895). *Movement* (Translated by Eric Pritchard). London: Heinemann Press.

Mead, M. (1995 [1974]). Visual anthropology and the discipline of words. In P. Hockings (Ed.), *Principles in Visual Anthropology* (2nd Edition) (pp. 3–10). Berlin and New York: Mouton de Gruyter.

Mondada, L. (2003). Working with video: how surgeons produce video records of their actions. *Visual Studies*, 18, 58–73.

Morphy, H., & Banks, M. (Eds). (1997). *Rethinking Visual Anthropology*. New Haven, CT: Yale University Press.

Peräkylä, A., & Ruusuvuori, J. (2006). Facial expression in an assessment. In H. Knoblauch, J. Raab, H.-G. Soefnner & B. Schnettler (Eds), *Video Analysis: Methodology and Methods* (pp. 127–142). Frankfurt: Peter Lang.

Pink, S. (2006). *Doing Visual Ethnography: Images, Media and Representation in Research* (2nd Edition). London: Sage.

Poech, R. (1907). Reisen in Neu-Guinea in den Jahren 1904–1906. *Zeitschrift für Ethnologie*, 39, 382–400.

Prodger, P. (2003). *Time Stands Still: Muybridge and the Instantaneous Photography Movement*. Oxford: Oxford University Press.

Relieu, M., & Licoppe, C. (2007). Entre système et conversation. Une approche située de la compétence des téléopérateurs dans les services d'assistance technique. In E. Kessous and J. L. Metzger (Eds), *Travailler avec les TIC*. Paris: Edition Hermès.

Rose, G. (2004). *Visual Methodologies: An Introduction to the Interpretation of Visual Materials*. London: Sage.

Sacks, H. (1992). *Lectures in Conversation* (Vols I and II). Oxford: Blackwell.

Sacks, H., Schegloff, E. A., & Jefferson, G. (1974). A simplest systematics for the organisation of turn-taking for conversation. *Language*, 50(4), 696–735.

Silverman, D. (1970). *The Theory of Organizations*. London: Heinemann.

Spencer, W. B., & Gillen, F. J. (1899). *The Native Tribes of Central Australia*. London: Macmillan.

Streeck, J., Goodwin, C., & Le Baron, C. (Eds). (Forthcoming). *Embodied Interaction: Language and Body in the Material World*. Cambridge: Cambridge University Press.

Suchman, L. (1996). Constituting shared workspaces. In Y. Engeström & D. Middleton (Eds), *Cognition and Communication at Work* (pp. 35–60). Cambridge: Cambridge University Press.

Suchman, L. (1997). Centers of coordination: a case and some themes. In L. B. Resnick, R. Säljö, C. Pontecorvo & B. Burge (Eds), *Discourse, Tools, and Reasoning: Essays on Situated Cognition* (pp. 41–62). Berlin: Springer-Verlag.

Suchman, L. A. (2007). *Human-Machine Reconfigurations: Plans and Situated Actions* (2nd Edition). Cambridge: Cambridge University Press.

Szymanski, M. (Forthcoming). *Making Work Visible*. Cambridge: Cambridge University Press

ten Have, P. (1999). *Doing Conversational Analysis: A Practical Guide*. London: Sage.

vom Lehn, D., Heath, C. C., & Hindmarsh, J. (2001). Exhibiting interaction: conduct and collaboration in museums and galleries interaction. *Symbolic Interaction*, 24(2): 189–217.

Whalen, J. (1995). Expert systems vs. systems for experts: computer-aided dispatch as a support system in real-world environments. In P. Thomas (Ed.), *The Social and Interactional Dimensions of Human-Computer Interfaces* (pp. 161–183). Cambridge: Cambridge University Press.

Whalen, J., & Vinkhuyzen, E. (2000). Expert systems in (inter)action: diagnosing document machine problems over the telephone. In P. Luff, J. Hindmarsh & C. Heath (Eds), *Workplace Studies: Recovering Work Practice and Informing System Design* (pp. 92–140). Cambridge: Cambridge University Press.

PART VII

QUALITATIVE DATA ANALYSIS

Some Pragmatics of Data Analysis 15

Tim Rapley

Abstract

This chapter aims to give you access to some of the routines, procedures, phases and tactics that are common in qualitative analytic reasoning and practice. Initially I focus on four routinely cited approaches to qualitative data analysis in order to explore their similarities and differences. I then describe some of the pragmatic issues you might need to consider alongside some of the qualities or states of mind you might seek to cultivate.

Keywords:

coding, memos, data reduction, sampling, deviant case analysis.

Some Initial Thoughts on 'Analysis'

Anyone new to qualitative analysis will be faced with a quandary: what should I do with all this data? You look at various journal articles, and often see the same key phrases again and again. People keep telling you they did 'grounded theory', or conducted a 'phenomenological analysis', and then give you various levels of details about what that did. Some are quite rich descriptions of things done to and with 'raw data'; others just use a couple of phrases and a single reference (often to the same small array of texts). Above all, whatever you read, you realize that it is de rigueur to have some kind of tag. You need the right kind of label in your methods section, ideally one that positions you as competent, so that your work can be nicely categorized.

The practices of good (or even adequate) qualitative data analysis can never be adequately summed up by using a neat tag. They can also never be summed up by a list of specific steps or procedures that have been undertaken. Above all, you need to develop a working, hands-on, empirical, tacit knowledge of analysis. This should enable you to develop what I can only think to call, 'a qualitative analytic attitude'.

Some Examples of Analytic Approaches

The novice is often faced with a second quandary: which of the many approaches I've read about should I use? Rather than offer you an exhaustive account and exploration of all the potential approaches available to you, I'm going briefly to focus on and compare four routinely cited approaches to qualitative data analysis. I'm only doing this to give you a flavour of the work that can be involved. In Table 15.1, you'll see that each column outlines, in very basic and procedural terms, some of the key actions related to each analytic method.

TABLE 15.1

Framework analysis (see Ritchie & Spencer 1994, Ritchie, Spencer & O'Connor 2003)	Thematic analysis (see Grbich 1999, Braun & Clarke 2006)	Interpretative phenomenological analysis (see Smith & Osborn 2008)	Constructivist grounded theory (see Charmaz 2000, 2006)
1 *Familiarize yourself with the dataset* (note initial themes or concepts)	1 *Familiarize yourself with the dataset* (note initial comments and ideas)	1 *Read single transcript* (note initial comments and ideas)	1 *Initial coding and memo writing* (line-by-line coding, compare new codes with old, evaluate, alter, adjust, write notes)
2 *Generate thematic framework* (themes, sub-themes from data and interview topic guide)	2 *Generate initial codes* (systematically code whole dataset)	2 *Generate initial themes* (transform comments into themes)	2 *Focused coding and memo writing* (select and then code key issues, keep comparing, write notes to refine ideas)

(Continued)

TABLE 15.1 *(Continued)*

Framework analysis (see Ritchie & Spencer 1994, Ritchie, Spencer & O'Connor 2003)	Thematic analysis (see Grbich 1999, Braun & Clarke 2006)	Interpretative phenomenological analysis (see Smith & Osborn 2008)	Constructivist grounded theory (see Charmaz 2000, 2006)
3 *Indexing* (apply thematic framework, label data with number or term)	3 *Search for themes* (collate similar codes into potential themes, gather all data for potential theme)	3 *Create initial list of themes*	3 *Collect new data via theoretical sampling* (strategically sample to further develop categories and their properties)
4 *Sort data by theme or concept and summarize* (create thematic charts)	4 *Review themes* (check if themes work in relation to the dataset, check for examples that do not fit, generate a thematic map/ diagram)	4 *Cluster themes* (order the list of themes into connected areas)	4 *Continue to code, memo and use theoretical sampling* (develop and refine categories until no new issues emerge)
5 *Develop descriptive accounts* (develop and then refine categories)	5 *Refine themes* (refine specifics of each theme and linkages between them, generate propositions, look for complexity, associations)	5 *Create a list/table with superordinate themes and sub-themes*	5 *Sort and integrate memos* (refine links between categories, develop concepts, write an initial draft of a theory)
6 *Develop explanatory accounts* (look for patterns, associations, clustering and explanations)		6 *Go to new transcript* (repeat above process and refine list/ table of themes)	
		7 *Create a final list/table with superordinate themes and sub-themes*	

I've chosen two quite popular and relatively discipline-free approaches, 'thematic analysis' and 'grounded theory',[1] alongside 'framework analysis', which is often tied to applied and/or policy research, and a relative newcomer, 'interpretative phenomenological analysis' (IPA), which is increasingly cited in qualitative psychology. These four were chosen, in part, as they already have quite clear, accessible, 'guidelines' about the key phases or tactics researchers might employ.

I need to add a health warning here. The table is a heuristic device. Do not simply follow the phases I've outlined in the table if you intend to use any of these approaches. Following the phases in a stepwise way will *not* ensure you are conducting the analysis in the ways the authors intended, as it does not render the specific practical action and reasoning that you are meant to employ. If you like the look of any of them, go and read about them.

As you'll see, in their most basic terms they all share some family resemblances, in that they seek to move from the particular to the abstract. By that I mean they all start with a close inspection of a sample of data about a specific issue. This close inspection is used to discover, explore and generate an increasingly refined conceptual description of the phenomena. The resulting conceptual description therefore emerges from, is based on, or is grounded in the data about the phenomena. The focus shifts from:

- what is said by participants, what you've observed them doing or what you read in a text (the level of description and summary); to
- exploring and explaining what is 'underlying' or 'broader' or to 'distil' essence, meaning, norms, orders, patterns, rules, structures, et cetera (the level of concepts and themes).

I'm going to do something quite naive now. I'm going to ask: what, if anything, can we learn from all these different approaches to qualitative data analysis? We can learn some quite useful lessons from looking at them as a whole, rather than as totally distinct approaches. I'm going to attempt to reduce them to some quite mundane and generic analytic practices. The central methods that appear to cut across these (and other forms of data-analysis methods like analytic induction, alongside data-analysis phases in things like ethnography, discourse analysis) appear to be as follows:

---

[1]Note that I've used Charmaz's version of 'constructivist grounded theory'. Grounded theory is a broad church. Novice readers should make themselves aware of the differences between Glaser's 'classical' grounded theory (1992), Strauss and Corbin's approach (1990) and the more constructivist ones (see Charmaz and Bryant, this volume).

Some Fundamentals

- *Always start by engaging in some kind of close, detailed, reading of a sample/section/ bit of your archive of data.*

  - And close, detailed, reading means looking for key, essential, striking, odd, interesting things people or texts say or do as well as repetition.
  - You should make notes, jottings, markings, et cetera, either on the pages or somewhere else.

- *Always read and systematically label your archive of data.*

  - Label[2] key, essential, striking, odd, interesting things.
  - Label similar items with the same label.
  - These labels can be drawn from ideas emerging from your close, detailed, reading of your data archive, as well as from your prior reading of empirical and theoretical works.
  - With each new application of a label, review your prior labelling practices and see if what you want to label fits what has gone before. If yes, use that label. If no, create a new one. If it fits somewhat, you may want to modify your understanding of that label to include this.

- *Always reflect on why you've done what you've done.*

  - Come up with a document that lists your labels. It might be useful to give some key examples, to write a sentence or two that explains what you are trying to get at, what sort of things should go together under specific labels.

- *Always review and refine your labels and labelling practices.*

  - For each label, collect together all the data you've given that label to. Ask yourself whether the data and ideas collected under this label are coherent, and ask yourself what are the key properties and dimensions of all the data collected under that label?
  - Try to combine your initial labels, look for links between them, look for repetitions, exceptions and try to reduce them to key ones. This will often mean shifting from more verbatim, descriptive, labels to more conceptual, abstract and analytic labels.
  - Keep evaluating, adjusting, altering and modifying your labels and labelling practices.
  - Go back over what you've already done and relabel it with your new schema or ideas.

---

[2]Labels are what you use to enable easy identification and retrieval of things of note.

- *Always focus on what you feel are the key labels and the relationship between them.*
  - o Make some judgments about what you feel are the central labels and focus on them.
  - o Try to look for links, patterns, associations, arrangements, relationships, sequences, et cetera.

The above fundamentals should be read as quite general statements about the analytic process, rather than as a stepwise guide about how to conduct analysis. They seem to be embedded, to various degrees, in the writing (and lived practices) of a whole range of traditions. Interestingly, they are all quite accessible, mundane and, above all, quite doable. Some other methods, although I personally feel they are central, only appear in some how-to discussions.

Some Options

- *Always make notes of your thinking behind why you've done what you've done.*
  - o Make notes on ideas that emerge before, during or while you're engaged in labelling or reading related to your research project.
  - o Make some diagrams, tables, maps, models that enable you to conceptualize, witness, generate and show connections and relationships between labels.

- *Always return to the field with the knowledge you have already gained in mind and let this knowledge modify, guide or shape the data you want to collect next.*

Despite some apparent family resemblances in the table, even a brief reading, without any knowledge of the actual analytic methods, shows that there are some telling differences. You should note that each approach has its own analytic language. So, for example, grounded theory talks in terms of moving from 'codes' to 'categories and their properties' (and, at times, to 'concepts'), whereas IPA talks of moving from 'themes' to 'superordinate themes'.

Each approach also has its own specific norms and rules of application. For example, both IPA and framework assume that the dataset is made up of some kind of recorded interviews. Given IPA's commitment to the specifics of each case, it is suggested that the analyst focus on a very small number of qualitative interviews. With framework, they suggest that you work with a range of 'thematic charts'. So, for example, you'd initially establish a table where you list all the themes and sub-themes and quotes from each interview. These tables enable you to divide the data into topics, you then begin to finely label that data, and then you refine those labels to more abstract, over arching, labels. In the case of constructivist grounded theory (and grounded theory as a whole) the focus is on developing substantive theory of a particular process, situation, or (inter)actions. Central to this style of work is constantly noting and developing your ideas in memos, encouraging you to shift your thinking from just this moment of data to more abstract reasoning. The iterative process of rounds of data collection, coding and memo writing is meant to encourage conceptual development, as new rounds of fieldwork are undertaken to explore, and ultimately confirm or discard, analytic ideas. Unlike the other approaches, thematic analysis, although referenced widely, suffers as it has no coherent groups of academics claiming, defining and shaping its trajectory. So, the specific analytic etiquette of doing thematic analysis seems to vary broadly between authors.[3]

Some Observations on Aspects of a Qualitative Analytic Attitude

I now want to focus on some descriptions of some aspects of qualitative analytic practice and reasoning. Rather than follow or champion a specific tradition or style of analysis, I'm interested in trying to give you access to some of the very practical things you might need to consider or do alongside some of the qualities or states of mind you might seek to cultivate.

On Uncertainty, Intuition and Hunches

Above all, when undertaking analysis you need to be prepared to be led down novel and unexpected paths, to be open and to be fascinated. Potential ideas can emerge from any quarter – from your prior and ongoing reading, your knowledge of the field, from engagements with your data, from conversations with colleagues, and from life beyond academia – and from any phase in the life-cycle of the project. Whatever you do, remember to write it down! You also need to listen to and value your intuition and hunches. At some points you follow up a hunch, you go back over the data, and look again at your archive (your project related transcripts, texts, field notes, labelling practices, notes to self, memos, journal articles, books, et cetera) with a sense of joy as you feel you might be on to something.

Sometimes this ends in frustration, as your idea does not hold water; either the interviewee did not say something that radically different, or your idea echoes something already well developed in the literature. Sometimes the idea only comes to fruition much later in the project, or acts as a spark that instigates a new trajectory of thought. Centrally, try and cultivate a sense of creative, even playful, engagement with your archive. If you spot a potential pattern, then search your archive to

---

[3]Even the definition of what a 'theme' is varies dramatically. See DeSantis & Ugarriza (2000).

see if this is coherent. Ideas emerge in all sorts of ways, but you *must* be immersed in the detail of your archive to be really able to generate and fully explore them.

On Labelling

There is something very interesting about adding some sort of label to your data archive. In learning to label, you begin to develop, to borrow a phrase from Goodwin (1994), a 'professional vision' directed at your data. By that I mean you make some analytic choices about which lines, chunks or sections of data to highlight. In highlighting some things as belonging to a particular label, you begin inductively to create a local coding schema, a specific way to see and understand the phenomena. It does involve quite a lot of skill and requires some degree of confidence, especially if you need to show and then discuss with others what you've done, when you are aware that your judgments may be examined.

At the start of the data-coding process, being faced with a large stretch of text to be highlighted and labelled can be quite scary, and adding your first 'official' label can be quite odd. If you are at all unsure, the trick is, rather than mark a specific day as 'the day I start coding', and maybe delay the process until you've collected some more data or done some more reading, just read the text and make some notes on it. Just underline or mark it in some way or add a note about whatever interests you. These initial engagements with your data archive, what Layder (1998) calls pre-coding, are vital, and enable you to start exploring some of the potential in your archive. Give yourself time to reflect and ponder. You may be inspired to write a note to yourself, or to go and do some reading to follow up something you've noticed.

On Your Initial Systematic Engagements

At some point, you need to start engaging in a more systematic, albeit tentative and preliminary, style of labelling. You are really doing this for three reasons:

1   It forces you to engage, word by word, line by line, section by section, with the detail, to ask specific questions about and of your data. Reading in and for detail is essential practice.
2   You simply will not be able to remember all the things you've seen that you feel are important, so labelling helps you to recall issues.
3   You can then easily gather all the data you've collected under a specific label and use this, alongside your related notes, to review the issue you are exploring, to help you to establish connections, commonalties and any overarching orders.

When starting to systematically label, I would always suggest working with a paper and pen over a computer. Computers can overly constrain the options you have for marking up a text, whereas with paper and pen you can scrawl all over the text. You will often find that initial marked-up text will be very messy, both in a practical sense – in that things will be underlined, crossed out, commented on, drawn on – and in a conceptual sense – in that you may have very large number of disparate, sometimes even competing or contradictory, labels. You need to remember that, especially at the start, what you choose to highlight and the label you choose to apply to it are the product of your understanding so far. Don't worry if the next day you feel you have to come back and do it again or if you think it's not quite right. At the start all you are trying to do is to establish the possible dimensions of the phenomena, so just try and make sense about what each word, line and section are about. Highlighting and labelling practices are always provisional and over the life of the project you will engage in continually modifying, refining and sometimes relabelling whole chunks of texts as your understanding shifts.

On Living in the Detail

Whether you prefer to think broadly and conceptually or prefer to live in the detail, with the first few rounds of highlighting and labelling texts, I would always recommend forcing yourself to start out doing line-by-line coding, and if you really can't face that, at least paragraph-by-paragraph coding. This initial tight focus can really help you concentrate on working with the data, and help avoid importing too many a priori presuppositions about what you think should be going on there. That is not say that you cannot draw on your prior reading, knowledge or experiences from the field. In thinking about and designing your interview schedule, setting up interviews or observations, or collecting documents or recordings you will already be making and forming certain analytic ideas. However, these ideas should never wholly overshadow or be the sole direction to your sense making as you engage with your data archive. They are tools which you can draw on to enable and enhance engagement with your archive. Above all, follow the data:

- When it comes to the early phases of acts of labelling and highlighting, you can learn a lot from disciplines like conversation analysis and discourse analysis. They often work with quite short extracts and focus on the specific work that is occurring with each utterance, word or section. You need to ask, with each line or paragraph: 'how is it the thing comes off?' (Sacks 1992).[4]

---

[4] You should note that conversation analyses engage in two quite distinct practices. First, they routinely work backwards from some outcome (e.g. an act of crying or shifting topic) and not downwards line by line, in order to explore how that action was produced. Second, rather than use a priori knowledge (e.g. that these people are a doctor and nurse) they focus on what people actually do, the identities that are invoked by the participants (e.g. they are doing being friends) (see Heritage, this volume).

The practicalities of coding are as simple as: highlight a word, line, sentence or paragraph and then give it a label. These labels can range from the quite descriptive to the abstract and conceptual. But what do you even use as a label? You have a whole array of possibilities, ranging from single 'key words' that do some nice summing up, to a few words, to phrases or even sentences. And these can emerge from using the specific words that people use, as well as modifying, somewhat, those phrases. This is often referred to as '*in vivo* coding' (see Charmaz 2006). You can also draw on your repertoire of ideas, using words or phrases that sum up or draw out the key issue or idea.

Some Words of Caution

Despite repeated warnings in the literature to retain 'the participant's voice', when it comes to the words you choose for your labels you really don't have to take this too far. Don't feel that you need to stick to exactly the phrase used, that to modify it, say by changing the tense or taking out an utterance, you are somehow being disrespectful to that person's 'lived experience'. This can lose the point of good analysis and can cause confusion. First, you need to remember that creating a list of key verbatim descriptions is not the end stage of analysis, it is the start. Second, it confuses the analytic phase with the phase of presentation of your argument to others. In notes to yourself and in publications, you will probably end up using verbatim quotes, and so give others access to these 'voices'.

Relatedly, grouping relatively large chunks of text together, using large theoretical labels like 'power' or 'identity work', is rarely a good way to start. Such grand, off-the-shelf labels are clearly the mainstay of a lot of academic writing and discussion, and such issues may be present, shaping or clearly visible in your data. However, this can easily close down the analysis far too quickly, in the sense that you've already decided that the specific focus is on issues such as this, and that these are the key examples that inform you about its properties or essential make-up. As such it can overly determine the shape and possibilities of your data. Such broad concepts are actually the end-point of a careful process of analytic work. By starting and only working with such theory-driven macro-labels, you often fail to grasp the specifics of the phenomena. The point is to try to make sense of how, when and why specific processes, practices and structures happen.

On Knowing How to see Things to Highlight and Label

How do you learn to read for the detail? Put simply, like most crafts, this takes practice and time. Alongside working with someone who has got some experience, and both working on the same data and then discussing your analytic reasoning and practices, it is worth looking at some of the texts available that offer you an overview of specific ways of labelling. For example, Bernard and Ryan (2010) offer 12 simple techniques to begin to identify what they call, following Opler (1945), themes. These include focusing on such aspects as 'repetitions', 'similarities and differences' and 'indigenous typologies and categories'. Saladaña (2009) describes 23 approaches to early-phase coding, with these grouped into seven different genres. For example, the genre 'elemental methods' includes *in vivo* coding, descriptive coding (use a label to describe the substantive topic of the line or lines of text), whereas the genre 'literary and language methods' includes narrative coding (so focus on aspects of narrative structure). Finally, Gibbs (2007) describes 12 aspects that you could focus on, from 'specific acts and behaviour', to 'relationship and interaction', and 'meanings'. What all these overviews share is a quite practical focus, offering a wide range of techniques for you to work with. Above all, read these and other texts, things that offer you quite practical and worked-through examples.

Finally, be aware that the initial stages of coding often take up a lot of time. It is routine to be hesitant, to find yourself pondering about what specific label to apply, about where the text connected to that label should begin and end. Keep asking yourself: does this make sense, is that really about X, Y or Z or something else? Remember, you are attempting to create your own coding scheme, your own professional vision, rather than apply someone else's. With that comes some responsibility; most importantly, that your schema actually has some connection to the data! However idiosyncratic your highlighting and labelling practice, others should be able to come to your data archive and, with your support, be able to follow your reasoning, to understand the logic of your practice.

On Splitting, Combining, Simplifying and Reducing

Alongside living in the detail, you also need to have your eye on the broader picture. You always need to be able to step back and think bigger and bolder, to think beyond just a single line, paragraph or case, and start to get a sense of connections between different parts of your archive. As Miles and Huberman (1994) argue, you always need to engage in a process of 'data reduction'. They describe this as:

> [t]he process of selecting, focusing, simplifying, abstracting and transforming the data that appear in written field notes or transcriptions [or texts]. ... As data collection proceeds, further episodes of data reduction occur (writing summaries, coding, teasing out themes, making clusters, making partitions, writing memos). ... Data reduction is a form of analysis that sharpens, sorts, focuses, discards, and organises data in such a way that 'final' conclusions can be drawn and verified. (p. 10)

Centrally, data reduction is an ongoing activity over the life of all research projects. The simple act of highlighting and labelling something, or of giving the same label to two distinct sections of the same or different texts, is in essence a way to reduce data.

Over the life of a project you are often moving through rounds of splitting the data into separate labels, reviewing those fragments (and notes about them) collected under specific labels, trying to see how and in what ways the ideas underlying each label combine, relate or diverge. You work to group certain labels together, to redefine and rename them, to drill down to explore the detail and dimensions of these new emerging issues. As you move through this process, you start to focus on specific issues and to discard some ideas as no longer central to your argument. As noted above, this may well mean you have to relabel parts or all of your data, in order to re-explore it, given your new concerns or ideas.

Over the life of a project the process of highlighting and labelling becomes quicker and you become less hesitant. With each new engagement with your archive, your coding schema needs less substantive tailoring and refining. You will generally reach a point when you've got a sense of what the key issues are so far. At the very least you now need to turn to a new, as yet unanalysed, piece of data or, even better, return to the field, to collect new data, to further refine your ideas. In an ideal world, as this process is going on you will be regularly meeting with others (be they colleagues or supervisors) to discuss, debate and challenge your emerging findings. People may not always agree with everything, but such discussions will definitely sharpen and direct your thinking.

Centrally you're aiming for something that is representative of your dataset, yet relatively abstract. To be utterly representative you'd need to give everyone all your data; instead you offer them 'categories' or 'themes' that demonstrate the key issues. Dey (2007), albeit speaking about grounded theory, outlines some aspects of the analytic attitude, the reasoning and practices, central to much qualitative work:

> [seek] the underlying logic of apparently disparate events, recognizing causal inferences at work through our categorizations, checking, revising, amplifying interpretations through comparisons across settings, and using representational techniques to evaluate and explore connections between categories. (p. 188)

You need carefully and creatively to conceptualize, abstract and render the central aspects of a phenomenon to make it available to others.

On Repetition and Boredom

Alongside moments of elation and frustration, at points, doing analysis can be quite boring. This may seem rather a negative thing to discuss but it is worth considering how it is that you get bored. Boredom can be your friend. There are two potential ways that you can find yourself 'bored'.

First, it emerges when you're seeing the same issues again and again and certain labels seem to be emerging as dominant. Discovering repetition can be a good thing. Qualitative research is in part about finding and describing patterns and structures, observing routines. When you've seen the same thing again and again, you may be onto something. In the early stages of analysis, seeing repetition can be useful. However, in these early stages, it can also mean that your labels are just too large, that you are not thinking with your data at an adequate level of detail. In the later stages, when you're trying to verify your ideas, being bored can be quite useful as it may signify that you've potentially hit gold.

Second, it can emerge as you are faced with an ever growing amount of data to analyse. This can lead you to cast too casual a glance at your data. When you are not expecting news, you can get into a habit of glossing over some sections of your data or just giving it a rather grand code. The trick is to be aware of potential surprises, to enable yourself to be interested by what is going on. This often emerges when you've collected a lot of data and have not had time to engage with it. In such cases, you're faced with having to manage large amounts of coding and related writing. This is, to be frank, a bad practice. Qualitative research is an iterative practice; its strength can lie in the process of collecting something, drawing out key issues, then going to discover, in your next round of data collection (or reading), how relevant that issue is in a different context, with a different person.

On Returning

For me, engaging in rounds or cycles of fieldwork (so data collection) and office-work (so analysis and note-taking) is essential practice. The reason we engage in qualitative research is to discover a phenomenon, in all its textures and nuances, to focus on and explore. The easiest way really to achieve this is to flip between phases of office- and fieldwork, so that they mutually inform each other. This means you need to think a lot about sampling. Our claims stand and fall on drawing out ideas from quite small (albeit deeply rich) collections of cases. As such we should work hard to choose those cases with some care. Only relying on convenience sampling, as in a sample of all those you have access to and that said 'yes' to taking part, is not good practice. Also, only relying on a retrospective conceptualization of your sample, discovering the diversity *post hoc* and then describing it as a 'maximum variation sample', is not that useful.

After your initial rounds of sampling that will often by design be a convenience sample, you really need follow that up with further rounds of sampling that are driven by your emerging analytic findings. Patton (2002) has a useful list of the 14 different styles of sampling to guide your choices (see also Draucker et al. 2007). Your emerging data and ideas about it suggest further criteria for selecting additional cases, texts or settings, and you specifically seek more data to develop those ideas.[5] You may want to go in search of similar cases or texts or visit similar settings, in order to further explore your ideas or more variable cases, texts or settings which may challenge your ideas.

At some point, you need to make the decision to stop collecting data. There are really no hard and fast rules about when this should happen. In an ideal world this would happen when you've had time to explore all the questions and issues that the office- and fieldwork raise, that you've generated a rich and coherent account, and further rounds will not generate any substantial new directions. However, given the nature of academic timelines and your willingness to devote your time to a single phenomenon, you'll never be able to answer all your questions, to follow up all the potential leads that your analysis raises. What is central is that the key ideas and claims have been thoroughly thought through and investigated.

On Writing

I cannot stress enough how key this is. The focus that writing enables is so incredibly helpful in both establishing what you know (and don't know) and assisting you in making conceptual leaps. Transforming your thoughts onto paper or onto the screen, throughout the life of the project, inscribes them with form and solidity. The act of writing is a rich and analytic process as you find yourself not only attempting to explain and justify your ideas, but also developing them. It is all very well to think with data in and through internal dialogues with yourself, brief jottings, or conversations with other interested people. However, thinking with data via some brief or extended period, either written or typed, will transform your ideas.

Making your ideas 'concrete' enables you to reflect, to see gaps, to explore, to draw other texts in. By writing, I mean as little as those moments when you're reading or thinking about your data, you have an idea and spend five minutes noting it down, to those moments when you might be spending hours writing. You should get into the habit of writing about anything that might be helpful. An idea may emerge from something you've read, seen, discussed or overheard. It is not only writing, but also working with diagrams, lists, tables, basically anything that offers you a way to conceptualize your ideas.

Two traditions of qualitative research already understand the value of writing. Writing in the form of memos is one of the essential foundations of all styles of grounded theory. For ethnographers, the practice of writing and working from field notes is vital. Irrespective of whether you're doing grounded theory, or ethnography, go and read some of the practitioners' discussion (see Emerson, Fretz and

---

[5] This is often referred to as 'theoretical sampling' (Glaser 1978).

Shaw 1995, Lempert 2007, Montgomery and Bailey 2007). Rather than read these accounts of writing-as-analysis as definitive guides about how to construct, manage and use writing, draw on them creatively. Whatever happens, you should never feel that writing is for the final stage of analysis, it is actually an essential practice at all stages of the analytic trajectory (see Marvasti, this volume).

On Exceptions

At the start of your analysis, it is not an understatement to say that exceptions will be *everywhere*. Analysis is, in some ways, about enacting a professional vision that focuses on 'similarity and difference'. As soon as you begin to look at a transcript, field note or text, you will be focusing not only on what it tells you about the phenomenon, but also on how it compares with what you already know. Exceptions can generally be found when you find yourself asking: where does that go?

In the early stages of analysis, finding 'exceptions' that make you change your ideas or labelling practices is a routine and everyday affair. Each new line or page of text can make you question your ideas, as something new often emerges which means you have to generate a new label or revise and expand your thinking about an old one. You often find something that could potentially fit into multiple labels and so you may need to refine it, or accept that it works for multiple labels.

Over time, as you begin to immerse yourself in your data, in rounds of data collection, labelling and writing, these exceptions become less visible. At this point, when you do notice something that does not really fit with what has gone before, it can really start to stand out, and in rarer case it can become vital for your argument, as it can either make you rethink your ideas or illuminate and strengthen your thinking.

At these later stages, exceptions really take three forms. These are what are known as the negative or deviant case (see Peräkylä, this volume) where the issue or case does not fit your current understanding of the phenomenon:

1 Those that, despite being different, *actually support your finding*, as people themselves understand them and orientate to them as 'exceptions to the rule' and in so doing show you the 'rule'.
2 Those that, through their difference, *mean you need to re-evaluate or change* your labelling or ideas.
3 Those that are different for *very specific, idiosyncratic and contingent reasons* that either do not support your findings or mean you need to re-evaluate your ideas.

You may want to go in search of them – some people do, in that they deliberately sample potentially atypical cases, in order to check and refine their ideas.

Some Closing Comments

An important thing to remember is that when you initially read about and start to apply a form of qualitative data analysis that is novel to you, you will find yourself engaging in it in a very procedural way. First, you might read some how-to descriptions, and maybe write down a reasonably step-by-step way of going about analysis. This initial 'recipe' is quite abstract and should contain the key stages and practices you need to go through. As you begin to apply this 'recipe' you'll generally find you have to go back to the how-to descriptions, to check if what you're doing makes sense in relation to the guidebooks. It is only through a process of 'getting your hands dirty' with data that some of the ideas you've read about begin to make sense. That is fine. No level of description can adequately prepare you for analysing your specific archive. Over time, you can begin to ad hoc, to follow the spirit of analytic principles of your chosen approach.

Summary

- There are a range of approaches to qualitative analysis, but they share a common focus on shifting from the level of description and summary to exploring and explaining the underlying essences, patterns, processes and structures.
- You should systematically label your data, constantly reviewing and refining your labelling practices. Initially, focus on a sample of your data archive and look at this in detail. As you analyse more data, try to see how the ideas underlying each label combine, relate or diverge. Focus on specific issues and discard those ideas that are no longer central. Drill down to explore the detail and dimensions of key issues.
- Writing short and extended notes – about your hunches, ideas, labelling practices, personal reflections, project related reading – over the life of the project can help develop your analytic thinking.
- Engaging in rounds of data collection and then analysis can enable you to explore, refine and check your emerging ideas.

Questions

- What are the core aspects of qualitative data analysis?
- Why does good analysis mean more than simply summarizing your data?
- Why should you bother to label your data?
- Why is writing part of the process of analysis?
- Why is looking for exceptions in your data important?

Recommended Reading

Bernard, H. R., & Ryan, G. W. (2010) *Analyzing Qualitative Data: Systematic Approaches.* Thousand Oaks, CA: Sage.

Miles, M. B., & Huberman, A. M. (1994) *Qualitative data analysis* (2nd edn). Thousand Oaks, CA: Sage.

Saladaña, J (2009) *The Coding Manual for Qualitative Researchers.* Thousand Oaks, CA: Sage.

Internet Links

http://onlineqda.hud.ac.uk/

www.hta.ac.uk/fullmono/mon216.pdf

References

Bernard, H. R., & Ryan, G. W. (2010) *Analyzing Qualitative Data: Systematic Approaches.* Thousand Oaks, CA: Sage.

Braun, V., & Clarke, V. (2006) Using thematic analysis in psychology. *Qualitative Research in Psychology*, 3 (2), 77–101.

Charmaz, K. (2000) Grounded theory: Objectivist and constructivist methods. In N. K. Denzin and Y. S. Lincoln (Eds), *Handbook of Qualitative Research* (2nd edn, pp. 509–536). Thousand Oaks, CA: Sage.

Charmaz, K. (2006) *Constructing Grounded Theory: A Practical Guide through Qualitative Analysis.* Thousand Oaks, CA: Sage.

DeSantis, L., & Ugarriza, D. (2000) The concept of theme as used in qualitative research. *Western Journal of Nursing Research*, 22 (3), 351–372.

Dey, I. (2007) Grounding categories. In A. Bryant & K. Charmaz (Eds), *The SAGE Handbook of Grounded Theory*. London: Sage.

Draucker, C. B., Martsolf, D. S., Ross, R., & Rusk, T. B. (2007) Theoretical sampling and category development in grounded theory. *Qualitative Health Research, 17*, 1137.

Emerson, R., Fretz, R., & Shaw, L. (1995) *Writing Ethnographic Fieldnotes.* Chicago: University of Chicago Press.

Gibbs, G. R. (2007) *Analysing Qualitative Data.* London: Sage.

Glaser, B. (1978) *Theoretical Sensitivity: Advances in Grounded Theory.* Mill Valley, CA: Sociology Press.

Glaser, B. (1992) *Basics of Grounded Theory Analysis: Emergence vs. Forcing.* Mill Valley, CA: Sociology Press.

Goodwin, C. (1994) Professional vision. *American Anthropologist*, 96, 606–633.

Grbich, C. (1999) *Qualitative Research in Health: An Introduction*. London: Sage.

Layder, D. (1998) *Sociological Practice: Linking Theory and Social Research*. London: Sage.

Lempert, L. (2007) Memo-writing in grounded theory. In A. Bryant & K. Charmaz (Eds), *The SAGE Handbook of Grounded Theory*. London: Sage.

Miles, M. B., & Huberman, A. M. (1994) *Qualitative Data Analysis* (2nd edn). Thousand Oaks, CA: Sage.

Montgomery, P., & Bailey, P. (2007) Field notes and theoretical memos in grounded theory. *Western Journal of Nursing Research*, 29 (1), 65–79.

Opler, M. E. (1945) Themes as dynamic forces in culture. *American Journal of Sociology*, 51 (3), 198–206.

Patton, M. Q. (2002) *Qualitative Research & Evaluation Methods* (3rd edn). Thousand Oaks, CA: Sage.

Ritchie, J., & Spencer, L. (1994) Qualitative data analysis for applied policy research. In A. Bryman & R. G. Burgess (Eds), *Analyzing Qualitative Data*. London and New York: Routledge.

Ritchie, J., Spencer, L., & O'Connor, W. (2003) Carrying out qualitative analysis. In J. Ritchie & J. Lewis (Eds), *Qualitative Research Practice: A Guide for Social Science Students and Researchers*. London: Sage.

Sacks, H. (1992) *Lectures on Conversation*, Volume 1. Oxford: Blackwell.

Saladaña, J. (2009) *The Coding Manual for Qualitative Researchers*. Thousand Oaks, CA: Sage.

Smith, J. A., & Osborn, M. (2008) Interpretative phenomenological analysis. In J. A. Smith (Ed.), *Qualitative Psychology: A Practical Guide to Methods* (2nd edn). London: Sage.

Strauss, A., & Corbin, J. (1990) *Basics of Qualitative Research: Grounded Theory Procedures and Techniques*. Newbury Park, CA: Sage.

Grounded Theory and Credibility 16

Kathy Charmaz and Antony Bryant

Abstract

Grounded theory is a method of theory construction in which researchers systematically develop a theory from the collected data. This method is the most widely claimed qualitative method yet questions have arisen about these claims as well as about its epistemological assumptions and methods of knowledge production. These questions have undermined the credibility of the method and veiled its innovative potential. We show why several major epistemological criticisms of the early versions of the method had merit but dismissal of the method did not. Credibility issues about grounded theory extend to research practice and encompass current debates in qualitative inquiry. Thus, we look at data collection and offer ideas for shaping it to enhance theory construction. We next show how grounded theory already contained underused strategies that increase both its methodological power and the credibility of the subsequent analysis. In particular, we illustrate how to code for actions and conduct line-by-line initial coding. We also explicate the benefits of theoretical sampling. Grounded theorists who take up the directions we outline here will increase the credibility of their studies and simultaneously become more impervious to being judged by the criteria of another form of inquiry.

Keywords:

grounded theory, constructivism, credibility, epistemology, data collection.

Grounded Theory and Credibility

Grounded theory is a method of qualitative inquiry in which researchers develop inductive theoretical analyses from their collected data and subsequently gather further data to check these analyses. The purpose of grounded theory is theory construction, rather than description or application of existing theories. Hence, grounded theorists pursue developing their analytic categories and use data in service of constructing these categories (Charmaz, 2010). The originators of this method, Barney G. Glaser and Anselm L. Strauss (1967), first argued that qualitative research could be used for theory construction at a time when qualitative research was imperilled. Yet they also articulated a powerful rationale for legitimizing conducting inductive qualitative research that inspired numerous scholars who neither understood the logic of grounded theory nor how to use it.

Several variants of grounded theory exist but all share a set of methodological strategies. Grounded theorists engage in data collection and analysis simultaneously in an iterative process that uses comparative methods. They compare data with data, data with codes, codes with codes, codes with tentative categories, and categories with categories. This method fosters analyzing actions and processes rather than themes and topics. Grounded theorists code their data for actions and study how these actions might contribute to fundamental processes occurring in the research site or in the research participants' lives. Through comparing data with codes and codes with codes, grounded theorists can decide which codes to treat and test as tentative theoretical categories. A defining strategy of grounded theory is theoretical sampling, which means sampling for developing the properties of a tentative category, not for ensuring representation of a sample of people with a particular demographic characteristic. Theoretical sampling involves gathering new data to check hunches and to confirm that the properties of the grounded theorist's theoretical category are filled out. Researchers may also use it to define variation in a studied process or phenomenon or to establish the boundaries of a theoretical category. When these properties are saturated with data, the grounded theorist ends data collection and integrates the analysis.

A contemporary version of grounded theory, constructivist grounded theory, adopts the methodological strategies above but also takes into account methodological developments in qualitative inquiry over the past 50 years. As a result, constructivist grounded theory takes a different stance toward the research process and product than earlier grounded theorists had adopted. We outline the constructivist stance here and take it up in more detail in the following sections. Earlier grounded theorists tended to treat inquiry as separate from its social conditions. In contrast, constructivist grounded theorists view research as occurring within specific social conditions and thus attempt to learn how these conditions influence their studies. This approach leads constructivist grounded theorists to locate themselves within inquiry whereas earlier grounded theorists' stance assumed they remained neutral observers outside of inquiry. Constructivists also locate themselves inside inquiry to get as close to the studied phenomenon as possible. While gaining a close view, constructivists aim to discern how participants' meanings and actions may be connected to larger social structures and discourses of which they may be unaware. Earlier grounded theorists seldom made such links.

Constructivist grounded theorists view data as constructed, not simply out there in the world waiting to be discovered and gathered. Similarly constructivists assume that conducting and writing research flows from views and values. These endeavors are not neutral activities. In this view, research products are not objective reports. Instead, researchers interpret findings. Earlier grounded theorists aimed to find patterns in social life and to create abstract generalizations that explain them. This quest for abstract generalization minimizes understanding difference and variation in the research site or among the research participants that constructivists aspire to learn.

In this chapter, we begin by examining major epistemological debates and methodological issues in critiques of grounded theory that raise questions about its credibility, but are not limited to the grounded theory method. As Karen Henwood (Charmaz and Henwood, 2007; Henwood and Pigeon, 2003) observes, grounded theory provides a useful nodal point around which researchers can debate contemporary issues in qualitative research. Specifically, we show how naive methodological claims, contested definitions of the grounded theory method, and unexamined epistemological assumptions have led to methodological misunderstandings that hide the power and innovative potential of grounded theory and undermine its credibility. Similar issues have arisen in other forms of inductive qualitative inquiry, albeit seldom as overtly (but see Wacquant, 2002). Our exploration of credibility emphasizes data collection, an area that many grounded theorists have treated as unproblematic, and shows how the logic of grounded theory can advance both data collection and analysis. We briefly discuss credibility in data analysis and theory construction, and conclude with reflections about establishing credibility.

We propose that constructivist grounded theory offers researchers a sound epistemology and makes using grounded theory strategies accessible. Unlike earlier versions of grounded theory, constructivist grounded theory acknowledges the influence of the researcher on the research process, accepts the notion of multiple realities, emphasizes reflexivity, and rejects assumptions that researchers should and could set aside their prior knowledge to develop new theories. Ironically, major criticisms questioning the credibility of grounded theory *as a method* have been based on its early statements of over 40 years ago, and on generalizations about what constitutes the method derived from readings of how early proponents have used it (Burowoy et al., 1991; Wacquant, 2002). These criticisms miss seeing that researchers can use grounded theory methodological strategies without accepting the epistemological assumptions of earlier versions of the method.

Methodological Claims, Knowledge Production, and Credibility

Grounded theory, or more correctly the grounded theory method (GTM), is far and away the most widely *claimed* qualitative method in recent and current sociological and social research literature (see, for example, Titscher et al., 2000). However, some grounds for scepticism have arisen that qualify what this level of popularity and these widespread claims actually mean. Credibility issues concerning methodological claims and knowledge production arise in three forms:

1. The highly misleading or questionable claims that many authors have made that they used GTM when they conducted a qualitative study. Many journal editors and research assessors view such claims with suspicion, since all too often these assertions are at best based on only a passing familiarity and adoption of the method; and at worst, amount to nothing more than an artifice, masking an ill-conceived and ill-prepared project.

2. The way GTM has developed in the hands of its two progenitors – Barney Glaser and Anselm Strauss. GTM itself originated in their three key texts published 1965–1968, particularly *The Discovery of Grounded Theory* (1967). These founding texts resulted from a genuine collaborative effort, but subsequent developments led to a major rift between them by the early 1990s. As a result, some GTM researchers have been more concerned with upholding one specific form of the method over the other than with stressing the outcome and value of the research itself and thus add to the misgivings of editors and research assessors already mentioned.

3. The 'fairy-tale' (Wacquant 2002, p. 1481) quality of early grounded theory epistemology, in which theories and concepts almost magically emerged from data. Many GTM users offer nothing more than mantra-like incantations along the lines of 'the researcher begins with an area of study and allows the theory to emerge from the data' (Strauss and Corbin, 1998, p. 12), and thus leave the method and its adherents open to the sort of ridicule that Wacquant intimates.

Taken together, these three issues have left GTM open to the accusation that the method lacks credibility, precision, and coherence. In our contributions to GTM, however, we have intended to demonstrate that the method is credible, rigorous, and highly practical because it is usable and produces valuable outcomes.

We will first take up the three areas of concern – in reverse order – to explain how these misconceptions and ambiguities derive from a partial or mistaken appreciation of the truly innovative characteristics of GTM. We will then demonstrate several ways in which the method can be employed, and, in so doing, will offer what we consider to be a clear and firm basis for the method that will prove useful both for researchers and those charged with assessing research proposals or publications which claim to employ GTM.

Whether or not Glaser and Strauss intended it, scholars took the initial formulations of GTM, and their subsequent individual versions of it, to imply that researchers discover truth rather than create it (Rorty, 1989). This reading of GTM placed it firmly in the positivist camp, but with the added twist that conceptual development and theoretical discovery appear to be the result of a process of emergence from the data, with the researcher acting in a passive or, at most, facilitative manner. Many of the actual statements in Glaser and Strauss's original monograph are, in fact, far more nuanced. For instance '[T]he sociologist should also be sufficiently *theoretically sensitive* so that he can conceptualize and formulate a theory as it emerges from the data' (Glaser and Strauss, 1967, p. 46; stress in the original), but the key words picked up by many researchers, and also continually quoted by Glaser himself, amount to the claim that 'theory emerges from the data'. When reading *Discovery*, it is understandable why this interpretation held sway: the previous page offers a somewhat ambiguous sentence that ends with the claim that 'data collection is *controlled* by the emerging theory' (emphasis in the original, p. 45). Strauss reinforces this idea in his later work, with Juliet Corbin:

> A researcher does not begin a project with a preconceived theory in mind (unless his or her purpose is to elaborate and extend existing theory). Rather, the researcher begins with an area of study and allows the theory to emerge from the data. (Strauss & Corbin, 1998, p. 12)

This view of the researcher as passive is exacerbated and extended with the image of GTM as research that takes place in a vacuum; Glaser (1998; 2003) enjoins researchers not to engage with the literature and not to formulate research questions or be guided by existing models or theories. Again several specific statements in this regard are somewhat more complex, but they have often been taken as a rationale for avoiding some of the time-consuming and detailed aspects of planning a research project. Hence, this rationale leads to judgments that claiming to use GTM is often simply an excuse for shirking necessary but somewhat mundane tasks of articulating a research question or hypothesis, and completing an initial literature review.

Not only some of GTM's harshest critics, but also others who claim to use it, see beyond this combination of epistemological make-believe and cognitive miasma. De Vreede et al.'s (1998) paper exemplifies this problem. The authors offer their version of the GTM mantra: 'This approach [GTM] aims to develop inductively derived grounded theories about a phenomenon. A grounded theory is not built *a priori*; rather, it emerges during study as data collection, analysis, and theory development occur in parallel' (1998, p. 205). De Vreede et al. state that the feat of cognitive plumbing – turning off the tap of prior knowledge – is simply an unproblematic procedure, as is the emergence of theory from collected data. In another instance, a surprising misuse of grounded theory became evident during a conference discussion.

An author happened to mention that the earlier versions of his paper had not specified any method, and that the journal editor suggested that since the approach was non-quantitative to retro-fit GTM to the paper, particularly since 'many qualitative researchers in IS [Information Systems] have to conduct and publish their research within the context of a positivist orthodoxy in North America ... and thus, the scientific (or perhaps scientistic) language of GTM is VERY valuable to them' (see Bryant, 2002).

So these two features of GTM were not specifically problematic, and indeed articulating them in this fashion actually helped them in getting published. The outcome may have occurred in part because the editors themselves did not have any great familiarity with GTM, something that would be less likely now, 10 years later.

This continuing incoherence in researchers' understanding of the method persisted in part as a result of the split between Strauss and Glaser in the 1990s. Researchers spent more energy in discussing the nature of the disagreement, and clarifying allegiance to either the Straussian or Glaserian version of the method, than in responding to critics from outside the two main camps. Researchers intent on using GTM do not need to engage with all the aspects of this disagreement, but they should at least be aware of it when discussing their use of the method and referring to the GTM literature.[1]

Glaser's (1992) invective directed at Strauss marked the split between them. Despite Glaser's rancor, the central points of his critique are well founded. Perhaps ironically, the popularity of the method dates precisely from the publication of Strauss's (1987; Strauss and Corbin, 1990; 1998) books separately and with Corbin (Titscher et al., 2000; Reichertz, 2007). Yet, with Strauss's death in 1996, Glaser has positioned himself as the voice of Classic GT, and his writings in the past 20 years offer his view of what the method ought to be.

To turn to the third of the above issues, the degree of misapprehension by some editors and research assessors also owes something to the large number of people who make questionable claims to use GTM. Given the split between the Straussian and Glaserian versions of GTM, in some cases questioning such assertions may actually be an argument centered on distinctions arising between these versions. Glaser certainly has contended that Strauss and Corbin's version no longer falls under the heading of GTM. But authors' claims to be using GTM when they simply use a limited and often conceptually pedestrian form of coding are far more widespread. Such authors fail to offer any conceptual development or theoretical insight. Thus, some commentators and critics challenge: where's the *theory* in grounded theory?

---

[1]The article by Smit and Bryant (2000) makes this point, and various chapters in Bryant and Charmaz (2007) point to the relevant literature.

This credibility gap concerning GTM became increasingly evident in the 1990s and, in some respects, still persists in some fields. In the light of all these issues, the truly innovative features of GTM can all too easily be forgotten. Fortunately in recent years sufficiently robust responses to the above issues ensure not only that the popularity of the method will continue, but that it can do so from a far stronger foundation. What is now often seen as the *constructivist* form of GTM, developed in the 1990s, was much more a case of a reinterpretation or restating of the principles of the method than a new formulation. The constructivist project has been further developed with the articulation of the pragmatist thread that runs through the method (Bryant, 2009; Charmaz, 2008).

Methodological Developments and Constructivist GTM

It is a truism that researchers must articulate their methodology and methodological practices in order to confirm an acceptable degree of methodological robustness and clarification of their research approach. This requirement applies particularly to PhD proposals, research proposals and publications. For those adopting qualitative approaches, meeting it can be problematic: indeed one of the key motivations in developing GTM was to provide a firm basis for qualitative research.

Unfortunately neither Strauss nor Glaser – either separately or in concert – ever offered a sustained engagement with the epistemological and methodological developments that can conveniently be dated from the appearance of Thomas Kuhn's book *The Structure of Scientific Revolutions* (1962; 2nd edition 1970). The result has been that throughout the 1980s and 1990s grounded theorists were open to attack from two sides. The orthodox, quantitatively oriented position regarded GTM as merely a veneer for largely descriptive, impressionistic work that at best simply laid the groundwork for 'real' research, preferably expressed in statistical terms. Simultaneously, interpretivists or constructivists challenged positivist orthodox, as Rorty's statement neatly encapsulated: truth is 'made' rather than 'discovered'. In response, grounded theorists, with their data-oriented mantra, simply remained mute.

We now respond to these problems by addressing, in turn, three issues:

1   Credible data
2   Analytic credibility
3   Theoretical credibility.

Credible Data

Epistemological and methodological developments inform the concrete practices of constructivist grounded theorists. We turn now to look at how data collecting, coding, and theoretical sampling shape grounded theory practice and to offer ideas about how grounded theorists and other qualitative researchers might use them to improve their studies.

The credibility of grounded theory starts from the ground up. The quality and sufficiency of the data for accomplishing the research goals matter. What stands as solid and sufficient data is currently contested throughout qualitative inquiry and also may be questioned in quantitative research. In the past, questions have arisen about the amount, depth, and quality (i.e., accuracy) of data in GTM as well as of the methods invoked for obtaining them. These questions eclipsed the untapped strengths of grounded theory for data collection.

GTM may be used with varied types of data including ethnographic materials, documents, and interviews, although interview data is the most common data collection method. Constructivist GTM answers earlier questions about credible data collection and offers directions for sharpening data collection that researchers have not yet fully explored, much less explicated. Constructivist GTM emphasizes choosing data collection methods that fit the research question and gathering sufficient data to construct a credible analysis to fulfill the research goals.

The hypothetical plausibility of specific data for theory construction interests grounded theorists more than ascertaining the complete accuracy of, say, a field note or interview statement. Glaser (2002) positions his version of grounded theory against the quest for 'worrisome accuracy' of other qualitative approaches. He emphasizes the 'transcending abstraction' (p. 3) of grounded theory categories and argues that the comparative process across many cases corrects such inaccuracies as caused by the influence of the researcher (p. 47). We agree that having many cases increases accuracy and enhances credibility. Yet Glaser (1978; 2001) and Stern (1985; 1991) defend small samples when they believe their data has saturated the properties of a theoretical category. But what makes a category theoretical? When is a category saturated? These questions have not been entirely resolved. Meanwhile, other researchers have adopted Glaser's and Stern's position to shortcut and shortchange data collection, and thus undermine the credibility of grounded theory.

Similarly, several GTM proponents' stance toward data collection has undermined the credibility of the method. GTM favors attending to data analysis more than examining data collection techniques. Glaser's (see, for example, 2002) slogan, 'All is data,' reinforces earlier views that grounded theorists were sloppy about data collection (Lofland and Lofland, 1984), as does his continued insistence on note-taking rather than transcribing interview data. The constructivist revision of grounded theory, however, attends to gathering detailed data and treats both data and data collection as located in temporal, spatial, social and situational conditions. Constructivists also take into account both researchers' and research participants' starting points and standpoints, and remain alert to how and when these shift during inquiry. Thus for constructivists, data do not simply reside in an external world but instead reflect the particular conditions of its production. This constructivist view of data encourages locating the data and analysis in these conditions. In contrast, Glaser treats data collection as unproblematic and aims for generalizations that transcend specific conditions.

We focus on interviewing here because of its predominance and our experience in using it. Interviews are, of course, retrospective accounts that often explain and justify behavior. Yet they may also be special social spaces in which research participants can reflect on the past and link it to the present and future in new ways. An interview is a performance, whether stories tumble out or are strategically calculated and enacted, but that does not disqualify interviews from providing rich data and sparking analytic insights (see Miller and Glassner, Gubrium and Holstein, and Riessman, this volume). An interviewer's questions may frame the research participant's performance and seem to make the co-construction of data explicit. However, much interaction and interpretation may proceed without words.

Becoming fascinated by people, their situations, and stories – and unflinching should their stories include tales of hardship, loss, or seeming moral transgression – encourages detailed responses and reflections. Kathy Charmaz's first interview with Karen, a 46-year-old woman, illustrates what may occur during an interview (see Figure 16.1). Karen viewed her devastating neck injury as leading to multiple health problems that included chronic fatigue syndrome and possible fibromyalgia. Note how a simple question, 'Were you married at the time then when your first accident occurred in '93', produced an elaborate response in Figure 16.1.

Karen's uninterrupted statement actually went on for three single-spaced pages when she paused and Kathy again asked an informational question for clarification. Clearly, Karen was open about her life, articulate about describing it, and found that the interview gave her space and time to tell her story – and to establish a view of the events that comprise it. Yet, for her, those events were unsettling and unsettled. Karen was dealing with identity questions, confirming her ex-husband's hidden identity, and was grappling with nagging questions about whom she might be.

The amount of non-stop detail belies the substantial non-verbal interaction that occurred and thus the co-construction of the interview. The content of this non-verbal interaction also challenges common assumptions about the researcher and participant's relative power to control the interview. Participants may have stories they want to tell and tales that they wish to sidestep or on which to tread softly.[2] Thus, they may exert control over the content of the interview – and the situation by avoiding areas that might elicit probing questions.

Simultaneously, a 'silent dialogue' (Olesen and Whittaker, 1968) ensues about the *interview* itself. This dialogue particularly arises when: (1) sensitive topics arise during the interview, (2) the interviewee believes that the interviewer might define him

---

[2]Social scientists (Charmaz, 2009b; Polkinghorne, 1997) have attended to silences in the interviewee's story, but examining Karen's interview brings the interviewer's seeming silence into focus, for the conversation includes more than words alone.

Examples of Codes	Initial Narrative Data to be Coded
	K: Were you married at the time then when your first accident occurred in '93?
	Yes, I was living in Springview and I was married to my third husband and we lived on a ranchette with a pasture, with farm animals, and a garden, and country
Describing life	life, pool, gym, it was very nice, and I was out there for
Evaluating living situation	six and a half years. My ex-husband had kind of a
Telling the time length	double life going on as it turns out; he would disappear
Living with ex-husband's double life	for two or three days at a time which became
Disappearing husband	increasingly worse. He had colitis...part of it was his
Escalating disappearances	colitis but part of it, [as] it turned out was a hidden
Accounting for husband's disappearances	cocaine addiction so I couldn't continue to–in my
Defining hidden addiction	chronic pain condition and his behavior, just kept me
Alluding to limits for self-explaining distress	so stressed out where I couldn't function emotionally
Being unable to function	and physically to a point. That's why I say my survival
Disintegrating self	was at stake...it hurt me. And there was no support
Questioning survival of self/of way of life	there for my pain issue. ...I always had to be the one
Feeling hurt/betrayed	who had to be strong because he'd be gone on these
Wanting husband's support for *her* pain	disappearing things and then somebody had to hold
Carrying doubled responsibilities	down the fort and keep everything going when this
Expressing resentments (in tone of voice)	would happen. And then sometimes it would take him
Keeping life (family and business) together	a week to recover because whatever he was doing
Detailing ex-husband's lapses	would cause his colitis to flare up, so I was always
Timing then husband's recovery/explaining his complicating illness	forced to be in the position of the emotional anchor in
Feeling forced to be family emotional anchor	the family and it was so exhausting to me and again I
Being exhausted	had to keep escalating that pain medication then to
Feeling forced to escalate pain meds	continue on and normally, then, at the time the disk
Seeing pain meds as allowing a normal life	was fully herniated so I was being treated for chronic
Explaining extent of injury	pain but there was still some questions to the validity
Externalizing questions about pain	of my pain factor whether it was emotionally induced
Revealing ambiguous cause of pain–physical and/or psychological	or physically and some question as to whether it was a
Questioning the possibility of addiction	lot psychological, that I was perhaps, you know, had a
Raising the specter of self over-medicating	painful addiction and was just self-medicating.
Disclosing a plausible identity	
Overlapping emotional and psychological pain	Most of this data excerpt appeared in Charmaz, 2008, p. 165.

FIGURE 16.1 *Initial grounded theory coding*

or her negatively,[3] or (3) the interviewer reveals signs of being disturbed about or disinterested in the content of the interview. At these points, the researcher and research participant may tacitly construct and negotiate meanings that influence what can and will be said. Kathy accounts for what happened in the following way:

> I was observing Karen and she was observing me – closely. I encouraged her to talk and she monitored my responses to her disclosures all along the way. As she began to reveal concerns about her use of prescription drugs, her expression and tone changed. Despite her non-stop story, Karen's face became impassive with her steady gaze focused on me and her voice took on a measured, matter-of-fact tone. I had the distinct feeling that she was gauging how I would view her and how much she could safely reveal.

From a grounded theory standpoint, asking few rather than many interview questions allows the interviewee to tell her story without the researcher preconceiving the content, or, for that matter, the direction the interview will take. Such a strategy is particularly useful during early interviews but may change as the researcher moves back and forth between data collection and analysis.

Constructivist grounded theory emphasizes going into emergent phenomena and defining their properties. By taking a phenomenon apart, researchers can build explicit 'What' and 'How' questions into the data collection, as other qualitative researchers do (Gubrium and Holstein, 2008). Grounded theorists, however, can use these questions to begin to shape a subsequent theoretical analysis. These questions elicit content that becomes the grist of the analysis and lead toward explicating processes. The question below gets at the properties of surrendering as well as this interviewee's meanings of it. When the researcher thinks analytically while interviewing, the lines blur between what constitutes data collection and what constitutes analysis. And thus here credibility is not simply a property of the data as separate from the *analysis*.

In addition to preparing an interviewee for questions that call for detailing meanings, the pacing and tone of a direct 'What' or 'How' question does much to defuse the interviewee's possible interpretation of the following question as confrontational.

Sara:	...But, fortunately, I had the experience of at some point surrendering, you know.
Interviewer:	**What does that mean to you, surrendering?**
Sara:	It means that I don't have, I can't control it and to look at what it has to teach me. Just, you know, let it tell me what it needs to tell me. You know, that willingness and that acceptance.

---

[3]This problem increases when, unlike Karen, interviewees have some memory loss, as did a number of Charmaz's.

In an interview on health narratives in schools, Lisa M. Perhamus's (2009) 'How' question (below) not only elicits the sequence of events following students' classroom disruptions, but also contributes to illuminating the process of trying to re-establish classroom control.

> Linda, a Hispanic kindergarten teacher at Wedgewood, talked about some of the personal tolls teaching can have.

> **Interviewer:** **And how does that [behavior problems] affect you as a teacher?**

> **Linda:** It drains me. It does. Because the amount of time that I have to take, when you've got a class of twenty-one kids and you have one or even two ... boys or girls, who are off and you know in part that they can't control it and this is what you've been told that they can't control it, and then they're off, and then I have to watch ... for the well-being of my other kids or in the situation where the child just doesn't want to do his work and he'll get up and make a spectacle moving around the room. I have to stop, redirect him, which takes attention away from everybody else, and it's just, it's draining and it's not fair to the other kids. (p. 110)

GTM made the iterative practice of moving back and forth between data and analysis a common strategy in inductive qualitative inquiry. Starting with 'What' and 'How' questions brings an analytic edge to the data collection, even in the very early stages of research, and maintaining the grounded theory emphasis on process helps the researcher to link events that otherwise might seem disparate. Inquiring about the person's circumstances, views, and priorities illuminates data about social locations, standpoints, and situations. Adding 'When' questions moves the data collection toward specifying conditions under which the studied phenomenon or process occurs or changes. Similarly, asking questions about sequence of actions gets at process and implications as well as uncovering specific meanings and actions. Whatever questions are asked, it is also important to study the sequences given in talk as the research participant tells his or her story (Silverman, 2007).

Generally, grounded theorists stick closely to patterns that they define in their data and treat as categories. From a constructivist perspective, such patterns develop as grounded theorists grapple with interpreting their data.

Analytic Credibility

The strength of grounded theory resides in its strategies for analyzing data but researchers have not taken full advantage of these strategies. Using explicit codes derives from grounded theory and has become part of qualitative inquiry. Many researchers code their data and believe that they are using grounded theory strategies to do it. However, grounded theory coding differs from other types of coding because it codes for actions, invokes comparative methods, and discerns meanings through studying actions and events. We compare bits of data within the same data such as an interview, between different pieces of data, and begin inductive analysis.

Grounded theory coding consists of at least two sequential types: an initial coding, in which researchers attempt to be open to defining whatever they see happening in fragments of data, and a focused coding that uses the most frequent and significant initial codes. The kind of data matters here. Researchers may prefer coding incidents or paragraphs with ethnographic data but use line-by-line coding with early intensive interviews and narratives. Line-by-line coding is a heuristic device to prompt the researcher to study each line of data and begin to gain a conceptual handle on them. Completing initial coding as quickly as possible fosters spontaneity and fresh ideas.

Using gerunds is pivotal in grounded theory coding. Gerunds move the analysis forward. A gerund is the noun form of the verb such as 'defining,' 'experiencing,' or 'questioning.' Conducting line-by-line coding with gerunds helps to capture, crystallize, and connect fragments of data – and thus to see processes. Gerunds help the researcher to define what is happening in the data, identify the theoretical direction implicit or explicit in the code, and discern lines of an emerging story in the data. Using gerunds is difficult at first for English-speakers who think in structural terms of topics and themes, not in processual terms, but practice builds speed.

gerunds?!

Observe that the codes in the figure reflect different levels of abstraction. The idea of a 'disintegrating self' is more abstract than the concrete interview statement. Is this legitimate? Yes, because the researcher tests the code against other data and writes memos explicating the comparisons involved in these tests. If the code does not hold up as a tentative conceptual category then the researcher drops it and pursues codes that do. Early coding allows time to ask analytic questions about the code and data that emerge from the material at hand, not from a preconceived coding framework. In this case, we could compare the data and code against other interview statements and ask questions such as:

- What are the properties of this self?
- How, when, and to what extent are these properties discernible?
- To whom?
- With which consequences?
- What happens when they are taken as real and discernible to certain key actors but not to others?
- How, if at all, is this code related to other codes?
- What kind of additional data do I need to explore this code?

Are the codes in Figure 16.1 the most fruitful for developing a grounded theory? Not necessarily. Another researcher from different perspectives, social locations, and situations might come up with more compelling codes. If we took experiencing a disintegrating self as a tentative category, we might ask how it is related to other codes such as 'questioning survival of self' and 'feeling forced to be family emotional anchor.' The latter might contribute to the former and both may contribute to experiencing a disintegrating self. Are these the only way to use these codes? Not at all. Other analytic directions could include reconstructing the past, questioning identity, accounting for and to self, or the properties and process of constructing disclosure and myriad additional possibilities depending on the relationship of the viewer to the viewed. Similarly, different researchers may develop dissimilar lines of coding of the same data, given their theoretical sensitivities and substantive interests.

Constructivist grounded theorists view coding as emergent and interactive. Therefore, coding has novel properties that draw on but are not wholly determined by the researcher's interests, standpoints, and relative and changing positions during data collection and analysis. A quest for inter-coder reliability does not make sense but a test of the robustness and usefulness of codes through comparative analysis does. Grounded theorists establish credibility by the strength of both the analytic concepts and claims and the evidence to support them.

Theoretical Credibility

Analytic credibility in the research process leads to theoretical credibility of the developed concepts. A major strength – and largely untapped potential – of grounded theory resides in theoretical sampling. Researchers use this form of later sampling to check and fill out the properties of their tentative categories, not to increase representativeness of their initial sample. In the excerpt below, Kathy Charmaz had already developed categories situating the self in time: the past, present, and future. Here, both the elusiveness of the category and her lengthy acquaintance with the interviewee influence taking an active role in shaping the conversation to pursue questions that pertained to her category. How and when a grounded theorist probes for meaning may change as both the relationship with a respondent and the iterative process of inquiry develop.

> I followed up on an earlier conversation about locating oneself in time. I asked her where she now located herself in time. Note how I follow her statements and return to key points that she raised.
>
> **Patricia:** I'm in the present.
>
> **Kathy:** You're in the present.
>
> **Patricia:** Oh yeah.

Kathy: And that's a change, isn't it?

Patricia: Where was I before?

Kathy: In the future.

Patricia: Future. Yeah. Yeah. [said thoughtfully] I'm right here – today.

Kathy: And has all this [what we had talked about in the preceding hour and a half] brought you to today?

Patricia: The whole process? Yeah.

Kathy: And what does tomorrow look like?

Patricia: Tomorrow's hopeful.

Kathy: How much of tomorrow do you see today with you [being] right here today?

Patricia: I see some. I can see quite a bit of tomorrow, I think. But what I see is that part...I feel like because I – I have much more control over my – my life today that tomorrow will be better as a direct result of how I live today. But I also know that there's a great deal of unknown in there. But I think there are a lot of unknowns for a lot of people, for everybody. And that I have the advantage over everybody else because I'll be able to deal with it.

Kathy: Hmm, that's interesting. And your today is, when your self is in today, what does that mean to you?

Patricia: When myself is in today, what I'm probably saying about today is, *today* – actually today. (Charmaz, 2009a, p. 54)

If researchers go back and forth to the same people or setting, they can use theoretical sampling to increase the depth and precision of their categories and their knowledge of the studied people and their situations. Because theoretical sampling often requires finesse, tacit negotiations may ensue about what researchers may ask and when they can ask it. It helps to listen to the stories participants want to tell before redirecting the conversation to ask questions pertaining to one's tentative theoretical categories. Such negotiations alleviate accusations of advocating the 'smash and grab' data collection approach that Dey (1999) wielded against Glaser and Strauss (1967) and that subsequently undermined the credibility of grounded theory data.

The analytic strength of grounded theory resides in how researchers use its iterative process. They can check hunches, follow leads in earlier data, select telling codes as tentative categories, develop categories, and demonstrate relationships between them. The point is to make these categories at once more abstract and useful by increasing their scope and interpretive power. Relatively few grounded theorists use theoretical sampling in a systematic way. Yet this strategy can help researchers to make their work distinctive and theoretically sophisticated and thus increase its credibility.

Summary and Future Prospects

- Grounded theory contains flexible methodological strategies that can be used effectively in contemporary qualitative inquiry.
- Methodological misunderstandings, questionable claims, and conflicting grounded theory approaches have undermined an extremely popular and innovative method.
- The constructivist revision of grounded theory resolves its earlier problematic epistemological assumptions and knowledge claims.
- Revisiting and revising areas of inquiry, such as collecting data that past GTM proponents had treated as unproblematic, fosters increasing the credibility of grounded theory practice and products.
- Adopting the strategies discussed above will not only increase the credibility of GTM studies but also decrease their likelihood of being judged by criteria imported from another form of inquiry.
- Explication of its methodological strategies makes the method more accessible and effective, thereby increasing its popularity and credibility.

In short, extending GTM strategies to explicitly address areas that early proponents of the method did not consider will contribute to the development of the method and to its credibility.

Questions

1 What is constructivist grounded theory?
2 How did misunderstandings about grounded theory contribute to questions about its credibility?
3 Which strengths of grounded theory increase its credibility?
4 What are the main features of grounded theory coding?
5 How does theoretical sampling differ from other forms of sampling?

Recommended Reading

Bryant, A. and Charmaz, K. (2007). Grounded theory in historical perspective: an epistemological account. In Antony Bryant and Kathy Charmaz (Eds.), *The Sage Handbook of Grounded Theory* (pp. 31–57). London: Sage.

Charmaz, K. (2006). *Constructing Grounded Theory: A Practical Guide Through Qualitative Analysis*. London: Sage.

Glaser, B. G. and Strauss, A. L. (1967). *The Discovery of Grounded Theory*. Chicago: Aldine.

Internet Links

Barney Glaser:

www.groundedtheory.com

Anselm Strauss:

http://sbs.ucsf.edu/medsoc/anselmstrauss

References

Bryant, A. (2002). Re-grounding grounded theory. *Journal of Information Technology Theory and Application, 4*(1), 25–42: www.computer.org/portal/web/csdl/doi?doc=abs/proceedings/hicss/2002/1435/08/14350253cabs.htm

Bryant, A. (2009). Grounded theory and pragmatism: The curious case of Anselm Strauss and GTM. *Forum for Qualitative Social Research, 10*(3), September: www.qualitative-research.net/index.php/fqs/article/viewArticle/1358

Bryant, A. and Charmaz, K. (2007). Grounded theory in historical perspective: an epistemological account. In Antony Bryant and Kathy Charmaz (Eds.), *The Sage Handbook of Grounded Theory* (pp. 31–57). London: Sage.

Burawoy, M., Gamson, J., Schiffman, J., Burton, A., Ferguson, A. A., Salzinger, L., Ui, S., Hurst, L., and Fox, K. (1991). *Ethnography Unbound: Power and resistance in the modern metropolis.* Berkeley: University of California Press.

Charmaz, K. (2008). Grounded theory as an emergent method. In S. N. Hesse-Biber and P. Leavy (Eds.), *The Handbook of Emergent Methods* (pp. 155–170). New York: Guilford.

Charmaz, K. (2009a). Recollecting good and bad days. In Antony Puddephatt, William Shaffir, and Steven Kleinknecht (Eds.), *Ethnographies Revisited: Constructing Theory in the Field* (pp. 48–62). London and New York: Routledge.

Charmaz, K. (2009b). Stories, silences, and self: dilemmas in disclosing chronic illness. (Expanded version). In D. E. Brashers and D. J. Goldstein (Eds.), *Communicating to Manage Health and Illness* (pp. 240–270). New York: Routledge.

Charmaz, K. (2010). Studying the experience of chronic illness through grounded theory. In G. Scambler and S. Scambler (Eds.), *Assaults on the Lifeworld: New Directions in the Sociology of Chronic and Disabling Conditions* (pp. 8–86). London: Palgrave.

Charmaz, K. and Henwood, K. (2007). Grounded theory in psychology. In Carla Willig and Wendy Stainton-Rogers (Eds.), *Handbook of Qualitative Research in Psychology* (pp. 240–259). London: Sage.

De Vreede, G., Jones, N., and Mgaya, R. J. (1998). Exploring the application and acceptance of group support systems in Africa. *Journal of Management Information Systems, 15*(3), 197–234.

Dey, I. (1999). *Grounding Grounded Theory.* San Diego: Academic Press.

Glaser, B. G. (1978). *Theoretical Sensitivity.* Mill Valley, CA: Sociology Press.

Glaser, B. G. (1992). *Basics of Grounded Theory Analysis*. Mill Valley, CA: Sociology Press.

Glaser, B. G. (1998). *Doing Grounded Theory: Issues and Discussions*. Mill Valley, CA: Sociology Press.

Glaser, B. G. (2001). *The Grounded Theory Perspective: Conceptualization Contrasted with Description*. Mill Valley, CA: Sociology Press.

Glaser, B. G. (2002). Constructivist grounded theory? Forum: Qualitative Social Research/Sozialforschung [On-line Journal], *3*: www.qualitative-research.net/fqs-texte/3-02/3-02glaser-e-htm. Accessed 3 December 2008.

Glaser, B. G. (2003). *The Grounded Theory Perspective II: Description's Remodeling of Grounded Theory*. Mill Valley, CA: Sociology Press.

Glaser, B.G. and Strauss, A.L. (1965). *Awareness of Dying*. Chicago, IL: Aldine.

Glaser, B. G. and Strauss, A. L. (1967). *The Discovery of Grounded Theory*. Chicago: Aldine.

Glaser, B.G. and Strauss, A.L. (1968). *Time for Dying*. Chicago, IL: Aldine.

Gubrium, J. F. and Holstein, J. A. (2008). From the individual interview to the interview society. In J. A. Holstein and J. F. Gubrium (Eds.), *Handbook of Constructionist Research* (pp. 3–32). New York: Guilford.

Henwood, K. and Pigeon, N. (2003). Grounded theory in psychological research. In P. M. Camic, J. E. Rhodes, and L. Yardley (Eds.), *Qualitative Research in Psychology: Expanding Perspectives in Methodology and Design* (pp. 131–155). Washington, DC: American Psychological Association.

Kuhn, T. S. (1970). *The Structure of Scientific Revolutions*, 2nd ed. Chicago: University of Chicago Press.

Lofland, J. and Lofland, L. (1984). *Analyzing Social Settings*, 2nd ed. Belmont, CA: Wadsworth.

Olesen, V. and Whittaker, E. (1968). *The Silent Dialogue: A Study in the Social Psychology of Professional Socialization*. San Francisco: Jossey-Bass.

Perhamus, L. M. (2009). In the name of health and wellness: An analysis of how young children, their families and school navigate the moralizing dynamics of health promotion. Unpublished Doctoral Dissertation. University of Rochester, Rochester, NY.

Polkinghorne, D. E. (1997). Reporting qualitative research as practice. In W. G. Tierney and Y. S. Lincoln (Eds.), *Representation on the Text: Reframing the Narrative Voice* (pp. 3–21). Albany, NY: State University of New York Press.

Reichertz, J. (2007). Abduction: The logic of discovery in grounded theory. In Antony Bryant and Kathy Charmaz (Eds.), *The Sage Handbook of Grounded Theory* (pp. 214–228). London: Sage.

Rorty, R. (1989). *Contingency, Irony, and Solidarity*. Cambridge: Cambridge University Press.

Silverman, D. (2007). *A Very Short, Fairly Interesting and Reasonably Cheap Book about Qualitative Research*. London: Sage.

Smit, K. and Bryant, A. (2000). Grounded theory method in IS research: Glaser vs. Strauss. *Research in Progress Papers*, 2000–7.

Stern, P. N. (1985). Using grounded theory in nursing research. In M. Leininger

(Ed.), *Qualitative Research Methods in Nursing* (pp. 149–160). New York: Grunne & Stratton.

Stern, P. N. (1991). Are counting and coding a capella appropriate in qualitative research? In J. M. Morse (Ed.), *Qualitative Nursing Research: A Contemporary Dialogue* (pp. 135–148). Newbury Park, CA: Sage.

Strauss, A. (1987). *Qualitative Analysis for Social Scientists*. New York: Cambridge University Press.

Strauss, A. and Corbin, J. (1990). *Basics of Qualitative Research: Grounded Theory Procedures and Techniques*. Newbury Park, CA: Sage.

Strauss, A. and Corbin, J. (1998). *Basics of Qualitative Research: Grounded Theory Procedures and Techniques*, 2nd ed. Thousand Oaks, CA: Sage.

Titscher, S., Meyer, M., Wodak, R., and Vetter, E. (2000). *Methods of Text and Discourse Analysis*. Thousand Oaks, CA: Sage.

Wacquant, L. (2002). Scrutinizing the street: Poverty, morality, and the pitfalls of urban ethnography. *American Journal of Sociology, 107*(6), 1468–1532.

What's Different about Narrative Inquiry?
Cases, Categories and Contexts[1]

Catherine Kohler Riessman

Abstract

Narrative inquiry is different in several ways from other qualitative approaches. It focuses closely on particular cases and the various contexts of production of data. After introducing some key narrative concepts, I illustrate them in action in two research examples. Narrative approaches are particularly useful in studying the performance of identity.

Keywords:

narrative analysis, narrative inquiry, storytelling, category-centered research, narrative form.

One of the questions students frequently pose in my research seminars is the difference between narrative inquiry and other qualitative approaches. Having used several analytic methods and combined them successfully with narrative in several studies (Riessman 1990, 2002a, 2002b, 2005), I always relish the question. This chapter allows me to take up the question again, articulating several dimensions of narrative analysis that distinguish it from the data analytic phase of grounded theory and other thematically oriented qualitative methods that work from interviews.

There is great diversity in modes of narrative inquiry and how they can be evaluated that I cannot survey here (see Riessman 2007). My approach to the methods was initially shaped by the sociolinguistic tradition that influenced scholars in the

[1] I thank The Leverhulme Trust for support during writing, and colleagues in the US and UK who commented on an early draft.

social sciences in the 1980s and by a network of colleagues since. But the field of narrative inquiry has mushroomed into something that is now very broad. As in other qualitative approaches, epistemological positions differ; both constructivists and logical positivists take up the idea of data as a 'story,' the widely used popular term. There is an increasing unfortunate trend to celebrate biographical accounts instead of systematically analyzing them (Atkinson and Delamont 2006). The softening of boundaries between the humanities and the social sciences has drawn many to a narrative vocabulary in interpreting diverse materials (not always critically, as discussed below). My focus in this chapter will be limited to narratives taken from interviews. Research interviews are not the only environment in which narratives appear as Example 1 below suggests; there is work influenced by conversational analysis that looks at storytelling in everyday settings (Polanyi 1989). Following a brief introduction to several key concepts that should guide a narrative inquiry, I present two research examples below that illustrate concepts in practice.

Category vs. Case-centered Research

The vast majority of contemporary qualitative research is category-centered rather than case-centered. In the former – grounded theory is a familiar example – detail and specificity slip away in favor of general statements about the phenomenon of interest. Interview data are fractured into segments that are coded into conceptual categories, grouped and compared to similar segments from other observations. The goal is to generate theoretical categories inductively, that is, generalizations about human processes that hold across individual participants (see Charmaz and Bryant, this volume). By contrast, in case-centered research – practiced in oral history, auto/biographical studies and narrative inquiry – the investigator preserves and interrogates particular instances, sequences of action, the way participants negotiate language and narrative genres in conversations, and other unique aspects of a 'case,' which could be an individual, family, community, group, organization, or other unit of social life. As Mishler (1996: 80) writes, case-based methods grant research participants 'unity and coherence through time, respecting them as subjects with both histories and intentions' (for a discussion in illness research, see Radley and Chamberlain 2001). Human agency, consciousness – socially constructed, to be sure – and particularity are preserved. This becomes difficult when cases are pooled to generate general statements about the group as a whole.

Case-centered methods nevertheless can generate 'categories,' that is, theoretical concepts and observations about general processes. The history of medicine is filled with studies of particular instances – cases where pathologies were noted and studied closely, leading to new disease categories. Similarly, in social research, knowledge about general aspects of social organization has sprung from the close study of particular action in a specific instance. Garfinkel's (1967) case study of Agnes, for example, generated theory that challenged, and eventually transformed, the binary concept of gender. Narrative analysts frequently compare cases to construct arguments about a process of social change (for examples from the women's health movement, see Bell 1988, 1999).

Narrative analysis opens up a 'methodological repertoire' (Quinn 2005: 6), rather than a canon, that investigators can draw upon and expand to suit the demands of a particular project. In this spirit of methodological diversity, I have developed elsewhere a typology and illustrative exemplars of four general approaches to interpreting narrative: thematic, structural, dialogic/performative, and visual analysis methods (www.qualitative-research.net/index.php/fqs/article/view/1418). In different ways, these analytic approaches resist narrative seduction and a preoccupation with content: primary attention to what is communicated substantively by a research participant.

There is a philosophy of language, of course, underlying the focus on content that many qualitative researchers share: viewing language as a transparent unmediated container of meaning. Such research assumes a direct connection between a speaker's words and the objects to which language refers. In everyday life, we operate with such a view, but, in analyzing data, we can problematize meaning and the seemingly easy relationship between sign and signifier. We can ask, for example:

- How was this account generated?
- Why was the story told *that* way?
- What do the specific words a participant uses carry on their backs from prior uses?
- What other readings are possible, beyond what the narrator may have intended?

A central feature of narrative seduction (Chambers 1984) is the illusion created by a skilful narrator that 'a story "is as it is" and needs no interpretation' (Bruner 1991: 9). The artifice predisposes the listener to one and only one way of understanding meaning. By resisting seduction, narrative research can challenge the 'automatic interpretive routine' of everyday life and begin 'unrehearsed interpretive activity' (Bruner 1991: 9). Readers can be invited to question the omniscient narrator and focus instead on how an account was generated, its effects, the positioning of characters and other aspects of narrative construction (see Holstein and Gubrium, this volume). Language use can come into view – an angle of vision typically missing from grounded theory studies.

A Narrative Vocabulary

Narrative terminology is important for anyone contemplating a narrative project, especially given the explosion of a literary vocabulary into everyday life. Take the terms 'narrative' and 'story,' which originated of course in literary studies but in the contemporary period have taken on commonsense meanings. Journalists now use the two words interchangeably to refer to what in the past would have been called an ideological position or argument. Many qualitative researchers are appropriating a narrative vocabulary to refer to interview segments of any kind and to all research reports. If investigators plan to use narrative concepts analytically, terminology needs to be taken seriously.

Sociolinguists generally make a sharp distinction between narrative and story. Narrative refers to the broad class of discourse types that have certain properties in common (identified below). A story is one prototypic form of narrative that recounts a discrete set of events with 'sequential and temporal ordering' (De Fina 2003: 13). I would add spatial ordering – *where* a sequence of events unfolded. Following Aristotle, De Fina reserves the term 'story' for oral discourses 'that include some kind of rupture or disturbance in the normal course of events…an action that provokes a reaction and/or adjustment' (2003: 13). All scholars, particularly those working with the subtype 'story,' owe a debt to the canonical work of Labov (1972, 1982) and prior work of Labov and Waletzky (1967), even if they did not always make a distinction between 'narrative' and 'story,' and the field has moved beyond their theory of narrative. As narrative studies have developed over the decades, our language and conceptual apparatus have grown more precise.

Accepting that narrative refers to a broad class of discourse types (of which the 'story' is only one), what are the defining features that distinguish narrative from other kinds of interview discourse, such as brief question and answer exchanges, expository statements of beliefs, chronicles, listings, and other speech acts? Bell builds on Hinchman and Hinchman (1997) to define narrative as:

> a sequence of ordered events that are connected in a meaningful way for a particular audience in order to make sense of the world or people's experience in it…. This definition assumes one action is consequential for the next, that a narrative sequence is held together with a 'plot,' and that the 'plot' is organized temporally and spatially…. More than a list or chronicle, a narrative adds up to 'something…'
> (Bell 2009: 8)

Determining that 'something', of course, is a central task for the listener and subsequently the analyst as they interpret meaning, or the 'point' the speaker wishes to make. A long story about a particular moment must be worth telling to take up so much space in a conversation.

Rather than thinking in binary terms – a segment is either narrative or not – and yet preserving some distinctions, Paley and Eva argue for degrees of narrativity, with the 'story' meeting the highest threshold: 'an arrangement of events [plot] and people [characters] designed to elicit a response [a reaction from an audience]' (2005. 89). Storytelling in conversational settings typically recapitulates discrete moments, whereas other forms of narrative telling are better suited for eliciting a response from the listener/question about the general course of things, or 'experience.' These discourse forms – not always event-centered or temporarily or spatially organized – include habitual, hypothetical, associative/episodic narrative, and other forms (Riessman 1993). A participant's causal claim – 'this is what x is like for me' – can be made more persuasively perhaps with a form other than a story about a particular incident.

Form Follows Function

To resist the pull toward narrative seduction, the investigator can interrogate what the narrative accomplishes and precisely how the form of telling achieves that end. Drawing on the familiar modernist architectural adage, form follows function.

There are many ways we can narrate an experience. It is the analyst's role to interrogate what is being accomplished with the particular choices a speaker makes. There are recognizable genres for narrating – farce, tragedy, the travel saga, the conversion tale, among others – which serve as cultural resources for any speaker. They provide familiar models for constructing 'human plights [and] they achieve their effects by using language in a particular way' (Bruner 1991: 14). We can ask why a narrative segment was developed *that* way at *that* point in an unfolding conversation. More generally, what does the speaker accomplish by adopting a particular narrative form? Does a story of a particular moment serve to persuade the listener of a preferred position perhaps, or put the speaker in an advantaged moral light ('I am a good person despite what I did')?

Personal narratives contain many performative features that enable the 'local achievement of identity' (Cussins 1998). Tellers intensify words and phrases; they enhance segments with narrative detail, reported speech, appeals to the audience, gestures, and even sound effects (Wolfson 1982; Bauman 1986). Analysts can ask additional questions of a performance:

- in what kind of a story does a narrator place herself?
- how does she position herself to the audience, and vice versa?
- how does she position characters in relation to one another, and in relation to herself?
- how does she position herself to herself, that is, make identity claims? (Bamberg 2005)

Social positioning in stories – how narrators position audience, characters and themselves – is a useful point of entry because 'fluid positioning, not fixed roles, are used by people to cope with the situations they find themselves in' (Harre and van Langenhove 1999: 17).

Narrators can position themselves, for example, as victims of one circumstance or another in their tales, giving over to other characters the power to initiate action. Alternatively, narrators can position themselves as active beings that assume control over events and actions: they purposefully initiate and cause action. They can shift among positions, giving themselves agentic roles in certain scenes, and passive roles in others. To create these fluid semantic spaces for themselves, narrators rely on particular grammatical resources to construct how they want to be known – verbs, for example, that frame actions as voluntary rather than compulsory, or grammatical forms that intensify their vulnerability (Capps and Ochs 1995).

These positionings in the performance of identity are enacted in an immediate discursive context – for an audience. Put differently, narratives are not simply a record of experience; they are composed for the listener/questioner and perhaps other audiences to accomplish something – to have an effect. In a word, narratives *do things*; they are motivated and purposeful, if not always consciously (Freeman 2002: 9). Echoing the warning about narrative seduction, Atkinson and Delamont (2006) caution us to avoid the assumption we have 'captured' someone's private experiences through our interviews. There is no unmediated access to a participant's 'lived-experience' – a claim often made in the qualitative research literature to describe what in-depth interviewing yields (see Holstein and Gubrium, this volume).

Interactional Context

Narratives in everyday life develop in dynamic conversations with listeners/ questioners. Yet many qualitative researchers ignore the audience and constraints of the setting in their analysis. In interview research the unfortunate practice follows from the view that a participant's 'story' is the focus of interest, which is independent of the conditions of production. If investigators believe they can gain unmediated access to a life story, they will not attend to the interactional and institutional contexts that shaped the particular version of it.

In contrast to the naive position, many of us in narrative studies attend to the research relationship, the unfolding interview conversation and the positioning of a story in it. We interrogate the influence of the setting, historical context and other dimensions that shape any speech act. The extent to which an investigator represents these dimensions will vary of course with the purpose of a project, but to neglect them entirely strips context from a piece of research.

Interviewers are active participants in interviews, subtly prodding participants to 'say more' about a topic or by pausing at key points in the expectation that 'more' could be said. By our receptive stance narrative interviewing encourages a degree of seduction; we invite stories rather than discourage 'digressions' from a predetermined focus of interest (Mishler 1986). Attention to the actions of all participants brings the dynamics of conversation into view – an essential element of the local context that is illustrated in the examples below. Excluding the action of the questioner/listener and other aspects of the production of narrative reflects a rationalist and monologic philosophy of language, and it can encourage essentialist thinking: the properties of an 'experience' as conveyed in a narrator's speech exist independent of context, that is, when, how, and to whom it is described.

It is particularly odd that qualitative researchers in the symbolic interaction theoretical tradition neglect the particular interactions that produce the knowledge then taken to be real. It seems that the 'story' is not important in this tradition, only the manifest content reflected in it. What happens to the reality construction process that happens when speakers and listeners interact during fieldwork, that is, during the simple act of dialogue where meaning is created in dynamic conversations with an 'other?' Verbal interactions occurring in specific settings produce stories that, depending on how they are composed, constrain meaning – how a reported experience can be interpreted. Arguably, narrative seduction is more likely when the content of speech is the exclusive focus.

If we accept that the research interview is a collaborative conversation, a discursive event involving give and take between speakers who operate within the constraints of broader social discourses (a topic illustrated in the second example), it is hard to justify excluding the listener/questioner. Perhaps the omission reflects unacknowledged power relations in the research relationship (see DeVault 1999; Gubrium and Holstein 2002) – all too common in qualitative research.

Many narrative researchers are incorporating visual technologies into their recording practice, thus expanding understandings of the context of an utterance. Particularly in ethnographic studies taking place in institutional settings (schools, health care settings, etc.), the use of video recording is increasing. What is commonly called 'body language' – relational positioning of the speakers in space, gaze and gesture – can come into the analysis, aiding greatly the interpretation of spoken discourse. (For recent examples, see Riessman 2007: 141–182; Örluv and Hydén 2006; Luttrell 2010; Heath, this volume).

In sum, my argument points to several key concepts for the beginning investigator who wants to incorporate narrative methods in a case study:

- Be precise in your use of a narrative vocabulary.
- In analyzing particular narrative segments, think about form and function – the way a segment of data is organized and why.
- Do not neglect the local context in your analysis, including the questioner/listener, setting and position of an utterance in the broader stream of the conversation.

Taken together, these dimensions (among others) distinguish narrative analysis from other forms of qualitative inquiry, particularly the analytic phrase of grounded theory. Research examples to follow illustrate the concepts in action. The first shows what narratives do in the institutional setting of a clinic. The second shows how a preferred identity is performed in a research interview.

Stories in Medical Settings

How is the clinical task (diagnosis, treatment and management of a chronic illness) actually accomplished in talk between patients and doctors in routine medical encounters? Clinical interviews are typically structured in fixed-alternative sequences that make it difficult for patients to tell stories about an episode in an illness trajectory. Building on a long tradition in conversation analysis on medical work, Clark and Mishler (1992) use contrasting case studies to show what collaborative storytelling accomplishes: in one case it facilitates the clinical task, in the second the physician's interruption of a potential narrative hinders illness management. I present the first part of the 'successful' case in Transcript 1 (see Appendix) and, after briefly summarizing its content, draw readers' attention to Clark and Mishler's microanalytic work related to narrative concepts introduced above.

A middle-aged African-American man with a seizure disorder comes to a scheduled appointment with a primary care physician, a third-year male resident[2] in an outpatient clinic of a large public teaching hospital in the northeastern US. In the conversation the patient and doctor each try to make coherent sense of a recent seizure. The physician's pause during his opening question ('Okay so you said you ha:d a-seizure… yesterday?'), which he follows with 'Hmm,' a long pause and then another question: 'At work?' (see Appendix for transcription conventions). This opening invites the story the patient then begins with an abstract – he is not 'really worried' because it is another instance of 'gettin upset and aggravated' – a precipitant apparently leading to seizures that the parties share. The patient then develops a detailed account of a challenging brake job on an Audi that required several days to complete – 'you get right up on the caliper.' He hit his eye on the caliper, got a black eye and headache, his boss failed to secure the necessary parts, and the next day he had to move on to a second car. The repeated frustrations ('It never took me that long before to finish up a brake job') led to aggravation to the point of having a seizure.

Notice how the story is invited and interactionally built, becoming a situated interactional accomplishment. The physician's long pauses cede the floor to the patient, creating the space to narrate. The patient then takes up the active role, developing a plot sequence embedded in his life world as an auto mechanic. The physician assumes the receptive stance and becomes an attentive listener. By remaining silent, indicating confusion and, in non-lexical utterances (um hum, hh hh), his interest,

---

[2]The authors do not specify the race of the physician.

he collaborates in the construction of a fully realized story (Labov 1982) that pivots on a rupture in the expected course of a day at work.

The story of frustration concludes with a summarizing coda that resolves the plot ('That's when I ended up having the seizure.') and returns the floor to the co-participant – the doctor – who then invites the patient to elaborate the story: 'Okay uhm.hh so: did your boss or someone else see the seizure happen?' From a clinical point of view, the finely coordinated activity of doctor and patient assures a precise history is obtained and a collaborative relationship established – necessary for good patient care. The incident demonstrates how medical work is done collaboratively.

For the narrative analyst, the co-participant's actions in producing the story are of particular interest. Clark and Mishler (1992) are not much interested in content – the report of a seizure – but rather in *how* the story is composed collaboratively. They draw attention to how the physician's clarifying questions and non-lexical utterances indicating attentiveness encourage the patient to elaborate the precise sequence of events (plot), setting and relevant witnesses (characters). The coherent story that is finally produced is jointly constructed in the give and take between speakers, rather than a 'patient's story' about an illness episode. The authors use the brief segment to identify components of attentive medical interviewing, but for narrative analysts the case offers an excellent example of the co-construction process – how stories are introduced and interactionally built in clinical settings. Detailed transcription practices allow us to see precisely how the story is invited, elaborated and resolved in a collaborative interchange between participants.

The conversation allows the patient something more: he can make an identity claim, developing the theme of his personal responsibility. More than merely a report of a seizure, the patient can position himself in a story as the diligent and responsible worker who was frustrated in his attempt to meet a challenge at work. His experience becomes the center of attention; the story functions, as personal stories often do, to make an explanatory argument and presentation of 'self.' He can construct a positive identity in the face of what might have been a stigmatizing illness episode on the job. He can ward off the stigma of epilepsy and any possible blame for precipitating the seizure by his behavior.

For the physician, the story provides something different: the historically connected facts needed to evaluate a clinical problem in a way that takes account of the life world of the patient. Shaped by the constraints of the medical setting, the story is recipient designed; it provides the detail and specificity needed to make clinical sense of a problem. In what follows in the conversation (not reproduced here, see Clark and Mishler 1992), the seizure story becomes the frame of reference to reorganize the treatment plan and adjust medication. The clinical task of diagnosis, treatment and illness management is completed in this instance by collaborating in the development of a story, which Clark and Mishler contrast with another case study in which the physician repeatedly interrupts a patient's account, thus missing crucial contextual cues about her illness.

Returning to the narrative concepts introduced earlier, I draw readers' attention to the principle of co-construction and the detailed recording practices the authors use to analyze it. The interactional work that goes on in all storytelling situations is visible when the speech actions of both participants are represented in detail, which makes for a complex transcript but one that allows for microanalysis of the story construction process. Coherent stories are the outcome of finely coordinated activity of speaker and listener/questioner; they are not simply carriers of content. Although Clark and Mishler's primary focus is on how the clinical task is accomplished through talk, it is also possible to read the data extract from the point of view of the patient and what the story allows him to accomplish – an identity claim.

The Social World in a Personal Narrative

The second example takes up more fully identity construction in the face of stigma and powerful social discourses. My research on childless women was conducted in Kerala, South India, and elsewhere (Riessman 2000, 2005). I describe the fieldwork in detail, which included an ethnographic component. Analysis of the interview data was initially category-centered, looking thematically across more than 30 conversations. Several case studies were added when I noticed a deviation from the general pattern among older women. There were very few in my sample but they appeared to have constructed successful lives that defied the master narrative of compulsory motherhood for married women in India (for a comparison of three case studies, see Riessman 2002a).

One of the participants was a woman I call 'Gita': 55 years old, married and childless, Hindu, and from a lower caste.[3] Because of progressive social policies and related opportunities in her South Indian state, Gita is educated, has risen in status, and works as a lawyer in a small municipality. The particular interview segment represented in the transcript (see Transcript 2 in the Appendix) took place after she and I had talked in English for nearly an hour in her home about a variety of topics, most of which she introduced – her schooling career, how her marriage was arranged, and her political work in the 'liberation struggle of Kerala.' We enter the interview as I reintroduce the topic of fertility. My transcription conventions are adapted from Gee (1991): lines about a single topic are grouped into stanzas, which I then group into scenes. Except for my opening question, I have not represented my brief utterances (they are marked '=' in the transcript) but bring my participation into the analysis in other ways.

Although Gita could have answered my question ('were you ever pregnant?') directly ('yes'), she chose instead to develop a complex narrative. She describes terminated

---

[3]The case study is adapted from Riessman (2002a).

pregnancies, going to a political demonstration, coming home to her husband's anger, whereupon the scene shifts to the actions of in-laws and her husband's refusal to be examined for infertility. This account was unlike others: although temporally organized, Gita's plot spans many years and social settings – she does not tell a Labovian story about a discrete sequence of events (as in the first example). Also unlike other women's accounts, there is no reference to sadness, disappointment, or other emotions common to narratives of miscarriage and infertility.

In an effort to interpret the segment, I struggled to define some boundaries, initially deciding to end my representation of the narrative with what seems like a coda at the end of Scene 4: 'But afterwards I never became – [pregnant].' The utterance ends the sequence about pregnancy – the topic of my initial question. Eventually, as I began to focus on identity construction and narrative form, I decided to include the next scene. As a general rule, the choice of a segment for closer analysis – the textual representation of a spoken narrative and the boundaries chosen – is strongly influenced by the researcher's evolving research questions. In these ways, the investigator variously 'infiltrates' a transcript (see Riessman 2007: chapter 2).[4]

Infertility in the Indian context is loaded with stigma for women and, consequently, was a major theme in my interviews, especially with younger women. I turned to sociological theory to think critically about stigma and its management. As Goffman (1963, 1969) suggests, social actors can stage performances of a desirable self to preserve 'face' in difficult situations, thus managing potentially 'spoiled' identities. These identity performances are situated and accomplished as I noted earlier: participants negotiate in conversation how they want to be known. Rather than 'revealing' an essential self, they perform the preferred self, selected from the multiplicity of selves or persona that we all switch between as we go about our lives. Approaching identity as a 'performative struggle over the meanings of experience' (Langellier 2001: 3) opens up analytic possibilities that are missed with static theories of identity that assume a singular unified 'self.'

Returning to my conversation with Gita, the absence of motherhood did not seem to be a particularly salient topic for her (I was always the one to introduce it); nor did she express negative self-evaluation, as younger women did. Gita had built a life around principles other than motherhood – as a lawyer and political activist. Close examination of the conversation reveals precisely how she constructs this preferred (positive) identity, solving the problem of stigma and subordination as a childless woman in South India.

---

[4]The narrative could be analyzed with a primary focus on cultural context – the prominent role of the wife's in-laws, for example, in defining and managing infertility in India. (For an example, see Riessman 2000.) Investigators interested in psychological processes might explore Gita's account of infertility for its closed, sealed-off features – she displays a set of understandings that seem to defy redefinition and she is silent about emotions. What remains unsaid – the fissures and gaps in the account – could be explored: do they suggest a defensive process? No analysis of discourse can be expected to do a multiplicity of tasks.

Gita carefully positions the audience (me) and various characters in the discursive construction of the story – a complex performance that I have represented in five 'scenes.' Each offers a snapshot of action, located in a different time and setting. Unlike the discrete story in the first example, there is a complex organization to Gita's narrative. Let us look at how the scenes are organized within the performance.

The first two scenes are prompted by a request ('were you ever pregnant?') – my attempt after an hour's conversation to position Gita in a world of fertility. She reluctantly moves into the role of pregnant woman in these brief scenes, quickly chronicling two pregnancies several years apart – the outcomes of which I have to clarify (in lines marked '=' on the transcript). She does not provide narrative detail or elaborate meanings – the audience must infer a great deal. The first two scenes contain only one character – a doctor – aside from Gita herself. She 'approached' the doctor, who 'asked' her to have a D and C. A quick aside states the doctor wanted to examine the husband, but we infer this did not happen. (With this utterance, Gita prefigures her husband's responsibility, anticipating the final scene and the point of the narrative.) She casts the doctor as the active agent again in Scene 2: she 'wanted' and 'advised' bed rest. By choice of verbs and positioning of characters, Gita constructs scenes in which she plays a relatively minor role. The audience infers from the lack of narrative detail that the events in the plot up to this point are not particularly salient for her.

The narrator's position and the salience of events radically change in the third scene. Gita shifts topics, from pregnancy to 'to what I already told you' – the primacy of her political world. She constructs a scene where she is the central character and agent of action: a 'political leader' in her Kerala community who 'had to' participate in a demonstration in Delhi against Mrs. Indira Gandhi, who was seeking re-election. A well-known component of her policy was forced sterilization. Ironically, this public discourse intersects a personal narrative about fertility.

Notice how in Scene 3 verbs frame the narrator's intentional actions,[5] situated in the political exigencies of the time. There is considerable narrative elaboration in sharp contrast to the spare, 'passive' grammar of the previous scenes, where she was the object of the doctor's actions. Gita locates her private fertility story in the public story of 'Mother India' and its socialist movement – the audience is not left wondering which is most important. Ignoring her doctor's advice 'to take bed rest' during her second pregnancy, she travels to Delhi to participate in a mass demonstration, which probably involved a three-day train trip in 1975. Despite her return by plane and a 16-day nursing home stay for 'bleeding,' we infer Gita lost the pregnancy (a fact I confirm a few lines later). She constructs a narrative around oppositional

---

[5]The verb construction 'had to' is ambiguous. It might refer to others' expectations that Gita participate in the political demonstration as a leader in the community; or it might refer to a personal desire to participate, arising out of her own political convictions and priorities. The narrative context supports the latter interpretation.

worlds – family life, on the one hand, and the socialist movement of India on the other. The personal and the political occupy separate spheres of action.

Gita shifts the action in the next two scenes to the family world. In Scene 4, she again introduces her husband as a character, and reports that he was 'very angry' at her 'social work,' meaning her political activism. She communicates a one-way conversation: not giving herself a speaking role, she positions herself as the object of her husband's angry speech. We do not know what she said to him, if anything. Her passive position in this scene is in sharp contrast to her activity in the previous one. Is she displaying here the typical practice in South Indian families – wives are expected to defer to husbands' authority (Riessman 2000)? If so, her choice of language is intriguing – he said 'this and that.' Could she be belittling his anger and directives here? She concludes Scene 4 with a factual utterance ('But afterwards I never became – [pregnant]').

In the fifth and final lengthy scene, Gita introduces new characters (her parents-in-law, an infertility specialist, a sister-in-law) and an intricate plot, before the narrative moves toward its point: infertility is not Gita's responsibility. The final scene has the most elaboration, suggesting importance, and the performance of identity is most vivid here. Gita begins by constructing a passive, stigmatized position for herself: in-laws 'brought' her for treatment to a gynecologist in the major South Indian city where the parents live, because 'they thought I had some defect.' As in earlier scenes involving pregnancy, others suggest or initiate action. She intensifies meaning and thematic importance with repetition ('defect') in the next stanza – the gynecologist determined after a lengthy examination that Gita has 'no defect at all.' She is 'perfectly' normal. Blame for infertility, Gita intimates, resides elsewhere. Using the linguistic device of reported speech, she performs several conversations on the topic of getting her husband tested. Everyone is enlisted in the effort – gynecologist, sister-in-law – but he refuses: 'No, no, I will not go to a lady doctor.' Nor is he willing to have his sperm tested in a laboratory. (Gita returned several other times in our interview to his refusal to be tested.) The narrator has crafted a performance – akin to a legal brief reviewing the evidence – where she has no responsibility whatsoever for infertility.

Looking critically at the conversation, we can wonder. By resisting seduction the analyst can interrogate the narrator's attributions. Gita ignored her physician's advice to 'take bed rest' during her second pregnancy, choosing to travel instead to Delhi. She gave primacy to political commitments, valuing work in the socialist movement over her gendered position in the home. She was also '40 or 41' years old when she was finally examined by a specialist. Age may have been a factor. Gita had conceived twice, but could not sustain pregnancies – suggesting a possible 'defect.'

The performance, however, signals how Gita wants to be known: as a 'perfectly' normal woman 'with no defect at all.' This is the point of the narrative, realized through its form. How she organizes scenes within the performance, choices about positioning, and the grammatical resources employed have effects and put forth her preferred identity – committed political activist, not disappointed would-be mother. Later in the interview, she supported my interpretation here. In a clear statement she resisted once again my positioning of her in the world of biological fertility: 'Because I do not have [children], I have no disappointments, because mine is a big family.' She continued with a listing of many brothers, their children, and particular nieces who 'come here every evening...to take their meals.' With these words, I become the defective subject with naive bipolar notions of parental status – either you have children or you do not. Although I did not 'get it' at the time of our conversation, I sense that she did get it and worked to counter my positioning of her in the world of fertility. She performed a gender identity that defied the master cultural narrative – biological motherhood is the central axis of identity for married women. With time, I was able to historicize Gita's life chances, and locate her in an evolving cultural discourse about women's 'proper' place in modern India, a 'developing' nation that is developing new spaces (besides home and field) for women to labor (Riessman 2000, 2002a, 2002b).

Conclusion

The analytic strategies demonstrated in the two examples are generalizable to other narrative projects. Identity construction was a common interest – particularly so in the second – and both projects were case-centered rather than category-centered. Also, unlike grounded theory and other thematically oriented methods, both examples paid considerable attention to how the narratives were composed, to whom, and with what effect. By resisting narrative seduction, the analysts actively *interpreted* the accounts for meaning in the specific situations, which in the second example may have been quite different than what the speaker intended.

The two examples differed in form of data and research setting: the first example analyzed the joint construction in a medical consultation of a 'simple' story; the second analyzed a complex narrative from a research interview that moved across vast expanses of time and space. In both, form and function were related – what the narrative was *doing* in the particular interactional context and setting in which it was produced. Though both examples emphasized the local context, there were big differences in how audience participation was displayed.

Research participants can emplot their lives in a variety of ways; they 'select and assemble experiences and events so they contribute collectively to the intended point of the story...why it is being told, in just this way, in just this setting (Mishler 1999: 8). As we resist seduction into the manifest content of narratives, form and function can come into view.

Summary

Narrative scholars and grounded theorists have both added to the burgeoning literature on identity construction. How narrators accomplish their situated accounts in interaction conveys a great deal about the process. Identity is constructed in situ. To make it visible, we can analyze scenes, the positioning of characters, self and audience, and we can 'unpack' the grammatical resources narrators select to make their points. We can analyze how narrators position their audience (and, reciprocally, how the audience positions the narrator). Preferred identities are constituted through such performative actions.

Future Prospects

Narrative inquiry offers opportunities for the disciplined study of interviews, naturally occurring conversations, political discourse, as well as epistolary and visual materials. There is a need for culturally sensitive applications of the methods in non-Western contexts with focused attention to language translation issues.

Questions

1 What are some key differences between grounded theory and narrative analysis of data?
2 What are some of the key points to keep in mind in analyzing transcribed texts as narrative?

Recommended Reading

Riessman, C. K. (2008). *Narrative Methods for the Human Sciences*. Thousand Oaks, CA: Sage.

An accessible introduction to some analytic approaches with exemplars from several social sciences.

Andrews, M., Squire, C. and M. Tamboukou, eds. (2008). *Doing Narrative Research*. London: Sage.

A guide to inquiry including forms of narrative analysis, reflexivity, interpretation and research contexts.

Emerson, P. and S. Frosh (2009). *Critical Narrative Analysis in Psychology: A Guide to Practice*, rev. ed. London: Palgrave Macmillan.

Working with a single 'case,' the reader learns levels of analysis from micro to macro.

Internet Links

Website for narrative researchers looking for courses, papers and colleagues:
www.uel.ac.uk/cnr

Website for narrative events and colleagues in Australia/New Zealand:
www.narrativenetworkaustralia.org.au

Website for model program in working with epistolary narrative:
www.oliveschreinerletters.ed.ac.uk

Review: Catherine Kohler Riessman (2008) by Duque, R. L. (2010). Forum: Qualitative Social Research:
www.qualitative-research.net/index.php/fqs/article/view/1418.

Appendix

Transcript 1

R: Okay so you said you ha:d a-"seizure yesterday?
{ }
P: Uh u yesterday yesterday about
* about eleven o'clock yeah
R: Hmm*. . Atwork?
P: (h)um hum
R: Okay, uh
{
P: Well I'm not really worried itz same thing you told me not gettin
ya-know not upset and aggravated and ". I couldn't have-ta uhm my
{}
/?:hh.hh
boss give me a car Tuesday right? *. . . . and I workin-on it was an
Audi I never did brakes on an Audi before, ya-know front wheel drive?
{}
/?:hh.hh
R: Yeah
P: And * it was a problem, ya-know and I was down all day long * you know
wË back like this-here. Like the car's on a lift,
R: Yeah
P: But it's two bolts ya-know ya just can't get to-em unless you get right up

on the caliper * and ah twis- jus can twist a little bit with a
screwdriver. * And I was going like (gangbust) when (it) ya see I got a
black e(h)ye .hhuh
R: (O-)Oh from the "seizure
P: No. From the caliper. One of em fell, to "the eye
/?: Oh I see
{}
P: And it hit me there so Tuesday night and 1 had this terrible
headache and all. * So 1 slept with a ya-know with a ice pack
over-it all night to keep- tryin to keep it from swelling and all.
*. . And then I went back in * yesterday to try to finish it up. It
never took me that long before to finish up a brake job
R: .hhhh.
P: And * my boss hadn't got all the parts for it so I start working
on another car-ya-know? * That's when I ended up having the seizure.
R: Okay uhm .hh so: did your boss or someone else see the seizure happen

Source: Clark and Mishler, 1992, p. 349.

Transcript conventions

. ? Punctuation marks indicate intonation. A period marks sharply
falling intonation; a question mark indicates rising intonation.
Carats indicate marked emphasis.
() Enclosed words spoken softly,
: Colons indicate elongated vowel sounds.
Hyphens indicate abruptly truncated portions of utterances.
= Equal signs indicate latching of successive utterances with no
discernible gap.
.hh hh An '.hh' indicates an audible inhalation; 'hh' indicates an
audible exhalation.
. . . * Series of periods indicate pauses, with each period a tenth of a
second. Pauses of one second are marked with an asterisk.
{ } Braces mark the location of simultaneous speech.

Source: Clark and Mishler (1992: 369)

Transcript 2

Cathy: Now I am going to go back and ask some specific questions.
Were you ever pregnant?

Gita: Pregnant means-You see it was 3 years [after the marriage]   Scene 1
then I approached [name of doctor]
then she said it is not a viable–[pregnancy].
=
So she asked me to undergo this operation, this D&C
and she wanted to examine him [husband] also.

Then the second time in 1974-in 75,   Scene 2
next time – four months.
Then she wanted [me] to take bed rest
advised me to take bed rest

Because I already told you   Scene 3
it was during that period that [name] the socialist leader

led the gigantic procession against Mrs. Indira Gandhi,
the Prime Minister of India, in Delhi.

And I was a political leader [names place and party]
I had to participate in that

So I went by train to Delhi
but returned by plane.
After the return I was in [name] Nursing Home
for 16 days bleeding

And so he [husband] was very angry   Scene 4
he said 'do not go for any social work
do not be active' this and that
But afterwards I never became – [pregnant]
=
Then my in-laws, they are in [city]   Scene 5
they thought I had some defect really speaking
So they brought me to a gynecologist,
one [name], one specialist.

She took three hours to examine me
and she said 'you are perfectly-[normal], no defect at all'
even though I was 40 or 41 then.
'So I have to examine your husband.'

Then I told her [doctor] 'You just ask his sister.'
She was – his sister was with me in [city].
So I asked her to ask her to bring him in.
He will not come.
Then we went to the house
So then I said 'Dr. [name] wants to see you.'

Then he [husband] said 'No, no, I will not go to a lady doctor.'
Then she [sister-in-law] said she would not examine him
they had to examine the – what is it? – the sperm in the laboratory.
But he did not allow that.

Source: Riessman (2002a: 700)

References

Atkinson, P. and P. Delamont. 2006. 'Rescuing Narrative from Qualitative Research.' *Narrative Inquiry* 16:164–72.

Bamberg, M. 2005. '"I Know it May Sound Strange to Say This, but We Couldn't Really Care Less about Her Anyway": Form and Function of "Slut-Bashing" in Male Identity Constructions of 15-Year-Olds.' *Human Development* 47: 331–353.

Bauman, R. 1986. *Story, Performance, and Event: Contextual Studies of Oral Narrative.* Cambridge: Cambridge University Press.

Bell, S. E. 1988. 'Becoming a Political Woman: The Reconstruction and Interpretation of Experience through Stories.' pp. 97–123 in *Gender and Discourse: The Power of Talk*, edited by A. D. Todd and S. Fisher. Norwood, NJ: Ablex.

— 1999. 'Narratives and Lives: Women's Health Politics and the Diagnosis of Cancer for DES Daughters.' *Narrative Inquiry* 9: 1–43.

— 2009. *DES Daughters: Embodied Knowledge and the Transformation of Women's Health Politics*. Philadelphia: Temple University Press.

Bruner, J. 1991. 'The Narrative Construction of Reality.' *Critical Inquiry* 18: 1–21.

Capps, L. and E. Ochs. 1995. *Constructing Panic: The Discourse of Agoraphobia.* Cambridge, MA: Harvard University Press.

Chambers, R. 1984. *Story and Situation: Narrative Seduction and the Power of Fiction.* Minneapolis: University of Minnesota Press.

Clark, J. A. and E. G. Mishler. 1992. 'Attending to Patients' Stories: Reframing the Clinical Task.' *Sociology of Health and Illness* 14: 344–370.

Cussins, C. M. 1998. 'Ontological Choreography: Agency for Women Patients in an Infertility Clinic.' In *Differences in Medicine: Unraveling Practices, Techniques and Bodies*, edited by M. Berg and S. Mol. Durham, NC: Duke University Press.

De Fina, A. 2003. *Identity in Narrative: A Study of Immigrant Discourse.* Amsterdam and Philadelphia: John Benjamins.

DeVault, M. L. 1999. *Liberating Method: Feminism and Social Research.* Philadelphia: Temple University Press.

Freeman, M. 2002. 'The Presence of What is Missing: Memory: Poetry and the Ride Home.' pp. 165–176 in *Critical Incident Narratives in the Development of Men's Lives*, edited by R. J. Pellegrini and T. R. Sarbin. New York: Haworth Clinical Practice Press.

Garfinkel, H. 1967. *Studies in Ethnomethodology.* Englewood Cliffs, NJ: Prentice Hall.

Gee, J. P. 1991. 'A Linguistic Approach to Narrative.' *Journal of Narrative and Life History/Narrative Inquiry* 1: 15–39.

Goffman, E. 1963. *Stigma: Notes on the Management of Spoiled Identity*. Englewood Cliffs, NJ: Prentice Hall.

— 1969. *The Presentation of Self in Everyday Life*. New York: Penguin.

Gubrium, J. F. and J. A. Holstein. 2002. 'From the Interview to the Interview Society.' pp. 3–32 in *Handbook of Interview Research: Context and Method*, edited by J. F. Gubrium and J. A. Holstein. Thousand Oaks, CA: Sage.

Harre, R. and L. van Langenhove, editors. 1999. *Positioning Theory*. Malden, MA: Blackwell.

Hinchman, L. P. and S. K. Hinchman, editors. 1997. *Memory, Identity, Community: The Idea of Narrative in the Human Sciences*. Albany: State University of New York Press.

Labov, W. 1972. *Language in the Inner City: Studies in the Black English Vernacular*. Philadelphia: University of Pennsylvania Press.

— 1982. 'Speech Actions and Reactions in Personal Narrative.' pp. 219–47 in *Analyzing Discourse: Text and Talk*, edited by D. Tannen. Washington, DC: Georgetown University Press.

Labov, W. and J. Waletzky. 1967. 'Narrative Analysis: Oral Versions of Personal Experience.' pp. 12–44 in *Essays on the Verbal and Visual Arts*, edited by J. Helm. Seattle: American Ethnological Society/University of Washington Press.

Langellier, K. 2001. '"You're Marked": Breast Cancer, Tattoo and the Narrative Performance of Identity.' pp. 145–184 in *Narrative Identity: Studies in Autobiography, Self, and Culture*, edited by J. Brockmeier and D. Carbaugh. Amsterdam and Philadelphia: John Benjamins.

Luttrell, W., with J. Dorsey, C. Shalaby and J. Hayden 2010. 'Transnational Childhoods and Youth Media: Seeing With and Learning from One Immigrant Child's Visual Narrative.' In *International Perspective on Youth Media: Cultural Production and Education*, edited by J. Fisherkeller. Berne: Peter Lang.

— 1986. *Research Interviewing: Context and Narrative*. Cambridge, MA: Harvard University Press.

Mishler, E. G. 1996. 'Missing Persons: Recovering Developmental Stories/Histories.' pp. 74–99 in *Ethnography and Human Development: Context and Meaning in Social Inquiry*, edited by R. Jessor, A. Colby and R. A. Shweder. Chicago: University of Chicago Press.

Mishler, E. G. 1999. *Storylines: Craftartists' Narratives of Identity*. Cambridge, MA: Harvard University Press.

Örluv, L. and L. C. Hydén. 2006. 'Confabulation: Sense-Making, Self-Marking and World-Making in Dementia.' *Discourse Studies* 8: 647–673.

Paley, J. and G. Eva. 2005. 'Narrative Vigilance: The Analysis of Stories in Health Care.' *Nursing Philosophy* 6: 83–97.

Polanyi, L. 1989. *Telling the American Story: A Structural and Cultural Analysis of Conversational Storytelling*. Cambridge, MA: MIT Press.

Quinn, N. 2005. *Finding Culture in Talk: A Collection of Methods*. New York: Palgrave Macmillan.

Radley, A. and K. Chamberlain. 2001. 'Health Psychology and the Study of the Case: From Method to Analytic Concern.' *Social Science & Medicine* 53: 321–332.

Riessman, C. K. 1990. *Divorce Talk: Women and Men Make Sense of Personal Relationships*. New Brunswick, NJ: Rutgers University Press.

— 1993. *Narrative Analysis*. Newbury Park, CA: Sage.

— 2000. 'Stigma and Everyday Resistance Practices: Childless Women in South India.' *Gender & Society* 14: 111–135.

— 2002a. 'Analysis of Personal Narratives.' pp. 695–710 in *Handbook of Interview Research*, edited by J. A. Gubrium and J. F. Holstein. Newbury Park, CA: Sage.

— 2002b. 'Positioning Gender Identity in Narratives of Infertility: South Indian Women's Lives in Context.' pp. 152–170 in *Infertility Around the Globe: New Thinking on Childlessness, Gender, and Reproductive Technologies*, edited by M. C. Inhorn and F. van Balen. Berkeley: University of California Press.

— 2005. 'Exporting Ethics: A Narrative about Narrative Research in South India.' *Health: An Interdisciplinary Journal for the Social Study of Health, Illness and Medicine* 9: 473–490.

— 2007. *Narrative Methods for the Human Sciences*. Thousand Oaks, CA: Sage.

Wolfson, N. 1982. *The Conversational Historical Present in American English Narrative*. Dordrecht: Foris.

Systematic Reviews and Qualitative Methods ⬤18

Mary Dixon-Woods

Abstract

This chapter focuses on methods for conducting overviews of bodies of evidence that include qualitative research studies. Systematic review methodology has emerged partly to counter the apparent fallibilities of traditional literature reviews. This methodology treats the production of a review as a scientific process. It typically uses pre-specified protocols for the conduct of a review, which formalise and codify: the review question; eligibility criteria for studies to be included; searching strategies to be used; quality appraisals to be undertaken; and methods to be used in synthesising the included studies. This approach poses a number of challenges when the aim is to include qualitative research studies. Methodological approaches for incorporating qualitative research in systematic reviews vary along a spectrum from those that remain fairly close to the conventional systematic review template to those that seek a redefinition of systematic review as an approach.

Keywords:

systematic review, research synthesis, literature review, qualitative research.

Introduction

Undertaking reviews of the literature is perhaps one of the most fundamental and routine tasks of any academic. Such reviews are used, for example, to identify gaps in knowledge, theory or evidence, or to provide an overview of a field or sub-field. The question of how literature reviews should best be conducted has become a focus of increasing interest and debate. In tracing the outlines of these debates, it is useful, to begin with, to characterise the various approaches to conducting reviews in terms of caricatures. Two are especially helpful in introducing the area, and I will term these:

- the 'authorship' approach;
- the 'contractual' approach.

The authorship approach is one that has long dominated much of the social sciences. Here, the literature review is seen as the product of a special kind of expertise and scholarly sensibility, gained by gradually internalising the modes of conduct proper to competent members of the scholarly community. The skill of literature reviewing is learned as part of long and difficult effort aimed at gaining mastery not only over a body of knowledge, but also over the rhetorical tactics needed to persuade readers of the correctness of the author's interpretation. These tactics may include:

- showing that the author is aware of what are generally held to be the 'key papers' in a field and can mount a satisfying critique of these;
- demonstrating that the argument being fashioned is coherent and plausible;
- showing that persuasive modes of vocabulary and organisation are mobilised.

Memorably described by Howard Becker (2007), the process of skill acquisition in this form of literature review is one of acculturation and socialisation, part of the larger project of developing the ability to write social science. The annotation 'stink! stink! stink!' by way of comment on one of his manuscripts was just one of the purgatories Becker endured on his way to acquiring this ability.

In contrast to this is the 'contractual' approach to literature reviewing. The defining characteristic of this approach is a proceduralisation of the process of review. Here, the literature review is viewed as a scientific process governed by a set of explicit and demanding rules oriented towards demonstrating comprehensiveness, immunity from bias, and transparency and accountability of technique and execution. This is the idea that finds its concrete expression in the methodology of the systematic review. Systematic reviews are conventionally understood to have specific characteristics (Box 18.1).

Box 18.1   Characteristics of a systematic review

- explicit study protocol;
- address a formal, prespecified, highly focused question;
- define the eligibility criteria for studies to be included in the review in advance;
- are explicit about the methods used for searching for studies, including any efforts to track down unpublished work or studies published in foreign languages;
- screen publications for inclusion in the review against a priori criteria;
- conduct formalised appraisals, assess their scientific quality and otherwise limit the risk of bias;
- use explicit methods to combine the findings of studies.

In systematic review, method is a way of expunging the author through a regime of accountability; the various techniques are intended to operate as a means of distancing the author from the material on which he or she works by disciplining and calling to account what he or she does and how he or she reports it. Learning how to do a literature review, in the contractual approach, involves learning the formal rules and displaying their conscientious application; systematic review is therefore just as much engaged in using rhetorical devices as a means of persuasion as the author-based review, but the nature of the rhetoric is different. A judgement about whether a systematic review has been done well will depend on an assessment of the extent to which it conforms to the procedural requirements governing its conduct. It can thus be understood as a contract-based form of activity, in which performance is assessed against specific standards. It is markedly distinct from a view of the literature review as a product of the author's innate, tacit skill, a form of cultural competence to be judged by attending to the quality of the argument and the aesthetics of the presentation. In this chapter, we examine what the turn towards systematic review means for reviews of qualitative studies.

The Rise of Systematic Review Methodology

The rise of 'systematic review' as a distinct methodology for conducting reviews of evidence has an interesting and instructive history. The need to produce unbiased overviews of the results of empirical studies was recognised as far back as 1753, when James Lind's treatise on scurvy noted the need to have a full and impartial view of the evidence. Methods for summarising and synthesising bodies of research have since taken several forms.

One important strand has been the development of statistical methods for aggregating and comparing the results of different quantitative studies. The statistician Karl Pearson (1904) is thought to have been the first to combine the findings of independent studies to produce an overall estimate, when he sought to compare infection and mortality among soldiers who had and had not volunteered for inoculation against typhoid fever. Techniques for statistical pooling of quantitative data continued to develop throughout the twentieth century, particularly within the fields of psychology and education studies. They were christened with the term 'meta-analysis' by the educationalist Gene Glass, who sought an alternative to what he saw as 'casual, narrative discussions of research studies' (1976: 3). Though sometimes (mis)appropriated, the term 'meta-analysis' is now properly used in a circumscribed way to describe the quantitative pooling of study findings. Meta-analysis is just one of the techniques that can be used in a systematic review: meta-analysis and systematic review are far from synonymous, and it is possible (indeed, very common) to have a systematic review without a meta-analysis.

The more general significance of the development of meta-analysis was in adding to a growing view throughout the 1980s and 1990s that unstructured and poorly disciplined reviews of quantitative studies were likely to be flawed because, confronted with a large body of evidence, reviewers are susceptible to a range of heuristics, biases, prejudices and sloppy practices. Reviewers may, for example:

- focus on a small sub-set of studies but not describe how they selected them;
- be influenced by their own perspective and expert opinions;
- fail to address the quality of studies they review;
- combine the findings of studies in inappropriate ways;
- not adequately account for publication bias (the problem that studies with positive findings are more likely to be published than those with negative findings);
- marshal the evidence in support of their preferred theories.

The correct remedy to the fallibilities of the author-based approach was seen to lie in the routinisation of processes of review. This argument gained particular force in medicine, where both the failure to conduct systematic reviews and the lack of scientific rigour in published reviews came to be seen as an unacceptable threat to patient safety. For example, tens of thousands of babies are thought to have suffered or died unnecessarily because of a failure to conduct a systematic review and meta-analysis of clinical trials of steroids for premature labour (Evans et al., 2006). The discovery of many similar examples, together with the increasingly rapid development of methods for systematic review, helped fuel the rise of what came to be known as the evidence-based practice and policy movement, which has now spread from its initial origins in medicine to many diverse fields.

This highly influential movement has taken a number of institutionalised forms, including the founding of organisations engaged in publishing guidance on how to undertake systematic reviews and coordinating the production of reviews. In healthcare, the Cochrane Collaboration and the UK NHS Centre for Reviews and Dissemination (NHS CRD) are among the best known of these. The newer Campbell Collaboration has used the Cochrane model as the basis of an international network to produce systematic reviews on the effects of social interventions, particularly in the areas of education, crime and social welfare. The evidence-based approach has also become popularised through blogs and columns such as Ben Goldacre's *Guardian* column (see www.badscience.net/), which, among other things, has exposed the ways in which commercial interests may influence scientific findings. The James Lind Library (www.jameslindlibrary.org) and the freely available book *Testing Treatments* (www.jameslindlibrary.org/testing-treatments.html) have also sought to bring principles of systematic review and evidence-based policy and practice to a wider audience.

Controversy about Systematic Reviews

Much of the work within the broad church of the evidence-based movement focuses on addressing questions of effectiveness or 'what works?', and it is perhaps unsurprising that it has had considerable appeal to policy-makers and decision-makers. The production of systematic reviews is now a large-scale activity, undertaken in support of a wide range of important areas of policy and practice, and increasingly relied upon to support decision-making in areas as diverse as anti-bullying interventions, the effects of interview and interrogation methods on confession rates in criminal suspects, and the health and social effects of housing improvements.

Systematic review has become established as a scientific research methodology in its own right, but it has also become a political and social force to be reckoned with, to the extent that systematic reviews are now seen, in many influential quarters, as having a special kind of scientific authority. This has led to considerable controversy and conflict within the social science community (and beyond). The debates to some extent represent the perpetuation of long-standing tensions about what should count as scientific method in the social sciences.

One side of the debate sees immense benefit in using systematic review methodology to synthesise bodies of available evidence, revealing to external scrutiny the basis of decisions about which studies have and have not been included in a review; making explicit and systematic the processes of summarising data across multiple studies; and, where appropriate, increasing the statistical power of estimates of effect.

The other side is critical of the argument that systematic review is the only evidence that counts as evidence. This criticism is particularly strong when systematic reviews are extended beyond the evaluation of therapeutic interventions in healthcare to address questions with the higher level of uncertainties and ambiguities that are characteristic of the social world. Systematic review methodology has been attacked for allegedly positivist, reductionist leanings, its rigidities and the apparently limited, or even absurd, nature of the conclusions of some reviews (MacLure, 2005; Hammersley, 2005).

A particular (though not exclusive) focus of criticism of early forms of systematic review methodology was that they offered little or no place for qualitative research. The original 'hierarchy of evidence' approach that ranked different study designs in terms of the quality of evidence they yielded typically excluded qualitative research altogether, or put it at (or close to) the bottom of the pyramid. There is no doubt that this can lead to a number of important problems, including:

- the risks that the question of the review might be inappropriately defined;
- the outcomes of interest might be inappropriately specified;

- the variables to be studied might be inappropriately selected;
- potentially relevant data might be excluded;
- inappropriate conclusions might be reached (Dixon-Woods et al., 2001).

The arguments in favour of including qualitative research in reviews might be stated briefly as follows: not everything we need to know about the world can be measured or counted, and other forms of data are often needed to form a comprehensive view or understanding of an area.

The last decade has seen explicit acknowledgement of the relevance and utility of qualitative research in systematic reviews, and a number of developments aimed at enabling qualitative research studies to be synthesised or summarised either on their own or with quantitative research findings. Recent guidance from both the NHS CRD (2008 – freely available from www.york.ac.uk/inst/crd/systematic_reviews_book.htm) and from the Cochrane Collaboration (Higgins and Green, 2009, freely available from www.cochrane-handbook.org/) devotes considerable attention to discussing the inclusion of qualitative research studies in or alongside systematic reviews of effectiveness.

Methods for Conducting Reviews of Research Evidence

The recognition that qualitative research might have a role to play in systematic reviews has led to considerable methodological innovation. Multiple methods for conducting reviews of qualitative (or qualitative and quantitative) studies are now available (Box 18.2), though they are at varying stages of development and evaluation (an overview of a selection of these methods is freely available from www.nice.org.uk/aboutnice/whoweare/aboutthehda/evidencebase/keypapers/papersthatinformandsupporttheevidencebase/integrative_approaches_to_qualitative_and_quantitative_evidence.jsp). Some represent 'new' methods specifically designed to tackle the issue of synthesis, or modifications of these methods; others are primary research methods that have been adapted for the purpose of review and synthesis. The scale and pace of methodological development have meant, however, that there are now several approaches that are, practically, very similar, but have different names and slightly different variants; the same terms are sometimes used to describe quite different things ('meta-synthesis' being one of these); some publications claim to use particular methods, but on more detailed inspection turn out not to have done so, or to have done so very poorly; and, overall, confusion about terminology and defining features abound. This poses many challenges for those seeking to conduct (or publish) a review.

Box 18.2   Examples of methods that may be used in conducting a synthesis of qualitative studies

Bayesian meta-analysis
Content analysis
Case survey methods
Case–case analysis
Qualitative comparative analysis
Narrative summary
Thematic analysis
Grounded theory
Meta-ethnography
Realist synthesis
Critical interpretive synthesis
Meta-narrative mapping

In describing the current state of the methodological landscape, it is again useful to distinguish broadly two extremes in terms of approaches to incorporating qualitative studies in systematic reviews, and that many of the methods to some extent can be characterised as part of a spectrum between these extremes. At one end, methods remain broadly within the frame or template offered by what we may term 'conventional' systematic review. Referring to 'conventional' systematic review does, of course, obscure the many complexities and debates within the paradigm, but it nonetheless has a useful function in clarifying what is an approach that accepts, in broad terms, the contractual commitments involved. It thus uses the methodological template of pre-specified protocols; a priori question definition; formalised searching strategies; standardised quality appraisal; and formal methods of synthesis.

A number of approaches mobilise this same methodological template, in broad terms, as the basis of systematic reviews of qualitative research (or mixed methods research). For instance, the NHS CRD guidance, which is focused on reviews of evidence of effects, outlines a number of ways in which qualitative research may be incorporated in a conventional systematic review. Methodological work by the EPPI Centre (the Evidence for Policy and Practice Information Centre at the Institute of Education, University of London) is characteristic of this kind of approach (Thomas and Harden, 2008). Some approaches involve hybrids of conventional systematic review methodology and more interpretive strategies. Thus meta-ethnography, originally proposed by Noblit and Hare (1988) solely as a method for interpretive synthesis, has been hybridised within a systematic review model in much of the recent methodological work in this area.

At the other end of the spectrum are methods that make a more fundamental challenge to the idea, premises and methods of conventional systematic review (though some of these continue to lay claim to the label of 'systematic review' as a means of legitimation). This second approach attempts to redefine in some sense what is meant by a systematic review, and may therefore modify or otherwise reject some or all of the requirements of the methodology. This latter situation arises because, as we outline below, there often is an uneasy fit between the frame offered by conventional systematic review methodology and the kinds of epistemological assumptions and research practices more usually associated with qualitative research. Towards this end of the spectrum lie approaches including realist synthesis, critical interpretive synthesis and meta-narrative mapping, though again many of these methods include some elements of conventional systematic review, and thus may also be considered hybrids.

The critical determinant of a choice of method, when conducting a review of literature involving qualitative research (or both qualitative and quantitative research), is the nature of the review question to be addressed. Just as primary research requires different methods and different theoretical perspectives depending on the purpose of the research, so too will reviews. This may seem rather an obvious point, but it tends to be one that gets rather lost in many of the controversies.

Conventional systematic reviews have often (though not exclusively) focused on assessing the effectiveness of various interventions or programmes: the 'does it work?' question. A number of roles for qualitative research studies can be identified in this regard, and some techniques – such as Bayesian meta-analysis – can be used to allow qualitative evidence to have a different influence on estimates of effects. Scholars often, of course, have many other motivations for conducting a review of qualitative studies, or qualitative and quantitative studies, in a particular area. A review might aim to do one, or a number, of the following, for example: listing; identifying all of the relevant issues in a particular area; describing and characterising; creating taxonomies; determining stages; finding factors implicated in relationships; theorising and explaining; critiquing and challenging extant orthodoxies. Clarifying the particular purpose of the review is critically important, because it determines almost all of the decisions that follow.

One useful way of thinking about the purpose of a review is to consider whether your aim is primarily aggregative or interpretive. *Aggregative syntheses* focus on *summarising data* (for example, does the evidence suggest that providing mentorship for young offenders reduces reoffending rates?). Both qualitative and quantitative forms of evidence can contribute to this kind of review, and a contractual-type systematic review approach might be best suited to ensuring that all the relevant evidence has been identified and included, and moreover that attention has been given to the quality of the available data.

Interpretive syntheses are concerned with the development of concepts and the specification of theories that integrate those concepts (for example, how can we best explain the impact of mentorship on offending behaviours?). Interpretive synthesis involves processes similar to primary qualitative research, in which the concern is with *generating* concepts that have maximum explanatory value. This approach achieves synthesis through incorporating the concepts identified in the primary studies into a more subsuming theoretical structure. This structure may include concepts which were not found in the original studies but which help to characterise the data as a whole. This kind of work may be best undertaken using something closer to an authorial approach, but perhaps disciplined by some explicit rules.

The distinction between an aggregative and an interpretive synthesis is very much a heuristic one; the difference is one of emphasis. It is important not to exaggerate how secure, in an integrative synthesis, the categories and their underlying concepts are. Indeed, stabilising the categories so that a summary under these headings can be achieved can be challenging and demand significant interpretive work – is this data type sufficiently like that data type; is this type of research subject sufficiently like that kind, and so on?

It is important also to recognise that aggregative syntheses can fulfil theoretical or interpretive functions. Aggregative syntheses may be especially likely to produce theories of causality, and may also include claims about generalisability. Similarly, an interpretive synthesis should not be seen as floating free of any empirical anchor: an interpretive synthesis of primary studies must be grounded in the data reported in those studies. Further, many reviews will attempt hybrids of aggregative and interpretive activities. The discussion that follows will briefly consider some of the issues that arise when working with different approaches within the methodological template offered by systematic review methodology.

Defining the Review Question

Defining the review question is one of the principal tasks of conventional systematic review. The normal procedure is to specify a clear set of criteria focused around a specific question. These criteria will usually define the study designs to be included (for example, randomised controlled trials, case control studies, etc.) as well as characteristics related to the question, including populations of interest and outcomes of interest. These may be very precisely specified – for example, 'young' offenders may be defined as those under the age of 18. If the aim of a review is aggregative, then it may be important to define the question in a way that conforms to expectations of a conventional systematic review. This, however, is far from straightforward, even for those conducting conventional systematic review, and will often require some kind of scoping exercise before the parameters of the review are determined. Even then, challenges may continue to arise about definitional decisions and choices about categorisation.

If the question is one requiring an interpretive account of the literature, there are good reasons for adopting a position closer to that of primary qualitative research than to conventional systematic review. A more iterative approach to question specification might be used. This would treat the question and its parameters as fundamentally unsettled and open to critique. For example, it might question the idea of 'an offender' and look at how definitions are applied to categorise some individuals as offenders, but not others (such as so-called 'white collar' criminals). Such a review might seek to modify the question in response to search results and findings from retrieved items, and might search across disciplinary boundaries or fields of study. Thus, rather than something defined very precisely in advance, the precise terms of an interpretive review question might not be determined until closer to the end of a review.

Finding Qualitative Research

Conventional systematic review methodology, in keeping with its highly protocolised model, strongly emphasises the importance of rigorous and systematic searching to identify the population of relevant material for the parameters of the review. An effort is then made to identify all studies relevant to the criteria specified in the review question. Making sure that the entire set of relevant studies has been identified is usually seen as important to avoiding bias, especially if a meta-analysis is to be conducted, as leaving out studies could lead to an inappropriate estimate of effect. This approach places particular stress on having a clear account of how searching was conducted, with the aim of ensuring that the search methods can be inspected and potentially reproduced. Searching may involve a range of strategies, but typically relies heavily on electronic bibliographic databases. The development and evaluation of search strategies is itself a sub-field of systematic review methodology. Characteristically, searching utilises the indexing systems of controlled keywords (known as thesaurus terms or subject headings) that catalogue records on major bibliographic databases. Other strategies such as referencing chaining (where the list of references for papers already identified is checked) and contact with experts in the field may also be used. It is usual, in reporting systematic reviews, to give full details of the search strategies used, including lists of keywords.

When the aim is to apply such approaches to qualitative research, a number of challenges arise. Some are essentially technical in nature. Despite some improvements in recent years, attempts to identify qualitative studies using formalised search strategies are often frustrating; the thesaurus terms that describe qualitative methodologies are still limited and vary across databases, and qualitative researchers do not always provide the kinds of abstracts and keywords that facilitate ready identification of the study designs they have used.

When the interest is in producing a more interpretive review, where the review question and its parameters are not well defined from the outset, practical problems may arise in trying to use a formalised and easily audited search strategy. Subjecting a question to continual review and refinement may make it much more difficult for those conducting reviews of qualitative research to demonstrate, as required by conventional systematic review methodology, the transparency, comprehensiveness and reproducibility of search strategies. These problems go beyond being merely technical. Those used to more authorial forms of scholarship may find it constraining and frustrating to have to work within tightly defined parameters, especially if their embodied expertise means that they are aware of the relevant literature but cannot find a way to show the inclusion of that literature to be legitimate within the frame of conventional systematic review. For example, a reviewer looking at ways of reducing 'inappropriate' admissions to hospitals through accident and emergency departments might recognise the relevance of literature in the completely different area of police processing of suspects because of the conceptual similarity of the nature of the tasks of classification and categorisation that both settings undertake. At the same time, such a reviewer might struggle to find a way of showing that such work could meet formalised criteria for inclusion under conventional systematic review methodology.

Selection of Material for Inclusion

One of the important principles of conventional systematic review is that all possible data that might contribute to the synthesis should be identified, as exclusion of relevant data might affect estimates. A meta-analysis, for instance, is concerned with quantifying how successful a particular intervention is on average, and will therefore want to include all relevant data that might assist in estimating that average. Inappropriate exclusion of relevant data might lead to the wrong estimate being made. As a check on the impact of including and excluding certain studies, quantitative syntheses use methods such as sensitivity analysis.

For interpretive syntheses, it could be argued that the same logic that governs sampling for primary qualitative research might apply. Here, the notion of theoretical saturation might have value. In primary research, theoretical sampling is conducted with a view towards the evolving theoretical development of the concepts. A researcher continues sampling until theoretical saturation is reached – where, after each new interview or observation, no new relevant data seem to emerge regarding a category, either to extend or contradict it (Strauss and Corbin, 1998). Under such a process, a reviewer might identify the papers that, on the basis of intuitive 'feel', are the most significant in a particular field, and might even deliberately sample outside of that field in order to test or refine the emerging synthesis.

There are, however, several problems with using theoretical sampling as a means of limiting the number of papers to be included in a review. First, within the frame of conventional systematic review methodology, it could be argued that once systematic reviews fail to be *explicit* and *reproducible*, and allowed to include (apparently) idiosyncratically chosen literatures and to use non-transparent forms of interpretation to determine the synthesis of the included studies, they are no longer systematic. In fact, it could be asserted, reviews of this type are nothing new: they are simply literature reviews of the type that have always been done. Second, in employing sampling as an alternative to *comprehensiveness*, it has to be acknowledged that sampling research papers is fundamentally not like sampling people. Unlike people, research papers have a vested interest in being different from one another, and are (in theory at least) only published if they are saying something new. Missing out some papers may therefore risk missing out potentially important insights. But precisely how a sensitivity analysis for an interpretive synthesis could be undertaken is unclear. Once a paper has made its contribution to the development of concepts and theories, it may be difficult to simply extract it to see what the synthesis would look like without that paper. With little available guidance on this area, this will be an important focus for future research.

Appraising Qualitative Research

Systematic appraisal of quality of evidence is undertaken by those conducting systematic reviews to reduce the possibility of bias. For quantitative systematic reviews, it is usual to devise broad inclusion criteria – for example, adequate randomisation for randomised controlled trials – and to exclude studies that fail to meet these. More detailed assessments of papers that are included in the review may also be undertaken to identify specific defects. If a meta-analysis is to be undertaken as part of the systematic review, techniques such as sensitivity analysis may be used to explore the effects of such defects on the conclusions of the synthesis, or the synthesis may be adjusted in other ways. For example, a randomised controlled trial (RCT) with only a very small number of participants would be given a lower 'weighting' than a bigger trial.

Whether or how to make judgements of the quality of qualitative research reports has been much contested in the context of both conventional systematic review and more interpretive reviews. No consensus has yet emerged. Some propose that there is an obligation to exclude 'weak' studies, but others disagree.

A decision to exclude qualitative studies from a review on the grounds of quality is not straightforward to execute. Because of the diversity of qualitative study designs and approaches, it is at present impossible to specify universally agreed a priori defects, equivalent to inadequate randomisation for RCTs, that would indicate that a qualitative study is fatally flawed. Assessment of the quality of qualitative papers has therefore traditionally relied on much more detailed appraisals, often using checklist-type approaches. The use of such checklists has been the subject of heated debate and criticism. Nonetheless, a striking proliferation continues of checklists, quality criteria and standards for qualitative research, often adopting non-reconcilable positions on a number of issues (Dixon-Woods et al., 2004). Few have distinguished between different study designs or theoretical approaches, thereby tending to treat qualitative research as a unified field; many represent attempts by their developers to impose a dominant view of what 'good' qualitative research should be like.

Appraisal checklists have themselves rarely been systematically appraised, but one study that compared two checklist-type approaches to unprompted judgement found that agreement between reviewers and between methods of appraisal was slight (Dixon-Woods et al., 2007). Reviewers disagreed not only on the quality of papers, but also on whether papers were reporting qualitative research and whether the paper was relevant to the topic of the review. Greatest agreement between reviewers appeared to occur when they used expertise-based judgements.

While the exclusion from systematic reviews of qualitative studies judged to be too weak might be one strategy for dealing with poor quality research, it is less clear what to do about assigning weights to studies which, while included, are not all of the same quality. Precisely how 'weak' qualitative findings should be attenuated or excluded in any synthesis is not yet clear. The feasibility and value of attempting some form of sensitivity analysis – where the effects of including or excluding particular qualitative findings are evaluated – remains to be assessed.

Conducting a Synthesis

Choices about methods for summarising and/or synthesising bodies of evidence will be strongly influenced by the purpose of the review. The methods listed in Box 18.2 vary in their degree of procedural specification and in the kinds of interpretive and aggregative work they require. Some require the conversion of one form of data into another. For example, Bayesian meta-analysis uses qualitative research to improve quantitative estimates. Other methods, such as meta-ethnography, proceduralise some aspects of the review process, but still rely on some level of interpretation by the reviewer. Some, such as realist synthesis, require a high level of creativity and critical interpretation on the part of reviewers; indeed, critical interpretive synthesis is in many (though not all) ways a codification and formalisation of the traditional authorial approach to reviewing.

Data extraction is one problem worth mentioning. In conventional systematic review, quantitative data are extracted onto pre-specified forms that have categories under which data are entered (for example, male, female, tumour type, treatment a, treatment b). Standardised data extraction of this type is considerably more difficult to use with qualitative research reports. It is often not really clear what *are* the data – are they just quotations or extracts for field notes, or are they interpretations? Should material in the discussion sections of papers be included, or just findings? How or should standardised headings be devised under which such data can be assigned, and in what format should they be extracted? There is no consensus yet on these issues.

Conclusions

Systematic review is important both scientifically and politically; overviews of evidence conducted using conventional systematic review methodology enjoy special kinds of authority, but have not escaped criticism and challenge. Many debates can be understood as a playing out of the inherent tensions between the 'authorial' and 'contractual' models of review, but more generally reflect the long history of epistemological contest between different paradigms. Different sides of the debate often have legitimate criticisms to make of the other. While the contractarians point to the tendency of authors to be chaotic, negligent, or simply biased in their selection and assembly of literature, the 'authors' may condemn the apparently mechanical and stifling effects of systematic review methodology.

It is now accepted that qualitative research does have a valuable role to play in reviews of research evidence, and a plurality of methodological approaches to review is now beginning to emerge. Questions can be asked about whether apparent differences between the strategies reflect superficial differences in terminology and the degree to which methods have been specified. At least some differences may reflect how approaches have developed in isolation, rather than more fundamental points of divergence. Work comparing the results of applying different methods of synthesis is now beginning to appear, and will be increasingly useful in distinguishing trivial from non-trivial differences between methods.

One key question concerns the extent to which conventional systematic review methodology, with its origins in the 'what works?' template and its focus on estimating the effectiveness of a particular intervention on average, can be consistent with aspirations of those aiming to produce more interpretive forms of overview of bodies of research evidence. Many innovations in attempting to incorporate qualitative research strain the epistemological and methodological assumptions that underlie systematic review, and raise questions about the precise remit and defining characteristics of this form of scientific activity. There is therefore a need for sustained reflection on whether 'systematic review' describes a very specific methodology with very well-defined characteristics, or whether it is becoming a broad framework that allows multiple forms of evidence synthesis to be undertaken. With the diversity of techniques now beginning to appear, those using 'new' or evolving techniques will need to be highly reflexive and critical, and to produce critical accounts of their experiences of using the methods (Dixon-Woods et al., 2006). By doing so, they will allow others to benefit from their learning and for the methods to be improved and become more sophisticated.

Summary

- Conventional systematic review methodology has emerged in response to criticisms that informal reviews may be incomplete or misleading.
- Systematic review requires a priori specification of the review question, the methods of searching, methods of quality appraisal and methods of synthesis.
- Methodological innovations aimed at including qualitative research in systematic reviews vary from those that remain fairly close to the conventional systematic review template to those that offer a more fundamental challenge to the approach.

Questions

- Identify a question that would be well suited to conventional systematic review. What makes it a good candidate for this approach?
- What are the advantages and disadvantages of the 'authorial' approach to reviewing literature?
- Why can it sometimes be difficult to work with highly specified protocols when including qualitative research in a review?

Acknowledgements

This chapter is based on work funded by ESRC Research Methods Programme grant H333250043. I thank my co-investigators Bridget Young, Andrew Booth, David Jones, Alex Sutton, Tina Miller and Jonathan Smith.

Recommended Reading

Evans I, Thornton H, Chalmers I (2006) *Testing treatments: better research for better healthcare.* London: British Library. This book can be downloaded from: www.jameslindlibrary.org/testing-treatments.html

Petticrew M, Roberts H (2006) *Systematic reviews in the social sciences: a practical guide.* Oxford: Blackwell.

Pope C, Mays N, Popay J (2007) *Synthezising qualitative and quantitative health evidence: a guide to methods.* Maidenhead: Open University Press

Sandelowski M, Barroso J (2007) *Handbook for synthesizing qualitative research.* New York: Springer.

References

Becker H (2007) *Writing for social scientists*. Chicago: Chicago University Press

Dixon-Woods M, Fitzpatrick R, Roberts K. (2001) Including qualitative research in systematic reviews; opportunities and problems. *Journal of Evaluation in Clinical Practice* 7: 125–133

Dixon-Woods M, Shaw RL, Agarwal S, Smith JA (2004) The problem of appraising qualitative research. *Quality and Safety in Healthcare* 13: 223–225

Dixon-Woods M, Bonas S, Booth A, Jones DR, Miller T, Sutton AJ, Shaw RL, Smith JA, Young B (2006) How can systematic reviews incorporate qualitative research? A critical perspective. *Qualitative Research* 6: 27–44

Dixon-Woods M, Sutton A, Shaw R, Miller T, Smith J, Young B, Bonas S, Booth A, Jones D (2007) Appraising qualitative research for inclusion in systematic reviews: a quantitative and qualitative comparison of three methods. *Journal of Health Services Research and Policy* 12: 42–47

Evans I, Thornton H, Chalmers I (2006) *Testing treatments: better research for better healthcare*. London: British Library. This book can be downloaded from: www.jameslindlibrary.org/testing-treatments.html

Glass GV (1976). Primary, secondary, and meta-analysis of research. *Educational Researcher* 5: 5–8

Hammersley M (2005) Is the evidence-based practice movement doing more good than harm? Reflections on Iain Chalmers' case for research-based policy making and practice. *Evidence and Policy* 1: 85–100

Higgins JPT, Green S (editors). *Cochrane Handbook for Systematic Reviews of Interventions* Version 5.0.2 [updated September 2009]. The Cochrane Collaboration, 2008. Available from: www.cochrane-handbook.org.

MacLure M (2005) 'Clarity bordering on stupidity': where's the quality in systematic review? *Journal of Education Policy* 20: 393–416

NHS Centre for Reviews and Dissemination (2008) *Systematic reviews: guidance for undertaking reviews in health care*. York: NHS CRD. This book may be downloaded from www.york.ac.uk/inst/crd/pdf/Systematic_Reviews.pdf

Noblit GW, Hare DR (1988) *Meta-ethnography: synthezising qualitative studies*. Newbury Park, CA: Sage

Pearson K (1904) Report on certain enteric fever inoculation statistics. *British Medical Journal* 3: 1243–1246

Strauss AL, Corbin J (1998) *Basics of qualitative research: techniques and procedures for developing grounded theory*. London: Sage

Thomas J, Harden A (2008) Methods for the thematic synthesis of qualitative research in systematic reviews. *BMC Medical Research Methodology* 8: 45

Secondary Analysis of Qualitative Data 19

Clive Seale

Abstract

Secondary analysis is usually understood to be the analysis of data originally collected by another set of researchers. Qualitative archives are in place in various countries, but QUALIDATA in the UK is the most developed archive. Although secondary analysis is just one use for archived data, the prospect of this usage has been subject to many reservations from elements of the qualitative research community. I take the view that, particularly in relation to secondary analysis, data collection and data analysis are best separated conceptually. Knowledge of the local context in which data is collected is relevant for all forms of research, not just that which is labelled 'qualitative'. The different forms of qualitative research also deserve recognition. These views have implications for debates about the value and advisability of secondary analysis of qualitative data.

The chief reservation expressed about secondary analysis of qualitative data is that secondary analysts will not have the kind of detailed contextual knowledge about the circumstances of data collection possessed by the primary researcher, knowledge which is deemed essential for good qualitative work to proceed. In various respects this objection is shown to be a rather partial view. It rests in part on an unexamined stereotype of the way secondary analysis of quantitative data sets proceeds, and does not recognise that archived data may be analysed with methods and for purposes that do not require in-depth knowledge of context. The value of secondary analysis of archived qualitative data is demonstrated by two case studies which show the degree to which general methodological debates are relevant to this form of research practice.

Keywords:

secondary analysis; archives, QUALIDATA, data analysis, quantitative and qualitative research.

Introduction: What is Secondary Analysis?

The secondary analysis of qualitative data, according to Janet Heaton (whose 2004 survey of this field is one of the most substantial and significant expositions of this method):

> involves the utilisation of existing data, collected for the purposes of a prior study, in order to pursue a research interest which is distinct from that of the original work. (1998: 1)

Heaton's definition is designed to include situations where a researcher at a later point returns to data which they have collected in order to do some further work on it. A less inclusive definition might have restricted the term to situations where the secondary analyst is a different person from the one who collected the data in the first place, as is classically the case when an archived data set is accessed.

Yet even this narrower definition covers a range of possibilities. Analysing data deposited in archives represents the most 'formal' end of various arrangements that might be classified as secondary analysis. Researchers often share their data informally, so that analysing data without having had the experience of collecting it is not unusual. In addition, where teams of people are involved in research projects, it is often the case that some of the analysis involves data that results from fieldwork done by just one member of the team.

Pursuing this matter of what 'secondary analysis' might be, it is also possible to take issue with some later definitional work by Heaton (2004), who, in an understandable attempt to narrow down the field, takes the view that the term ought not to be applied to such 'naturalistic' data as the recordings used by conversation analysts. She argues that such data 'are "found" or collected with minimal structuring by researchers' (2004: 5) unlike 'non-naturalistic' material such as interviews. Yet this definition misses the fact that audio recordings of interviews can and have been studied by conversation analysts (Rapley 2001), demonstrating that the application of the label 'naturalistic' is the product of the researcher's analytic stance rather than an inherent property of data. In addition, no data can be regarded as wholly 'found', since any 'find' is directed by the particular intentions of the finder (see the discussion of the status of 'naturally occurring data' in Silverman 2007: chapter 2).

Heaton wants to exclude collections of documents, photographs, letters, autobiographies and life stories from the possibility of being subject to secondary analysis. Yet all such collections, if made for the purposes of an analysis by one researcher, will have been shaped in some way by the act of collection, and might be considered as materials for secondary analysis.

So we run into definitional difficulties straightaway with this subject. Perhaps the most that can be said is that some situations are more clearly examples of 'secondary analysis' than others. Classically, secondary analysis involves analysis by one set of researchers of data deposited in data archives by different researchers who originally collected the data. Seeing an example at this stage may help, and it is one to which we will return later in the chapter.

An Example

This project is reported by Mike Savage (2007) who used material from the UK Mass Observation Archive (www.massobs.org.uk) to investigate changes in the way social class was narrated in 1948 compared with 1990. Hosted at the University of Sussex, this archive contains the writings of those participating in this long-standing project to document everyday life in the UK since 1937. Because of the large amount of material available, he studied only 10% of the replies written at each time point.

In the 1948 sample, it was common for observers to contest the value of talking about class, although most would identify as belonging to one if pushed. Examples include:

> I hate class distinctions and do not think any definite lines can be drawn between social classes, but if there has to be a division, I consider myself to belong to the upper middle class.

> I try to eliminate all class distinctions from my social life…however I suppose I have been brought up with a middle class outlook as… For the most part of ten years my father has been a regular army officer.

Observers wrote brief statements which identified themselves as belonging to a class (usually the middle class) because of 'ties of birth, through having appropriate manners, and other social ties' (Savage 2007: 4.13). For example:

> From a materialistic point of view, I would place [myself] in the middle class. Whereas we do not live in a large mansion with a staff of servants, have a 'Rolls Royce' and mix socially with 'country folk', we possess a house plus one acre of garden, two cars, and enough money to give us a good annual holiday at a first class hotel. This type of living could hardly, I think, be called that of a working class family.

In 1990, replies on this subject were much more extensive, prompting observers in several cases to tell detailed stories about their lives and their continuing negotiation of class identity. A number of respondents narrated hybrid family histories in which different members of a family were regarded as belonging to different classes. Others remarked that their class identity was related to whether they lived in a working class or middle class location, suggesting that this had been a choice they had exercised. Observers in 1948 did not regard their class identity as fluid in this way, portraying it as something which was fixed by virtue of birth or occupation.

Several observers demonstrated knowledge of sociological discussions of class, suggesting to Savage that the double hermeneutic (Giddens 1991), whereby social science ideas about a subject themselves become incorporated into lay thinking about that subject, is at play. For example, one mass observer wrote:

> Mary Daly, in her book Gyn-ecology, suggests that the setting up of divisions or barriers is typical of patriarchy, so I am always reluctant to fit my thinking into what, tangibly and socially exists, circumscribing, nay defining my life.

Savage comments: 'respondents use class talk reflexively to show their sophistication – very different to the Mass-Observers of 1948 who saw talking about class as a sign of vulgarity' (2007: 5.6). Savage ends by commenting that such qualitative sources enable a better appreciation of the complexities and ambiguities through which class is lived at certain points in time than is provided by survey research which simply asks people whether they believe they belong to a particular class.

Clearly, then, archives like Mass Observation can support innovative studies – in this case comparing change over time – by building on the work done by previous generations of researchers. But to do this, data archives must be set up where researchers can deposit data for future use by others, so a consideration of qualitative data archiving is therefore relevant.

Qualitative Data Archives and Secondary Analysis

The Qualitative Data Archival Resource Centre (QUALIDATA) was established at the University of Essex in 1994, later becoming a part of the Economic and Social Data Service (ESDS) which also archives quantitative data sets. At the last count (November 2009) QUALIDATA displayed details of 309 data sets on its website, some of which were added to the archive as a result of the policy adopted by the UK Economic & Social Research Council (ESRC) which requires researchers funded by ESRC to offer their data for archiving at the end of projects.

Other archives containing qualitative social research data include the Murray Research Archive in the US and the Finnish Social Science Data Archive, both of which contain both quantitative and qualitative data sets. There are links on the QUALIDATA website to qualitative data archives in Finland, Northern Ireland, Germany, France and Switzerland. At the time of writing, a national qualitative data archive is being set up in Australia.

The rationale for archiving social science data for secondary analytic purposes is straightforward: a great deal of work goes into producing social science data sets, and it is not always possible for the original researchers to find the time to analyse these fully. It is both economical and ethical to analyse existing data sets rather than collecting new ones, if these data sets are adequate to answer the research questions being asked. As well as being ethical to save public money, it is also ethical to avoid overburdening participants with too many research enquiries. Ethical arguments, of course, go both ways, as the interests of research participants may not be served by making data about them widely available, especially if people's identities are not masked and the material is personally sensitive (see Johnson and Bullock (2009) for a fuller discussion).

A further benefit of secondary analysis relates to the size of some of these data sets, which means that students and those without access to significant funding for data collection may benefit from access to archived data (Silverman 2010: chapter 13). In the long run, data sets can be combined, or compared over time. In addition, as new methods of analysis develop, they can be applied to old data sets to gain new insights. In relation to the secondary analysis of quantitative data, a number of procedures have been described for assessing and modifying data sets so that they may answer questions for which they were not originally intended (Dale et al. 1988). In relation to the reuse of qualitative data, there is less consensus about how to proceed (for which see below).

Corti and Thompson (2004) have listed six main uses for archived qualitative data, shown in Box 19.1. Notably, only the first three may be categorised as secondary analysis, suggesting that archives have purposes that go beyond the reuse of data to answer research questions.

Box 19.1   Six uses for archived qualitative data (adapted from Corti and Thompson 2004)

1 *Description*: For example, a study of the City of London business district (Kynaston 2001) drew on interviews done by other researchers (Courtney and Thompson 1996) for accounts of working lives.

2 *Comparative research, re-study or follow-up*: For example, Franz et al. (1991) used data in the Murray Research Archive to follow up the children of mothers interviewed in 1951 about their child-rearing practices, comparing this later sample with the earlier one.

3 *Re-analysis*: For example, Fielding and Fielding (2000) re-analysed data collected by Cohen and Taylor (1972) on men in long-term imprisonment, identifying new themes in the material.

4 *Research design and methodological advancement*: For example, the interview guides of other researchers investigating similar topics can assist a researcher's own development of an interview.

(Continued)

(Continued)

5 *Verification*: If a study makes important claims, other researchers can examine its original data to assess the evidence in support of those claims.
6 *Teaching and learning*: Examining original research materials can be an important resource in learning how to do research. The 'Edwardians Online' project (containing interviews with people recalling life in the UK between 1900 and 1918) within QUALIDATA has been designed with this purpose in mind.

In addition to large general archives such as QUALIDATA, there are parallel small initiatives that concern the particular sub-specialty of researchers interested in analysing 'naturally occurring' data, often from the perspective of conversation analysis. The best known of these archives is TalkBank, a part of which contains a conversation analysis database with transcripts and audio files. Currently, no data sets are stored on QUALIDATA involving audio or video recordings of naturally occurring talk. There is a preponderance of studies involving research interviews, reflecting the dominance of this data source in qualitative research generally.

Some Assumptions

I must expose some underlying assumptions about research before proceeding further, since, if taken seriously, they have implications for the debates about the secondary analysis of qualitative data that I then review in this chapter. These are as follows:

- It is important to distinguish conceptually between data collection and data analysis, particularly when thinking about secondary analysis, but also more generally when thinking about social research. Relatedly, the particular form that data takes does not dictate the type of analysis that must be used. (Of course, in practice it is often useful to integrate data collection and data analysis in social research, and this is a feature of much qualitative work, as in the use of theoretical sampling in grounded theorising. Additionally, there is of course a sense in which all data is 'produced' by an implicit 'analysis' that any researcher will bring to a project because of background knowledge and preferences).
- The distinction between quantitative and qualitative research is, by contrast, overblown and recognition of both mixed methods and methods that cannot be categorised as either quantitative or qualitative is beneficial.

- Epistemological considerations, and knowledge about the local context in which data is collected, are relevant for all forms of research, including that which is labelled 'quantitative'.
- The label 'qualitative research' includes a large variety of data sources and analytic procedures. Differences between these may be as significant as differences between 'quantitative' and 'qualitative' approaches.

In the rest of this chapter I will review debates about secondary analysis of archived qualitative data. It will become clear that some existing general methodological debates about the value of data archives and about the possibility of doing secondary analysis of qualitative data are bypassed by applying the considerations listed above.

It will also become clear that, like Mason (2007), I believe a good way to make progress in these debates is to 'get on and do it' (2007: 1.3) so that particular examples of secondary analysis can inform general methodological discussion. As I have argued elsewhere (Seale 1999), general discussions can be useful in raising the methodological awareness with which particular research studies are carried out, but should not be treated as obstacles or fixed rulings governing researchers' conduct. Examples of two studies where the researchers have 'got on and done' secondary analyses of qualitative data are described in the final part of the chapter.

Reusing Qualitative Data: The Case Against

Hammersley (1997) was one of the first to identify problems in transferring the logic of secondary analysis of quantitative data to the analysis of archived qualitative data, arguing that:

> There is a difference between how ethnographers read the fieldnotes they have produced themselves and how someone else will read them. The fieldworker interprets them against the background of all that he or she tacitly knows about the setting as a result of first-hand experience, a background that may not be available to those without that experience.... The data collected by different researchers will be structured by varying purposes and conceptions of what is relevant. As a result, users of archives are likely to find that some of the data or information required for their purpose is not available. (1997: 139)

Additionally, Hammersley feels that if researchers are aware that their personal diaries and log books, as well as records of data, are likely to be scrutinised by outsiders, they will be 'tidied up' as they are written, in much the same manner as politicians often write their diaries in the certain knowledge that they will one day be published. Further, some types of qualitative research involve a strong sense of personal possessiveness about data, perhaps classically in traditional anthropology:

> [field notes are]...the anthropologist's most sacred possession. They are personal property, part of a world of private memories and experiences, failures and successes, insecurities and indecisions.... To allow a colleague to examine them would be to open a Pandora's box. (Bond 1990: 275)

The view that secondary analysts will be unable to draw on unrecorded knowledge and memories of the context in which data was originally collected is also raised as a significant problem by Parry and Mauthner (2004). These authors also argue that '[t]he construction of qualitative data [is] a joint endeavour' (2004: 142) between researcher and research participant, so that archiving that does not preserve the anonymity and copyright claims of both parties is counter to the interests of these joint producers of data. Some qualitative data, they argue, would be rendered almost useless by anonymising.

After Bishop (2005) pointed out that QUALIDATA is aware of these issues in assessing potentially archivable data sets, and sometimes turns them down for the archive if their content appears to raise these kinds of problems, Parry and Mauthner (2005) produce more reasons for questioning the value of archives. They complain that archiving is costly, and that there has been no economic analysis setting the cost of running QUALIDATA against the presumed savings made to data collection costs as a result of secondary analysis. They also say that, unlike ESRC, which requires a list of published outputs from all researchers it funds, QUALIDATA does not produce a list of publications that have involved use of its archive, so that one cannot know whether the deposited data is, in practice, used to any significant extent. Against this, Thompson (author of the 'Edwardians' data set featured prominently in QUALIDATA) reports anecdotally that:

> It was incredible how many other researchers came to use it. At least five times as many major publications came out of it as the original research team could have produced. That has been an enormous source of satisfaction to me as a researcher. I want to encourage anyone here who has not yet deposited, that it will give you great pleasure and pride in the longer run, to have your work used in that way too. (2004: 83–84)

Yet, in spite of this positive experience of Thompson's, doubts persist amongst some qualitative researchers about whether secondary analysis breaches a fundamental principle of (their version of) qualitative research. An investigation of Australian researchers' perceptions of secondary analysis and qualitative archiving (Broom et al. 2009) is revealing. One respondent, a professor of sociology, remarked:

I must say that I'm familiar with the quantitative data archives, and I think in my mind – and this may be because I'm just used to the idea – I found that they're uncontroversial. When my mind first started to focus on qualitative data, I decided that this is a completely different kind of fish. Now, you could ask why. (Broom et al. 2009: 1169)

The researchers who were respondents in this study perceived quantitative data to be 'mere data', transferable to other researchers without too much problem. Qualitative material, though, was different, as its production involved the researcher in a reciprocal relationship with research participants, with an accompanying feeling of ownership. This personal involvement in data collection became a resource when the knowledge of the context in which data collection occurred was required in order to make sense of data. Researchers felt that this could not be present in a secondary analysis:

I remember as I was doing it and watching this thing unfolding before me, I remember thinking no [other] researcher would actually understand what's going on here right now because I could just intuitively read what they were saying with their body language, but if you weren't there, it wouldn't be there...if I put that in an archive no one would have understood what was happening. (Broom et al. 2009: 1170)

Although archives may seek to provide 'metadata' – information about, for example, the circumstances under which a set of interviews was conducted, or in which fieldwork was carried out – in order to give some sense of context, this is seen as a weak substitute for the kind of detailed knowledge gained by a researcher who has 'been there' (Mauthner et al. 1998).

Reusing Qualitative Data: The Case For

There are a number of points that can be made to show that the problems listed above constitute a partial view, only applicable to certain kinds of secondary analysis, and not always as difficult to solve as is sometimes suggested.

First, running through many of the objections, there is a lack of appreciation of the processes involved in the secondary analysis of quantitative data sets. Dale et al. (1988), in a book advising those who wish to carry out secondary analyses of quantitative data sets, list six questions to ask about any such data set before proceeding. These are summarised in Box 19.2.

Box 19.2   Six questions to ask about a data set doing secondary analysis (adapted from Dale et al. 1988)

1 What was the purpose of the original study and what conceptual framework informed it?
2 What information has been collected and is it on subjects relevant to the concerns of the secondary analyst and in the form needed?
3 How was the sample drawn up and what biases in responders and non-responders were evident?
4 What sort of agency collected the data and how adequate were the agency's procedures for ensuring its quality?
5 Which population does the survey represent?
6 When was the data collected and is it still relevant to the circumstances the secondary analyst wishes to investigate?

Much of the rest of Dale et al.'s book consists of advice, based on extensive personal experience, on how to adapt data sets collected for one purpose so that the different purpose of the secondary analyst may be achieved. Compare this with the quote from Hammersley (1997) shown in the last section where he indicates concern that:

> The data collected by different researchers will be structured by varying purposes and conceptions of what is relevant. As a result, users of archives are likely to find that some of the data or information required for their purpose is not available. (1997: 139)

The difference here is that while researchers in the quantitative tradition have noticed a problem and devised procedures to get around it, some qualitative researchers are encouraging a view that the problem is insuperable.

Second, the concern that knowledge of the context of data collection is unavailable to the secondary analysis also reflects a stereotype about quantitative research. A great deal of concern about the 'context' of data collection lies behind the fourth point in Box 19.2. Good quality procedures in generating quantitative data sets involve careful piloting of research instruments and considerable expertise in ensuring that measurement devices reflect what they are supposed to measure, so that the influence of context is well understood. In addition, these procedures are often documented in writing so that others can assess their rigour.

By contrast, researchers who claim that personal experience of qualitative data collection provides knowledge of context that is essential for adequate analysis take the view that this cannot be adequately conveyed by trying to describe fieldwork experiences in writing. This is because of a reliance on memory and intuition that is regarded as a legitimate source of evidence by some researchers. Thus Hammersley's (1997) view is that this knowledge consists of what the researcher 'tacitly knows' because of field experience. The second researcher quoted in Broom et al. (2009) in the section above believes s/he could 'just intuitively read what they were saying with body language' and that memory of this would surely be unavailable to a secondary analyst.

Such arguments can prompt suspicion about the rigour of qualitative research by outsiders, who may take the view that reliance on the memories of a researcher who has 'been there' opens the door to the reporting of unsubstantiated opinion. The emphasis on personal fieldwork memories as sources of evidence is not shared by all qualitative researchers. Conversation and discourse analysts, for example, seek to validate their claims solely by reference to what is shown in the transcripts and documents which they display to readers of their work, and they try hard to exclude researcher 'intuition' (see for example Peräkylä in this volume). Body language, for example, can be videotaped, and tone of voice can be audio recorded, and such recordings can be deposited in a data archive.

Finally, the critics of secondary analysis of qualitative data appear to have a narrow view of the range of data sources and analytic procedures involved in 'qualitative' research. Regarding data sources, the concern about context largely seems to arise from studies that involve face-to-face methods of data collection, such as interviews, focus groups and participant observation. But qualitative data sets may also consist of documents, photographs, radio and TV programmes, things that happen on the internet, or artefacts used in daily life. The contexts in which some of these occur may be quite public ones, and are as well (or as badly) understood by the primary analyst as the secondary analyst.

Concerning data analysis, it appears that critics believe that any secondary analyst is bound to want to use the same analytic methods as they themselves employed in the primary analysis. Yet qualitative data can be analysed with a range of methods that are different from those used by the original researchers, even including quantitative analytic approaches, as well as the use of qualitative analytic methods not yet developed when the original researchers collected their materials.

Researchers deposit data in archives in part to fulfil an obligation to share publicly funded work; to impose restrictions on the methods used to analyse this data seems contrary to this public duty. Consider the following view from Moore:

> while it is clearly not possible to use multiple regression or visual analysis in interpreting the text of an interview, we might more usually be thinking about choosing

between different kinds of discourse analysis, narrative analysis, content analysis, for example, and the decision about which of these to choose is likely to be related to research questions and the epistemology and the ontology of the researcher (as well of course as disciplinary background, and particular training and predilections of the researcher). (2007: 2.4)

This was written in the context of an argument in support of secondary analysis, in which Moore points out that the method of analysis used by the primary researcher may not be the method used by the secondary analyst, and that some of the methods used by the secondary analysis will require less knowledge of context than others.

Yet even Moore's argument is limited by the view that multiple regression and visual analysis cannot be applied to the text of an interview. In fact, it is common for multivariate statistics to be used in quantitative text analysis (Weber 1990, Krippendorf 2004). Although I have not seen a published visual analysis of an interview transcript, I think the idea of doing one is an intriguing idea. I have often been struck by the visual appearance of transcripts and the manner in which these are arranged to convey the epistemological authority of authors working in various research traditions. An interview transcribed by a conversation analyst looks technical and 'sciencey'; an interview transcribed by a writer like Richardson (1994), who arranges her interviewees' words into stanzas, looks like poetry. These visual appearances reflect the preferred authorial image of the writers concerned. It seems like a good idea to retain this as a possible research project, rather than seeing it as something that is 'clearly not possible'.

Just Do It!

So is secondary analysis a good thing or a bad thing? There is a sense in which starting the debate at this level is unhelpful. The answer, as with a lot of methodological questions, must be 'sometimes yes and sometimes no' or 'it all depends'. The most that such generalised debates can do is alert us to issues that might (or might not) be experienced when we get involved in actually doing some secondary analysis. Arguably, the debate about the advisability of archiving and secondary analysis of qualitative data has begun, and become somewhat polarised, before significant practical experience of doing such analysis has accumulated. To help counter this tendency, the final part of this chapter will reflect on the example outlined at the start of this chapter, where Savage (2007) drew on the Mass Observation Archive to re-analyse data about the changing meanings of social class in the UK, and will then describe a second project. In different ways, each of these illustrates issues raised in the general debate.

Project 1: Social Class Identities Compared Over Time

Reflecting back on the example of Savage's work, it is clear that this shows the value of an archive in enabling comparison over time. Significantly for the arguments about context rehearsed earlier, Savage's knowledge of the context in which Mass Observation data is collected was similar to that which anyone may have – the original data collectors do not have privileged knowledge here, since contributors of data ('observers') respond in writing to written requests for information. The wording of these written requests is reported in Savage's paper so that readers can also share in knowledge of context. Savage reflects on the way in which question wording may have influenced responses at the different time points, and notes the consequences of relying on a sample consisting largely of middle class respondents.

Clearly, Savage's investigation benefitted from the foresight of the archivists who established the Mass Observation Archive without knowing all of the uses to which it might be put in the future. Worries about the secondary analyst not having 'been there' when the data was collected are not relevant, as the primary researchers were also not 'there' in a situation where the material was gathered in response to a written request (although it might be argued that, as they were themselves part of the generation of people who wrote comments in 1948, whereas Savage was not, their general understanding of the background to the comments will have been different from that of Savage). The awareness demonstrated by the analyst of the ways in which the social environment may have influenced the nature of the data is very much in the foreground of the analysis nevertheless.

Project 2: The Interaction of Gender with Age and Social Class in Illness Narratives

This project, carried out by myself and a collaborator from linguistics, illustrates how a new method of analysis, different from the method employed by the primary researchers and which was not available at the time of primary data collection, can be applied to archived data. It also illustrates the benefits of analysing a very large qualitative data set, involving a combination of data from many studies, each of them of a size which would normally be regarded as quite substantial in the ordinary practice of qualitative research. Only a data archive can assemble this volume of material under normal research funding conditions.

The data archive was purchased by me from the DIPEx organisation (see www.healthtalkonline.org) with the aid of a grant from the ESRC. Healthtalkonline displays edited video clips from longer qualitative interviews with people talking about their experiences of a wide variety of illnesses and health-related issues, and is a public information resources as well as being widely used in the training of health care professionals.

Clearly the ESRC, in spite of funding QUALIDATA, was not very familiar with the practice of secondary analysis, as one of the first things I discovered on starting the project was that I was required by ESRC to guarantee that I would deposit the data from the project with QUALIDATA, otherwise I would not receive instalments of the grant. After a series of phone calls and emails in which I explained to ESRC staff progressively higher up in seniority that neither I nor the ESRC had ownership rights over this archive, and that this was a project which involved funding from the ESRC to purchase access to someone else's archive, not a grant for original data collection, the ESRC officials finally got the picture and stopped asking.

The data set consisted of 1035 transcribed qualitative interviews with people talking about their experience of a variety of illness and illness-related conditions. Because the age, gender and in many cases the occupation of the respondents had been recorded, it was possible to use this information to select a subsample of 102 interviews so that the gender differences in language usage across three different age groups could be assessed without being confounded by the type of illness being discussed (Seale and Charteris-Black 2008a). Similarly, 96 interviews were selected to form four sub-groups of higher and lower socio-economic men and women respectively, keeping constant and therefore controlling for the influence of type of illness and age of respondent (Seale and Charteris-Black 2008b).

The project facilitated discoveries that have extended knowledge about the performance of gender identities in the sociological and sociolinguistics literature (Charteris-Black and Seale 2010), which is itself very large but mostly based on a series of studies of quite small samples of qualitative data undifferentiated by other social variables. The study showed that older men, for example, perform a rather different gender identity from younger men with illness. Young men are in many respects more like women in the way in which they express themselves, referring frequently to family relationships and feelings of vulnerability. Older men do less of these things and focus much more on their relationship with their doctors. Higher social class men appear to be particularly skilled in varying their linguistic repertoire, being able to adopt an informal and self-revealing style that most of the literature on gender and language, and the women in the data set, show to be characteristic of women's linguistic style. This then represents a way of 'doing' masculinity which enables some higher social class men to claim new sources for their social authority in the face of feminist critiques of traditional masculinity, and this repertoire appears to be less available to working class men.

This quasi-experimental design relied on having a very large archive of interviews from which to select, and is a design that the researchers who collected the original data would not have envisaged. The project also used a new method of data analysis based on corpus linguistics known as comparative keyword analysis (Seale et al. 2006). This method uses the computational power of modern personal computers and Wordsmith Tools software (www.lexically.net/wordsmith/), which supports the creation and comparison of lists of words appearing in different texts, to perform a conjoint 'quantitative' and 'qualitative' analysis of text. Hence it is a method that breaks free of the division between these forms of research that underlies much debate about qualitative secondary analysis, and indeed methods in general.

Summary

The starting assumptions of this piece were that data collection and data analysis are best separated conceptually, whereas a firm distinction between quantitative and qualitative research is less valuable. Knowledge of the local context in which data is collected is relevant for all forms of research, not just that which is labelled 'qualitative'. The different forms of qualitative research also deserve recognition.

Qualitative archives are in place in various countries, but QUALIDATA in the UK is the most developed archive, supported by ESRC. It is not clear how heavily it is used, although there are clearly some popular data sets such as 'The Edwardians' which receive considerable attention. Although secondary analysis is just one use for archived data, the prospect of this usage has been subject to many reservations from elements of the qualitative research community. The chief problem that such critics perceive is that secondary analysts will not have the kind of detailed contextual knowledge about the circumstances of data collection possessed by the primary researcher, knowledge which is deemed essential for good qualitative work to proceed.

In various respects this objection has been shown in this chapter to be a rather partial view. The critical view rests in part on an unexamined stereotype of the way secondary analysis of quantitative data sets proceeds, and does not recognise that archived data may be analysed with methods and for purposes that do not require in-depth knowledge of context. The value of secondary analysis of archived qualitative data is demonstrated by two case studies of such work which demonstrate through practical example how general methodological concerns may or may not relate to this form of research practice.

Conclusion and Future Prospects

In conclusion, much of the general debate about whether it is wise to archive qualitative data and subject it to secondary analysis is bypassed if the assumptions laid out at the start of this chapter are taken seriously. Secondary analysts of quantitative data sets have confronted and solved some of the difficulties that qualitative critics raise, and I have argued that we need greater experience of projects involving secondary analysis of qualitative data sets before concluding that such analysis is unwise. Once one gets involved with a data set it is often possible to show the value of this kind of work without falling into the pitfalls imagined by the critics. I hope that this chapter has freed up the spirit to engage in this kind of work with an open and adventurous mind so that the exciting opportunities made available by underused qualitative data archives are more fully taken up.

Questions

1   What is secondary analysis?
2   In what ways is the secondary analysis of qualitative and quantitative data similar? How do they differ?
3   What concerns have been raised about the analysis of archived qualitative data?
4   What are the arguments in favour of the secondary analysis of archived qualitative data?
5   What points about secondary analysis are supported by the case studies of the work done by (a) Savage and (b) Seale and Charteris-Black?

Recommended Reading

Corti, L. and Thompson, P. (2004) 'Secondary analysis of archived data', in C.F. Seale, G. Gobo, J.F. Gubrium and D. Silverman (eds), *Qualitative Research Practice*. London: Sage. pp. 327–343.

Heaton, J. (2004) *Reworking Qualitative Data*. London: Sage.

Internet Links

QUALIDATA:
www.esds.ac.uk/qualidata/
Murray Research Archive:
www.murray.harvard.edu/
TalkBank:
http://talkbank.org/
DIPEx/Healthtalkonline
www.healthtalkonline.org/

References

Bishop, L. (2005) 'Protecting respondents and enabling data sharing: reply to Parry and Mauthner', *Sociology*, 39(2): 333–336.

Bond, G.C. (1990) 'Fieldnotes: research in past occurrences', in R. Sanjek (ed.), *Fieldnotes*. New York: Cornell University Press. Pp. 278–290.

Broom, A., Cheshire, L. and Emmison, M. (2009) 'Qualitative researchers' understanding of their practice and the implications for data archiving and sharing', *Sociology*, 43(6): 1163–1180.

Charteris-Black, J. and Seale, C. (2010) *Gender and the Language of Illness*. London and Basingstoke: Palgrave Macmillan.

Cohen, S. and Taylor, L. (1972) *Psychological Survival: The Effects of Long-term Imprisonment*. London: Allen Lane.

Corti, L. and Thompson, P. (2004) 'Secondary analysis of archived data', in C.F. Seale, G. Gobo, J.F. Gubrium and D. Silverman (eds), *Qualitative Research Practice*. London: Sage. Pp. 327–343.

Courtney, C. and Thompson, P. (1996) *City Lives*. London: Methuen.

Dale, A., Arber, S. and Proctor, M. (1988) *Doing Secondary Analysis*. London: Unwin Hyman.

Fielding, N. and Fielding, J. (2000) 'Resistance and adaptation to criminal identity: using secondary analysis to evaluate classic studies of crime and deviance', *Sociology*, 34(4): 671–689.

Franz, C., McClelland, D. and Weinberger, J. (1991) 'Childhood antecedents of conventional social accomplishment in midlife adults: a 36-year prospective study', *Journal of Personality and Social Psychology*, 60(4): 586–595.

Giddens, A. (1991) *The Consequences of Modernity*. Cambridge: Polity Press.

Hammersley, M. (1997) 'Qualitative data archiving: some reflections on its prospects and problems', *Sociology*, 31(1): 131–142.

Heaton, J. (1998) 'Secondary analysis of qualitative data', *Social Research Update* Issue 22: http://sru.soc.surrey.ac.uk/SRU22.html (accessed 23 November 2009).

Heaton, J. (2004) *Reworking Qualitative Data*. London: Sage.

Johnson, D. and Bullock, M. (2009) 'The ethics of data archiving: issues from four perspectives', in D.M. Mertens and P.E. Ginsberg (eds), *The Handbook of Social Research Ethics*. Thousand Oaks, CA: Sage. Pp. 214–228.

Krippendorff, K. (2004) *Content Analysis: An Introduction to Its Methodology*, 2nd edition. Thousand Oaks, CA: Sage.

Kynaston, D. (2001) *The City of London, IV: A Club No More, 1945–2000*. London: Pimlico.

Mason, J. (2007) '"Re-using" qualitative data: on the merits of an investigative epistemology', *Sociological Research Online*, 12(3). Available at: www.socresonline.org.uk/12/3/3.html (accessed 5 November 2009).

Mauthner, N.S., Parry, O. and Backett-Milburn, K. (1998) '"The data are out there, or are they?" Implications for archiving and revisiting qualitative data', *Sociology*, 32(4): 733–745.

Moore, N. (2007) '(Re)using qualitative data', *Sociological Research Online* 12(3). Available at: www.socresonline.org.uk/12/3/1.html (accessed 5 November 2009).

Parry, O. and Mauthner, N.S. (2004) 'Whose data are they anyway? Practical, legal and ethical issues in archiving qualitative research data', *Sociology*, 38(1): 139–152.

Parry, O. and Mauthner, N.S. (2005) 'Back to basics: who re-uses qualitative data and why?', *Sociology*, 39(2): 337–342.

Rapley, T. (2001) 'The art(fulness) of open-ended interviewing: some considerations on analysing interviews', *Qualitative Research,* 1(3): 303–324.

Richardson, L. (1994) 'Nine poems: marriage and the family', *Journal of Contemporary Ethnography*, 23: 3–14.

Savage, M. (2007) 'Changing social class identities in post-war Britain: perspectives from Mass Observation', *Sociological Research Online*, 12(3). Available at: www.socresonline.org.uk/12/3/6.html (accessed 5 November 2009).

Seale, C.F. (1999) *The Quality of Qualitative Research*. London: Sage.

Seale, C. and Charteris-Black, J. (2008a) 'The interaction of age and gender in illness narratives', *Ageing and Society,* 28(7): 1025–1043.

Seale, C. and Charteris-Black, J. (2008b) 'The interaction of class and gender in illness narratives', *Sociology,* 42(3): 453–469.

Seale, C., Charteris-Black, J. and Ziebland, S. (2006) 'Gender, cancer experience and internet use: a comparative keyword analysis of interviews and online cancer support groups', *Social Science and Medicine*, 62(10): 2577–2590.

Silverman, D. (2007) *A Very Short, Fairly Interesting, Reasonably Cheap Book About Qualitative Research*. London: Sage.

Silverman, D. (2010) *Doing Qualitative Research*, 3rd edition. London: Sage.

Thompson, P. (2004) 'Pioneering the life story method', *International Journal of Social Research Methodology*, 7(1): 81–84.

Weber, R.P. (1990) *Basic Content Analysis*, 2nd edition. Newbury Park, CA: Sage.

Validity in Research on Naturally Occurring Social Interaction

20

Anssi Peräkylä

Abstract

The validity of research concerns the interpretation of observations: whether or not the inferences that the researcher makes are supported by the data, and sensible in relation to earlier research. This chapter describes processes of validation in research based on audio or video recordings of social interaction. Although it uses examples drawn from conversation analysis, it discusses validation issues relevant to many different kinds of qualitative research. Such issues include the analysis of the next speaker's interpretation of the preceding action as an instance of validation of the researcher's interpretations, deviant case analysis, specifying with reference to data the claims concerning the relevance of an institutional context of interaction, comparisons within and between institutional settings, generalizing results of case studies as possibilities of social interaction, as well as use of quantitative techniques. Some procedures of validation in conversation analysis are used in this particular approach only, while others are shared between conversation analysis and other qualitative approaches. At a more general level, the considerations of validity in all qualitative research are the same, involving meticulous testing and consideration of the truthfulness of analytic claims.

Keywords:

validity, conversation analysis, deviant cases, comparisons, generalization.

The aim of social science is to produce descriptions of a social world – not just any descriptions, but descriptions that in some controllable way correspond to the social world that is being described. Even though all descriptions are bound to a particular perspective and therefore represent the reality rather than reproduce it (Hammersley, 1992), it is possible to describe social interaction in ways that can be subjected to empirical testing. *Reliability* and *validity* are the technical terms that refer to the objectivity and credibility of research.

In research practice, enhancing objectivity is a very concrete activity. It involves, on one hand, efforts to ensure the accuracy and inclusiveness of recordings that the research is based on, and, on the other hand, efforts to test the truthfulness of the analytic claims that are being made about those recordings. The former effort has to do with reliability. Even though it is of utmost importance, it will not be discussed in this chapter (see, however, Peräkylä, 2004). The latter effort involves validity, and it will be the topic of this chapter.

The researcher's efforts to ensure validity takes different shapes according to the type of data on which the research is based. Questions that arise, for example, in research based on interview data are partially different from questions that arise in observational research. In interview research, one key question of validity is whether the views expressed by the interviewees reflect their experiences and opinions outside the interview situation, or whether they are an outcome of the interview situation itself (see Silverman, 2010: 225–229). In observational research, such questions do not arise because the researcher does not manufacture data but observes naturally occurring situations. In observational research, on the other hand, one key issue is the reconstructive nature of the field notes and descriptions based upon them: that is that the descriptions to a degree are bound to represent the researcher's (and not the participants') cultural and cognitive perspectives (Hammersley and Atkinson, 2007: 203–205).

This chapter will deal with issues of validity in research based on audio or video recordings and transcripts, and, in particular, in conversation analysis (CA). I will focus this discussion on one specific type of qualitative research only, mainly because, as stated above, the questions of validity take a different form in different qualitative methods. Although the chapter focuses on a specific type of qualitative research , the basic issues raised here are relevant in the context of any qualitative method. Therefore, readers who are not primarily interested in CA are encouraged to treat this chapter as an *example* of the kinds of considerations that need to be addressed by any qualitative researcher. Even though the specific questions and answers concerning validity are different in other qualitative methods, the basic concerns are the same. At the conclusion of the chapter, I will return to some comparisons between questions of validity across different qualitative methods.

What is Validity?

The validity of research concerns the interpretation of observations: whether or not 'the researcher is calling what is measured by the right name' (Kirk and Miller, 1986: 69; see also Guba and Lincoln, 2005: 205–209; Silverman, 2010: 275–286). In discussions about validity, especially in the context of quantitative research, there is an underlying background assumption about a separation between the 'raw' observations and the issues that these observations stand for or represent. Responses to questionnaires, for example, can be more or less valid representations of underlying social phenomena, such as the respondents' attitudes or values (see Bryman, 2004: 72–74). In CA, the questions of validity are articulated in a rather different way. The core aim of conversation analytical research is to investigate talk-in-interaction, not as 'a screen on which are projected other processes', but as a phenomenon in its own right (Schegloff, 1992a: xviii). This commitment to naturalistic description of interaction gives a distinctive shape to the issues of validation in CA. These include:

- the transparency of analytic claims;
- validation through 'next turn';
- deviant case analysis;
- questions about the institutional character of interaction;
- the generalizability of conversation analytic findings;
- the use of statistical techniques.

The Transparence of Analytic Claims

In *Tractatus Logico-Philosophicus*, Wittgenstein pointed out that philosophy, rightly understood, is not a set of propositions but an activity, the clarification of non-philosophical propositions about the world. The method of this activity is complex because the 'knots' in our thinking are complex, but the results of philosophy are simple (see Kenny, 1973: 18, 101–102). A similar kind of paradox between the complexity of method and the simplicity of results is characteristic of CA, too.

The results of (good) conversation analytic research exhibit, in a positive manner, what Kirk and Miller (1986: 22) called *apparent validity*: once you have read them, you are convinced that they are transparently true. A conversational activity called 'fishing' may serve as an example. Anita Pomerantz showed in a classical paper published in 1980 how participants in a conversation can indirectly 'fish' for information from one another by telling what they themselves know. Descriptions of events displaying their producer's 'limited access' to the relevant facts may work as a device for inviting the other party to disclose his or her authorized version of the same issues (assuming, of course, that the other party is in a position of having privileged access to the relevant facts). Such dynamics are at work in cases like the following:

(1)

```
1 B:   Hello::.
2 A:   HI:::.
3 B:   Oh:hi:: 'ow are you Agne::s,
4 A:   Fi:ne. Yer line's been busy.
5 B:   Yeuh my fu (hh)- .hh my father's wife called me
6      ..hh So when she calls me::, .hh I can always talk
7      fer a long time. Cuz she c'n afford it'n I can't.
8      hhhh heh .ehhhhhh
```
                                                    (Pomerantz, 1980: 195)

In Extract 1 above, the description based on limited access to relevant facts given by A (bolded) works as what Pomerantz called 'a fishing device', successfully eliciting B's insider's report in the next turn. By telling her observations about the line having been busy, A makes it relevant for B to disclose to whom she was talking.

The description of an activity like 'fishing' tends to 'ring a bell' as soon as anyone stops to think about it. 'Fishing' is something in which everybody has participated in different roles. But until Pomerantz's article, this activity had not been described formally. The results of Pomerantz's analysis are very simple. Her argument is transparently true, or, in Kirk and Miller's (1986) terms, it has a genuine 'apparent validity'.

But just as in Wittgenstein's philosophy, 'although the *result* [...] is simple, its method cannot be if it is to arrive at that result' (Wittgenstein, 1975: 52). In CA, the complexities of the method involve other kinds of issues of validation.

Validation Through 'Next Turn'

Even though the meaning of any expression, if considered in isolation, is extremely open ended, any utterance that is produced in talk-in-interaction will be locally interpreted by the participants of that interaction. In the first place, their interpretation is displayed in the next actions after the utterance. Hence, any interpretations that conversation analysts may suggest can be subjected to the 'proof procedure' outlined by Sacks et al. (1974: 728–729): the next turn will show whether the interactants themselves treat the utterance in ways that are in accordance with the analyst's interpretation.

Therefore, in Extract 1 shown above, the utterance produced by B in lines 5–8 provides a proof procedure for the interpretation suggested by Pomerantz concerning A's turn in line 4. (What Pomerantz suggested was that 'telling my side' (what A did in line 4) can operate as a 'fishing device', which indirectly elicits an authoritative version of the events from the interlocutor.) And as we see, Pomerantz's interpretation passes the test: in lines 5–8, B gives her first-hand account of what had happened.

In much everyday conversation analytic work, things are not as nice and simple as in Extract 1: the next turns may be ambiguous in relation to the action performed in the preceding turn. However, the 'proof procedure' provided by the next turn remains the primordial criterion of validity that must be used as much as possible in all conversation analytic work.

Deviant Case Analysis

By examining the relations between successive turns of talk, conversation analysts aim at establishing *regular patterns* of interaction (Heritage, 1995 and in this volume). The patterns concern relations between actions (such as the relations between 'telling my side' and 'giving an authoritative report' in the case of 'fishing' described above). After having established a pattern, the analyst's next task is to search for and examine *deviant cases*: cases where 'things go differently' – most typically, cases where an element of the suggested pattern is not associated with the other expected elements. The deviant case analysis in CA closely resembles the technique of 'analytic induction' often used in ethnographic studies (see Silverman, 2001: 237–238). For the analyst, those cases that do not fit the inductively constructed pattern are deviant. Rather than putting aside these discrepant cases, the analyst is encouraged to focus particular attention on them.

In her paper on 'fishing', Pomerantz (1980: 186–187) presents a deviant case in which a description of events displaying its producer's 'limited access' does *not* lead the other party to disclose her authorized version of the event:

(2)

1 A: …dju j'see me pull us?=

2 B: =.hhh No:. I wz trying you all day. en the line

3   wz busy fer like hours

4 A: ohh:::::, oh:::::, .hhhhhh We::ll, hh I'm g'nna

5   c'm over in a little while help yer brother ou:t

6 B: Goo:d

7 A: Goo.hhh Cuz I know he needs some he::lp,

8   ((mournfully))

9 B: .hh Ye:ah. Yeh he'd mention' that tihday.=

10 A: =M-hm,=

11 **B: .hhh Uh:m, .tlk .hhh Who wih yih ta:lking to.**

(Pomerantz, 1980: 186–187)

In Extract 2 above, B reports her experience about A's line having been busy (lines 2–3). In terms of the interactional pattern identified by Pomerantz, this kind of telling should make relevant a subsequent disclosure of the details of the event by the other, more knowledgeable party. In the extract above, however, this does not happen. Instead, A shifts the topic in her subsequent turn (lines 4–5). Therefore, within the framework of the analysis of 'fishing', we can consider Extract 2 as a deviant case.

In an insightful paper, Clayman and Maynard (1994) have outlined three different ways that deviant cases, like Extract 2, can be dealt with:

1   Sometimes deviant cases can be shown to exhibit the interactants' orientation to the *same* considerations and normative orientations that produce the 'regular' cases. In those cases, something in the conduct of the participants discloses that they, too, treat the case as one involving a departure from the expected course of events. If the deviant cases show this kind of property, they provide *additional support* for the analyst's initial claim that the regularities found in the first phase of the data analysis 'are methodically produced and oriented to by the participants as normative organizations of action' (Heritage, 1988: 131). Extract 2 above is an example of this type of deviant case. After A has failed to respond to B's initial 'fishing' turn by an authorized report of the events, B asks directly to whom A had been talking (line 10). Through her question, she openly requests the information which the fishing device (lines 2–3), according to Pomerantz's analysis, solicited indirectly. This shift to open information seeking after an unsuccessful 'fishing' attempt indirectly confirms B's initial orientation to the 'fishing' as a device which can be used in indirect solicitation of information.

2   Clayman and Maynard (1994) point out, however, that there are also deviant cases that cannot be integrated within the analysts' construction of the participants' orientations that normally produce the regular cases. In dealing with these cases, the analyst may need to change his or her construction of the participants' orientations. A classical example is Schegloff's (1968) analysis of a single deviant case in his corpus of 500 telephone call openings. In this single case, unlike the other 499, the caller spoke first. The analysis of that single case

led Schegloff to abandon his initial hypothesis (according to which there is a norm obligating the answerer to speak first) and to reconceptualize the very first moves of telephone calls in terms of the adjacency pair 'summons (telephone ringing)–answer'. In the deviant case, the answerer did not produce the relevant second pair part, and, accordingly, the caller reissued the summons by speaking first.

3 There are also, however, deviant cases which cannot be integrated either into the existing or into a reconceptualized hypothesis concerning the participants' orientations (Clayman and Maynard, 1994). In these cases, an explanation can be sought from the individual contingencies of the single case. Normative orientations or strategic considerations other than those that usually inform the production of the pattern may be invoked by the participants in single cases, and these other orientations or considerations may explain the deviance.

In sum, deviant case analysis constitutes a central resource for testing hypotheses in conversation analytic work. Therefore, the researcher should consider the deviant cases not a nuisance, but a treasure. The meticulous analysis of those cases gives impetus, strength and rigour to the development of the analytic arguments.

Validity of Claims Concerning the Institutional Character of Interaction

In both qualitative and quantitative research, a central dimension of validity involves the correspondence between a theoretical paradigm and the observations made by the researcher. 'Construct validity' is a term that is often used in this context (Kirk and Miller, 1986: 22; Bryman, 2004: 73). It involves the relations between theoretical concepts and the observations that are supposed to represent those concepts. As was pointed out above, the primary emphasis that CA places on naturalistic description de-intensifies the relevance of many ordinary concerns of construct validity. However, the expansion of conversation analytic research on institutional interaction (see Heritage, this volume; Drew and Heritage, 1992; Arminen, 2005; Heritage and Clayman, 2010) has reinforced the need to consider the relation between observations and concepts also in conversation analytic studies.

In conversation analytic research on institutional interaction, a central question of validity is this: what grounds does the researcher have for claiming that the talk he or she is focusing on is in any way 'connected to' some institutional framework? The fact that a piece of interaction takes place in a hospital or in an office, for example, does not per se determine the institutional character of that particular interaction (Drew and Heritage, 1992: 18–21). Institutional roles, tasks and arrangements may or may not be present in any particular interactions; they may or may not be present at particular *moments* in particular interactions. If they are, the conversation analytic programme presupposes their presence is observable to the participants and the analyst alike.

Schegloff (1987, 1991, 1992b) points out that there are indefinitely many aspects of context potentially available for any interaction: we may categorize one another on the basis of gender, age, social class, education, occupation, income, race, and so on, and we may understand the setting of our interaction accordingly. In the momentary unfolding of interaction, Schegloff argues, 'the parties, singly and together, select and display in their conduct which of the indefinitely many aspects of context they are making relevant, or are invoking, for the immediate moment' (1987: 219).

Awareness of this 'problem of relevance' requires the professional analyst to proceed with caution. There is a danger of 'importing' institutional context to data. The professional analyst may be tempted to assume, without going into the details of data, that this or that feature of talk is an indication of a particular context (such as 'medical authority' or 'professional dominance') having affected the interaction. Such stipulation for context may, Schegloff (1991: 24–25) argues, result in the analysis being terminated prematurely, so that the inherent organization within the talk is not thoroughly understood. Phenomena which in the beginning may appear as indications of the workings of an 'institutional context' may in a more thorough examination be even better understood without reference to the 'institutional context'.

A case in point is provided by a recent study by Curl and Drew (2008) on the choice between two request forms: in asking for services, we can say either '*could you do X?*' or, in a more complex and apparently deferential way, '*I was wondering if you could do X*'. In the beginning of their analytic work, Curl and Drew paid attention to the fact that the choice of request form seemingly and broadly corresponded to the nature of the encounter – *could you do X* format was used in everyday encounters, and the more complex format in medical encounters (the patient making requests to the doctor). So, one might suggest, was the institutional context the 'reason' for the choice? But Curl and Drew did not terminate their analysis there. By exploring both everyday and institutional data, they eventually came to the conclusion that there is a more local explanation. The choice between two request forms embodied the speaker's orientation to her *entitlement to make the request* and the *contingency of granting* of the request. Crucial evidence for this more local explanation was cases from medical encounters where the more simple format was used (in which cases the speaker observably oriented herself to her entitlement and to non-contingency of granting) and cases from everyday encounters where the more complex format was used, and in which the speaker observably oriented herself to her lack of entitlement to ask, and to the granting being contingent. Thus, by not terminating their analysis prematurely by using the 'institutional context' as an overall explanation,

Curl and Drew were able to show in detail what the participants locally oriented to in their choice of request form. This is not to say that institutional context did not have any relation to this choice. In distributional terms, it clearly did. But the actual vehicle of this relation, the participants' consideration which, as it were, mediated or embodied their institutional relations, was their orientation to entitlement and contingency.

Schegloff (1991, 1992b) also maintains that it is not sufficient to say that a particular institutional context is oriented to 'in general' by the participants in interaction, but, instead, it has to be shown how specifiable aspects of the context are consequential for specifiable aspects of the interaction. What is said, when it is said, and how, and by whom, and to whom, may invoke the context; the goal of the conversation analytic research is to explicate exactly how the things said brought forward the context.

Schegloff's emphasis on the procedural consequentiality of the context has an important corollary. If a piece of research can pin down specific procedural links between a context and talk-in-interaction, it is likely that these observations not only are relevant in terms of analysis of detailed organization of interaction, but also contribute to the understanding of the context per se. Standard social scientific understandings of professional and other contexts are often based on rough generalizations concerning the professionals' tasks, clients' roles and the relations between the two. Conversation analytic research goes far beyond such generalizations. Thus, for example, the studies of Heath (1992), Maynard (1992) and myself (Peräkylä, 2006) on the delivery of diagnostic news have involved not only a detailed description of the specific practices found in medical consultations, but also a specification of a central aspect of that context, namely the dimensions and character of medical authority.

Thus, the relevance and consequences of institutional context are to be demonstrated by the researcher. In demonstrating them, the researcher will focus on particular phenomena in interaction, such as lexical choice, turn design, sequence organization and overall structural organization (Drew and Heritage, 1992: 29–45; Heritage, this volume). Where the workings of context will be found in a particular piece of research cannot be predicted in advance. This unpredictability arises from the inductive character of the conversation analytic enterprise; it causes both the fundamental difficulty and the exceptional fascination of conversation analytic research.

Generalizability of Conversation Analytic Findings

A crucial dimension of validity in any research concerns the generalizability of findings (Bryman, 2004: 76–77, 284–285). Owing to their work-intensive character, many conversation analytic studies are based on relatively small databases. How widely can the results, derived from relatively small samples, be generalized? This character of the problem is closely dependent on the type of conversation analytic research. In studies of ordinary conversation (everyday interactions outside specific institutional settings), the baseline assumption is that the results are or should be generalizable to the whole domain of ordinary conversations, and to a certain extent even across linguistic and cultural boundaries. Recent studies where conversational practices in different cultures are compared suggest that, unlike some earlier anthropological research has presumed, there are indeed universal features in conversation, such as avoidance of overlapping talk and minimization of silences between turns (see Stivers et al., 2009; Sidnell, 2007).

In conversation analytical study of institutional interaction, the problem is posed in different terms. The key question regarding generalization is this: do the findings of a particular study hold true in settings other than the one that was studied in this particular case? The answer to this question can be articulated in different ways, depending on the institution that has been studied.

Some types of institutional setting are, by now, covered by set of cumulative studies of CA. Primary care medical consultation is a case in point. There are strings of studies of CA on different phases of the consultation: opening, verbal and physical examination, diagnosis, treatment recommendation, and the like (see Heritage and Maynard, 2006). Any new study on medical consultation can, and has to, reflect its findings in the light of the earlier studies, specifying the results of the earlier ones. One thing that makes this cumulativeness possible is, it needs to be added, the universality of the medical institution. In many ways, medical consultations in Finland, the US or India are likely to be similar, and therefore one study can add new details of the picture drawn in the earlier ones.

Comparison across institutions is another avenue for generalization. What is being compared can be an action or a practice that can be found in different institutional settings, and which takes somewhat different shapes in these different settings. Drew (2003), for example, focuses on *formulations*, i.e. utterances that propose a gist or upshot of the preceding talk (cf. Heritage and Watson, 1979). He compares the uses of formulations in four settings – news interviews, workplace negotiations, radio call-in programmes and psychotherapy – and shows how this practice is shaped differently in each setting, so as to serve its specific contingencies. In similar vein, Ruusuvuori and Voutilainen (2010; see also Voutilainen, et al., 2010) compare professionals' responses to patients' emotional expressions in general practice, homeopathy and psychotherapy, showing how the different responses are geared to facilitate the different professional tasks in each setting. Thus, for example, in general practice, the professionals' empathizing utterances are geared to close down the discussion on emotional experiences (and to move on to medical business), whereas in psychotherapy they project topicalization and further talk of that experience.

It is likely that as the databases and analyses of institutional interaction gradually accumulate, studies like Drew's and Ruusuvuori and Voutilainen's will become more common. The comparative approach directly tackles the question of generalizability by demonstrating the similarities and differences across a number of settings. For the time being, however, many studies on institutional interaction are more like case studies.

Many case studies on institutional interaction are based on data collected from one or a only a few sites. The number of subjects involved in such studies usually is relatively small. There are perhaps two overlapping ways in which issues of generalization can be tackled in case studies. One involves *finding the generic from the particular*: through the study of a single case, the researcher can come up with results that constitute claims or hypotheses regarding the organization of human interaction in a most generic level. Some studies by Charles Goodwin are a case in point. In studies that focus on particular occasions in interaction, such as a school-child doing homework with her father (2007), students and scholars undertaking archaeological excavation in a field school (2003) or chemists undertaking an experiment (1997), Goodwin shows 'the constellation of language, environment, body and action' in bringing about joint attention, action packages and, ultimately, human social and cognitive worlds (see esp. Goodwin, 2007: 61). In other words, Goodwin is not primarily trying to tell us what is peculiar in doing homework, archaeological excavation or chemistry. Instead, he uses activities in these settings as specimens on the ways in which humans (in general) employ the resources of language, body and physical environment in bringing about their shared worlds that they attend to and know about. In this way, we might say, Goodwin finds the generic from the particular.

The other way to tackle the problem of generalization in case studies involves the notion of *possibility*. In terms of the traditional 'distributional' understanding of generalizability, case studies on institutional interaction cannot offer much. Studying one or a few sites only does not warrant conclusions concerning similarities in the professionals' and their clients' conduct in different settings. The problem may be particularly acute if the professional practice that is studied is informed by specific professional theory: for example, psychotherapists working in the framework of 'solution-oriented therapy' interact with their clients in ways that are distinctively different from those of psychoanalysts or other different theoretical inclinations (see Peräkylä et al., 2008). The concept of possibility, however, gives a new perspective to this. *Social practices that are possible*, i.e. *possibilities of language use*, are the central objects of all conversation analytic case studies on interaction in particular institutional settings. The possibility of various practices can be considered generalizable even if the practices are not actualized in similar ways across different settings. For example, in my study on AIDS counselling in a London teaching hospital (Peräkylä, 1995), the research objects were specific questioning practices used by the counsellors and their clients. These practices arose from a particular therapeutic theory and they were to a large extent developed in the particular hospital that my data were from. Therefore, it is possible that they are not used anywhere else exactly in those specific ways that were analysed in my study (see Silverman (1997) for some observations on the wide variety of approaches in AIDS counselling in the UK). Hence my results cannot be directly generalizable to any other site where AIDS counselling is done.

However, the results of my study can be considered descriptions of questioning techniques that are possible across a wide variety of settings. More specifically, the study involves an effort to describe in detail how these questioning techniques were made possible: what kind of management of turn-taking, participation frameworks, turn design, sequence organization, and so on, was needed in order for the participants to set up scenes where 'circular questioning', 'live open supervision' and 'hypothetical future-oriented questioning' were done? The study showed how these practices are made possible through the very details of the participants' action. As possibilities, the practices that I analysed are very likely to be generalizable. There is no reason to think that they could not be made possible by any competent member of (at least any Western) society. In this sense, this study produced generalizable results. The results were not generalizable as descriptions of what other counsellors or other professionals do with their clients, but they were generalizable as descriptions of what any counsellor or other professional, with his or her clients, *can* do, given that he or she has the same array of interactional competencies as the participants of the AIDS counselling sessions have.

Quantification

Use of large databases and quantification involves another kind of strategy for ensuring the generalizability (and also other aspects of the validity) of the conversation analytical research findings. Some of the practices studied by conversation analysts lend themselves to 'coding and counting'. For example, in Clayman and Heritage's (2002) study on question design in presidential press conferences in the US, the journalists' questions were coded regarding the degree of 'adversarialness' that they exhibited. Calculations were made to show how the relative proportions of questions, showing different degrees of adversarialness, changed over time. It was shown that the journalists have become much less deferential and more aggressive in their treatment of the president. Another example of successful quantification is offered in Stivers and Majid's (2007) study on racial bias in routine paediatric medical consultations. Their focus of attention was whether the doctor addressed his or her questions to the parents or to the children in such consultations. Through statistical analysis, they demonstrated that black children and Latino children of low-education parents were less likely to be selected to answer questions than their white peers of the same age, irrespective of education. Thus, there was an implicit race bias in the doctor's way of conducting interaction.

At least two issues are critical regarding the applicability of quantitative techniques in CA. First, straightforward coding of interactional practices is not always possible. Many practices involve such complexity that large numbers of cases cannot be subsumed under simple (and mutually exclusive) categories. If complex cases are forced under simple categories, something that is analytically important may be lost from sight. This kind of consideration has led Schegloff (1993: 117) to propose the possibility that interaction might be orderly 'at the level of the singular occurrence only' and not orderly, in any relevant way, at the aggregate level. The other problem concerns sampling (Silverman, 2001: 249). In order for quantitative analysis to provide a basis for generalization, the selection of cases to be studied should follow adequate statistical procedures so as to ensure their representativeness. In studies of CA, anything like random sampling is rarely possible. The data collection is too laborious and institutional conditions too strict. In researching medical consultations or psychotherapy, for example, the researcher may have to work with the kind of data to which he or she can get access. If the relation between the sample and the population remains unclear, statistical tests, if they are used, may yield results that should be understood heuristically only (as in Peräkylä, 2006). This does not need to be a reason not to use quantitative techniques at all, but it is a consideration that restricts their import in terms of generalizability of findings.

Bearing these restrictions in mind, statistical analysis may be useful in particular conversation analytical research designs. These include research designs that concern relations between distinct interactional variables in standardized forms of encounters (like the studies on diagnosis by Peräkylä, 2006), or historical change in such encounters (like the changes of presidential press conferences studied by Clayman and Heritage, 2002), or relations between social categories and interactional practices (like the relations between race and interactional practices studied by Stivers and Majid, 2007). (For a more thorough account on this, see Heritage, 1995.) In any case, however, the backbone of conversation analytical work involves qualitative case-by-case analysis.

Conclusion

At the beginning of this chapter, I pointed out that the specific procedures of securing validity in different types of qualitative research are not always the same. The aim of this chapter has been to give an overview of the imperatives faced and solutions found in conversation analytic research. The main procedures of validation of the researcher's analytic claims in all conversation analytic research include the analysis of the next speaker's interpretation of the preceding action, and deviant case analysis. Validation also involves the anchoring in data of the claims concerning the relevance of an institutional context of interaction, comparisons within and between institutional settings, issues of generalizability of the results of case studies, as well as use of quantitative techniques.

Some of these procedures of validation have to do with CA only. Especially, that is the case in the use of the speaker's utterance as an instance of validation for the researcher's interpretation of the import of the preceding action. This 'next turn proof procedure' is a 'fingerprint' of conversation analytical data analysis: it is a procedure of validation that is available only to an approach based on sequential analysis of recorded interaction. However, as Silverman (2007: chapter 3) has argued, *all* qualitative research can be improved by paying attention to data sequences.

Questions about the specific particulars of interaction that may or may not convey the participants' orientation to institutional context might not arise in many other approaches, which are not concerned with the details of speech and other action in the same way as CA. But some other procedures of validation are shared between CA and other approaches. Deviant case analysis has its origins in ethnographic research, and the procedures employed in CA are quite similar to those employed there. Furthermore, questions about comparison within and between institutions, as well as other issues related to generalization of research results, might well arise for example in ethnographic studies. And, at a more general level, the considerations of validity in CA are indeed similar to those in any other kind of qualitative research: all serious qualitative research involves meticulous testing and consideration of the truthfulness of analytic claims.

Summary

The specific procedures of securing validity in different types of qualitative research are not the same, even though there is a considerable overlap between them. This chapter offered an overview of the imperatives faced and solutions found in conversation analytic research. The main procedures of validation of the researcher's analytic claims in all conversation analytic research include the analysis of the next speaker's interpretation of the preceding action, and deviant case analysis. Validation also involves the anchoring in data of the claims concerning the relevance of an institutional context of interaction, comparisons within and between institutional settings, showing generic patterns of interaction or possibilities of language use, in the results of case studies, as well as use of quantitative techniques. Validation through consideration of the next utterance is a procedure used mainly in CA, whereas analysis of deviant case is used also in ethnography and other types of qualitative research.

Future Prospects

Regarding techniques of validation, the use of quantitative techniques will become more frequent, as well as the comparisons within and between institutions. The case study design will prevail especially in video-based analysis of complex working environments (see Heath, this volume).

Questions

- What does 'validity' mean?
- Why might there be different techniques of validation in different qualitative approaches?
- What procedures of validation do conversation analysis and ethnography share?

Recommended Reading

ten Have, P. (2007) *Doing Conversation Analysis: A Practical Guide.* Second Edition. London: Sage. Chapters 3, 7 and 8.

Hutchby, I. and Wooffit, R. (1998) *Conversation Analysis: Principles, Practices and Applications.* Cambridge: Polity Press. Chapters 4–5.

Silverman, D. (2010) *Doing Qualitative Research.* Third Edition. London: Sage. Chapter 15.

Internet Links

Ethnomethodology and conversation analysis newsletter *Ethno/CA News:* www2.fmg.uva.nl/emca/

The International Institute for Ethnomethodology and Conversation Analysis: www.iiemca.org/

References

Arminen, I. (2005) *Institutional Interaction: Studies of Talk at Work*. Aldershot: Ashgate.

Bryman, A. (2004) *Social Research Methods*. Second Edition. Oxford: Oxford University Press.

Clayman, S.E. and Heritage, J. (2002) 'Questioning presidents: Journalistic deference and adversarialness in the press conferences of Eisenhower and Reagan', *Journal of Communication*, 52 (4): 749–775.

Clayman, S.E. and Maynard, D.W. (1994) 'Ethnomethodology and conversation analysis', in P. ten Have and G. Psathas (eds), *Situated Order: Studies in the Social Organization of Talk and Embodied Activities*. Washington, DC: University Press of America. pp. 1–30.

Curl, T. and Drew, P. (2008) 'Contingency and action: A comparison of two forms of requesting', *Research on Language and Social Interaction*, 41: 1–25.

Drew, P. (2003) 'Comparative analysis of talk-in-interaction in different institutional settings: A sketch', in P.J. Glenn, C.D. LeBaron and J. Mandelbaum (eds), *Studies in Language and Social Interaction: In Honor of Robert Hopper*. Mahwah, NJ: Erlbaum.

Drew, P. and Heritage, J. (1992) 'Introduction: Analyzing talk at work', in P. Drew and J. Heritage (eds), *Talk at Work: Interaction in Institutional Settings*. Cambridge: Cambridge University Press. pp. 3–65.

Goodwin, C. (1997) 'The blackness of black: Color categories as situated practice', in I.B. Rescnick, R. Säljö, C. Pentecorvo and B. Burge (eds), *Discourse, Tools and Reasoning: Essays on Situated Cognition*. Berlin: Springer. pp. 111–140.

Goodwin, C. (2003) 'The body in action', in J. Coupland and R. Gwyn (eds), *Discourse, the Body, and Identity*. Houndmills and New York: Palgrave/Macmillan.

Goodwin, C. (2007) 'Participation, stance and affect in the organization of activities', *Discourse & Society*, 18 (1): 53–73.

Guba, E.G. and Lincoln, Y.S. (2005) 'Paradigmatic controversies, contradictions, and emerging confluences', in N.K. Denzin and Y.S. Lincoln (eds), *The Sage Handbook of Qualitative Research*. Third Edition. Thousand Oaks, CA: Sage, pp. 191–216.

Hammersley, M. (1992) *What's Wrong with Ethnography: Methodological Explorations*. London: Routledge.

Hammersley, M. and Atkinson, P. (2007) *Ethnography: Principles in Practice*. Third Edition. London: Routledge.

Heath, C. (1992) 'The delivery and reception of diagnosis in the general practice consultation', in P. Drew and J. Heritage (eds), *Talk at Work: Interaction in Institutional Settings*. Cambridge: Cambridge University Press. pp. 235–267.

Heritage, J. (1988) 'Explanations as accounts: A conversation analytic perspective', in C. Antaki (ed.), *Analysing Everyday Explanation: A Case Book of Methods*. London: Sage. pp. 127–144.

Heritage, J. (1995) 'Conversation analysis: Methodological aspects', in U.M. Quatshoff (ed.), *Aspects of Oral Communication*. Berlin: Walter de Gruyter. pp. 391–418.

Heritage, J. and Clayman, S. (2010) *Talk in Action: Interaction, Identities, and Institutions.* Chichester: Wiley-Blackwell.

Heritage, J. and Maynard, D. (eds) (2006) *Communication in Medical Care: Interaction between Primary Care Physicians and Patients.* Cambridge: Cambridge University Press.

Heritage, J. and Watson, R. (1979) 'Formulation as conversational objects', in G. Psathas (ed.), *Everyday Language. Studies in Ethnomethodology.* New York: Irvington. pp. 123–162.

Kenny, A. (1973) *Wittgenstein.* London: Allen Lane.

Kirk, J. and Miller, M.L. (1986) *Reliability and Validity in Qualitative Research.* London: Sage.

Maynard, D.W. (1992) 'On clinicians co-implicating recipients' perspective in the delivery of diagnostic news', in P. Drew and J. Heritage (eds), *Talk at Work: Interaction in Institutional Settings.* Cambridge: Cambridge University Press. pp. 331–358.

Peräkylä, A. (1995) *AIDS Counselling: Institutional Interaction and Clinical Practice.* Cambridge: Cambridge University Press.

Peräkylä, A. (2004) 'Reliability and validity in research based on naturally occurring social interaction', in D. Silverman (ed.), *Qualitative Research: Theory, Method and Practice.* London: Sage. pp. 283–304.

Peräkylä, A. (2006) 'Communicating and responding to diagnosis', in J. Heritage and D. Maynard (eds), *Communication in Medical Care. Interaction between Primary Care Physicians and Patients.* Cambridge: Cambridge University Press. pp. 214–247.

Peräkylä, A., Antaki, C., Vehviläinen, S. and Leudar, I. (eds) (2008) *Conversation Analysis and Psychotherapy.* Cambridge: Cambridge University Press.

Pomerantz, A. (1980) 'Telling my side: "Limited access" as a "fishing device"', *Sociological Inquiry*, 50: 186–198.

Ruusuvuori, J. and Voutilainen, L. (2010) 'Comparing interaction in different types of health care encounter', in M. Haakana, M. Laakso and J. Lindström (eds), *Talk in Interaction. Comparative Dimensions.* Helsinki: Finnish Literature Society.

Sacks, H., Schegloff, E.A. and Jefferson, G. (1974) 'A simplest systematics for the organization of turn-taking for conversation', *Language*, 50: 696–735.

Schegloff, E.A. (1968) 'Sequencing in conversational openings', *American Anthropologist*, 70: 1075–1095.

Schegloff, E.A. (1987) 'Between macro and micro: Contexts and other connections', in J. Alexander, B. Giesen, R. Munch and N. Smelser (eds), *The Micro–Macro Link.* Berkeley and Los Angeles: University of California Press. pp. 207–234.

Schegloff, E.A. (1991) 'Reflections on talk and social structure', in D. Boden and D.H. Zimmerman (eds), *Talk and Social Structure: Studies in Ethnomethodology and Conversation Analysis.* Cambridge: Polity. pp. 44–70.

Schegloff, E.A. (1992a) 'Introduction', in H. Sacks, *Lectures on Conversation*, Vol. 1, ed. G. Jefferson. Oxford: Blackwell. pp. ix–Lxii.

Schegloff, E.A. (1992b) 'On talk and its institutional occasion', in P. Drew and J. Heritage (eds), *Talk at Work: Interaction in Institutional Settings.* Cambridge: Cambridge University Press. pp. 101–134.

Schegloff, E.A. (1993) 'Reflections on quantification in the study of conversation', *Research on Language and Social Interaction*, 26: 99–128.

Sidnell, J. (2007) 'Comparative studies in conversation analysis', *Annual Review of Anthropology*, 36: 229–244.

Silverman, D. (1997) *Discourses of Counselling*. London: Sage.

Silverman, D. (2001) *Interpreting Qualitative Data: Methods for Analysing Talk, Text and Interaction*. Second Edition. London: Sage.

Silverman, D. (2007) *A Very Short, Fairly Interesting, Reasonably Cheap Book about Qualitative Research*. London: Sage.

Silverman, D. (2010) *Doing Qualitative Research*. Third Edition. London: Sage.

Stivers, T. and Majid, A. (2007) 'Questioning children: Interactional evidence of implicit bias in medical interviews', *Social Psychology Quarterly*, 70 (4): 424–441.

Stivers, T., Enfield, N.J., Brown, P., Englert, C., Hayashi, M., Heinemann, T. et al. (2009) 'Universals and cultural variation in turn-taking in conversation', *Proceedings of the National Academy of Sciences of the United States of America*, 106 (26): 10587–10592.

Voutilainen, L., Peräkylä, A. and Ruusuvuori, J. (2010) 'Recognition and interpretation: Responding to emotional experience in psychotherapy', *Research on Language and Social Interaction*, 44 (1): 85–107.

Wittgenstein, L. (1975) *Philosophical Remarks*. Edited from his posthumous writings by R. Rhees and translated by R. Hargreaves and R. White. Oxford: Blackwell.

Three Aspects of Writing Qualitative Research: Practice, Genre, and Audience

21

Amir Marvasti

Abstract

Focusing on writing as both a process and the outcome of qualitative research, this chapter offers novice researchers a framework for assessing their work. In particular, writing qualitative research is presented as a three-facet enterprise that involves practice, genre, and audiences. Practice refers to the ongoing, fluid dimensions as was well as the basic skills or craft of writing. The discussion of genre deals with the various stylistic choices available to social scientists, particularly to qualitative researchers. Finally, audience selection addresses the strategic choices authors have to consider as they try to publish their work and make it accessible to various audiences. It is argued that a 'perfect paper' is one that strikes a balance between these three dimensions.

> **Keywords:**
>
> writing, genre, audience, researcher roles, peer review.

Introduction

The field of qualitative research is rich with analytical options, representational styles, and publication outlets. Questions about how much data, how to analyze the data, how to write it all down, and what to include in the final manuscript become progressively more difficult as one learns about the variety of qualitative paradigms. Many of these issues have been addressed elsewhere in this book and are beyond the focus of this chapter. Here I focus on writing qualitative research.

I think it is possible to locate points of common interest across the diverse landscape of qualitative research. For example, while there are many styles of interviewing (structured, open ended, ethnographic, etc.), we would all agree that, at a minimum, an interview requires questions and respondents. Similarly, while representational choices may seem infinite, the practice and logic of writing itself is not entirely without boundaries. In this chapter, I borrow from the insights of reader response and genre theories, to offer a vision of 'good writing' in qualitative research based on three interrelated themes: (1) the ongoing practice and craft of writing, (2) writing genres, and (3) external evaluation of writing.

In keeping with my own emphasis on audience expectations and purposeful writing, I should begin by noting that the intended audience for this chapter is novice qualitative researchers and graduate students. Therefore, my examples and citations were chosen to serve the interests of this specific group. I should also note that although I have avoided reifying a strict qualitative–quantitative distinction, the material presented here does vary in its relevance to conventional methodo- logical camps. In particular, the discussion of genre goes furthest in addressing the specific needs of qualitative researchers whereas other sections may be useful to novice writers, in general.

The Craft and Practice of Writing

Writing is typically thought of as a unique, creative form of self-expression, and that myth may be a large part of the problem. Even in its most self-consciously creative manifestations, writing is a craft that involves endless practice and the mas- tery of techniques. Creativity and technical know-how are not mutually exclusive dimensions of the craft of writing; great ideas, no matter how profound, cannot be expressed without the basic skills of writing. Fortunately, for social scientists interested in the technical conventions of writing, there is no shortage of instruc- tional books. For qualitative researchers, in particular, there is a growing market of how-to texts that include at least a chapter on writing theses and dissertations, with some entirely devoted to the basics of writing qualitative research (see, for example, Wolcott 2009).

However, technical know-how develops in tandem with actual, ongoing practice. Specifically, writing could be envisioned and taught as a fluid process of organizing and articulating loosely connected observations. In this context, the researcher/ writer (embedded in time and place and in interaction with others) has to con- stantly reevaluate initial ideas. Let me illustrate this point using an example from my own research. At the beginning of my ethnography of a homeless shelter, I wanted to organize my dissertation around the notion that the homeless are 'the postmodern heroes of our time.' The idea was inspired by interviews with homeless men who had said things like 'It sucks to be a citizen' or 'I feel sorry for the poor bastards who're enslaved by their work. I'm free to sleep where I want and go where I want.' I interpreted such statements as clear rejections of the modern, capitalist premise of productive labor. Chatting in coffee shops with fellow students, I championed the cause of the homeless by quoting their anti-work statements, translating my field notes into political slogans. However, when it came to writing the dissertation, aside from a few broad declarations like 'It appears that some homeless people reject conventional notions of work,' I had little else to write on the topic.

Fortunately, as my writing and analysis progressed, with the help of my peers and dissertation director, I focused on another idea that seemed more in synch with the empirical evidence and my sociological training. In particular, my data seemed to show that the very notion of 'the homeless' was problematic. The men and women on the streets and in shelters viewed their circumstances from many different standpoints. Some thought of their situation as a type of personal freedom whereas others said they were 'miserable.' This way of analyzing and writing about my fieldwork became the foundation of my research and was further polished as the writing went on.

As this example shows, one practices writing over time, in association with others (e.g., mentors, peers, and reviewers) and in specific settings. Qualitative research texts are not written overnight and 'independently,' but they emerge in a context and in collaboration with others, much like any other practice. Thinking about writing as an ongoing practice in this way balances the emphasis on technical know-how (e.g., spelling and grammar) with the fluid and varied contexts, which, as shown in the next two sections, further expand and limit the author's choices.

Organization and Genre

There are many ways to write social science research. As Howard Becker puts it:

> Scholarly writers have to ... express an argument clearly enough that readers can follow the reasoning and accept the conclusions. They make this job harder than it need be when they think there is only One Right Way to do it .... They simplify their work, on the other hand, when they recognize that there are many effective ways to say something and that their job is only to choose one and execute it so that readers will know what they are doing. (1986: 43)

In this section, I consider the range of writing choices, alluded to by Becker, in two ways. I begin by discussing how a research manuscript can be organized in terms of varying emphasis on method, theory, and findings. I then turn to variations in genre as another way of mapping the landscape of writing qualitative research.

Organization

The most widely used mode of writing a research paper, whether qualitative or quantitative, organizes the text into four elements: *introduction, methods, analysis,* and *conclusion*. Think of each section as answering a different set of questions, as outlined below.

> **Introduction**: What is the topic of your paper? Have there been previous studies on this topic?
> **Methods**: What was the size of the sample for the study? How and where was the sample collected? How is the data to be analyzed?
> **Analysis**: What is the empirical evidence for this study? What social processes are revealed by the data? How does it support the researcher's claims about a particular sociological topic or process?
> **Conclusion**: How is the study of interest to ordinary people or policy makers? In what ways could it be improved or expanded (i.e., the proverbial call for 'further research')?

Most other styles of writing research papers are variations of this standard theme. What changes is the degree of emphasis placed on each of the four components (i.e., introduction, methods, analysis, and conclusion).

Genre and the Alternative Ways of Writing

In the social sciences, there is a growing awareness of the rhetorical dimensions of writing and representing facts, particularly among ethnographic researchers (see, for example, Alasuutari 1995 and Gubrium and Holstein 1997). Perhaps the work that is mostly widely cited in this context is James Clifford and George Marcus's *Writing Culture: The Poetics and Politics of Ethnography* (1986), which states in its introduction: 'the making of ethnography is artisanal, tied to the worldly work of writing' (p. 6). John Van Maanen's *Tales of the Field* is another important analysis of the stylistic features of qualitative writing. Through secondary analysis, Van Maanen (1988) identifies different genres of ethnographic texts (e.g., realist, confessional, and impressionist). He argues that rather than describing a single social reality seen from multiple perspectives, variations in writing construct realities of their own.

While some have dismissed the textual shift as a passing fad, others have embraced it as the new logic of social science and have proposed alternative writing strategies that go beyond the traditional organization of a research paper outlined earlier. In the remainder of this section, I offer a brief survey of these alternative writing practices by focusing on the following three genres: (1) writing with pictures, (2) writing the story, and (3) writing the author. I end the section with a critical assessment of these genres.

Writing with Pictures

While the visual has always had a place in the social sciences, its use and analysis have fluctuated over the history of various disciplines (see Emmison, this volume). For example, more than a hundred years ago, the *American Journal of Sociology*, the flagship journal of the discipline, published a number of articles that used photos as data (see Stasz 1979). According to Elizabeth Chaplin (1994: 201), the first manuscript of this type was F. Blackmar's 'The Smoky Pilgrims' published in 1897. The study depicted poverty in rural Kansas using posed photographs. Yet, this earlier interest in the visual waned as the written word accompanied with numerical analysis became the dominant mode of analysis. In a way, statistical figures, charts, and tables became the visual centerpieces of professional sociological publications.

In the broad context of writing in the social sciences, one can think of the visual in two ways: (1) writing about pictures and (2) writing with pictures. Writing about pictures involves the analysis of existing images, often for the purpose of cultural critique. For example, in his landmark sociological study *Gender Advertisements* (1979), Erving Goffman analyzed how gender roles and expectations are reflected in magazine ads. Using over 500 photos, he critiqued the taken-for-granted nature of gender relations in Western societies. Specifically, Goffman showed that magazine ads in the late 1970s depicted men in active roles (doing things like helping patients or playing in sports) and the women as mere spectators, passively watching the men's activities.

By contrast, writing with pictures involves creating first-hand visual material for the purpose of illustrating, complementing, or even transcending the written text. In the social sciences, anthropology is a leader of the use of pictorial and filmic materials for illustrative purposes. For example, Gregory Bateson and Margaret Mead's *Balinese Character: A Photographic Study* (1942) juxtaposes text and the visual in a complementary way so that one would enhance the meaning of the other.

As Douglas Harper (2005) notes, emerging computer technologies have facilitated the use of visual material in social research. Particularly, multimedia texts can now easily combine pictures and written material in the same context. Additionally, multimedia texts can be posted on internet websites accessible to users virtually from any location in the world. A key feature of internet-posted multimedia text (e.g., 'hypertext') is that the material does not have to be read or viewed linearly like a bound book. So-called 'hot links' or 'hyperlinks' allow the readers to jump from one passage to another. For example, while reading a hypertext ethnography, the reader can click on pictures from the field, see an image of a respondent, and click on his name to see excerpts from an interview with that respondent.

Writing the Story

Some qualitative researchers approach writing as a type of storytelling. In this genre of writing, the researchers narrate the characters and the 'scenes' in which the data was collected. Additionally, the author's reflections and the roles he or she assumed in the study can become part of the story. For example, Carolyn Ellis and Arthur Bochner's (1992) personal experience with abortion is told using the following familiar narrative headings:

The Story
Scene 1: The Pregnancy Test and the Test of Pregnancy
Scene 2: Making the Decision
Scene 3: Dealing with the Decision
Scene 4: The Preabortion Procedure
Scene 5: The Abortion
Epilogue

(Adapted from Ellis and Bochner 1992: 70–101)

The decision to write in a narrative style tends to hinge on the data and data collection method. For example, ethnographic methods are better suited for storied writing as the research procedures readily lend themselves to the mainstays of storytelling (e.g., characters and settings). Conceivably, any ethnography can be written as the story of someone entering a site and reporting their experiences. For example, William Whyte's classic ethnography *Street Corner Society* (1949) can be reduced to the story of a white man living with Italian immigrants in the inner city.

Writing the Author

Writing the author into the field notes, or autoethnography, is another genre of representing qualitative research. A thorough survey of this type of writing can be found in the introductory chapter of Deborah Reed-Danahay's *Auto/Ethnography* (1997), which presents autoethnographic writing as essentially a self-reflexive account of social experience. Accordingly, autoethnographic texts explicitly aim to include the author and embed his or her experiences in a broader social context, or as Reed-Danahay puts it: autoethnography is a 'self-narrative that places the self within a social context' (1997: 9).

However, how this is achieved and for what purposes is the subject of considerable debate and contention. In Reed-Danahay's chapter there seems to be a continuum of representational strategies for autoethnographers. On the one hand, there is the minimally self-referential text that simply adds the author's own subjective voice to the many voices and observations from the field. On the other hand, there is 'pure,' 'native' experience represented with little or no intervention from academic sources.

In the field of autoethnography, the works of Carol Rambo are exemplary because of her ability to combine the best analytical innovations of this genre with superior aesthetic sensibility. Her story, 'My mother is mentally retarded' (Rambo 1996), is a classic example of what she calls a 'multi-layered account.' In this particular form of autoethnography, the author's experiential account is juxtaposed with academic and popular discourses. The descriptions are layered and deliberately disjointed using a set of asterisks.

Words of Caution on Genre and the Aesthetics of Writing

The status of 'alternative' does not exempt these texts from critical assessment. For example, some critics point out that some representational experiments simply result in bad writing. For example, in her review of Ellis's *The Ethnographic I: A Methodological Novel about Autoethnography*, Pamela Moro writes:

> The real question is, perhaps, whether Ellis is a good enough writer to pull off this heartfelt endeavor. Writing good fiction is hard; writing compelling dialogue is extremely hard. I am not entirely sure if what Ellis has written is a 'novel.' . . . It is as though she has taken the shell of a novel and poured into it the material of textbook. (2006: 266)

Others question whether alternative writing forms are effective in achieving their emancipatory goals. For example, Paul Atkinson and Sara Delamont caution that some writing experimentations inadvertently (1) re-center the social scientist as the all-knowing author and (2) promote an individualized rather than an interactive view of social experience:

> we warn against the wholesale acceptance of aesthetic criteria in the reconstruction of social life. In many contexts, there is a danger of collapsing the various forms of social action into one aesthetic mode—that is, implicitly revalorizing the authorial voice of the social scientist—and of transforming socially shared and culturally shaped phenomena into the subject matter of an undifferentiated but esoteric literary genre. (2005: 823)

Similarly, Jay Gubrium warns against 'self-referential writing' that 'eclipses' or loses sight of the subject matter of research. In his words:

> I know that the subject matter can be the experience of the researcher, but what I'm concerned with here is the emphasis this can take in the final written product. If you do aim to feature your place in a project in writing, in particular yourself and your relation with others, then write about how that relates to broader issues of personal and interpersonal experience in the circumstances. (2009)

Finally, some argue that alternative writing and related genres are trendy tropes that lack substance. This position is best articulated by David Silverman who warns:

- Contemporary qualitative research has been infiltrated by two elements: the experience game of Romanticism and (as we'll see in a moment) the pastiche of Post-Modernism.
- Both these elements derive from an unthinking adoption of certain features of contemporary culture [Silverman suggests that following this path is dangerous and reminds us of the perverted versions of science in the twentieth century when Soviet science and Nazi science flourished].
- Under these auspices, qualitative research can amount to 'bullshit' conceived, not in its pejorative and vernacular sense, but as overly kitsch, overly-jargonised and over-theorised.

(2007: 119)

Audiences: Publication Outlets and Reviewers

Research texts are not intended for researchers' own consumption but for external audiences. To illustrate this point, let's begin with a form of writing that is largely intended for self-use (i.e., personal diaries). What goes into such documents is traditionally considered self-directed and private, so much so that the unauthorized reading of them is considered taboo in Western cultures. In a diary the words can appear in any order and have many meanings, and no external authority is expected to proofread it or demand clarification.

Of course, the 'private diary' as an ideal type is fast changing (web-based forums such as Twitter and text-messaging now make it possible for the personal to become public, and diaries of famous people have always been of interest to the public and publishers). Nonetheless, if we were to think of writing on a continuum of audiences, private diaries would fall on the extreme where the audience is essentially reduced to the self. On the other hand, we would find research reports that are explicitly tailored to the needs of an external audience, which could vary from small committees overseeing a dissertation to editors and reviewers evaluating a manuscript for publication. The next section offers some how-to, as well as analytical, guidance for navigating the world of audiences for qualitative research with an emphasis on journal publications.

Strategic Choices

The two common choices for publishing social science research are books and journal articles. As you consider the two choices, it is important to keep in mind that book and journal publications are given different weights in the tenure process, and for one's professional career in general. For example, in 'Books vs. articles: Two ways of publishing sociology' Alan Wolf (1990) shows that the balance between book and article production fluctuates considerably across academic institutions, at least in the United States. As Wolf notes, that pluralism in scholarly publications is useful and necessary; books and articles allow for different treatments of topics under analysis and they allow sociologists to reach different audiences. However, it is unlikely that a qualitative researcher will pass the tenure requirements at major academic institutions without journal publications. With that in mind, the remainder of this section considers the basic requirements of journal publishing.

Responding to Editors' and Reviewers' Comments

Most journal articles are rejected or returned with a request for substantial revision from the reviewers whose comments are returned to the author along with a letter from the editor. If the editor's letter contains the phrase 'revise-and-resubmit,' especially when preceded by 'strongly encourage you to,' that is very good news. In revising the paper, authors are advised to give special attention to the reviewers' comments that were echoed by the editor. In other words, one may ignore some of the reviewers' comments, but it would be a huge mistake to set aside the editor's suggestions.

After submitting several papers, it is possible to see a pattern among the reviewers. Some are undoubtedly more helpful than others. It is important to keep in mind that reviewers provide their services to editors free of charge, often spending hours reading and commenting on a paper. Indeed, it might be empowering for writers to think of their reviewers as people with diverse motivations and interests. To this end, here is a loose categorization scheme of reviewers to help further contextualize the writing and publication process for novices:

- *Editor impressers*: Their comments tend to be directed more at the journal editor than the authors. These reviewers write detailed (sometimes irrelevant reviews) with the hope of being invited to contribute their own manuscript to the journal.
- *Ego bruisers*: These reviewers seem to receive pleasure from attacking the competition in their field. They have elevated their insulting and backhanded comments to an art form (one can almost hear them giggling at their own handywork in between the lines).
- *Ego bruised*: These reviewers are primarily concerned with the critique of their own work or that someone neglected to cite them. Their comments sometimes include direct references to their own articles.
- *Shoddy reviewers*: These folks (usually well-established scholars in their field) do not really read the papers they are asked to comment on. Their reviews contain comments so brief and perfunctory as if to suggest to the editor, 'Don't bother me with this kind of submission again.'
- *Helpful reviewers*: These are the ideal reviewers. They actually read the papers carefully and provide specific suggestions for improving them.

Research Roles and Audiences

Envisioning reviewers as audiences with different roles and expectations of their own puts the qualitative researcher in the position of an actor, and the writing itself becomes a type of interaction, initially with an audience of reviewers and editors and eventually the readership of the journal as a whole. The next logical question then is: What role should the researcher assume in the course of this interaction? For example, should researchers allow personal or political values to enter their writing as a method of persuasion? As in the case of genre, and perhaps as an extension of it, here too qualitative researchers have many choices.

David Silverman (2006: 351–359) suggests that researchers can assume one of three roles in this context. First, there is the position of the 'scholar.' In this capacity, the researcher is interested in science for the sake of science. The second research role is that of a 'state counselor.' Here, the goal is to work closely with interested policy makers. In this role, sociologists might be viewed as social engineers who assist state bureaucrats in a joint effort to create a 'better' society. Finally, there is the 'partisan' role, where the sociologist sides with a particular group. In Silverman's words, 'the partisan seeks to provide the theoretical and factual resources for a political struggle aimed at transforming the assumptions through which both political and administrative games are played' (p. 265). The partisan role is best captured in an often quoted statement by Howard Becker in which he asks sociologists, 'Whose side are we on?' (1967: 239). Table 21.1 summarizes Silverman's three research roles.

Along with reflecting on their specific research roles, writers should also be responsive to the demands of their audience(s). As Anselm Strauss and Juliet Corbin put it, researchers should ask, 'What style can I use to reach each audience [i.e., academics, practitioners and laymen]?' and be aware that 'the style and shape of presentation should be sensitive to and reflect the targeted audience(s)' (1998: 256). Indeed, it is the absence of such awareness that characterizes novice technical writers. In her review of *Interacting with Audiences* (Blakeslee 2001), Janet Zepernick offers this useful list of audience-related problems that plague novice writers:

TABLE 21.1   *Silverman's three research roles*

Role	Politics	Commitment
Scholar	Liberal	Knowledge for knowledge's sake, protected by scholar's conscience
State counselor	Bureaucratic	Social engineering or enlightenment for policy makers
Partisan	Leftwing Rightwing	Knowledge to support both a political theory and political practice

Source: Adapted from Silverman (2006: 353)

- insufficient understanding of the audience's expectations,
- inability to predict the kinds of claims the audience will be prepared to accept, and
- unwillingness (or inability) to subordinate aspects of the work that the writer personally finds most interesting or most difficult to the interests and informational requirements of the audience. (2003: 245)

Summary

It can be argued that the ideal type of qualitative writing is a text that incorporates the following three elements into a well-balanced report:

- *Practice and craft of writing:* Conveying research ideas coherently.
- *Organization and genre:* Structuring the manuscript and presenting findings in line with one's chosen writing conventions and style.
- *Audience expectations and researcher role:* Being aware of and accountable to the demands of intended publication outlet and its consumers.

Attending to these criteria simultaneously amounts to understanding writing as rhetorical practice aimed at persuading a particular audience. In this context, writing is an ongoing and socially embedded practice (Van Maanen 2006: 14). More than just a means to convey ideas, writing becomes what Pertti Alasuutari calls a 'literary process' that

resembles riding a bicycle. Not in that once you have learned it you'll master it, but because riding a bike is based on consecutive repairments of balance. The staggerings or whole detours of the text have to be repaired over and over again so that they do not lead the story line in the wrong direction; and the rambling of the first draft cannot be seen in the final product. (1995: 178)

At the same time, it is worth considering that the 'perfect paper' is in some ways a fiction. In the words of Howard Becker: 'No report in any medium or genre, following no-matter-how-strict rule, will solve all problems, answer all questions, or avoid all potential troubles' (2007: 131). Thus, the best advice for writing good social science may be to keep writing and always be prepared to make compromises and adapt your text to suit the needs of your audience.

Future Prospects

There are, of course, numerous theoretical issues in the context of writing that demand further attention and point to the very philosophy of science. For example, we can ask: To what extent should researchers try to change audience expectations by experimenting with new genres and, in a sense, reinvent their field? This question relates to the larger issue of writing as an instrument of disciplinary change. One answer would be that the progress of science is one gradual accumulation of knowledge. Or as Karl Popper (1963) would put it, science follows a process of 'conjectures and refutations' whereby new knowledge tests and replaces old knowledge. In this context, writing is viewed as a medium for conveying facts. By contrast, if we adopt Thomas Kuhn's notion of 'paradigm shifts' (1996), writing social science becomes more politicized. Kuhn departs from Popperian philosophy by approaching scientific knowledge as a human activity that is conditioned by particular socio-historical forces. Therefore, to the extent that alternative writing challenges mainstream tropes, it should be encouraged as the fuel for change, or scientific progress. Whether the landscape of writing practices and expectations should be expanded or curbed will likely remain a matter of contention in the field of qualitative research.

A related area of interest, whose impact is yet to be fully understood, is the so-called information revolution and its effect on the genres, organization, and audiences of qualitative research. Specifically, the use of personal web pages and hypertext make it possible for authors to invent new non-linear texts that are instantly accessible by a global audience. The response from traditional publication outlets (i.e., book and journal publishers) to this challenge could dramatically transform the review process and audience expectations.

Questions

- What are the different ways in which a qualitative research manuscript could be organized?
- What are the different genres of writing qualitative research?
- What are some of the criticism against so-called alternative methods of writing qualitative research?
- What is the relationship between researcher role and audience expectations?

Recommended Reading

Becker, H. (1981) *Exploring Society Photographically*. Chicago: University of Chicago Press.

Behar, R. and D. Gordon (1995) *Women Writing Culture*. Berkeley, CA: University of California Press.

Denzin, N. (2000) Aesthetics and the practices of qualitative inquiry. *Qualitative Inquiry* 6: 256–265.

(Continued)

(Continued)

Gubrium, J. (2009) Curbing self-referential writing. Durham University: www.dur.ac.uk/writingacrossboundaries/writingonwriting/jaygubrium/

Moro, P. (2006) It takes a darn good writer: A review of ethnographic I. *Symbolic Interaction* 29(2): 265–269.

Rose, G. (2001) *Visual Methodologies*. London: Sage.

Silverman. D. (2006) *Interpreting Qualitative Data* (3rd ed.). London: Sage.

Van Maanen, J. (1988) *Tales of the Field*. Chicago: University of Chicago Press.

Wolcott, H. F. (2009) *Writing Up Qualitative Research* (3rd ed.). Thousand Oaks, CA: Sage.

Internet Links

Durham University's 'Writing on Writing': www.dur.ac.uk/writingacrossboundaries/writingonwriting/jaygubrium/

Durham University's 'Writing Across Boundaries':

www.dur.ac.uk/writingacrossboundaries/

The University of Queensland's PhD Writing Tips:

www.uq.edu.au/student-services/phdwriting/

References

Alasuutari, P. (1995) *Researching Culture: Qualitative Method and Cultural Studies*. London: Sage.

Atkinson, P. and Delamont, S. (2005) Analytic perspectives, in N. Denzin and Y. S. Lincoln (eds.) *The Handbook of Qualitative Research* (3rd ed.). Thousand Oaks, CA: Sage.

Bateson, G. and Mead, M. (1942) *The Balinese Character: A Photographic Analysis*. New York: New York Academy of Sciences.

Becker, H. (1967) Whose side are we on? *Social Problems*, 14: 239–247.

Becker, H. (1986) *Writing for Social Scientists: How to Start and Finish Your Thesis, Book, or Article*. Chicago: University of Chicago Press.

Becker, H. (2007) *Telling about Society*. Chicago: University of Chicago Press.

Blakeslee, A. (2001). *Interacting with Audiences: Social Influences on the Production of Scientific Writing*. Mahwah, NJ: Lawrence Erlbaum.

Chaplin, E. (1994) *Sociology and Visual Representation*. London: Routledge.

Clifford, J. and Marcus, G. (eds.) (1986) *Writing Culture: The Poetics and Politics of Ethnography*. Berkeley, CA: University of California Press.

Ellis, C. and Bochner, A. (1992) Telling and performing personal stories: The constraints of choice in abortion, in C. Ellis and A. Bochner (eds.) *Investigating Subjectivity*. Newbury Park, CA: Sage.

Goffman, E. (1979) *Gender Advertisements*. Cambridge, MA: Harvard University Press.

Gubrium, J. (2009) Curbing self-referential writing. Durham University: www.dur.ac.uk/writingacrossboundaries/writingonwriting/jaygubrium/

Gubrium, J. and Holstein, J. (1997) *The New Language of Qualitative Method*. New York: Oxford University Press.

Harper, D. (2005) What's new visually?, in N. Denzin and Y. S. Lincoln (eds.) *The Handbook of Qualitative Research* (3rd ed.). Thousand Oaks, CA: Sage.

Kuhn, T. (1996) *The Structure of Scientific Revolutions*. Chicago: University of Chicago Press.

Moro, P. (2006) It takes a darn good writer: A review of ethnographic I. *Symbolic Interaction*, 29(2): 265–269.

Popper, K. (1963) *Conjectures and Refutations: The Growth of Scientific Knowledge*. London: Routledge.

Rambo, C. (1996) My mother is mentally retarded, in C. Ellis and A. Bochner (eds.) *Composing Ethnography*. Walnut Creek, CA: Altamira Press.

Reed-Danahay, D. (1997) *Auto/Ethnography: Rewriting the Self and the Social*. Oxford: Berg.

Silverman, D. (2006) *Interpreting Qualitative Data* (3rd ed.). London: Sage.

Silverman, D. (2007) *A Very Short, Fairly Interesting and Reasonably Cheap Book about Qualitative Research*. London: Sage.

Stasz, C. (1979) The early history of visual sociology, in J. Wagner (ed.) *Images of Information: Still Photography in the Social Sciences*. Beverly Hills, CA: Sage.

Strauss, A. and Corbin, J. (1998) *Basics of Qualitative Research: Techniques and Procedures for Developing Grounded Theory* (2nd ed.). Thousand Oaks, CA: Sage.

Van Maanen, J. (1988) *Tales of the Field*. Chicago: University of Chicago Press.

Van Maanen, J. (2006) Ethnography then and now. *Qualitative Research in Organizations and Management*, 1(1): 13–21.

Whyte, W. F. (1949) *Street Corner Society*. Chicago: University of Chicago Press.

Wolcott, H. F. (2009) *Writing Up Qualitative Research* (3rd ed.). Thousand Oaks, CA: Sage.

Wolf, A. (1990) Books vs. articles: Two ways of publishing sociology. *Sociological Forum*, 5(3): 477–489.

Zepernick, J. S. (2003) Review of the book *Interacting with Audiences: Social Influences on the Production of Scientific Writing* by A. Blakeslee, 2001. *Journal of Business and Technical Communication*, 17(2): 243–247.

PART VIII

THE WIDER COMMUNITY

Addressing Social Problems through Qualitative Research

22

Michael Bloor

Abstract

This chapter explores two case studies which provide illustrative details of two different but related approaches for researchers who wish to address social problems and who are also sceptical of the possibilities of extensive influence among the policy-making community. Both of the approaches aim to influence practitioners rather than policy-makers and both link particularly well with qualitative research methods. In the first case study, an ethnographic research project is viewed as an analogue or partial paradigm of successful practitioner work, in this case outreach work among male prostitutes: in effect, the ethnography may be viewed as a demonstration or pilot outreach project. In the second case study, ethnographic work provides the material and the stimulation for practitioners to evaluate and revise particular facets of their own service provision.

Keywords:

ethnography, social problems, practice-relevant research, policy-relevant research, case study.

Social Researchers as Social Engineers?

In Carey's (1975) social history of the 'Chicago School' of sociology he writes that in the 1920s the foremost practitioners of the foremost school of sociology were divided about how sociological knowledge should be applied. Should it be used to influence policy-makers? Or (and here lies a surprise) should sociologists intervene in social problems directly as consulting professionals, like clinicians or architects? Some hundred years earlier Auguste Comte had proposed a similar priestly cadre of sociologists to direct society along enlightened (and Enlightenment) paths. But I was shocked to realize that, as late as the 1920s, my intellectual forebears could hanker after the power to re-engineer social life and institutions to their nostrums. It was the absence of that power, rather than humility, which thwarted them: in Carey's analysis (1975: 71–94), it was the lack of the kind of institutionalized authority which medicine exercises over a lay clientele, rather than any acknowledged deficiency in knowledge or in technical competence, which determined the path along which sociology would develop. Sociologists and other social researchers eventually opted to set out their stalls as scientists rather than professionals, and the West was largely spared the directive intervention of social experts (the peoples of the Soviet Union were less fortunate).

Social Researchers as 'Enlighteners' of Policy-Makers?

Since the 1960s, the more limited aspiration of sociologists to influence policy-makers has also been under attack. It was pointed out by various critics that the policy community rarely sought *policies* from researchers: instead, research would be commissioned to confirm a preferred policy option, or perhaps to delay a necessary but inconvenient intervention. Bulmer (1982), in *The Uses of Social Research*, was one of those who sought to redefine an influential role for social science in the face of these criticisms. Taking up Janowitz's (1972) distinction between the 'engineering' and 'enlightenment' models of policy research, Bulmer argued that research cannot engineer changes of policy, but it can have an important indirect impact on the policy climate through processes of intellectual association and influence. Silverman (2001) has termed this the 'state counsellor' role and has gently ridiculed how Bulmer's book on 'the uses of social research' turns out to be solely about the uses of social research for policy-makers.

Both the 'enlightenment' and 'engineering' models have long been under attack from advocates of the 'critical social research' model. Becker (1967), for example, posed the rhetorical question 'whose side are we on?' and argued for a partisan sociology that spoke up for the underdogs against the elites, elites which would include policy-makers in their number. Today Becker's question is widely believed to defy a simple answer, with researchers experiencing cross-cutting responsibilities to their research participants, to funding agencies, to gatekeepers and to their colleagues in the scientific community (Social Research Association, 2003). And Becker's rhetoric of sides is thought to be intellectually disabling, embracing what Silverman (2001: 260) has called 'its prior commitment to a revealed truth' (the plight of the underdog, and so on).

Hammersley (1995) has characterized all three models (engineering, enlightenment and critical) as different varieties of Enlightenment models with a capital E, since they all endorse certain Enlightenment ideas originating with the French 'Encyclopaedists' of the eighteenth century, namely that social life can be improved by planned intervention derived from accumulated scientific knowledge, itself the product of social research. In late modern society all three tenets of the Enlightenment paradigm have come under postmodernist criticism: it is no longer universally accepted that planned intervention is capable of bringing about desirable social change, or that scientific knowledge can facilitate this, or that social research can produce such knowledge. Hammersley's review of these postmodernist criticisms leads him to the assessment that they serve to qualify, rather than demolish, the possibility of a social impact for social research: the scope for and feasibility of successful policy intervention has been overestimated in the Enlightenment Project and the role of research in bringing change about has been exaggerated and misunderstood, but this does not mean that social improvement is impossible or that knowledge lacks all authority.

A Practitioner Audience for Social Research?

The policy community is not the sole audience for qualitative social research. Silverman (2010) has written about the needs of lay audiences for qualitative social research: the general public want ideas for reform, suggestions on how to manage better and get better services, and assurances that others have shared similar experiences and problems to their own. In addition, sociologists who have conducted research on sociological aspects of health and medicine have long been aware that there are also audiences of practitioners (clinicians and other health professionals) for social research. Practitioner-oriented social research has also been the subject of revisionist criticisms, which are considered below, but first this chapter reports on two quite different pieces of qualitative research designed for practitioner audiences.

The first case study reported in this chapter is a street ethnography of HIV-related risk behaviour among Glasgow male prostitutes. Safer and unsafe commercial sexual encounters were compared: unsafe encounters were found to be associated with control of the sexual encounter by the clients of prostitutes; safer sex was associated with particular techniques of power exercised by prostitutes. These findings indicate possible lines of successful intervention for those engaged in sexual health promotion, while the fieldwork methods and experience offered lessons for the design of successful outreach work in this area. The second case study is a comparative ethnography of variations in therapeutic community practice. The comparative design highlighted a number of features of good therapeutic practice found in particular communities that could profitably be adopted elsewhere, while the researcher's close fieldwork relationships with local therapeutic community practitioners encouraged the practitioners to experiment with particular new methods of working.

Case A: Male Prostitutes' HIV-Related Risk Behaviour

The Need for Services

Prior to the HIV epidemic, targeted services for male prostitutes hardly existed in the UK and did not exist at all in Glasgow. Not all male prostitutes have much need of services, but others have multiple and complex problems (legal problems, health problems, housing problems, financial problems) which are sometimes unpresented to, or inadequately addressed by, service-providers. The illegality of male prostitution made specialist service development difficult: most Glasgow male prostitutes contacted in our study were below the then age of consent for homosexual acts and many of these acts did not occur in private; although the police adopted a stance of qualified toleration to female street prostitution, whereby female street prostitution was 'policed' rather than suppressed, that toleration was never extended to male street prostitution. And male service-providers with an interest in providing services for male prostitutes were vulnerable to misconstructions of their motives.

The HIV epidemic, along with its toll on lives and health, represented an opportunity to change the policy climate in respect of male prostitution. The situation was analogous to that in the drugs services, where a range of services (most notably syringe exchanges) was put in place for existing drug injectors who were not motivated to abstain from drugs. This new drugs policy, which became known as that of 'harm reduction', argued that 'the spread of HIV is a greater danger to individual and public health than drug misuse . . . [and that] services that aim to minimize HIV risk behaviour by all available means, should take precedence in development plans' (Advisory Council on the Misuse of Drugs, 1988). In similar fashion, it became possible to argue the case for services targeted at male prostitutes which had as their priority not the elimination of prostitution, but the minimization of individual and public health risks.

Study methods and service provision

The findings and the methodology of the study have been described elsewhere (Bloor, 1995; Bloor et al., 1993). After pilot work, six different sites – two parks, two pubs and two public lavatories – were selected for time-sampling; non-streetworking prostitutes (escorts, masseurs and call men) were contacted through their advertisements and the study's own advertisement in the gay press. The ethnographic fieldwork was conducted in pairs for security purposes. Participants were contacted by a combination of cold-contacting and snowballing. It was recognized from the outset that the fieldwork also offered opportunities for health promotion: relations between fieldworkers and research participants can never be scientifically neutral (Hammersley and Atkinson, 1995) and an attempt to preserve a fictional neutrality should never be used as an excuse for failing to attempt to save lives. The Greater Glasgow Health Board provided condoms suitable for oral and for anal sex for the researchers to distribute (when the fieldwork started condoms suitable for anal sex were not freely commercially available); an advice leaflet was also handed out which gave advice on HIV prevention and also gave contact numbers for HIV/AIDS counselling and for other relevant services such as welfare rights and homelessness.

Study Findings

If the handing-out of condoms and advice leaflets could be thought to generate a 'reporting bias', discouraging the reporting of unsafe commercial sex, then such discouragement can only have been marginal because at least a third of those prostitutes contacted reported unsafe sex with at least some of their current commercial partners (unsafe sex was defined, following the Terrence Higgins Trust, as anal sex with or without a condom, because of the greater risk of condom failure in anal sex). Unsafe commercial sex was associated with client control. In contrast to female street prostitution, where safer commercial sex was almost always practised and the women assumed directive control of the encounter (McKeganey and Barnard, 1992), in many male prostitute–client encounters it was the client who assumed control and decided on matters such as the type of sex and its location. Safer commercial sex among male prostitutes was associated with particular strategies of power to wrest the initiative away from clients. Seeking payment up front (universally practised by female prostitutes) was one such successful strategy. Getting payment up front was not popular with the clients, who feared (with some justification) that the prostitute might 'do a runner', but the minority of male prostitutes in the sample who *did* insist on prior payment were all currently practising safer commercial sex.

However, getting the money up front was not the only successful countervailing strategy of power used by male prostitutes to insist on safer sex. Male prostitution was often a highly covert and ambiguous activity, few words were exchanged and it is not even always clear to both parties that the encounter is a commercial one. Safer sex was likely to be associated with any techniques that served to dispel the ambiguity that surrounded the encounter and made type of sex (and prices) a matter for overt discussion, as in the following field note:

> His procedure was to stand at the urinal. The client would come and stand beside him. When the coast was clear, the client would put out a hand and he would immediately say 'I'm sorry but I charge.' Some would leave at that point. With the remainder he'd negotiate a rate. He would accept 10 pounds but sometimes got 20 pounds… He always did hand jobs or oral sex. … If clients asked him for anal sex he told them to eff off.

The substitution of overt negotiations between prostitutes and clients for the furtive and largely non-verbal exchanges characteristic of many encounters would have advantages beyond the prevention of HIV infection and of other sexually transmitted diseases. One considerable advantage might lie in an attendant reduction in the levels of violence surrounding male prostitution. Rapes, muggings and assaults (of clients by prostitutes, of prostitutes by clients and of both prostitutes and clients by 'queer bashing' third parties) were commonplace; during the 16-month fieldwork period, 3 of our 32 research subjects were charged with assault and a fourth was imprisoned. Many (but not all) of these violent altercations were disputes about money. There were no 'going rates' for the various sexual services on offer: prostitutes took what money they could and, without prior agreement on charges (sometimes without even prior agreement that a charge was to be levied), the scope for violent disputes was considerable, as is illustrated in the following field note:

> ['Sammy' said he'd] never been cheated out of his money: he'd make sure he always got his money (this was said with a sudden hard emphasis ...). He and 'Kenny' laughingly recalled an altercation with one of 'Colin's' punters [i.e. clients]. Colin was demanding twenty-five pounds and the punter swore he was only due fifteen pounds, refusing to hand over the extra ten pounds. Kenny, in his cynical way, was disinclined to believe Colin, but Sammy said he'd rather believe a mate than some dirty old punter. Sammy had intervened, whipped a knife out and held it in front of his face (this was mimed out for our benefit). The punter instantly pulled out the extra cash, shot off and had never been seen at the toilets since.

Implications for Service Provision

This research project had two possible policy pay-offs. First, it indicated how both unsafe commercial sex and violence could be reduced, namely through encouraging male prostitutes to engage in overt negotiations with clients. And, second, it indicated a possible medium for that encouragement, namely outreach work associated with condom distribution at regular prostitution sites.

Outreach work, taking services to clients rather than waiting for clients to attend at agencies, is the only means of delivering services to clients who are unable or unwilling to attend agencies. At the time this study was conducted, Glasgow had no outreach project targeted at male prostitutes: there was a drop-in centre for female prostitutes, but no outreach workers were attached to it and no men were admitted to the drop-in premises. Ethnographic fieldwork, in its protracted and regular contacts with research subjects, has much in common with services outreach work and it was therefore possible for the ethnographic study to take on the character of a local feasibility study for a male prostitute outreach service, demonstrating to the sceptical that appreciable numbers of male prostitutes were working in Glasgow, that levels of HIV-related risk behaviour were high and that outreach contact could be established. Moreover, the nature of the fieldwork contact that was established augured well for a future outreach service: large quantities of condoms were distributed (to clients as well as prostitutes); even highly socially isolated individuals with no contact with other prostitutes proved contactable; working relationships were established with important local individuals such as bar-owners and managers, toilet attendants and (at an appropriate distance) the police; and the project proceeded without threat to the safety of the ethnographers.

Throughout the fieldwork period I had briefed public health personnel, social work staff and AIDS charity workers about project developments and provisional findings. At the conclusion of the fieldwork period, I had arranged (with the permission of my research participants) to introduce them to a local social worker who was to be employed as an outreach worker, covering the same prostitution sites that I had covered during ethnographic fieldwork. The introductions were accomplished but the planned outreach post was 'frozen' (along with other local authority posts) owing to a local authority budgetary crisis associated with non-payment of the 'poll tax' (aka 'the community charge', a form of local authority taxation that was abandoned soon after its introduction because of widespread unpopularity and widespread non-payment). Nevertheless, the commitment to a male prostitution outreach service had been made and the establishment of such a service was merely postponed, taking place at a later date.

Case B: Principles of Good Therapeutic Community Practice

Study Methods

Therapeutic communities are found in a variety of shapes and sizes (residential and non-residential, long term and short term), catering for a range of client groups (psychiatric patients, ex-psychiatric patients, children with learning difficulties, adults with learning difficulties, drug users and alcoholics, prisoners, and so on), with a range of different staffing arrangements, but having in common an approach to therapeutic work as an essentially cognitive activity which can transform any mundane event in the community (be it lavatory cleaning, or complaining about the noise) by redefining that event in the light of some therapeutic paradigm (Bloor et al., 1988). The nature of the paradigm may vary from community to community (Association of Therapeutic Communities, 2009), but the redefinition of the event (as showing responsibility, say, or seeking out a new and less pathogenic way of relating to others) as an occasion or a topic for therapy sets it apart and transforms it, much as the profane is transformed into the sacred by religious belief and ceremony.

I and two colleagues (Neil McKeganey and Dick Fonkert) conducted a comparative ethnography of eight different therapeutic communities studied by one or another of us over a period of about 10 years. Because all the individual studies involved the collection of similar (participant observation) data on the same general topic (the treatment process), it was possible to reuse those data for a single comparative study which avoided the usual constraint of qualitative methods, namely that breadth of coverage must be sacrificed for depth. As a result, we were able to compare practice across a wide range of contrasting therapeutic community settings – two contrasting residential psychiatric units (studied by McKeganey), a Camphill Rudolf Steiner school for children with learning difficulties (McKeganey), a 'concept house' for drug users (Fonkert), a 'foster family' care facility (Bloor), two contrasting halfway houses for disturbed adolescents (Bloor), and a psychiatric day hospital (Bloor). The research methods have been described elsewhere (Bloor et al., 1988).

Comparison as a Stimulus to Practice Change

Any ethnography is essentially comparative in approach. When the ethnographer is making field notes, he or she is selecting from a cornucopia of continuing sense data those moments that seem to him or her to be of special significance. When analysing the field notes, the ethnographer is juxtaposing and comparing numerous similar and contrasting field note accounts. And when writing the ethnography the writer is weighing various different accounts in order to illustrate and develop the argument in the text. Of course, these comparative judgements are not confined to ethnography: similar evaluative judgements are made on a continuing and routine basis by all research participants. It therefore follows that one possible *use* of ethnography is to assist in these everyday comparative judgements: rich description of particular kinds of therapeutic practice, for example, can assist practitioners in making evaluative judgements about their own practices, preserving what seems to them good practice and experimenting with the adoption of new practices where this seems appropriate. Lincoln and Guba (1985) have termed this the 'transferability' of research findings. In effect, reading an ethnography of therapeutic communities can be like visiting other communities and being drawn to reconsider one's everyday routines in the light of contrasted experience: McKeganey has described how a group visit to a second community led staff and residents at the 'Faswells' psychiatric unit to try to make mealtimes much more of a community and therapeutic occasion, such as the group had observed to be the case at the visited community (Bloor et al., 1988: 180). Drawing practitioners' attention to contrasting practices in research feedback sessions can stimulate changes in practitioner practice.

Provided that the practitioner audience retains some autonomy of function and judgement in their everyday work (arguably a minimum definition of professional practice (Freidson, 1970)), then any ethnography can thus serve as a stimulus to practice change and a number of sociological ethnographies have found their way onto professional training courses for this reason (indeed our comparative ethnography was used on at least one therapeutic community training course). However, my fellow researchers and I wished to go beyond merely passively providing opportunities for such comparative practitioner judgements; we wished actively to draw the attention of readers to particular features of practice in one or two communities which, it seemed to us, might be adopted with profit by other communities. The utility of ethnographic texts for practitioner audiences can be enhanced by making explicit for readers those silent and implicit researcher judgements that have led to particular practices being recorded and analysed in the first place. No authoritative scientific judgement is intended here, I simply list below some practices that seemed to my colleagues and myself to be worthy of wider dissemination. The final test of their utility would lie in whether practitioners themselves shared our judgement and found themselves able to adopt the practices successfully; successful adoption in the unique circumstances of individual communities may not always be possible, perhaps because of a clash with other valued practices, or inadequate resources, or time-tabling problems. The practices we commended were as follows (in no particular order of importance):

1   giving fellow residents the responsibility for keeping residents in treatment;
2   ways of increasing residents' awareness of the changeability of the community structure;
3   the 'after-group' as a way of promoting resident reflectivity;
4   the attendance of residents at staff change-over meetings;
5   the 'tight house' as a way of countering institutionalism;
6   resident selection of participating staff;
7   the offering of alternative sources of satisfaction to junior staff.

There is no space here to enlarge on all these possible means of improving therapeutic community practice (see Bloor et al., 1988: 172–185, for a fuller account); instead I shall simply expand upon the first listed practice, that of giving residents the responsibility for keeping residents in treatment, as was the case in a therapeutic community in a psychiatric day hospital.

Keeping Residents in Treatment

All non-custodial treatment institutions face problems associated with the premature departure or self-discharge of residents. In studies of 'concept houses' for the treatment of drug users, for example, high reported success rates in remaining drug-free among those ex-residents who *complete* their courses have to be set against the fact that up to three-quarters of enrollees may discharge themselves prematurely, against staff advice (see, e.g., Volkman and Cressey's (1963) evaluation of the first concept house, Synanon).

No therapeutic community is more vulnerable to premature self-discharge than a psychiatric day hospital, where patients who wish to drop out have the simple expedient of failing to turn up for treatment on the following day. Treatment at the day hospital was conducted on a group basis and followed the principle of 'reality confrontation' (Morrice, 1979), the reflection back to patients, informally and in formal group therapy sessions, that their conduct is unacceptable and the depiction of the therapeutic community as a locale where new and less pathogenic social behaviours can be experimented with and adopted. Although confrontation could be manifest in many forms other than angry denunciation, staff were aware that the treatment method put pressures on patients which could lead to self-discharge or even to suicidal impulses. To avoid premature discharge and self-harm, there was a convention in the day hospital (understood by staff and all but novice patients alike) that fellow-patients should provide the necessary comfort and support for patients to remain in treatment, as in the fieldnote extract below:

> This afternoon considerable pressure was put on 'Dawn': she had spoken of her feelings of hopelessness and depression, her failure to 'work' in the group, and her feeling that she ought to leave the day hospital. Several staff members had already left for prior appointments. 'Edith' (staff) said she had seen Dawn glance at the clock several times: now was her chance to end it (the group). Her voice breaking, Dawn picked up her bag, said she'd end it all right, and rushed out of the room. Edith did nothing to stop her. At 'Harry's' (patient) bidding, 'Olive' (patient) went after her, caught her up in the toilets and made her promise to come again tomorrow. Once before she'd dashed off and her fellow-patients set off after her. Indeed, this dashing after bolting patients is a fairly common occurrence – Edith could predict that Dawn would be looked after.

Moreover, patients who did silently discharge themselves by failing to return to the day hospital could expect a delegation of fellow-patients visiting them at their homes, urging them to return. Determined would-be defaulters had either to announce and defend their decisions in the formal groups or to resort to subterfuge – failing to answer the door and even, in one case, leaving the country.

The patient or resident culture plays an important, even crucial, part in the treatment process in all therapeutic communities. Thus, requiring that patients/residents undertake the responsibility for keeping their fellows in treatment would be simply an extension of the active patient/resident therapeutic role. Nevertheless, such an extension of patients'/residents' responsibilities, if successful, could have an appreciable influence on patterns of self-discharge in many communities. At 'Ashley', for example, one of the two halfway houses for disturbed adolescents in the study, although the residents were prepared to welcome and support new arrivals, established residents who chose to self-discharge/abscond were never confronted or persuaded otherwise by their fellows. In one celebrated instance during my fieldwork at the house, almost the entire resident group knew beforehand of one resident's planned 'escape', which involved hanging around on the street outside to intercept the postman and appropriate his 'giro' (welfare benefits cheque) before catching an inter-city bus. No one chose to dissuade him and one fellow-resident even helped him carry his possessions to the bus station.

Feeding Back Findings

Not only were these findings reported in the academic and practitioner press and in a paper to an international conference of practitioners, but also findings were fed back to individual communities involved in the research. At Ashley halfway house, this impressionistic feedback focused on how one might combat premature self-discharge:

> I had previously said that I would give the staff some feedback on my thoughts about the house before I left ... I'd given some thought to this in advance and had decided to concentrate on one problem I thought was perhaps inadequately attended to – premature departure by residents ... and a possible solution – a stronger resident culture. I spent an evening talking about this with the warden last night ... and she brought it up in the staff group this afternoon.
>
> It led to a lot of discussion: general agreement that the problem was there.
>
> At the end of the [weekly] community meeting [the warden] said that she'd like (after her return from holiday) a special meeting of the community to discuss the problem of people leaving.

Ashley was not the only study community where the comparative analysis acted as a spur to modifications in practice. Sociological description of everyday therapeutic work can act as a stimulus to practitioners to re-examine their practice and perhaps modify it in response to comparative data. This stimulus to change can be increased by choosing certain forms of dissemination in preference to others, for example by explicit highlighting of examples of good practice, and by personal briefings as well as written reports.

Conclusion

Policy influence for social researchers is quite possibly a chimera, a 'unicorn among the cedars' which is glimpsed tantalizingly from time to time but is always elusive. Some might say that policy-makers themselves are a chimera: a distinguished epidemiologist of my acquaintance claims never to have met one. He searched in vain for the fountainheads of health service policy until in old age the truth struck him that no one knowingly makes policy; for reasons perhaps of protective coloration everyone is convinced that they are mere policy-implementers, simply interpreting and elaborating edicts passed down from some more august authority. Analogous, if less colourful, arguments have been constructed by some empirical researchers of policy processes (Manning, 1989; Rock, 1987), namely that policy is a situated discourse, a set of tacit assumptions and implicit meanings found within particular offices and occupational groupings.

It is this policy discourse, this amalgam of committee asides, gossip and unspoken assumptions, that Bulmer would seek to influence through the gentle diffusion of ideas and research findings. But social researchers are rare visitors to these corridors and committee rooms: their capacity for cultural diffusion is minimal. The argument in this chapter has been that the real opportunities for social research influence lie closer to the coalface than they do to head office, that the real opportunities for influence lie in relations with practitioners, not with the managers of practice.

This role for qualitative researchers as practitioner helpmeets will not be found by some to be wholly satisfactory. All practitioner–client relationships (be they outreach worker–prostitute relationships, or therapeutic community staff–resident/patient relationships) are power relationships. In a Foucauldian analysis (see, e.g., Foucault, 1980), power cannot be wished or legislated away, it is inherent in all relationships. Therapeutic advance has as its corollary the extension of the controlling therapeutic gaze: the growth of public health medicine since the nineteenth century, for example, has brought great health benefits, but it has also subjected populations to increasing surveillance and regulation (Armstrong, 1983). Surveillance as a technique of power is increasingly complemented by other techniques, most notably that of 'pastoral care' (Foucault, 1981), whereby clients of agencies find themselves 'shepherded' into disciplinary relationships with practitioners whose avowed goals are merely those of care and advice. Assisting in the extension of outreach work to new populations, or suggesting ways to increase the effectiveness of therapeutic community practice, are each alike analysable as endeavours which tighten the disciplinary grip of experts on citizens. In a new twist on Becker's old 'whose side are we on?' question, it may be argued that researchers should be assisting not in the extension of power, but in the extension of resistance – resistance to meddlesome interference in prostitutes' street dealings, and resistance to expert orchestration of patients' private lives. The opposite of power is not its absence, but the resistance it provokes; researchers, so the argument goes, should be laying the groundwork for citizen resistance rather than fostering the extension and effectiveness of expert power. Foucault himself did not did not follow up his celebrated analysis of prisoner surveillance, *Discipline and Punish* (Foucault, 1977), with attempts to influence prison staff, but with work for prisoners' groups such as the 'CAP', the Prisoners' Action Committee (Major-Poetzl, 1983: 46–54).

However, this critical view of sociological influence on practitioners is a new version of an old song, the song of the Leninist vanguard party which always knows best, having learned the Lessons of History. It matters not, in this critical view, that male prostitutes may welcome the provision of a service where there was none before, or that patients/residents in therapeutic communities may welcome the chance to play a fuller part in the treatment process by providing comfort and support to their fellows. What matters is resistance to experts' disciplinary power. Yet if the critical analysts are themselves experts, what kind of disciplinary relationship do they have with their audience? Should not they too be resisted? It follows that we can skirt these sophistries: where citizens themselves commend the work of practitioners, then it is not the place of researchers to murmur of false consciousness and demand resistance to pastoral care.

Unsustainable suggested roles for researchers	Problems
Researchers as 'social engineers'	• Low technical competence • Lack of institutional authority
Researchers as policy formulators/evaluators	• Policy-makers rarely seek policies from researchers • Policy-makers may commission research on policies in order to delay evaluation
Researchers as 'enlighteners' of policy-makers	Researchers have few opportunities to mingle with policy-makers, as opposed to practitioners
Researchers as emancipators	Involves a prior commitment to an objective reality revealed to the researcher, but not to policy-makers, practitioners or laity

This issue (of whether or not social research should seek to assist the resistance of clients and patients) is part of a broader debate about the epistemological status of social research, about whether value neutrality can and should remain a constitutive principle of social research. The claim that social research can and should be value neutral is under attack from two sides. On one side, battle has been joined by those who argue that research should be explicitly politically participatory, embracing particular political aims, such as combating racism or patriarchy. On the other side, battle has been joined by those who argue that *no* practice or policy prescriptions can be offered by researchers under any circumstances, since all knowledge is socially constructed and there are no grounds for the researcher to claim superior knowledge.

The argument about participatory research is perhaps seen most clearly in the responses which greeted the publication of Foster's (1990) findings on the lack of evidence for racist practices in British schools. Foster found little evidence that black pupils were treated unfairly in lessons or that they were misallocated to ability groups; moreover, he re-examined the evidence of racism found in earlier studies and found it methodologically flawed. The study generated a considerable critical response from those committed to some version of anti-racism. Hammersley's (1995) review of the controversy firmly supports Foster's position against various implicit and explicit charges, notably that as a middle-class white male he was experientially disabled from collecting and understanding evidence of institutional racism, and that the primary objective of research is not the production of knowledge but the changing of society.

The argument of the 'strict constructivists' (the term is Best's, 1989) that researchers should be silent on social problems (having no basis for claiming superior knowledge, or 'reality claims') was stated succinctly by Woolgar and Pawluch (1985). Best's edited volume (and especially his own concluding chapter) relates some of the responses to Woolgar and Pawluch's paper. He argues the case for a 'contextual constructivist' position in distinction to the 'strict constructivist' position. Best is doubtful about whether it is practically possible to achieve the strict constructivists' goal of analyses wholly free of assumptions about objective reality; he cites various examples of how such assumptions may creep in at the backdoor of such analyses – all our writing and thinking is saturated in reality claims. Contextual constructivists, in contrast, may collaborate with collectivity members in examining and debating competing policy claims.

It seems, therefore, that qualitative researchers *may* address social problems and that they can address them most effectively by influencing practitioner practice. Qualitative research has a two-fold advantage in these processes of influence: one advantage relates to influencing practitioners who are the researcher's research participants, and the second advantage relates to influencing practitioners who are the wider audience for the research findings. In respect of practitioners who are research participants, qualitative researchers can call upon their pre-existing research relationships with their research subjects as a resource for ensuring an attentive and even sympathetic response to their research findings. In respect of other practitioners (who are not research subjects), the qualitative researcher has the advantage that the research methods allow rich descriptions of everyday practice which enable practitioner audiences imaginatively to juxtapose their own everyday practices with the research description. There is therefore an opportunity for practitioners to make evaluative judgements about their own practices and experiment with the adoption of new approaches described in the research findings. Relatedly, where specialist services (such as male prostitute outreach services) do not currently exist, qualitative research can provide detailed descriptions of the circumstances and behaviour of potential service-users such that material assistance is given with the design of targeted services. Shaw (1996) has developed at length the argument that qualitative methods can provide a paradigm or exemplar for practitioners seeking to reflect upon and modify their work practices.

Practitioners may not always have the local autonomy to develop new services to new target populations of clients, but all practitioners have the autonomy to modify their everyday work practices. In seeking the chimera of policy influence, sociologists rather neglected how research findings can address social problems through the encouragement of modifications and developments in practitioners' everyday practices.

Summary: Qualitative Researchers Addressing Social Problems through Influence on Practitioners' Practices

Advantages	Alleged disadvantages
• Qualitative researchers can capitalize on fieldwork relationships with practitioners to stimulate interest in their findings	• Assisting practitioners in improving service delivery may be viewed as conspiring with experts against the laity
• The rich descriptions of everyday practice found in qualitative research allow practitioners to compare their own practices with those reported in the research	• Researchers should be silent on social problems having no basis for superior knowledge
• New practices can be adopted from research descriptions	• The scope for successful changes in practice is frequently overestimated
• Ethnographies may even provide a partial model for new outreach services	• Practitioner autonomy is limited, especially in the creation of new services

Questions

- What is meant by the 'Enlightenment models' of social policy research and what are the main problems with each model?
- What kinds of sociological research might attract a 'practitioner' audience? Why might they be attractive to practitioners? Illustrate your answer with examples.
- Whose side are social researchers on and why?

Acknowledgements

I wish to thank Ian Shaw, Anssi Peräkylä, Clive Seale and David Silverman for their helpful comments on an earlier draft of this chapter. All the research reported on here was supported by the Medical Research Council. I wish to thank Marina Barnard, Andrew Finlay and Neil McKeganey for their help as my co-fieldworkers in the male prostitution study and I wish to thank Dick Fonkert and Neil McKeganey for their help in the comparative analysis of the therapeutic communities data.

Recommended Reading

The section on 'generalizability' in Anssi Peräkylä's chapter elsewhere in this volume addresses cognate issues.

Hammersley, M. (1995) *The Politics of Social Research*. London: Sage.

A comprehensive guide to the inevitable limitations researchers face in influencing policy.

Heath, C. and Luff, P. (1992) 'Collaboration and control: crisis management and multimedia technology in London Underground line control rooms', *Journal of Computer Supported Cooperative Work*, 1: 69–94.

A good early example of 'workplace studies', analysing workplace interaction and claimed by conversation analysts and video analysts to have high practical utility for practitioners and managers.

Shaw, I. (1996) *Evaluating in Practice*. Aldershot: Ashgate.

Offers suggestions on a closer relationship between research and practice.

Silverman, D. (2010) *Doing Qualitative Research: A Practical Handbook*. London: Sage.

Chapter 27 considers the different audiences for social research.

References

Advisory Council on the Misuse of Drugs (1988) *AIDS and Drug Misuse: Part One*. London: Department of Health and Social Security.

Armstrong, D. (1983) *Political Anatomy of the Body: Medical Knowledge in Britain in the Twentieth Century*. Cambridge: Cambridge University Press.

Association of Therapeutic Communities (2009) 'What is a TC?': www.therapeuticcommunities.org/index.php?option=com_content&view=article&id=76&Itemid=94 (accessed 22 December 2009).

Becker, H. (1967) 'Whose side are we on?', *Social Problems*, 14: 239–248.

Best, J. (ed.) (1989) *Images of Issues: Typifying Contemporary Social Problems*. Hawthorne, NY: Aldine de Gruyter.

Bloor, M. (1995) *The Sociology of HIV Transmission*. London: Sage.

Bloor, M., McKeganey, N. and Fonkert, D. (1988) *One Foot in Eden: A Sociological Study of a Range of Therapeutic Community Practice*. London: Routledge.

Bloor, M., Barnard, M., Finlay, A. and McKeganey, N. (1993) 'HIV-related risk practices among Glasgow male prostitutes: Reframing concepts of risk behaviour', *Medical Anthropology Quarterly*, 7: 1–19.

Bulmer, M. (1982) *The Uses of Social Research*. London: Allen & Unwin.

Carey, J. (1975) *Sociology and Public Affairs: The Chicago School*. London: Sage.

Foster, P. (1990) *Policy and Practice in Multicultural and Antiracist Education*. London: Routledge.

Foucault, M. (1977) *Discipline and Punish*. London: Allen Lane.

Foucault, M. (1980) 'The eye of power', in C. Gordon (ed.), *Power/Knowledge: Selected Interviews and Other Writings 1972–1977*. Brighton: Harvester.

Foucault, M. (1981) 'Omnes et singulatim: Towards a criticism of political reason', in S. McMurrin (ed.), *The Tanner Lectures on Human Values II*. Salt Lake City: University of Utah Press.

Freidson, E. (1970) *Profession of Medicine*. New York: Dodds Mead.

Hammersley, M. (1995) *The Politics of Social Research*. London: Sage.

Hammersley, M. and Atkinson, P. (1995) *Ethnography: Principles in Practice* (2nd edn). London: Routledge.

Janowitz, M. (1972) *Sociological Models and Social Policy*. Morristown, NJ: General Earning Systems.

Lincoln, Y. and Guba, E. (1985) *Naturalistic Enquiry*. Beverley Hills, CA: Sage.

Manning, P. (1989) 'Studying policies in the field', in J. Gubrium and D. Silverman (eds), *The Politics of Field Research: Sociology Beyond Enlightenment*. London: Sage. pp. 213–235.

Major-Poetzl, P. (1983) *Michel Foucault's Archaeology of Western Culture*. Chapel Hill: University of North Carolina Press.

McKeganey, N. and Barnard, M. (1992) *AIDS, Drugs and Sexual Risk: Lives in the Balance*. Milton Keynes: Open University Press.

Morrice, J.K. (1979) 'Basic concepts, a critical review', in R. Hinshelwood and N. Manning (eds), *Therapeutic Communities: Reflections and Progress*. London: Routledge & Kegan Paul. pp. 94–111.

Rock, P. (1987) *A View From the Shadows: Policy Making in the Solicitor General's Office*. Oxford: Oxford University Press.

Shaw, I. (1996) *Evaluating in Practice*. Aldershot: Ashgate.

Silverman, D. (2001) *Interpreting Qualitative Data: Methods of Analysing Talk, Text and Interaction* (2nd edn). London: Sage.

Silverman, D. (2010) *Doing Qualitative Research: A Practical Handbook* (3rd edn). London: Sage.

Social Research Association (2003) Ethical Guidelines: www.the-sra.org.uk/documents/pdfs/ethics03.pdf

Volkman, R. and Cressey, D. (1963) 'Differential association and the rehabilitation of drug addicts', *American Journal of Sociology*, 64: 129–142.

Woolgar, S. and Pawluch, D. (1985) 'Ontological gerrymandering: The anatomy of social problems explanations', *Social Problems*, 32: 214–227.

23 Ethics and Qualitative Research[1]

Anne Ryen

Abstract

Ethnographers rely on rich data in order to understand participants' practices and perspectives. This makes long-lasting research relations a core element, but the quest for rich data is undisputedly accompanied with ethical dilemmas which are somewhat different from survey research. These issues cannot be sorted out at the outset because they are not simply either–or. Many of the dilemmas are emergent and contextual and call for situational responses. This means that the underlying biomedical model of most guidelines may unduly simplify the social world as understood by qualitative researchers.

This chapter offers a brief review of some major contemporary ethical issues in qualitative research. I use my data on Asian businesses in East Africa as a point of departure to illustrate and discuss the complexity of research ethics in the qualitative ethnographic field. The chapter is written from a constructionist position. I argue that what we come to see as challenges and solutions in research ethics is informed in practice by the interconnection between methodology and epistemology, and that research ethics itself is a socially constituted and situated field.

Keywords:

qualitative research, research ethics, epistemology, cross-cultural contexts, paired identities.

[1]Thanks to Nufu for funding the programme Governance, Gender and Scientific Quality (GGSQ) where I hold the position of Programme Coordinator on the Norwegian side.

The 'Omnipresence' of Research Ethics

In 1999, Hammersley coined the term 'ethicism' when he characterised ethical considerations as one of the contemporary tendencies in qualitative research diverting attention away from knowledge production to social justice (also see 2000). If, as a playful though lazy exercise, we 'google' some relevant terms, research ethics is shown to be a topic that has become increasingly important in discussions of research methodology.[2] The professional web pages offer a varied menu from check lists to further links to other organisations' guidelines, authoritative sources, discussion groups, contacts, cases and publications on relevant topics (like the UK Social Research Association in www.the-sra.org.uk/documents/pdfs/ethics03.pdf and many more). They reflect the extensive organisational efforts in recent years to hammer out an agreement on moral practice in the social sciences.

However, for some guidelines like informed consent there is a (surprisingly) long historical track. In 1880, the Norwegian Gerhard Armauer Hansen, the man who discovered the leprosy bacillus, was destined to lose his position as a medical doctor after having put a needle in the eye of a woman (Ruyter, 2009). He had failed to ask her consent to be involved in his experiment and disregarded her protests. This shows an early intervention by an external body where harm to an individual was seen as unacceptable despite generating new knowledge (by experimental research) to the benefit of the many. The support from his medical colleagues and the limited practical impact at the time are of less importance here.

Research Ethics: from Medical to Social Science Research

According to Ruyter (2009), scientific communities have always operated with some kind of self-imposed ethical regulations in respect of societal norms and general ethics. Nazi war crimes stimulated much discussion about research ethics with the court coming up with 10 rules to prevent any recurrence of such atrocities conducted in the name of science (Ruyter et al., 2000: 254). This paved the way for

---

[2]A Google Scholar search for 'research ethics' shows 1,540,000 hits, 'research ethical guidelines' 1,040,000 hits and 'research ethical practice' 1,850,000 hits compared to 681,000 for 'social sciences and knowledge production', 2,060,000 for 'qualitative research' and 2,265,000 for 'ethnographic research' (all web addresses in references). These links open access to research ethics in disciplines like medicine and health, psychology, education, sociology, engineering and to guidelines in social science research associations like the American Psychological Association (APA), the American Sociological Association (ASA), the Association of Social Anthropologists of the UK and Commonwealth (ASA), the British Sociological Association (BSA), the German Sociological Association (GSA), the (Norwegian) National Committee for Research Ethics in the Social Sciences and the Humanities (NESH), as well as to funding agencies like the European Commission's Seventh Frame Programme (FC7).

internal regulations in biomedical research with The Geneva Declaration and the Helsinki Declaration passed by the World Medical Association (WMA, www.wma.net/en/10home/index.html) in 1947 and 1964 respectively. Observations of further medical misdemeanours led the WMA also to recommend reviews by ethical committees (1975), later to be adopted by social science research institutions across the Western world. The social science lag compared to medical research is reflected in the response from an elderly professor on the question of how he got access to the data for one of his earlier projects. 'In those days', he said, 'we didn't ask. We just taped.'

Contemporary social scientists have taken two opposed positions over ethics. Some wonder whether any research is ethically correct because the very nature of much qualitative research inevitably invites ethical dilemmas into the qualitative research *process* (de Laine 2000; Mauthner et al., 2002; Shaw, 2008; Mertens and Ginsberg, 2009) related to issues such as recruiting participants, ownership of data, compensation, etc. The second group of comments refers to the worry expressed by Hammersley whether 'the stirring up of moral panic works against the benefits of qualitative methods' (Van den Hoonaard, 2002: 176). Hammersley's scepticism raises a number of concerns partly motivated by the internal controversies within qualitative research with its many methods, paradigms and conflicting stances.

Classic and Frequently Raised Concerns

Briefly, the three main issues most frequently raised in the Western research ethical guidelines and by the professional associations are:

- codes and consent
- confidentiality
- trust.

For different reasons each topic raises more questions than answers.

Codes and consent refer in particular to 'informed consent'. This means that research subjects have the right to know that they are being researched, the right to be informed about the nature of the research and the right to withdraw at any time. In some countries this means that it is mandatory that research participants sign an informed consent form. Other places accept oral consent unless the researcher is working with certain groups like children, pupils, clients, patients, etc. In many cases, the researcher will need to follow special and lengthy procedures for approval of the theoretical sample and for approval to contact potential research participants (for dilemmas with informed consent in oral communities, see Ryen, 2007).

The relationship between informed consent and covert research serves as the ultimate illustration of ethical dilemmas in data collection. On the one hand, the distinction between overt and covert research is often unclear, as pointed out by

Robert Dingwall (1980). On the other hand, as argued by Punch (1994), to make written informed consent mandatory would mean the end of much 'street-style' ethnography. Other dilemmas refer to qualitative data archives that may call for 'process-consent' because the very point of such archives is to make use later of the same data for different research problems. This makes it difficult for research participants to know what they are consenting to. Based on my own research from East Africa, I refer to 'layers of consent' where the major gatekeeper in rural areas most often is a local government representative who actually provides the researcher with a sample of people who always tend to consent (how smart is it to oppose an official representative's decision?) (Ryen, 2004, 2007). Finally, we also need to ask ourselves what the field is from which we seek our consent in our multiple places and spaces in virtual and non-virtual realities (from chatting to Google Maps: did anyone ask for your consent? See Markham, this volume).

As much as we appreciate proper practice on consent, it does raise issues about how and if we may be able to study phenomena such as crime, elites and private groups. If we accept that what we find out is a result of how we find it, then this is a good illustration of the close but at times not unproblematic relationship between research ethics and knowledge production. A great moral responsibility rests with decision makers here.

There are no standard answers to these dilemmas, and this was the very argument why they have been found too important to be left to researchers alone. We need to be prepared for all these challenges, which demand that we put them on the agenda from the very start of our projects and ask ourselves how they relate to our own particular project.

But, what should we do? A good piece of advice is always to invite experienced researchers with particular knowledge in research ethics and in your field to discuss matters with you (invite your supervisor or your project colleagues to a meeting or a departmental seminar before you proceed).

Confidentiality means we are obliged to protect the participants' identity, the place and the location of the research. However, do we know whether all participants want to be treated anonymously? What do we do if they want their names included? Again, we need to talk to experienced researchers in the area where our research takes place. However, we also need to be aware that Western research ethical guidelines are not necessarily universal. The recommended order if you do research in another country than your own is to identify the relevant guidelines in your home country and in the country in which you do your research (you are governed by both), then compare them and discuss with colleagues before you act.

Trust, the third classic concern, refers to the relationship between the researcher and the participants, and to the researcher's responsibility not to 'spoil' the field for others in the sense that potential research subjects become reluctant to further study (Ryen, 2004). In this way trust also applies to the report or the discursive practices defining the standards for presenting both the researcher and the work as trustworthy (Fine, 1993). Trust is the classic key to good field relations and is a constantly unfolding challenge during the research process, though more so in ethnographic studies than in other kinds of fieldwork.

At times we come across delicate situations that involve hidden or problematic information that someone may be harmed or put at risk (like crimes being planned), or that certain findings may be discomforting (like job evaluations or health information) or even dangerous to some subjects (like some kinds of illegal activities). These issues call for decisions on whether we should do such projects (alone or with someone else) or not at all; when to decide there are data we do not want to get (is it okay just to turn off the tape recorder, to move the conversation on to another track, or do we need more explicit strategies?); or if we simply need to shut down the whole project.

Undoubtedly the three ethical issues of consent, confidentiality and trust are closely linked. If you intervene by calling in an external person, you show the participant that s/he no longer is treated anonymously and no longer can trust you. Probably the participant will be very hesitant to work with other researchers later. The general advice is not to make such dilemmas your own individual load but to invite others to discuss how to be prepared and ways to react before (make an informed decision), during (discuss possible challenges, worst case included, and in the particular contextual and cultural setting of your fieldwork) and after fieldwork (communicating your research).

However, such recommendations often tend to reflect a rather simplistic approach to qualitative research practice. Let us therefore look at the more fundamental assumptions on which the institutional management of such issues is based.

Our Moral Responsibility in Complex Realities

In this section we will look at some of the main arguments in the contemporary discussion of research ethics. Later this feeds into a discussion on concerns regarded as specific to qualitative research. These also constitute the background to claims that ethical guidelines and much institutional governance are problematic, particularly in ethnographic research.

Any model based on a pre-fixed rather naive ideal research subject (or rather, object), embedded in a classic research relationship and in need of protection from harm, will fail to capture what is special about qualitative research. With reference to the classic 'Can we trust them?', questions of validity and research ethics such as confidence and trust become closely entangled, especially in the data collection phase.

The response in positivism is based on the assumption that language refers to an external reality 'out there' that makes access to the assumed reservoir of stocked information crucial. In the constructionist model, social reality is a more complex phenomenon where we examine how members produce recognisable forms that are treated as real or 'worlding' to cite Gubrium and Holstein (1997: 42; also see Silverman, 2006) or simply, how they do this. The stories we get are produced *with* rather than *by* someone; they are contextually produced, designed for a particular audience, serve locally produced purposes and are embedded in wider cultural contexts. As researchers we have a responsibility for producing rigorous research. However, just as immoral research may provide us with data that is otherwise difficult to get (such as in covert research, or the fine balance in our information when recruiting informants etc. (Fine, 1993)), naive simplified assumptions about field relations pose another dilemma.

This does not mean we dissociate ourselves from research ethics, but rather that we fully acknowledge our moral responsibility. For qualitative research informed by constructionist epistemologies and other than utilitarian ideas, social reality is a much more complex, multi-dimensional and contextual phenomenon. This makes research ethics more, not less, complex.

The debate about moral responsibility should be grounded on a critical meeting of philosophy, epistemology and research practice. The absence of pre-fixed answers is no entitlement for postmodern relativism or Durkheimian anomie. Rather it adds to the researcher's continuous moral responsibility.

Contemporary Research Ethical Issues

Ernest House reminds us that 'qualitative research does not live in a state of methodological grace' (1991, in Shaw, 2008: 403), and researchers' misdemeanours remain the main source of the more intensive restrictions (such as Humphreys, 1975, or Milgram, 1963; for more examples see Ryen, 2004). However, alternative reactions were always available, such as more research ethics and philosophy on the students' timetable, more systematic use of mentors or stronger links between individual researchers and research communities. We have ended up with external control; the social sciences copied the medical profession (Johnson and Altheide, 2002; Adler and Adler, 2002).

Ethical Models and Qualitative Inquiry

Instead of basing ethics upon abstract principles, Kvale (1996) calls for a contextual and situational position and emphasises the skill of the researcher in reflexively negotiating ethical dilemmas. As suggested by Edwards and Mauthner (2002: 21), this leaves us with two opposing positions: a universalist versus a contingency approach.

Critics of universalist models have questioned the basis upon which institutional review takes place (Van den Hoonaard, 2002) and its competence in assessing the nature of ethical issues raised by non-positivist research paradigms (like Mauthner et al., 2002; Leisey, 2008; McIntosh and Morse, 2009: 84; and many more) or by researchers working in cross-cultural contexts (Riessman, 2005; Sewpaul, 2003; Mertens, 2007; Ryen, 2007, 2008a, 2008b). This has generated a range of alternative ethics models like an 'ethics of care' (Gilligan, 1983; Nodding, 1984; Porter, 1999), 'ethics of epistemology' (Maynard, 1994), 'the feminist, communitarian ethical model' (Denzin, 1997) and others. They all reject basic assumptions inherent in universalist models, such as that ethical issues can be sorted out by the start of a project and the either–or assumptions as with informed consent and harm. The concern with specificity and context reflects the different positions as in the feminist focus on care, power, relationships and 'the Other' mirroring the set of ethical values underlying their situated approach.

In Defence of What?

Research ethics tends to be associated with a concern for research participants. However, the accentuated pressure for external funding necessitates a concern also with the contracting and governance of research activities. This has made Edwards and Mauthner (2002: 16–18) point to litigation as a relevant issue. Ethical guidelines can protect researchers from any funder's attempt to limit academic freedom by restricting the publication or findings or by demands to submit first drafts. If researchers do break contractual obligations they, as well as their institutions, may find such obligations more pressing than ethical issues. They also accentuate the framework now embedding research activities, like pressures on time, funding and internal bureaucracy as well as training that may take precedence over ethics. Indeed the role of the present research ethics bureaucracy may become less important for researchers than funding institutions (Adler and Adler, 2002).

An Illustration: Researching Across Cultures

I now want to demonstrate how the complex issues discussed so far can be illustrated by my own research in East Africa. In research practice there are few simple answers. Rather the ethnographer often finds him- or herself squeezed between definitions of the ethical and the acceptable as well as the workable. As you will see, I position myself within the non-universalist research ethical position.

When qualitative researchers claim that the very nature of qualitative research calls for more flexible, emergent perspectives compared to the dominating model of the research ethical regime, we need to make this a credible statement. I will do so in two steps. First, I will present a few data extracts to illustrate what is emergent and flexible in research relations. Second, I will discuss the implications for research ethics in qualitative research and how these differ in what follows from the underlying assumptions of the structured positivist-informed perception of such relations and challenges.

Transcending the Geographically Bound

Recently we have seen a global revival of oral communication earlier associated with traditional communities. The global mobile network allows relations to continue in the spaces between classic field visits. This encourages a continuous relationship across transnational spaces making the geographically bound 'field' more complex and decentred with no 'clear-cut distinction between *the here* and *the elsewhere*' as put by Stake and Rizvi (2009: 525). Interestingly, when the field changes this calls for a more nuanced debate on communication.

My data on Asian business in East Africa consists of mobile talk, text messages, taped talk and notes from casual talk across contexts. As I have been accepted into my informant Mahid's network of regular contacts, we never lose complete track of each other despite the months between our meetings. In a more classic perspective, it is this connectedness so prominent in qualitative research and so crucial to successful ethnographic fieldwork that paradoxically also poses its own moral concerns as relations evolve and fluctuate.

The Emergent and Contextual Side of Ethnographic Field Relations

According to the classic model, fieldwork is an activity between the ethnographer and the respondent or the key informant. It is these pre-fixed, structural field roles that are the main target of textbook protocols. They also tend to be the main point of reference for much present research ethics governance in their concern for field interaction as well as the final report. However, the claim that the social world can be discovered by being 'there', as in traditional ethnography, has for long been disputed by those who argue that social reality is accomplished rather than experienced.

According to Harvey Sacks, the central research question is how societal members 'see' or 'hear' particular activities and therefore offers a way of describing 'methods persons use for doing social life' (Sacks, 1984; Silverman, 1998). This makes language more than a passive medium for transferring external meanings or experiences and Sacks' 'apparatus' or machinery represents one way of analysing such talk in a way that works to illustrate how 'participants orient and respond to each other in an orderly, recognizable way' (Gubrium and Holstein, 1997: 55). This machinery is not the actual categories that members use (like 'culture' or other sociological variables), but rather what allows the phenomenon, whatever it is, to be done. Members collaboratively make social order happen in their unfolding sequences of talk and the researcher's job is to describe how this reality is being done.

By using Sacks' membership categorisation device (MCD) (Silverman, 1998: chapter 5), we can describe how people come to hear things the way they do in everyday life based on assumptions about what people are doing. This is possible because each of the pairs (of MCDs) or paired identities, as shown in the extracts below, implies common expectations about what sort of activity is appropriate. However, as clearly stated by Carolyn Baker, attributions may be explicitly pronounced or just hinted at, 'indicating the subtlety and delicacy of much implicit categorisation membership work' (Baker, 2004: 174).

Let me present a few examples of the paired identities invoked by Mahid and myself. Altering the way we see field relations has, as I will shortly make clear, crucial implications for research ethics in qualitative research. Let us start with the classic image.

Emergent Relational Identities

The Classic Researcher–Key Informant

Mahid is my key informant. This implies much everyday talk about his business activities and unstructured interviews about his life history. Here is a sequence about employing a professional hotelier in one of his businesses:

Extract 1

1 A: so why did you hire the person?

2 M: I hired the person because I needed a professional hotelier here

3 A: ehe

4 M. Ok, none of us were professional hoteliers, ok. And hotel is a job where the kitchen has to be looked

5 after which is very important, the bar has to be looked after, the clients' interests have to be looked

6 after. I had no time for that eh nobody wanted to come forward and I had employed [my cousin] she

7 was working here. Just because she did not have any hotel experience

8 A: mhm

9 M: ok, UNDP came up and said, No, we want to hire a professional…

(Taped talk, Kenya 2002) (Ryen, 2008c: 90)

Following Sacks, my 'ehe' and 'mhm' are activities that prompt Mahid's recipient-designed elaborations and should therefore not be ignored. In the classic way, the researcher here (line 1) asks a question and the key informant responds (line 2), followed by the researcher's cues (lines 3 and 8) to prompt further elaborations (lines 4–7 and 9). The point here is that in this particular extract we jointly invoke the standard pair researcher–key informant traditionally portrayed as the only legitimate roles in the field (Ryen, 2004, 2008a). In a constructionist approach, however, this is but one of an array of relations as fieldwork unfolds.

As claimed by Holstein and Gubrium, to see the process of meaning making as important as the meaning that is produced 'resonates well with the critique offered by feminist scholars' (2004: 142) and their concern with subjectivity and complexity that they share with poststructuralists, postmodernists and ethnomethodologists. However, their worry is with their prioritised focus on how lived experience is constituted rather than with the experience itself or the 'whats' of it (see Holstein and Gubrium, this volume).

Let us now look at alternative relations invoked in the activity of doing being in the field. My task now is to show the constitutive character of field relations and how this makes such relations active and emergent rather than structured and inflexible.

Tight schedules and tough conditions with some of the big international contracts make business in this region a risk, and this is in its own way being imported into our relationship. Careful analysis of my tapes also shows a further paired identity:

Patient–Counsellor

In the interval between our first and second meeting, Mahid had experienced severe economic problems. He started to call me rather frequently, explicitly expressing his request to be available simply as a listener, a classic virtue in ethnography. Rather than his explanation (what) let us again look at the process whereby we do being Mahid and myself:

Extract 2

M: I was so depressed this morning. You were not here when I needed you the most.

A: I am so sorry.

M: I tried calling you again and again, and I must have sent you 6 sms.

$$\text{(Mobile 2003, related to extract 3 in Ryen, 2009: 233)}$$

Financial problems beyond a certain scale are not easily overcome. This means that negotiations run parallel to other businesses and project portfolio activities across the region. Deadlines have to be met to avoid penalties and the best deals to make a profit must be secured, while handling hassles by local tax inspectors (who may expect bribes). The paired identity of patient and counsellor tended to emerge when problems accumulated. This made us alternate between identities as we went along. Here he is telling me a story from his early days in business:

Extract 3

I said 'No'...and simultaneously tears were just running down my eyes because how my parents had reacted [very emotional voice] (3.0) Till this day, It breaks my heart' (3.0)... It is very bad for you' [crying] (7 pages later)... I said 'I made you go there 4–5 times. I won't embarrass you. You come there and you find the money is not there. It is very bad for you [crying, I'm giving him a napkin]... (4 pages later) Now I just want to say goodbye to you [whispering, sniffling]... You know, staying in the house makes me feel suffocation' (5.0), and she [mother] started crying and I said [crying, I take his hand] 'For your sake I'll stay in the house (4,0), [sniffling]... (1 page later) She said 'I told you [father] at that time not to tell things like these things'. Looking at me: 'I am sorry. I am emotional right now because those words, they still hurt me till today' [sniffling].

(Taped talk, Uganda, 2003)

This is a story that evokes strong emotions. First, such narratives challenge categories or labels such as 'elite' studies and the vulnerability associated with non-privileged groups, and, second, this analytic approach makes visible the dynamics and actively emergent side of social life most relevant to the moral responsibility of research. Let us look at another example from our dataset.

Friend–Friend

After having worked together for a few years, we have also come to share events in our lives associated with health and illness. Independent of whatever explanation we use for this, it means we (at times) also recognise the other as a good listener and a competent and emphatic co-member. One morning I found a new text message on my mobile sent by Mahid in the middle of the night when his son died from cancer:

Extract 4

Hi got a bad news [my son] passd away i am in shock wil talk 2morow.

(Text message 2005, his son's name kept anonymous; Ryen, 2008c: 238)

When I called him the next morning I offered to stay in more regular contact, which made him respond positively and appreciate my emotional support, albeit a member's explanation. The contextual and reciprocal side of our relationship is reflected in his considerate text messages after one of my medical operations:

Extract 5

R u ok pls tel me.

(Text message 31 January 2007; Ryen, 2008c: 93)

Extract 6

Did u have a comfortable nite u worry me u rest and get wel soon.

(Text message 4 February 2007; Ryen, 2008c: 93)

Despite the protocol on emphatic and smooth relations, long-lasting field relations also invite unforeseen eruptions. Here is his rather humorous response to my efforts to repair:

Extract 7

I am glad. I must kneel down. I told u to listen to the great man.

(Text message 26 January 2006; Ryen, 2008c: 94)

Man–Woman

The focus on the meaning-making process opens up for display the contextual, the active and dynamic (eruptions included) field relations as opposed to being stuck in fixed roles. At times we also actively construct our relationship as relaxed, joyful and of mutual interest, aspects of vital importance in keeping up the good relationship. Here we see a good rhythm of mutual response to light-hearted flirtation:

Extract 8

1 A: would you accept me if I came to your office asking?
2 M: why not? (a bit aggressive). Would I accept you (warm)?
3 A: as an interviewer
4 M: no, you know, I don't, if you came to my office and said you wanted to inter-
       view me, I'd say Why?
5   (aggressive) Don't you know enough of me? (warm) (both laughing)
6 M: do you want to stand outside and do, if you want to do the talking outside?
7 A: eh, I think we should go inside. I need to make the dough for the rolls.
8 M: oh ok.

(Taped talk, Norway, 2004; Ryen, 2008d: 154)

Mahid's question, line 6, and my response, line 7, reflect the local, situated and contextual side of our talk – we are standing by the car in my driveway (in Norway) with shopping bags. Within a second, the relationship changes from light-hearted flirtation to friends going inside to prepare dinner for my family. This switch makes possible what Frederick Erickson refers to as the multimensionality of social identities (2009: 29). I will comment on this later. Let us now look at how this relates to what is claimed to be the particulars of research ethics in qualitative research.

Research Ethics In Research Practice: Complex Fields

According to the professional guidelines, the researcher is responsible for informed consent, for trust and protection, and for protecting participants' privacy by confidentiality (Ryen, 2004: 231–236). A signed consent form then becomes a guarantee that participants are informed about the research and consent to participate. Unfortunately, this procedure leads us to perceive moral responsibility as something to get done initially, something to be ticked off as 'done', a symbol of goodness. This undermines the qualitative side of qualitative research (see Ryen, 2004, 2007, for illustrations from East Africa; see Miller and Bell, 2003, on access, consent, power and feminism). This external policing also tends to turn research ethics into an either–or issue (Edwards and Mauthner, 2002: 20): participants either consent or they do not, things are good or bad, harmless or not. And it presupposes a clear, static research problem typical of a positivist-informed epistemology.

If we accept the constitutive nature of qualitative research or knowledge production as a meaning-making process, inevitably there are issues unfamiliar or problematic to positivist-informed notions of correct or acceptable research relations and whatever they might bring about. The idea of the professional–private divide works well to pinpoint the particulars of qualitative inquiry and moral responsibility. Prominent examples of dilemmas associated with good rapport are friendship/deception, privacy/intrusion and emotional stress. Despite their interconnectedness, I will discuss them in separate subsections. They refer to the whole process from negotiating access to the field to data gathering and analysis, and they all relate in different ways to the classic issues of consent, confidentiality and trust of research ethics.

The Professional–Private Divide: Is Good Rapport a Problem?

Interviews and ethnographic studies are dependent on building up rather long-lasting relations in the field to get access to 'there'. To do this we draw on mundane practices; we link up with people, spend time together and build up a stock of joint experiences. Friends do the same. Is the ethnographer a friend? Is such friendship fake? Is our niceness instrumental? When some years ago I called Mahid and found him in the middle of a tough bout of malaria, did my worry express care or rather concern for the possible loss of data? Do we deceive them?

Duncombe and Jessop (2003: 107) discuss the parallel between interviewing skills and 'doing rapport' and refer to Hochschild's (1983) 'emotion work' and her argument of the commercialisation of human feelings. She argues that those who do such jobs may feel and even become 'inauthentic', like women employees in service jobs when simulating empathy to make people feel well. If textbook prescriptions for successful interviews encourage good rapport, they see such friendships as detached and opposed to Ann Oakley's advocacy of minimal social distance between feminist researchers and research subjects in order to offer 'an emotionally emphatic, egalitarian and reciprocal rapport' (1981: 108). Despite a somewhat naive assumption of authenticism, there is a good resonance with research ethics.

The commercialisation of interviewer skills on 'doing rapport' into 'management of consent' implies a more personalised approach to building trust. However, if power inequalities in 'faking friendship' are ignored, Duncombe and Jessop see it as 'a disturbing ethical naivety' (2003: 110). Qualitative interviewers even adopt counselling skills and language to increase the interviewee's personal insight to improve introspection. Rightly, Duncombe and Jessop critically ask if this is the kind of disclosure to which the interviewee consented. Also, they are quite right about the danger that such talk could escalate into a quasi-therapeutic interview and create severe problems in drawing boundaries around the 'friendship' or 'intimacy'. So, we could argue that it is as important to know the boundaries around one's skills as it is to know one's skills. Ethnographers are trained in ethnography, not therapy.

While in the field, we do not yet know about the relevant and irrelevant, the interesting and uninteresting. We may invite or reject agendas. I could have cut off Mahid's narrative in Extract 3 or not responded to his text messages in Extracts 2 and 4. I decided to 'stay'. Anything else would have violated norms in both cultures. However, Mahid and I have explicitly discussed dilemmas associated with disclosure, confidentiality and trust. I do listen, but I do not explicitly prompt for more (see Extracts 2 and 3, though inevitably my sounds, silences or movements are communicative devices too).

Fieldwork is a delicate balance between the interesting, the workable and the acceptable, all ingredients in our search for knowledge. The alternatives are neither stricter rule, nor to call in a committee. I share Kant's ethical concern with the individual over the group (deontology as opposed to utilitarianism, Ryen, 2004) – and with research participants over committees. However, for analytic purposes we need to explore occasions and contexts but we do not need to go 'deep' for 'authentic' experiences. I will come back below to the emotional and private as in Extracts 3 and 8.

This accentuates the qualitative of qualitative research, so let us explore further how such issues relate to knowledge.

Interpersonal Distance and Comprehensibility: Are Qualitative Researchers Intruders?

Robert Stake and Brinda Jegatheesan (2008: 1–13) have shown that the road to understanding participation is assumed to go via reduced interpersonal distance, hence the importance of rapport, but at some point we may intrude into that person's zone of privacy. 'The points that bound these zones are not points at all. They are shadings, passages...Through empathy, intuition, experience, something, we need to rely on ourselves to back off' (2008: 8), and quite rightly emphasise that 'Privacy is not defined only by the content of disclosure, but also in terms of audiences and circumstances involved' (2008: 2).

Prescriptions or external control mechanisms cannot solve this dilemma, though the tilt towards revelation is more prominent in some qualitative paradigms (like emotionalism and postmodernism) than in others (see table 15.1 in Ryen, 2004: 244, for an overview of values and ethics in some contemporary paradigms). However, a positivist-informed belief in an external reality is no guarantee that the researcher will avoid undue introspection or intruding into the private lives of participants. External control is not necessarily the answer to emergent challenges.

Cross-cultural contexts make some challenges more visible with long narratives (I have some more than three hours long) assumingly depicting 'authentic' experiences. Also, participants are active and may in different ways exercise power in relations with the researcher from withholding information to over-enthusiasm. What then about the informants? Did Mahid text-message me in the hospital because he feared he might lose his free 'counsellor'? Was it convenient to have me around when he was broke so I could pay for lunches at times, even with his contacts? How come informants volunteer (Ryen, 2008c)? Exploring the meaning-making process will better enable us to recognise problematic zones. They are not standardised.

By 'transgressions' Duncombe and Jessop refer to participants exercising power (2003: 119). This makes power, trust and protection from harm complex phenomena in qualitative research (Ryen, 2008c). Bourne-Day and Lee-Treweek's concept of 'transaction' (2008: 36, 55) recognises participants as instrumental in having their own agendas and goals for their participation, seeing the researcher as a gatekeeper to attractive assets, convenient mediator, alibi or trying to transform relations into private ones (see Ryen, 2004, 2008d, on flirtation). This makes power, abuse and intrusion complex and stresses the ordinary, unfolding and upcoming of qualitative data collection calling for an alert researcher.

In Stake and Jegatheesan's reference to zones of privacy as shadings and passages, they see moral responsibility as intrinsic. This accentuates the situatedness of field-work across and within emergent contexts, and puts moral responsibility upon the researcher to recognise 'intruding' passages. My conclusion is that I must listen to so-called private stories because I have been sanctioned for not listening and spent days managing eruptions. Interestingly, this has been very informing about our Western notions of 'privacy', how narratives change, etc. It has also taught me to recognise local shades or passages in gendered ethnographies of Third World organisations, passages more complex and explicit than the flirtation in Extract 8 (Ryen, 2008d).

Emotional Stress: Do Qualitative Researchers Cause Harm?

It is common knowledge that a good rapport in long-lasting relations may invite participants to disclose emotional experiences as Mahid did in Extract 3. The question is whether or not this is harmful to our participants and thus ethically problematic (despite participants' efforts at times also to intrude into the ethnographer's privacy).

Michele J. McIntosh and Janet M. Morse argue that 'emotional distress motivates purposive participation, creates relational connections, facilitates self-knowledge of participants and their experiences, and expresses its voice in the emotional space afforded by the interview' (McIntosh and Morse, 2009: 91). This makes it an integral part, not a by-product, of unstructured interview research and reflects how emotions in the West are associated with valence and polarity. But this is too simplistic to account for the complex, multidimensional and contextual nature of pain and pleasure.

Mahid's story about his painful experience from his early business life illustrates emotional distress as part of a wider emotional repertoire participants may evoke during fieldwork. The pain evoked is contextual and displayed in stories told and retold across contexts. The experience is narrated as a tellable story, recipient oriented and tailored for a particular audience. The emotional stress is subjective and interpretive and the story works to connect and relate, calls for attention and relieves the stress.

I have stories that come up in different versions, emotional and unemotional, depending on audience and setting. This challenges the assumed 'authenticity' of experiences. We still have to relate to the storyteller's emotional state of mind in one way or another while being aware of the cultural and situated ways of interpreting emotions. Such stories may serve different ends and reflect complicated transactions in the field. Our research participants lead us. If they are in need of an audience, who are we to reserve the right to 'the meaty (research-relevant) stuff' only? There is also a time for boundaries, but no documents tell us exactly when or where.

There is no simple formula for the link between qualitative research and emotional stress. Harm or harmless is a complex phenomenon.

Summary and Future Prospects: What about Vulnerability?

Knowledge production comes with moral responsibility towards research participants. The rich literature on research ethics and qualitative research reflects the multitude of approaches informed by parallel, alternative epistemologies. This makes the question of how moral responsibility can be best attended to. This is contested terrain. The contemporary governance of research ethics may itself actively participate in constituting qualitative research as a vulnerable field. My chapter is another effort to avoid naive assumptions about the nature of ethical dilemmas in qualitative research. It would be immoral to underestimate the complexity of research ethics. What we come to see as challenges and solutions to dilemmas in research ethics in practice is informed by epistemology (Ryen, 2004, 2009), and ethics is itself a field socially constituted and situated (Ryen, 2004).

In our global times, with extensive international research activities, we have to be cautious not to reiterate the colonial trap. For the future, we will need to be more aware of variations in the basics of ethics and research ethics. If you go abroad for your project, then what about African philosophy, or Asian? If they collide or if our own set of research ethical guidelines is inadequate, what do you do? If local research ethics claims national ownership of data just as of other resources, under what condition can you still export data to your home country? 'Whose field is it?' and 'Whose ethics?' How is research ethics intertwined with power? What about the controversies of non-secularised contexts (Ryen, 2008b)? This calls for more knowledge of the philosophy and culture of the context of your research whether abroad or at home. These issues will add to the contemporary debate when we no longer can take 'the taken-for-granted' for granted (Ryen, 2007). The contextual side of allegedly universal Western research ethics shows the limits of the either–or perspective.

Quite rightly, qualitative research is not in a state of methodological grace, though as Shaw (2008: 402, footnote 2) argues, the harm we cause may be less harmful compared to other areas. Simply, we need to recognise the social processes through which things come to be seen as ethical or not. As claimed by Zygmunt Bauman: 'The foolproof – universal and unshakeably founded – ethical code will never be found' (1993: 2–27, also cited in Ryen, 2004: 230). Qualitative research calls for moral responsibility in a field littered with dilemmas, not for quick pre-fixed answers.

Questions

1 What research ethical guidelines are you compelled to follow in your own research? Look them up.
2 Think of your research problem: try to identify possible ethical dilemmas. Which ones can be sorted out *before* you start your fieldwork, and which ones may come up *during* fieldwork? How can the guidelines in question 1 help you?
3 If your field is located in another country, what are the research ethics guidelines there? Look them up and compare with 'your own'. Any difference? If so, what do you do?

Recommended Reading

For an introduction to the standard ethical issues (consent, confidentiality and trust) and a table overview of the link between values, ethics and paradigms in qualitative research:

Ryen, A. (2004) 'Ethical issues', in C. Seale, G. Gobo, J.F. Gubrium and D. Silverman (eds) *Qualitative Research Practice*. London: Sage, pp. 158–174.

Books that also discuss ethical dilemmas across the research *process*:

de Laine, M. (2000) *Fieldwork, Participation and Practice. Ethics and Dilemmas in Qualitative Research*. Thousand Oaks, CA: Sage.

Mauthner, M., Birch, M., Jessop, J. and Miller, T. (eds) (2003) *Ethics in Qualitative Research*. London: Sage.

Publications where authors write about and discuss ethical dilemmas in their own research: *Qualitative Social Work. Research and Practice*, Vol. 7(4). Special issue on research ethics guest edited by A. Ryen (http://qsw.sagepub.com/content/vol7/issue4/). Offers an overview article and some good illustrations on Institutional Review Boards (IRBs), informed consent, trust, etc.

Jegatheesen, B. (ed.) (2008) *Access: A Zone of Comprehension, and Intrusion*. Bingley: Emerald.

Offers good illustrations on topics such as closeness, privacy, deception, IRBs, indigenous research, flirtation and self.

Overview for the more advanced:

Mertens, D.M. and Ginsberg, P.E. (eds) (2009) *The Handbook of Social Research Ethics*. Los Angeles: Sage.

You will also find the rich lists of references in these publications very helpful.

Internet Links

Ethnographic research:

http://scholar.google.no/scholar?hl=no&q=ethnographic+research&as_ylo. Retrieved 10 January 2010.

Qualitative research:

http://scholar.google.no/scholar?hl=no&q=qualitative+research&btnG=S%C3%B8k&as_ylo. Retrieved 10 January 2010.

Research ethical guidelines:

http://scholar.google.no/scholar?hl=no&q=research+ethical+guidelines&as_ylo. Retrieved 06 January 2010.

Research ethical practice:

http://scholar.google.no/scholar?hl=no&q=research+ethical+practice&btnG=S%C3%B8k&as_ylo. Retrieved 06 January 2010.

Social sciences and knowledge production:

http://scholar.google.no/scholar?hl=no&q=qualitative+research+and+knowledge+production+&btnG=S%C3%B8k&as_ylo. Retrieved 10 January 2010.

The American Psychological Association (APA):

www.apa.org/ethics/code/index.aspx. Retrieved 02 January 2010.

The American Sociological Association (ASA):

www.asanet.org/about/ethics.cfm. Retrieved 2 January 2010.

The Association of Social Anthropologists of the UK and Commonwealth (ASA):

www.theasa.org/ethics/guidelines.htm. Retrieved 02 January 2010.

The British Sociological Association (BSA):

www.britsoc.co.uk/equality/Statement+Ethical+Practice.htm. Retrieved 02 January 2010.

The European Commission's Seventh Frame Programme (FC7):

ftp://ftp.cordis.europa.eu/pub/fp7/docs/guidelines-annex5ict.pdf. Retrieved 02 January 2010.

The German Sociological Association (GSA):

www.soziologie.de/index.php?id=292&L=2. Retrieved 02 January 2010.

The National Committee for Research Ethics in the Social Sciences and the Humanities (NESH):

(Continued)

(Continued)

www.etikkom.no/no/Vart-arbeid/Hvem-er-vi/Komite-for-samfunnsvitenskap-og-humaniora/. Retrieved 15 January 2010. Click further for English version.

The Social Research Association:

www.the-sra.org.uk/documents/pdfs/ethics03.pdf. Retrieved 02 January 2010.

The World Medical Association (WMA):

www.wma.net/en/10home/index.html. Retrieved 02.01.10.

Qualitative research and knowledge production:

http://scholar.google.no/scholar?hl=no&q=qualitative+research+and+knowledge+ production&btnG=S%C3%B8k&as_ylo. Retrieved 10 January 2010.

References

Adler, P.A. and Adler, P. (2002) 'The reluctant respondent', in J.F. Gubrium and J.A. Holstein (eds) *Handbook of Interview Research. Context and Method.* Thousand Oaks, CA: Sage, pp. 515–536.

Baker, C.D. (2004) 'Membership categorization and interview accounts', in D. Silverman (ed.) *Qualitative Research: Theory, Method and Practice.* London: Sage, pp. 162–176.

Bauman, Z. (1993) *Postmodern Ethics.* Oxford: Blackwell.

Bourne-Day, J. and Lee-Treweek, G. (2008) 'Interconnected lives: examining privacy as a shared concern for the researched and researchers', in B. Jegatheesen (ed.) *Access: A Zone of Comprehension, and Intrusion.* Bingley: Emerald, pp. 29–60.

Denzin, N.K. (1997) *Interpretive Ethnography: Ethnographic Practices for the 21st Century.* London: Sage.

de Laine, M. (2000) *Fieldwork, Participation and Practice: Ethics Dilemmas in Qualitative Research.* London: Sage.

Dingwall, R. (1980) 'Ethics and ethnography', *Sociological Review*, 28(4): 871–892.

Duncombe, J. and Jessop, J. (2003) '"Doing rapport" and the ethics of "faking friendship"', in M. Mauthner, M. Birch, J. Jessop and T. Miller (eds) *Ethics in Qualitative Research.* London: Sage, pp. 107–122.

Edwards, R. and Mauthner, M. (2002) 'Ethics and feminist research: theory and practice', in M. Mauthner, M. Birch, J. Jessop and T. Miller (eds) *Ethics in Qualitative Research.* London: Sage, pp. 14–31.

Erickson, F. (2009) 'Inappropriate closeness in fieldwork? A view from anthropology of education', in N.K. Denzin and M.D. Giardina (eds) *Qualitative Inquiry and Social Justice*, Section I: Ethics, Evidence and Social Justice. Walnut Creek, CA: Left Coast Press, pp. 15–28.

Fine, G.A. (1993) 'Ten lies of ethnography: moral dilemmas in field research', *Journal of Contemporary Ethnography*, 22(3): 267–294.

Gilligan, C. (1983) *In A Different Voice: Psychological Theory and Women's Development*. Cambridge, MA: Harvard University Press.

Gubrium, J.F. and Holstein, J.A. (1997) *The New Language of Qualitative Research*. New York: Oxford University Press.

Hammersley, M. (1999) 'Some reflections on the current state of qualitative research', *Research Intelligence*, 70: 16–18.

Hammersley, M. (2000) *Taking Sides in Social Research*. London: Routledge.

Hochschild, A.R. (1983) *The Managed Heart: The Commercialization of Human Feeling*. Berkeley, CA: University of California Press.

Holstein, J.A. and Gubrium, J.F. (2004) 'The active interview', in D. Silverman (ed.) *Qualitative Research: Theory, Method and Practice*. London: Sage, pp. 140–161.

House, E. (1991) 'Evaluation and social justice: where are we now?', in M. McLaughlin and D. Phillips (eds) *Evaluation and Education: A Quarter Century*. Chicago: Chicago University Press.

Humphreys, L. (1975) *Tearoom Trade*, enlarged edn. Chicago: Aldine.

Jegatheesen, B. (ed.) (2008) *Access: A Zone of Comprehension, and Intrusion*. Bingley: Emerald.

Johnson, J. and Altheide, D.L. (2002) 'Reflections on professional ethics', in W.C. van den Hoonaard (ed.) *Walking the Tightrope: Ethical Issues for Qualitative Researchers*. Toronto: University of Toronto Press, pp. 59–69.

Kvale, S. (1996) *InterViews: An Introduction to Qualitative Research Interviewing*. Thousand Oaks, CA: Sage.

Leisey, M. (2008) 'Qualitative inquiry and the IRB. Protection at all costs', *Qualitative Social Work*, 7(4): 415–426.

Mauthner, M., Birch, M., Jessop, J. and Miller, T. (eds) (2002) *Ethics in Qualitative Research*. London: Sage.

Maynard, M. (1994) 'Methods, practice and epistemology: the debate about feminism and research', in M. Maynard and J. Purvis (eds) *Researching Women's Lives from a Feminist Perspective*. London: Taylor & Francis.

McIntosh, M.J. and Morse, J. (2009) 'Institutional review boards and the ethics of emotion', in N.K. Denzin and M.D. Giardina (eds) *Qualitative Inquiry and Social Justice*. Walnut Creek, CA: Left Coast Press, pp. 81–107.

Mertens, D.M. (ed.) (2007) *Mosenodi*. Journal of the Botswana Educational Research Association. Special issue on research ethics, 15(1&2).

Mertens, D.M. and Ginsberg, P.E. (eds) (2009) *The Handbook of Social Research Ethics*. Los Angeles: Sage.

Milgram, S. (1963) 'Behavioral study of obedience', *Journal of Abnormal and Social Psychology*, 67: 371–378.

Miller, T. and Bell, L. (2003) 'Consenting to what? Issues of access, gate-keeping and "informed" consent', in M. Mauthner, M. Birch, J. Jessop and T. Miller (eds) *Ethics in Qualitative Research*. London: Sage, pp. 53–69.

Nodding, N. (1984) *Caring: A Feminine Approach to Ethics and Moral Education*. Berkeley: University of California Press.

Oakley, A. (1981) 'Interviewing women: a contradiction in terms?', in H. Roberts (ed.) *Doing Feminist Research*. London: Routledge & Kegan Paul.

Porter, E. (1999) *Feminist Perspectives on Ethics*. Harlow: Pearson Education.

Punch, M. (1994) 'Politics and ethics in qualitative research', in N.K. Dentin and Y.S. Lincoln (eds) *Handbook of Qualitative Research*. Thousand Oaks, CA: Sage, pp. 83–97.

Riessman, C.K. (2005) 'Exporting ethics: a narrative about narrative research in South India', *Health: An Interdisciplinary Journal for the Social Study of Health, Illness and Medicine*, 9(4): 473–490.

Ruyter, K.W. (2009) 'Forskningsetikkens historie' (Last updated 12 May 2009). The National Research ethical committees [Online]. Accessible at: http://etikkom.no/no/FBIB/Introduksjon/Systematiske-og-historiske-perspektiver/Forskningsetikkens-historie/.

Ruyter, K., Førde, R. and Solbakk, J.H. (2000) *Medisinsk etikk: En problembasert tilnærming*. Gyldendal norsk forlag.

Ryen, A. (2004) 'Ethical issues', in C. Seale, G. Gobo, J.F. Gubrium and D. Silverman (eds) *Qualitative Research Practice*. London: Sage, pp. 158–174.

Ryen, A. (2007) 'Do Western research ethics work in Africa? A discussion about not taking "the taken-for-granted" for granted', *Mosenodi*, 15(1&2): 31–45, University of Botswana, guest edited by D.M. Mertens.

Ryen, A. (ed.) (2008a) *Qualitative Social Work. Research and Practice*, A guest edition on research ethics: http://qsw.sagepub.com

Ryen, A. (2008b) 'Trust in cross-cultural research. The puzzle of epistemology, research ethics and context', *Qualitative Social Work*, 7(4): 448–465.

Ryen, A. (2008c) 'Wading the field with my key informant: exploring field relations', *Qualitative Sociology Review*, Vol. IV, Issue 3: www.qualitativesociologyreview.org/ENG/archive_eng.php

Ryen, A. (2008d) 'Crossing borders? Doing gendered ethnographies of Third-World organisations', in B. Jegatheesen (ed.) *Access: A Zone of Comprehension, and Intrusion*. Bingley: Emerald, pp. 141–164.

Ryen, A. (2009) 'Ethnography: constitutive practice and research ethics', in D.M. Mertens and P.E. Ginsberg (eds.) *The Handbook of Social Research Ethics*. Los Angeles: Sage, pp. 229–242.

Sacks, H. (1984) 'Notes on methodology', in J.M. Atkinson and J. Heritage (eds) *Structures of Social Action: Studies in Conversational Analysis*. Cambridge: Cambridge University Press, pp. 21–27.

Sewpaul, V. (2003) 'Reframing epistemologies and practice through international exchanges: global and local discourses in the development of critical consciousness', in L.D. Dominelli and W.T. Bernard, (eds) *Broadening Horizons: International Exchanges in Social Work*. Aldershot: Ashgate.

Shaw, I. (2008) 'Ethics and practice of qualitative research', *Qualitative Social Work*, 7(4): 400–414.

Silverman, D. (1998) *Harvey Sacks: Social Sciences and Conversational Analysis*. Cambridge: Polity Press.

Silverman, D. (2006) *Interpreting Qualitative Data*. London: Sage.

Stake, R. and Jegatheesan, B. (2008) 'Access: a zone of comprehension, and intrusion', in B. Jegatheesen (ed.) *Access: A Zone of Comprehension, and Intrusion*. Bingley: Emerald, pp. 1–13.

Stake, R. and Rizvi, F. (2009) 'Research ethics in transnational spaces', in D.M. Mertens and P. Ginsberg (eds) *Handbook of Social Science Research in Ethics*. Thousand Oaks, CA: Sage, pp. 521–536.

Van den Hoonaard, W.C. (ed.) (2002) *Walking the Tightrope: Ethical Issues for Qualitative Researchers*. Toronto: University of Toronto Press.

Appendix
Transcription Conventions

The examples printed embody an effort to have the spelling of the words roughly indicate how the words were produced. Often this involves a departure from standard orthography. Otherwise:

→	Arrows in the margin point to the lines of transcript relevant to the point being made in the text.
( )	Empty parentheses indicate talk too obscure to transcribe. Words or letters inside such parentheses indicate the transcriber's best estimate of what is being said.
hhh	The letter 'h' is used to indicate hearable aspiration, its length roughly proportional to the number of 'h's. If preceded by a dot, the aspiration is an in-breath. Aspiration internal to a word is enclosed in parentheses. Otherwise 'h's may indicate anything from ordinary breathing to sighing to laughing, etc.
[	Left-side brackets indicate where overlapping talk begins.
]	Right-side brackets indicate where overlapping talk ends, or marks alignments within a continuing stream of overlapping talk.
°	Talk appearing within degree signs is lower in volume relative to surrounding talk.
> <	'Greater than' and 'less than' symbols enclose talk that is noticeably faster than the surrounding talk.
((looks))	Words in double parentheses indicate transcriber's comments, not transcriptions.
(0.8)	Numbers in parentheses indicate periods of silence, in tenths of a second – a dot inside parentheses indicates a pause of less than 0.2 seconds.
:::	Colons indicate a lengthening of the sound just preceding them, proportional to the number of colons.

becau-   A hyphen indicates an abrupt cut-off or self-interruption of the sound in progress indicated by the preceding letter(s) (the example here represents a self-interrupted 'because').

_____   Underlining indicates stress or emphasis.

dr^ink   A 'hat' or circumflex accent symbol indicates a marked pitch rise.

=   Equal signs (ordinarily at the end of one line and the start of an ensuing one) indicate a 'latched' relationship – no silence at all between them.

Fuller glossaries may be found in Sacks, H., Schegloff, E.A. and Jefferson, G. (1974) 'A simplest systematics for the organization of turn-taking for conversation', *Language*, 50: 696–735; and Atkinson, J.M. and Heritage, J. (eds) (1984) *Structures of Social Action: Studies in Conversation Analysis*. Cambridge: Cambridge University Press.

Name Index

Subject Index